THE CONCEPTION OF BUDDHIST NIRVĀṆA

THE CONCEPTION OF BUDDHIST NIRVĀNA

(*With Sanskrit Text of Madhyamaka-Kārikā*)

TH. STCHERBATSKY PH. D.

Professor in the University of Leningrad, Member of the Academy of Sciences of the USSR.

With Comprehensive Analysis & Introduction by

JAIDEVA SINGH

M. A., (Phil. and Sans.) D. Litt.

Formerly Principal, Y. D. College, Lakhimpur-Kheri

MOTILAL BANARSIDASS

Delhi Varanasi Patna

Bangalore Madras

First Indian Edition : Varanasi, 1968
Second Revised and Enlarged Edition : Delhi, 1977
Reprint: Delhi, 1978, 1989

MOTILAL BANARSIDASS
Bungalow Road, Jawahar Nagar, Delhi 110 007

Branches
Chowk, Varanasi 221 001
Ashok Rajpath, Patna 800 004
24 Race Course Road, Bangalore 560 001
120 Royapettah High Road, Mylapore, Madras 600 004

ISBN: 81-208-0529-1

PRINTED IN INDIA

BY JAINENDRA PRAKASH JAIN AT SHRI JAINENDRA PRESS, A-45 NARAINA INDUSTRIAL AREA, PHASE I, NEW DELHI 110 028 AND PUBLISHED BY NARENDRA PRAKASH JAIN FOR MOTILAL BANARSIDASS, DELHI 110 007.

PREFACE TO THE SECOND EDITION

Misprints in the first edition have been corrected. The Introduction has been enlarged by adding new matter.

I have consulted 'Nāgārjuna's Philosophy as presented in The Mahā-Prajñāpāramitā-Śāstra' by Shri K. Venkata Raman which was published some three years after the first edition of this book was out. I have now incorporated in the Introduction the most salient points of Mahā-Prajñāpāramitā-Śāstra. The Introduction thus improved would serve as a brief but lucid hand-book on Madhyamaka Philosophy.

An 'Analysis of Contents' is a special feature of this edition of Stcherbatsky's 'Conception of Buddhist Nirvāṇa'. By reading this, one can get a gist of the entire book.

The original of the Madhyamaka Kārikās together with Candrakīrti's commentary which has been translated by Stcherbatsky has been appended at the end of the book so that the reader may be able to profit by a comparative study of the translation and the original Sanskrit.

In the Introduction M. K. stands for Madhyamaka Kārikā and P.P. for Prasannapadā commentary of Candrakīrti published by the Mithila Institute, Darbhanga.

JAIDEVA SINGH

Varanasi
1977

CONTENTS

Part I

INTRODUCTION

ANALYSIS OF CONTENTS

Part II

Part III

Part IV

INTRODUCTION

Mahāyāna and Hīnayāna

There are two aspects of Mahāyāna Philosophy, viz. the Madhyamaka Philosophy or Śūnyavāda and Yogācāra or Vijñānavāda. Here we are concerned only with Madhyamaka Philosophy or Śūnyavāda.

Generally there are three names current for Hīnayāna and Mahāyāna. The three names for the former are Southern Buddhism, Original Buddhism, and Hīnayāna, and those for the latter Northern Buddhism, Developed Buddhism and Mahāyāna. The first two names are given by European scholars. Southern and Northern Buddhism are names used on Geographical basis. European scholars called Buddhism prevalent in countries to the north of India, viz., Nepal, Tibet, China, Japan etc., Northern Buddhism and that prevalent in countries to the South of India, viz., Ceylon, Burma, Siam etc. Southern Buddhism. This division is not quite correct, for, according to Dr. J. Takakusu, the Buddhism prevalent in Java and Sumatra which lie in a southern direction from India is similar to that prevalent in the North.

The division 'original and developed Buddhism' is based on the belief that Mahāyāna was only a gradual development of the original doctrine which was Hīnayāna, but this is not acceptable to Mahāyānists. Japanese scholars maintain that the great Buddha imparted his teachings to his pupils according to their receptive capacities. To some he imparted his exoteric teachings (*vyakta-upadeśa*) containing his 'phenomenological perception;' to more advanced pupils he imparted his subtle esoteric teachings (*guhya-upadeśa*) containing his 'ontological perception.' The Buddha generally gave an outline of both the teachings, and both were developed by the great *ācāryas*. It is, therefore, a misnomer to call one 'original Buddhism' and another 'developed Buddhism.' Both the teachings were delivered simultaneously. The exoteric teachings may be called well-known Buddhism and the esoteric less known, the latter being subtler than the former.

We have, however, to find out how the terms Hīnayāna and Mahāyāna came into vogue. According to R. Kimura, the Mahāsaṅghikas had retained the esoteric teachings of the Buddha and were more liberal and advanced than the Sthaviras. In the Vaisāli Council, the Mahāsaṅghikas or the Vajjian monks were excommunicated by the Sthaviras for expressing opinions different from those of the orthodox school, and were denounced as 'Pāpa Bhikkhus' and 'Adhammavādins.' The Mahāsaṅghikas, in order to show the superiority of their doctrines over those of the Sthaviras, coined the term Mahāyāna (the higher vehicle) for their own school, and Hīnayāna (the lower vehicle) for the school of their opponents. Thus the terms Mahāyāna and Hīnayāna came into vogue. It goes without saying that these terms were used only by the Mahāyānists.

Three Phases in Buddhism

Three phases can be easily marked in Buddhist philosophy and religion.

1. *The Ābhidharmic phase from the Buddha's death to Ist Century A. D.*

This was the realistic and pluralistic phase of Buddhism. The method of this school was one of analysis. The philosophy of this period consisted mostly of analysis of psycho-physical phenomena into *dharmas* (elements) *saṁskṛta* (compounded or conditioned) and *asaṁskṛta* (uncompounded or unconditioned). The main interest in this period was psychological-soteriological. The dominant tone of this school was one of rationalism combined with meditation practices. The language used in this period was Pāli, and the school is known as Hīnayāna.

2. *Development of Esoteric Teachings*

The second phase consisted of the development of the esoteric teachings of the Buddha which were current among the Mahāsaṅghikas, simultaneously with the Ābhidharmic phase. The main interest in this period was ontological-soteriological. The dominant tone of this school was one of supra-rationalism combined with *yoga*. The main attempt was to find out the *Svabhāva* or true nature of Reality and to realize it in oneself by developing Prajñā. The language used was Saṁskṛta or mixed Saṁskṛta. This school was known as Mahāyāna. The earlier phase was known as Madhyamaka philosophy or Śūnyavāda, the later as Yogācāra or Vijñānavāda. This phase lasted from 2nd century A.D. to 500 A.D.

3. *Development of Tantra*

The third phase was that of Tantra. This lasted from 500 A. D. to 1000 A.D. The main interest of the period was cosmical-soteriological. The dominant feature of this school was occultism. The main emphasis was on adjustment and harmony with the cosmos and on achieving enlightenment by *mantric* and occult methods. The language was mostly Saṁskṛta and Apabhraṁśa. The main Tāntric schools were Mantrayāna, Vajrayāna, Sahajayāna, Kālacakrayāna.

Here we are not concerned with the first and third phase. We are concerned only with the earlier phase of the second period. Stcherbatsky has provided a translation only of the first and twentyfifth chapters i.e. the chapter dealing with causality and that dealing with Nirvāṇa of the Madhyamaka Śāstra or the Madhyamaka-Kārikās of Nāgārjuna together with the commentary of Candrakīrti. In the Introduction, an attempt is made to give a brief resumè of the Madhyamaka system as a whole.

Madhyamaka Śāstra : life of Nāgārjuna and Āryadeva

The Madhyamaka philosophy is contained mainly in the Madhyamaka Śāstra of Nāgārjuna and the *Catuḥ-Śataka* of Āryadeva.

Books on Mahāyāna Buddhism were completely lost in India. Their translation existed in Chinese, Japanese and Tibetan. Mahāyāna literature was written mostly in Saṁskrta and mixed Saṁskṛta. Scholars who had made a study of Buddhism hardly suspected that there were books on Buddhism in Saṁskṛta also.

Mr. Brian Houghton Hodgson was appointed Resident at Kāṭhamāṇḍu in Nepal in 1833, and served in this capacity up to the end of 1843.

During this period, he discovered there 381 bundles of

manuscripts on Buddhism in Saṁskṛta. These were distributed to various learned societies for editing and publication. It was then found out that the Buddhism in the Saṁskṛta manuscripts was greatly different from that of the Pāli Canon, and that the Buddhism in China, Japan, Tibet etc. was very much similar to that of the Saṁskṛta works. Among the Saṁskṛta manuscripts was also found the *Madhyamakaśāstra* of Nāgārjuna together with the commentary known as *Prasannapadā* by Candrakīrti. This was edited by Louis de la Valleè-Poussin and published in the *Bibliotheca Buddhica*, Vol. IV. St. Petersburg, Russia in 1912. An earlier edition of this book was published by the Buddhist Text Society, Calcutta, in 1897 and edited by Śaraccandra Śāstrī. This was full of misprints. Poussin consulted this book, but he also used two other manuscripts, one from Cambridge and another from Paris. He also checked up the text of the Kārikās and the commentary with the help of Tibetan translation. Dr. P. L. Vaidya utilised Poussin's edition and brought out in 1960 *Madhyamaka Śāstra* of Nāgārjuna with Candrakīrti's commentary in Devanāgarī character. This has been published by Mithilā Vidyāpīṭha, Darbhaṅgā. Stcherbatsky had utilized Poussin's edition in writing out his Conception of Buddhist Nirvāṇa.

The Buddha used to characterize his teaching as *madhyamā-pratipad* (the middle path). When Nāgārjuna evolved his philosophy, he seized upon this important word, and called his philosophy *Madhyamaka* (*madhyamaiva madhyamakam*) or *Madhyamaka-śāstra*. The followers of this system came to be known as Mādhyamika (*madhyamakam adhīyate vidanti vā Mādhyamikāḥ*). The correct name for the system is Madhyamaka, not Mādhyamika. Mādhyamika means the believer in or follower of the Madhyamaka system.

Under the title of *Madhyamaka-śāstra*, Nāgārjuna wrote out his philosophical teaching in over 400 *kārikās* in *anuṣṭubha* metre, divided into 27 chapters.

Nāgārjuna

He was the teacher who developed and perfected the Madhyamaka system. He flourished in the second century A.D.

A. D. He was born in a Brahmin family in Āndhradeśa probably in Vidarbha (Berār). Śrīparvata and Dhānyakaṭaka were the centres of his activities in the south. In the north, he carried on his activities in many places of which Nālandā is said to be the most prominent. He was also connected with Amarāvatī and Nāgārjunakoṇḍa. *Rājataraṅgiṇī* (11th Century A.D.) says that he was a contemporary of Huṣka. Juṣka and Kaniṣka.

According to the biography of Nāgārjuna, translated into Chinese by Kumārajīva (about 405 A.D.), Nāgārjuna was born in a Brahmin family in Southern India, and studied the Vedas and other important branches of Brāhmanical learning. He was later converted to Buddhism.

One of his minor works, *Suhṛllekha* (Friendly Epistle) is said to have been addressed to the Āndhra king, Śātavāhana. Śātavāhana is, however, regarded not as the name of a particular king, but as the name of a family of Āndhra kings, founded by Simuka (vide, *Ancient India*, by R. C. Majumdar, p. 133). Some scholars maintain that *Suhṛllekha* was addressed to Kaniṣka.

There is a legend associated with his name. Nāga means a serpent or dragon. Arjuna is the name of a tree. It is said that he was born under an Arjuna tree, and he visited the submarine kingdom of the Nāgas, where the Nāga king transmitted to him the *Mahāprajñāpāramitā Sūtra* which had been entrusted to the Nāgas by the Buddha.

The word 'Nāga' however, is symbolic of wisdom. The Buddha is said to have remarked, "The serpent is a name for one who has destroyed the *āsavas* (passions)" (*Majjhima-Nikāya*, I.23.). The Nāgas may, therefore, have been certain Arhants to whom the *prajñāpāramitā* teachings may have been handed down. Nāgārjuna may have received the teachings from them.

The Buddhist Nāgārjuna should not be confused with the Chemist and Tāntrika Nāgārjuna who lived probably in the 7th century A.D.

The Tibetans ascribe 122 books to Nāgārjuna, but only the following seem to have been his authentic works.

(1) *Madhyamaka-Śāstra*, also known as Prajñā or Kārikās with the commentary, *Akutobhaya* by the author himself.

(2) *Vigrahavyāvartanī* with a commentary by the author.
(3) *Yuktiṣaṣṭikā.*
(4) *Śūnyatā-saptati* with a commentary by the author.
(5) *Pratītyasamutpādahṛdaya* with a commentary.
(6) *Catuḥstava.*
(7) *Bhāvanākrama.*
(8) *Suhṛllekha.*
(9) *Bhāvasamkrānti.*
(10) *Ratnāvalī.*
(11) *Prajñāpāramitā-sūtra-Śāstra.*
(12) *Daśabhūmivibhāṣā-śāstra.*
(13) *Eka-śloka-śāstra.*
(14) *Vaidalya sūtra* and *Prakaraṇa.*
(15) *Vyavahāra-siddhi.*

Only a few of these are available in the original. There is, however, a Tibetan translation of all these books.

Kumārajīva's biography of Nāgārjuna mentions the following works also as Nāgārjuna's.

1. Upadeśa in 100,000 gāthās 2. Buddhamārgālaṅkāraśāstra in 5,000 gāthās 3. Akutobhaya-śāstra in 100,000 gāthās.

The Chinese collection mentions the following also among the works of Nāgārjuna :

1. Mahāyānabhavabheda-śāstra (bhavasaṅkrāntiśāstra) 2. Buddhisambhāra-śāstra 3. Dharmadhātustava.

Āryadeva or Ārya Deva

He was born in Siṁhala (Ceylon) and became a pupil of Nāgārjuna. He travelled with him to various places and helped him greatly in propagating his doctrine.

His biography was translated into Chinese by Kumārajīva in about 405 A.D.

His most famous work is *Catuḥ-Śataka* which consists of 400 Kārikās. He defended the teachings of Nāgārjuna, and criticized the philosophy of Hīnayāna, Sāṁkhya and Vaiśeṣika. He was probably the author of *Akṣara-Śatakaṃ*. He is also said to have been the author of *Hastavala-prakaraṇa* and *Cittaviśuddhi-prakaraṇa*. Prof. Winternitz expresses his doubt whether *Citta-viśuddhi-prakaraṇa* was his work.

It is said that he was murdered by the pupil of a heretical teacher whom he had defeated in disputation.

The Original Sources of Mahāyāna

The origin of Mahāyāna may be traced to an earlier school known as *Mahāsaṅghika* and earlier literary sources known as *Mahāyāna sūtras*.

1. *Mahāsaṅghikas*

At the council held at Vaisāli (according to Kimura), certain monks differed widely from the opinions of other monks on certain important points of the *dharma*. Though the monks that differed formed the majority, they were excommunicated by the others who called them 'Pāpa Bhikkhus and Adhammavādins. In Buddhist history, these Bhikkhus were known as *Mahāsaṅghikas*, because they formed the majority at the council or probably because they reflected the opinions of the larger section of the laity. The Bhikkhus who excommunicated them styled themselves Sthaviras or the Elders, because they believed that they represented the original, orthodox doctrine of the Buddha. We have seen that the *Mahāsaṅghikas* coined the term *Mahāyāna* to represent their system of belief and practice, and called the Sthaviras' *Hīnayāna*.

Let us see what the main tenets of the *Mahāsaṅghikas* were. Their contributions can be summed up under four heads.

1. *The Status of the Buddha*

According to the Mahāsaṅghikas, the Buddha was not simply a historical person. The real Buddha was transcendental, supramundane, eternal, and infinite. The historical Buddha was only a fictitious person sent by Him to appear in the world, to assume a human body, to live like an ordinary human being and teach the *dharma* to the inhabitants of the world. The real Buddha is the Reality *par excellence* and will continue to send messengers to the world to teach the true *dharma* to mankind.

2. *The Status of the Arhat*

The *Sthaviras* had attributed perfection to the Arhats.

The *Mahāsaṅghikas* maintained that the Arhats were not perfect; they were troubled by doubts and were ignorant of many things. They should not be held up as ideals. Rather those should be emulated as ideals who during aeons of self-sacrifice and struggle attained to Buddhahood.

3. *The Status of Empirical knowledge*

According to the *Mahāsaṅghikas*, empirical knowledge could not give us an insight into Reality. Only *Śūnyatā* which transcends all worldly things can give us a vision of the Real. All verbal statements give us a false view of the Real; they are mere thought-constructions.

4. *The Unsubstantial Nature of the Dharmas*

The Sthaviras believed that the *pudgala* or a personal self was unsubstantial, but the *dharmas* or elements of existence were real entities. The Mahāsaṅghikas maintained that not only were the *pudgalas* unsubstantial (*pudgala-nairātmya*), but the *dharmas* (elements of existence) were also unsubstantial (*dharma-nairātmya*). Every thing was unsubstantial (*śūnya*).

It will be seen from the above account that the germs of practically all the important tenets of Madhyamaka philosophy were present in the system of the Mahāsaṅghikas.

It is the *Mahāsaṅghikas* who first of all gave expression to Buddha's ontological perceptions which were first embodied in the Mahāyāna sūtras and were later developed into Mahāyāna philosophy and religion.

11. *Literary Sources*

In Buddhism, *sūtra* literature is said to contain the direct, oral teachings of the Buddha, and *śāstra* is said to contain the scholarly and philosophical elaboration of the direct teachings of the Buddha.

We have a large bulk of literary works known as *Mahāyāna sūtras*. Being *sūtras*, they claim to be the direct teachings of the Buddha. Such bulky volumes, obviously, cannot be the spoken word of the Buddha. They are the elaboration of some 'seminal sūtras' which are so deeply embedded in the voluminous *Mahāyāna sūtra* literature that it is now almost impossible to disentangle them.

The most important of these works are the *prajñāpāramitā sūtras*. *Prajñā-pāramitā* is generally translated as 'perfect wisdom.' The word 'pāram-itā' i.e. 'gone beyond' suggests that it would be better to translate *prajñā-pāramitā* as 'transcendent insight' or 'transcendent wisdom'. The Tibetans translate it in this way. In all countries where Mahāyāna is a living religion, the following *prajñā-pāramitā mantra* is generally recited: *Gate*, *gate*, *pāraṁgate*, *pārasaṁgate Bodhi*, *svāhā* i.e. "O wisdom which has gone beyond the beyond, to thee Homage."

According to Dr. Edward Conze, the composition of the *Prajñā pāramitā* texts extended over about a thousand years which may be divided into four phases.

The first phase (C. 100 B. C. to A.D. 100) consists in the leaboration of the teaching in a basic text.

The second phase (C.A.D. 100-300) consists in the expansion of the teaching into three or four lengthy treatises.

The third phase (C.A.D. 300-500) consists in the abridgement of the teachings into a few shorter treatises.

The fourth phase (C. A. D. 500-1200) consists in its condensation into Tāntric *dhāraṇīs* and *mantras*.

(1) According to most scholars, the *Aṣṭa sāhasrikā*, consisting of 8,000 lines is the oldest of the *Prajñāpāramitā* literature. It had its origin probably among the Mahāsaṅghikas. The principal theme of this treatise is the doctrine of *śūnyatā* (void or emptiness).

(2) *Aṣṭa-sāhasrikā* seems to have been expanded in the three hundred years that followed into *Śatasāhasrikā* (of 100,000 lines), *Pañcaviṁśatisāhasrikā* (of 25,000 lines) and *Aṣṭādaśasāhasrikā* (of 18,000 lines). The last one was translated by Lokarakṣa in A. D. 172.

(3) Now began the abridgement of the *Prajñā-pāramitā* literature. The earliest abridgements are the *Hṛdaya-sūtra* and the *Vajracchedikā sūtra*. The *Vajracchedikā* was translated into Chinese probably in the 5th century A. D. This translation was printed in China on 11th May, 868. This is said to be the oldest printed book in the world.

Abhisamayālaṁkāra is said to be a summary of *pañcaviṁśatisāhasrikā* made by Maitreyanātha, the teacher of Asaṅga.

(4) Lastly *Prajñāpāramitā* was condensed into *dhāraṇīs* and *mantras*. One of these, viz., *Ekākṣarī* says that the perfec-

tion of wisdom is contained only in one letter, viz., 'a'. Ultimately *Prajñāpāramitā* was personified as a goddess to be worshipped.

Prajñāpāramitās are both philosophy and religion. They are not mere 'philosophy' in the Western sense of the word. In the West, philosophy cut itself adrift from religion and became a purely intellectual pursuit. In India, every philosophy was a religion, and every religion had a philosophy. Western religion became only a credal religion. Indian religion was a philosophical religion.

The principal theme of the *Prajñāpāramitā* literature is the doctrine of *śūnyatā*. The Hīnayānists believed only in *pudgala-nairātmya* or the unsubstantiality of the individual. They classified Reality into certain *dharmas* or elements of existence and thought that the *dharmas* were substantially real. *Prajñāpāramitā* gives a knock-out to this belief. It teaches *sarva-dharma-śūnyatā*, the unsubstantiality of all *dharmas*.

Phenomena are dependent on conditions. Being so dependent, they are devoid of substantial reality. Hence they are *śūnya* (empty).

Nirvāṇa being transcendent to all categories of thought is *Śūnyatā* (emptiness) itself.

Both *saṁsāra* and *Nirvāṇa*, the conditioned and unconditioned are mere thought-constructions and are so devoid of reality.

Ultimate Reality may be called *Śūnyatā* in the sense that it transcends all empirical determinations and thought-constructions.

Prajñā or transcendent insight consists in ceasing to indulge in thought-constructions. So *Prajñā* becomes synonymous with *Śūnyatā*.

One, however, acquires insight into *Śūnyatā* not merely by avowing it enthusiastically, nor by logomachy, but by meditation on *Śūnyatā*.

One has to meditate on *Śūnyatā* as the absence of self-hood, on the absence of substantiality in all the *dharmas*, on *Śūnyatā* as even the emptiness of the unconditioned. Finally one has to abandon *Śūnyatā* itself as a mere raft to cross the ocean of ignorance. This meditation will, however, be ineffective unless one has cultivated certain moral virtues.

Though this is a very brief summary of the *Prajñāpāramitā* texts, it is enough to show that this kind of literature contained all the important elements of the Mahāyāna system.

Thus we see that the Madhyamaka system was developed on the basis of the doctrines of the *Mahāsaṅghikas* and the *Mahāyāna sūtras* known as *Prajñāpāramitā sūtras*.

The Madhyamaka Works and Schools

The Madhyamaka system of philosophy was developed mainly by Nāgārjuna. He was one of the greatest geniuses the world has ever known. The system of which he laid the foundation was developed by his brilliant followers. It had a continuous history of development from the second century A.D. upto eleventh century A.D.

Three stages of its development can be easily marked. In the first stage, there was a systematic formulation of the Madhyamaka philosophy by Nāgārjuna and Āryadeva. The second stage is one of division of the system into two schools the *Prāsaṅgika* and the *Svātantrika*. The third stage is one of re-affirmation of the *Prāsaṅgika* school.

Nāgārjuna and Āryadeva (2nd Century A. D.)

First Stage—Nāgārjuna was the author of a voluminous commentary on *Prajñāpāramitā* known as *Prajñāpāramitā-śāstra*. This was translated into Chinese by Kumārajīva (A. D. 402-405). The original is not available now. He, however, formulated his main philosophy in *prajñā-mūla* or *Mūla-Madhyamaka-Kārikās* known also as Madhyamaka-Śāstra. His devoted pupil Āryadeva elaborated his philosophy in *Catuḥ-śataka*. We have already seen what other books were written by Nāgārjuna and Āryadeva.

Second stage—Nāgārjuna had used the technique of *prasaṅga* in formulating his Madhyamaka philosophy. *Prasaṅga* is a technical word which means *reductio ad absurdum* argument. Nāgārjuna did not advance any theory of his own, and therefore, had no need to advance any argument to prove his theory. He used only *prasaṅga-vākya* or *reductio ad absurdum* argument to prove that the theories advanced by his opponents only led to absurdity on the very principles accepted by them. This implied that Reality was beyond thought-construction.

Buddhapālita who flourished in the middle of the sixth century was an ardent follower of Nāgārjuna. He felt that *prasaṅga* was the correct method of the Madhyamaka philosophy and employed it in his teachings and writings. He wrote a commentary called *Madhyamakavṛtti* on the *Madhyamaka Śāstra* of Nāgārjuna. This is available only in Tibetan translation. The original is lost.

A junior contemporary of Buddhapālita, named Bhavya or Bhāvaviveka maintained that the opponent should not only be reduced to absurdity, but *svatantra* or independent logical arguments should also be advanced to silence him. He believed that the system of dialectics alone could not serve the purpose of pin-pointing the Absolute Truth.

He wrote *Mahāyāna-Karatala-ratna Śāstra*, *Mādhyamikahṛdaya* with an auto-commentary, called *Tarkajvālā*, *Madhyamārtha-Saṁgraha* and *Prajñā-pradīpa*, a commentary on the Madhyamaka Śāstra of Nāgārjuna. Only a Tibetan translation of these works is available. Dr. L. M. Joshi transcribed the *Madhyamārtha-Saṁgraha* into Nāgarī letters and translated it into Hindi which appeared in the *Dharmadūta*, Vol. 29, July-August, 1964.

N. Aiyswāmi Śāstri has restored *Karatalaratna* from the Chinese translation of Yuan Chwang into Saṁskṛta (Viśvabhārati Śantiniketan, 1949).

So we see that in the sixth century, nearly 400 years after the death of Nāgārjuna, the Madhyamaka school was split into two, viz. (a) Prāsaṅgika school, led by Buddhapālita and (b) Svātantrika School, led by Bhāvaviveka.

Y. Kajiama says that the problem which divided the Mādhyamikas was whether the system of relative knowledge could be recognised as valid or not, though it was delusive from the absolute point of view.

According to Yuan Chwang, Bhāvaviveka externally wore the Sāṁkhya cloak, though internally he was supporting the doctrine of Nāgārjuna.

Third Stage—In the third stage, we have two very brilliant scholars of the Madhyamaka system, viz. Candrakīrti and Śāntideva.

A large number of commentaries (about twenty) was written on Nāgārjuna's Madhyamaka Śāstra. They are available only in Tibetan translation. Candrakīrti's *prasannapadā* commentary is the only one that has survived in the original Saṁskṛta. It seems to have elbowed every other commentary out of existence.

He flourished early in the seventh century A. D. and wrote several works. He was born in Samanta in the South. He studied Madhyamaka philosophy under Kamalabuddhi, a disciple of Buddhapālita and probably under Bhavya also. His *prasannapadā* commentary on Nāgārjuna's *Madhyamaka Śāstra*, has already been mentioned. He wrote an independent work, named *Madhyamakāvatāra* with an auto-commentary. He frequently refers to *Madhyamakāvatāra* in his *Prasannapadā* which goes to show that the former was written earlier than the latter.

He also wrote commentaries on Nāgārjuna's *Śūnyatā Saptati* and *Yukti Ṣaṣṭikā* and on Āryadeva's *Catuḥśataka*. Two other *prakaraṇas* or manuals, viz., *Madhyamakaprajñāvatāra* and *Pañcaskandha* were also written by him. Of all his works, only *Prasannapadā* is available in the original; other works are available only in Tibetan translation.

Candrakīrti vigorously defends the *Prāsaṅgika* school, and exposes the hollowness of Bhāvaviveka's logic at many places.

He also supports the common-sense view of sense-perception and criticizes the doctrine of the 'unique particular' (*svalakṣaṇa*) and perception devoid of determination (*kalpanāpoḍha*).

He has also criticized Vijñānavāda and maintains that consciousness (vijñāna) without an object is unthinkable.

Śāntideva was another great pillar of the *Prāsaṅgika* school. He flourished in the seventh century A. D. According to Tārānātha, Śāntideva was the son of King Kalyāṇavarman of Saurāṣṭra and was the rightful successor to the throne. As a prince he was known as Śāntivarman. He was so deeply inspired by Mahāyānic ideal that he fled away from his kingdom and took orders with Jaideva in Nālandā after which he was known as Śāntideva.

He was the author of *Śikṣā-samuccaya* and *Bodhicaryāvatāra*. In the former, he has referred to many important Mahāyāna works, nearly 97 in number which are now completely lost. In the *Bodhicaryāvatāra* he has emphasized the cultivation of Bodhicitta. He was the greatest poet of the Madhyamaka school and his works evince a beautiful fusion of poetry and philosophy. He was the follower of the *Prāsaṅgika* method and has criticized Vijñānavāda vehemently.

It may be said in passing that Śāntarakṣita and Kamalaśīla represent a syncretism of the Madhyamaka system and Vijñānavāda and cannot be strictly called Mādhyamikas. Śāntarakṣita flourished in the eighth century A. D. His great work was *Tattvasaṁgraha* (Compendium of Reality). His celebrated pupil, Kamalaśīla wrote the *Tattvasaṁgraha-pañjikā*, a learned commentary on *Tattvasaṁgraha*.

The Mudhyamaka Dialectic : Its Origin, Structure And Development.

We have seen that nearly all the important tenets of the Madhyamaka philosophy were already adumbrated in the Mahāsaṅghika system and *Prajñāpāramitā* literature. Nāgārjuna only developed them. What was then the original contribution of Nāgārjuna ? His original contribution was the dialectic that he evolved. He certainly threw new light on the various doctrines of Mahāyāna foreshadowed in the Mahāsaṅghika thought and *Prajñāpāramitā* works, and provided a deeper and more critical exposition of those doctrines, but his most original contribution was the dialectic.

The mysterious silence of the Buddha on the most fundamental questions of Metaphysics led him to probe into the reason of that silence. Was the Buddha agnostic as some of the European writers on Buddhism believe him to be? If not, what was the reason of his silence? Through a searching inquiry into this silence was the dialectic born.

There are well-known questions which the Buddha declared to be *avyākṛta* i.e. the answers to which were inexpressible. Candrakīrti enumerates them in his commentary on the MK, 22, 12.

He begins by saying *Iha caturdaśa avyākṛta-vastūni bhagavatā nirdiṣṭāni*—The Lord announced fourteen things to be inexpressible," and then mentions them in the following order:

(1) Whether the world is (a) eternal, (b) or not, (c) or both (d) or neither-4

(2) Whether the world is (a) finite, (b) infinite, (c) or both, (d) or neither-4

(3) Whether the Tathāgata (a) exists after death, (b) or does not, (c) or both, (d) or neither-4

(4) Whether the soul is identical with the body or different from it-2 = 14 in all.

It will be seen that there are four alternatives in the first three sets of questions. There could be four alternatives in the last question also. These four alternatives formed the basis of *Catuṣkoṭi* or tetra-lemma of Nāgārjuna's dialectic. In each, there is (i) a positive thesis, opposed by (ii) a negative counter-thesis. These two are the basic alternatives. (iii) They are conjunctively affirmed to form the third alternative, and (iv) disjunctively denied to form the fourth.

The 'yes' or 'no' answer to these fundamental questions could not do justice to truth. Buddha called such speculations mere *diṭṭhivāda* and refused to be drawn into them.

Nāgārjuna had before him the structure of these questions and Buddha's silence, refusing to give any categorical answer to such questions. Buddha used to say that he neither believed in *Śāśvata-vāda*, an absolute affirmation, nor in *Ucchedavāda* an absolute negation. His position was one of *madhyamā pratipada* (literally, the middle position).

Nāgārjuna pondered deeply over this attitude of the Buddha, and came to the conclusion that the reason of Buddha's studied silence in regard to such questions was that Reality was transcendent to thought. He systematized the four alternatives (*antas* or *koṭis*), mercilessly exposed the disconcerting implications of each alternative, brought the antinomies of Reason luminously to the fore by hunting them out from every cover, and demonstrated the impossibility of erecting a sound Metaphysic on the basis of dogmatism or rationalism. This was his dialectic. The four alternatives were already formulated by the Buddha. His originality consisted in drawing out by the application of rigorous logic the implications of each alternative, driving Reason in a *cul de sac* and thus preparing the mind for taking a right-about-turn (*parāvṛtti*) towards *prajñā*.

To the unwary reader, Nāgārjuna appears to be either a cantankerous philosopher out to controvert all systems, or as a sophist trickster wringing from an unsuspecting opponent certain concessions in argument by artful equivocation and then chuckling over his discomfiture or as a destructive nihilist negativing every view brusquely, affirming none.

On a more careful study of his dialectic, it will appear that none of these fears is true, that he is, in all soberness, only trying to show up the inevitable conflict in which Reason gets involved when it goes beyond its legitimate province of comprehending phenomena, and enters the forbidden land of noumena.

The Meaning of Dialectic

What then does dialectic mean? In plain words, dialectic is that movement of thought which, by examining the *pros* and *cons* of a question, brings about a clear consciousness of the antinomies into which Reason gets bogged up, and hints at a way out of the impasse by rising to a plane higher than Reason.

Structure of The Dialectic

We have seen that the origin of the dialectic of the Mādhyamika lay in the four alternatives in each *avyākṛta* problem followed by a mysterious silence on the part of the Buddha. Nāgārjuna clearly systematized these and formulated them into the *catuṣkoṭi*, tetralemma or quadrilemma, also called the four-cornered negation. The structure of the clearly articulated dialectic finally stood thus:

The first alternative of the tetralemma consisted of (i) a positive thesis, the second of (ii) a negative counter-thesis, the third of (iii) a conjunctive affirmation of the first two, the fourth of (iv) a disjunctive denial of the first two.

The Technique of The Dialectic

The technique of the dialectic consisted in drawing out the implications of the view of the opponent on the basis of the principles accepted by himself and thus showing the self-contradictory character of that view The opponent was hoisted with his own petard. He was reduced to the position of absurdity when the self-contradictory consequences of his own assumptions were revealed. The dialectic was thus a rejection of views by *reductio ad absurdum* argument. Technically this was known as *prasaṅga*.

R. H. Robinson points out in his '*Early Mādhyamika* in India and China' that the stanzas in the Madhyamaka Śāstra of Nāgārjuna contain a large number of hypothetical syllogisms. In the stanzas, there are examples of the two valid types of hypothetical syllogism—modus ponens and modus tollens, and also the fallacious mode in which the antecedent is negated.

As an example of 'modus ponens', he cites 3.2. (Prasannapadā); and as an example of 'modus tollens', he cites 19, 6. (Prasannapadā).

He rightly maintains that in the stanzas, there are many dilemmas and the commonest type is of the form; "If *p*, then *q*; if not-*p*, then *q*" which is a special form of the "simple constructive dilemma" of Western Logic.

Another form of dilemma found in the stanzas is: "If *p*, then *q*; if not-*p*, then *r* which is a special form of "Complex constructive dilemma" of Western Logic.

The Purpose of The Dialectic

The purpose of the dialectic was to *disprove* the views advanced by others, not to prove any view of one's own. He who advances a view must necessarily prove it to others whom he wants to convince; he who has no view to advance is under no such necessity. Nāgārjuna states clearly in his *Vigrahavyāvartanī* (St.29) that no one can find fault with the Mādhyamika, for he has no view of his own to advance.

Yadi kācana pratijñā syān me tata eva me bhaved doṣaḥ./
Nāsti ca mama pratijñā tasmān naivāsti me doṣaḥ//

"If I had a thesis of my own to advance, you could find fault with it. Since I have no thesis to advance, the question of disproving it does not arise."

The dialectic was directed against the dogmatists and rationalists who maintained a definite view about Reality. By exposing the hollowness of their logic and the self-contradictory consequences of their assumptions, Nāgārjuna wanted to disprove the claims of Reason to apprehend Reality. Candrakīrti puts the whole position very clearly in the following words:

Nirupapattika-pakṣābhyupagamāt svātmānam eva ayaṁ kevalaṁ visaṁvādayan na śaknoti pareṣāṁ niścayam ādhātum iti. Idameva asya spaṣṭataraṁ dūṣaṇaṁ yaduta svapratījñātārthasādhanāsāmarthyam iti (P.P, p.6) "By his illogical assumption, the opponent only contradicts himself, and is unable to convince others. What could be more self-convicting than the fact that he is unable even to prove the premises on the basis of which he advances his arguments."

Nāgārjuna mercilessly demolished every philosophical opinion of his time, not because he derived a sadistic pleasure in doing so, but because he had a definite purpose. Negatively the dialectic was meant to prove that Reality could not be measured by the three-foot rule of discursive thought. But this was not all. It had some positive suggestions. Firstly, phenomenon or empirical reality is a realm of relativity, in which an entity is *śūnya* or *nis-svabhāva* i.e., devoid of independent reality or unconditionedness.

Secondly, one can comprehend Reality by rising to a plane higher than logical thought i.e., the plane of *prajñā*.

Thirdly, Reality cannot be expressed in terms of the 'is' 'is not'—dichotomising mind.

The Application of the Dialectic

Nāgārjuna rigorously examines all philosophical theories that were held by the thinkers in his time. He turns the battery of his dialectic against concepts like causality, motion and rest, the *āyatanas*, the *skandhas*, the *ātman* etc.

Stcherbatsky has included only his criticism of causality and nirvāṇa, for they are the most important. We shall, therefore, confine our observations only to these two. We shall consider Nāgārjuna's examination of the concept of causality here, and his examination of Nirvāṇa under a separate heading.

Nāgārjuna fires the first shot against causality, for that was the central problem of philosophy in his days.

Examination of Causality

Applying his tetralemma to causality, Nāgārjuna says that there can be only four views about causality, viz. (1) view of *svata utpattiḥ*, the theory of self-becoming (2) *parata utpattiḥ*, i.e. production from another (3) *dvābhyām utpattiḥ* i.e. production from both i.e from itself and from another (4) *ahetuta utpattiḥ* i.e. production without any cause, production by chance.

(1) *Svata utpattiḥ*—This means that the cause and effect are identical, that things are produced out of themselves. Nāgārjuna had evidently in view the Satkāryavāda of Sāṁkhya while criticizing the autogenous theory of causality.

The Mādhyamika's criticism of this theory may be summarized thus:

(i) If the effect is already present in the cause, no purpose would be served by its re-production. The Sāṁkhya may say that though the effect may be present in the cause, its manifestation (*abhivyakti*) is something new. This, however, does not mean that the effect is a new substance. It only means that it is a new form or state of the substance. But this difference of form or state goes against the identity of the underlying substratum.

(ii) If it is said that the cause is partly actual, and partly potential, it would amount to accepting opposed natures in one and the same thing.

If the cause is wholly potential, it cannot by itself become actual without an extraneous aid. The oil cannot be got out of the seed, unless it is pressed by a crusher. If it has to depend on an external aid, then there is no *svata utpattiḥ* or self-production. This amounts to giving up *satkāryavāda*.

(iii) If the cause and effect are identical, it would be impossible to distinguish one as the producer of the other.

The identity view of cause and effect (*Satkāryavāda*) is, therefore, riddled with self-contradiction.

(2) *Parata Utpattiḥ*. This means that the cause and effect are different. This view is known as *asatkāryavāda*. This was held by the Sarvāstivādins and Sautrāntikas or the Hīnayānists in general. Nāgārjuna had obviously these in view while criticizing this heterogeneous view of causality.

His criticism of this view makes out the following important points:

(i) If the cause is different from the effect, no relation can subsist between the two. In that case anything can be produced from anything.

(ii) The Hīnayānist believed that with the production of the effect the cause ceased to exist. But *ex hypothesi* causality is a relation between two. Unless the cause and effect co-exist, they cannot be related. If they cannot be related, causality becomes meaningless.

(iii) The Hīnayānist believed that the effect is produced by a combination of factors. Now for the co-ordination of these factors, another factor would be required, and again for the co-ordination of the additional factor with the previous one, another factor would be required. This would lead to a *regressus ad infinitum.*

(3) *Dvābhyām utpattiḥ*—This theory believes that the effect is both identical with and different from the cause. This is a combination of both Satkāryavāda and Asatkāryavāda, and so contains the inconsistencies of both. Besides this would invest the real with two opposed characters (identity and difference) at one and the same time.

(4) *Ahetutaḥ Utpattiḥ*—This theory maintains that things are produced without a cause, by chance. The Svabhāvavādins—Naturalists and Sceptics believed in such a theory. If no reason is assigned for the theory, it amounts to sheer, perverse dogmatism. If a reason is assigned, it amounts to accepting a cause.

Having exposed the inherent inconsistency in all the above views, Nāgārjuna comes to the conclusion that causality is a mere thought-construction superimposed upon the objective order of existence. In the words of Kant, causality is only a category of mind.

Positive Contribution of Nāgārjuna

From a reading of the Madhyamaka Kārikās, it appears that Nāgārjuna was only an intransigent negativist. In his *Mahāprajñāpāramitā Śāstra*, however, as ably expounded by Dr. K. Venkata Ramanan, Nāgārjuna states his positive views on the vexed question of Reality.

1. Both the *Madhyamaka Kārikā* and the *Mahāprajñā-*

pāramitā Śāstra point to the *naiḥsvābhāvya* or unsubstantiality, conditionedness, relativity as the basic import of *Śūnyatā* with regard to the mundane nature of things, but the *śāstra* brings out more clearly than the *kārikā* the deeper implication of the unsubstantiality of the mundane entities. It says that the tendency of man to seize the relative as the absolute is, at root, the secret-inchoate longing in the heart of man for the absolute (*dharmaiṣaṇā*). Owing to inveterate Ignorance, this longing is misapplied. Man clings to the relative as the absolute only to meet with frustration. But if he clings to the *distinction* of the absolute and the relative as *absolute separateness*, then again he commits the error of 'clinging' in another form. Nāgārjuna is at pains to bring home to man the deeper truth that the unconditioned', the absolute is not only the ground of the conditioned or relative, it is in fact the ultimate nature of the relative itself, and not another entity *apart* from it.

2. The absolute, the unconditioned is not only the ultimate nature of the conditioned mundane entities, it is also the ultimate nature of man. It is because of this that his hunger for the real acquires a deeper significance. As an individual, man is certainly related to the rest of the world, to phenomena, to his *skandhas*, to the contingent, conditioned environment, but he is not alienated from the unconditioned which is the ultimate nature of his very being; he is not bound for ever to his apparent fragmentariness. Being engrossed completely in the passing show of the conditioned entities, and asleep to the inner meaning of his being, he seizes the relative as if it were the absolute and thus invites inevitable suffering. Once he is awake to the conditionedness (Śūnyatā) of the conditioned, his sense of values changes. He becomes a transformed man and then his *dharmaiṣaṇā*, his mysterious longing for the Real finds its meaning and fulfilment. The Kārikā emphasizes the insufficiency, the incompleteness, the unsubstantiality of the *dharmas* (entities) and the *pudgala* (the empirical individual). The Śāstra emphasizes the axiological significance of this sense of incompleteness, and maintains that it is the keen realization of this insufficiency that fans man's tiny spark of longing for the Real, the absolute into the living flame of truth.

3. Practically all the basic concepts of Nāgārjuna's philosophy are found in the Kārikā but then they are over-

shadowed by the overwhelmingly negative character of approach. And it could not be otherwise, for in the Kārikā, Nāgārjuna has all along used the technique of *prasaṅga vākya*, argument of *reductio ad absurdum* character. His main concern is to expose the absurdities involved in accepting what is only relative (niḥsvabhāva) as absolute (sasvabhāva). Even in the Kārikā, Nāgārjuna avers with unmistakable forthrightness that the conditioned bespeaks the unconditioned as its ultimate ground. "That which is of the nature of coming and going, arising and perishing, in its conditioned aspect is itself Nirvāṇa in its unconditioned aspect". (XXV, 9)

Distinction Between Hīnayāna and Mahāyāna

There are several aspects of Buddhist philosophy and religion in which Mahāyāna differs from Hīnayāna. In what follows, we shall deal mostly with the Madhyamaka system of Mahāyāna.

(1) *Difference in the Interpretation of Pratītyasamutpāda*— The doctrine of Pratītyasamutpāda is exceedingly important in Buddhism. It is the causal law both of the universe and the lives of individuals. It is important from two points of view. Firstly, it gives a very clear idea of the impermanent and conditioned nature of all phenomena. Secondly, it shows how birth, old age, death and all the miseries of phenomenal existence arise in dependence upon conditions, and how all the miseries cease in the absence of these conditions.

We have seen what view the Mādhyamikas held of causality. Since Pratītyasamutpāda was the universal causal law, the Mādhyamikas undertook a critical examination of this law. Their interpretation of this law differs considerably from that of Hīnayāna. Pratītyasamutpāda is generally translated as 'conditioned co-production' or 'interdependent origination'.

According to Hīnayāna, *pratītyasamutpāda* means *prati prati ityānāṁ vināśinām samutpādaḥ* i.e. "the evanescent momentary things appear." According to it, *pratītya-samutpāda* is the causal law regulating the coming into being and disappearance of the various elements (*dharmas*).

According to the Mādhyamika rise and subsidence of the

elements of existence (*dharmas*) is not the correct interpretation of *pratītyasamutpāda*.

As Candrakīrti puts it *hetupratyayāpekṣo bhāvānām utpādaḥ pratītyasamutpādārthaḥ* (P. P., p. 2) i.e. *pratītyasamutpāda* means the manifestation of entities as relative to causes and conditions.

The Hīnayānists had interpreted *pratītyasamutpāda* as temporal sequence of real entities between which there was a causal relation.

According to the Mādhyamika, *pratītyasamutpāda* does not mean the principle of temporal sequence, but the principle of essential dependence of things on each other. In one word, it is the principle of relativity . Relativity is the most important discovery of modern science. What science has discovered to-day, the great Buddha had discovered two thousand five hundred years before. In interpreting *pratītyasamutpāda* as essential dependence of things on each other or relativity of things, the Mādhyamika means to controvert another doctrine of the Hīnayānist. The Hīnayānists had analysed all phenomena into elements (*dharmas*), and believed that these *dharmas* had a separate reality of their own. The Mādhyamika says that the very doctrine of *pratītyasamutpāda* declares that all the *dharmas* are relative, they have no separate reality (*svabhāva*) of their own. *Nis-svabhāvatva* is synonymous with *śūnyatā* i.e. devoid of real, independent existence. Phenemena are devoid (*śūnya*) of independent reality. *Pratītyasamutpāda* or Interdependence means Relativity, and Relativity connotes the unreality (*śūnyatā*) of the separate elements.

Candrakīrti says, *Tadatra-nirodhādyaṣṭa-viśeṣaṇa-viśiṣṭaḥ pratītyasamutpādaḥ śāstrābhidheyārthaḥ* (P. P. P. 2) i.e., "The subject matter or the central idea of this treatise is *pratītyasamutpāda* characterized by eight negative characteristics."

The importance of *pratītyasamutpāda* lies in its teaching that all phenomenal existence, all entities in the world are conditioned, are devoid of (*śūnya*) real, independent existence (*svabhāva*).

As Nāgārjuna puts it *Nahi svabhāvo bhāvānām pratyayādiṣu vidyate* (M. K. 1, 5)—"There is no real, independent existence of entities in the *pratyayas* i.e. conditions". As Dr. E. Conze puts it "All the concrete content belongs to the interplay of countless conditions" (*Buddhist Thought in India*, p. 240).

Nāgārjuna sums up his teaching about *pratītya-samutpāda* in the following words:

Apratītya samutpanno dharmaḥ kaścinna vidyate. Yasmāt tasmāt aśūnyo hi dharmaḥ kaścinna vidyate (M. K, 24, 19) "Since there is no element of existence (*dharma*) which comes into manifestation without conditions, therefore there is no *dharma* which is not *śūnya* (devoid of real independent existence)."

The *pratītyasamutpāda* becomes equivalent to *śūnyatā* or relativity. Nāgārjuna says *Yaḥ pratītyasamutpādaḥ śūnyatāṁ tām pracakṣmahe.* (M. K. 24, 18) "What is *pratītyasamutpāda* that we call *śūnyatā*".

Śūnya or *śūnyatā* is the most important concept of Madhyamaka philosophy. We shall, therefore, consider it under a separate heading in the sequel.

In the Kārikā, however, the main purpose of Nāgārjuna was to clear the ground for the exposition of his positive philosophy, viz., the role of *prajñā* in comprehending the different levels of understanding. He gives a detailed exposition of *prajñā* in the śāstra. Again in the Kārikā there is no direct reference to *dharmaiṣaṇā*, the secret longing for the Real imbedded in the human heart. In the Śāstra, this *dharmaiṣaṇā* becomes the burden of his song. In the Kārikā, there is hardly any description of the course of wayfaring towards the goal; in the Śāstra this is vividly described. In the Kārikā, the unconditioned as the immanent reality of the conditioned is only obliquely hinted at; in the Śāstra, it receives prominent attention. The chapter on *tathatā* particularly brings to light the immanence of the real in every being. The chapter on *bhūtakoṭi* gives an illuminating description of *upāya*, the skilfulness of non-clinging. Thus the Śāstra is complementary to the kārikā.

2. *Difference in the concept of Nirvāṇa*

The following points regarding Nirvāṇa are common between Hīnayāna and Mahāyāna.

(1) Nirvāṇa is inexpressible. It has no origin, no change, no decay. It is deathless (*amṛta*).

(2) It has to be realized within oneself. This is possible only when there is complete extinction of craving for sense-pleasure.

(3) Personal self as such ceases in Nirvāṇa. Access to Nirvāṇa is possible only on the extinction of the personal self.

(4) It is a peace (*śama* or *upaśama*) that passeth understanding.

(5) It provides lasting security.

The word 'nirvāṇa' literally means extinguished' and therefore 'tranquil'.

There are four ways in which Nirvāṇa is generally described in Buddhist literature; viz., (1) negative, (2) positive, (3) paradoxical and (4) symbolic.

1. Negative—The negative description is the most common. Nirvāṇa is (1) *amṛta* (deathless), (2) unchanging, (3) imperishable (*acyuta*), (4) without end (*ananta*), (5) non-production, (6) extinction of birth, (7) unborn, (8) not liable to dissolution (*apalokina*), (9) uncreated (*abhūtam*), (10) free from disease, (11) unaging, (12) freedom from transmigration, (13) *anuttaram* (utmost), (14) cessation of pain (*duḥkha-nirodha*), (15) final release (*apavagga*).

2. Positive : Nirvāṇa is (1) peace (*śama or upaśama*); The following verse of *Mahāparinirvāṇasūtra* brings out this idea very clearly:

anityā vata saṁskārā utpāda-vyaya-dharmiṇaḥ |
utpadya hi nirudhyante teṣām vyapaśamas sukham ||

"Impermanent, indeed, are all conditioned things. It is their very nature to come into being and then to cease. Having been produced, they are stopped. Their cessation brings peace and ease."

Śama or *upaśama* connotes extinction of craving, cessation of suffering and a state of calm.

(2) bliss—*Nibbānam paramaṁ sukham*
"Nirvāṇa is the supreme bliss."

(3) *Sambodhi or prajñā* (transcendental wisdom)

(4) *jñāna* (illumination) or *viññāṇam*—pure, radiant consciousness.

(5) security (*kṣamam*)

3. Paradoxical. This statement is mostly found in Prajñāpāramitā or Mahāyānika literature. Nirvāṇa is abiding in a state of non-abiding. The only way of reaching the goal is to

realize that in the ultimate sense there is no goal to be reached. Nirvāṇa is reality which is *śūnya* (void).

4. Symbolical: Symbolical description differs from the paradoxical in avoiding to speak in abstractions and using concrete images instead. From this standpoint, Nirvāṇa is (1) the cool cave, (2) the island in the floods, (3) the further shore, (4) the holy city, (5) the refuge, (6) the shelter, (7) the asylum.

A question that arises in this connexion is whether Nirvāṇa is only a transformed state of the mind or whether it is another dimension of being. The word has been used both for a transformed psychological state and for a metaphysical status.

Buddhist literature is full of statements which go to show that Nirvāṇa is a transformed state of personality and consciousness. The transformation is described in negative terms as the destruction of *taṇhā* (craving) and *āsavas* (obsessions) and in positive terms as the emergence of *prajñā* or *sambodhi* (transcendental wisdom) and *Śānti* (peace).

While the emphasis is on the transformed psychological state, there are also statements which go to show that Nirvāṇa has a metaphysical status, that it is a different dimension of being.

Two quotations will suffice.

The Buddha is said to have made the following remark about Nirvāṇa:

"There is an Unborn, Unbecome, Unmade, Uncompounded; for if there were not this Unborn, Unbecome, Unmade, Uncompounded, there would be apparently no escape from this here that is born, become, made, and compounded" (*Udāna*, VIII.3)

This goes to show that Nirvāṇa is not annihilation, that the aspirant enters a different dimension of being. Some have tried to explain it away as a mere transformed state of personality. The logic of the words does not permit such an interpretation. There is, however, another statement in Udāna which cannot, by any linguistic *tour de force* be interpreted as mere transformation of personality. It is as follows:

consideration as *bhāva* (ens) or *abhāva* (non-ens) of the real." It is above the relativity of existence and non-existence. Candrakīrti clinches the whole issue by saying *Tataśca sarvakalpanā-kṣayarūpam eva nirvāṇam* (P., P. p. 229) Nirvāṇa or Reality is that which is absolved of all thought-construction.

4. The Hīnayānist thinks that *Nirvāṇa* is the opposite of *saṁsāra* (phenomena). Nāgārjuna says that there is no difference between *Nirvāṇa* and *saṁsāra*.

Na saṁsārasya nirvāṇāt kiñcid asti viśeṣaṇam /
Na nirvāṇasya saṁsārāt kiñcid asti viśeṣaṇam. //

(M.K. XXV, 19)

"Nothing of phenomenal existence (*saṁsāra*) is different from *nirvāṇa*, nothing of *nirvāṇa* is different from phenomenal existence."

Nirvāṇasya ca yā koṭiḥ koṭiḥ saṁsaraṇasya ca /
Na tayor antaraṁ kiñcit susūkṣmam api vidyate //

(M.K. XXV, 20)

"That which is the limit of Nirvāṇa is also the limit of *saṁsāra*; there is not the slightest difference between the two".

Ya ājavaṁjavībhāva upādāya pratītya vā/
So' pratītya anupādāya nirvāṇam upadiśyate//

(MK., XXV, 9)

"That which when appropriating or relative (*upādāya*) or dependent (pratītya vā) wanders to and from (*ājavaṁja-vībhāva*)in its conditioned nature is declared to be Nirvāṇa when not depending (*apratītya*) or not appropriating or relative (*anupādāya*) i.e., in its unconditioned nature.

To sum up, there are two main features which distinguish the Mādhyamika conception of Nirvāṇa from that of the Hīnayānist.

(1) The Hīnayānist considers certain defiled and conditioned *dharmas* (elements) to be ultimately real, and also certain undefiled and unconditioned *dharmas* to be ultimately real. According to him, Nirvāṇa means a veritable change of the discrete, conditioned existences (*saṁskṛta dharmas*) and defilements ((*kleśas*) into unconditioned (*asaṁskṛta*) and undefiled *dharmas*. The Mādhyamika says that Nirvāṇa does not mean a change in the objective order, the change is only subjective. It is not the world that we have to change, but only ourselves. If the *kleśas* (defilements) and the *saṁskṛta dharmas* (conditioned existences) were ultimately real, no power on earth could

change them. The change is in our outlook; it is a psychological transformation, not an ontological one. Suzuki sums up the Mādhyamika position about Nirvāṇa in the following words: "Theoretically, Nirvāṇa is the dispersion of the clouds hovering round the light of Bodhi. Morally, it is the suppression of egoism and the awakening of love (*karuṇā*). Religiously it is the absolute surrender of the self to the will of the Dharmakāya." (*Outlines of M. Buddhism*, p. 369). It may be added that ontologically it is the Absolute itself. "Nirvāṇa is not something which can be abandoned or acquired, neither a thing annihilated nor a thing eternal; it is neither destroyed nor produced." (M.K., XXV, 3). No change can be effected in the Absolute or Reality. It is as it has always been. A change has to be effected only in ourselves.

2. The Absolute and the Empirical, the Noumenon and the Phenomena, Nirvāṇa and Saṁsāra are not two sets of separate realities set over against each other. The Absolute or Nirvāṇa viewed through the thought-constructions (*vikalpa*) is saṁsāra, the world or *saṁsāra* viewed *sub specie aeternitatis* is the Absolute or Nirvāṇa itself.

It may be said in passing that much of the confusion regarding Nirvāṇa is due to the fact that the same word Nirvāṇa is used for the psychological change consequent on the extinction of craving and the sense of ego, and also for the ontological Reality or the Absolute. It should be borne in mind that Nāgārjuna is using the word Nirvāṇa throughout the twenty-fifth chapter of the *Madhyamaka Karikā* in the sense of the Absolute Reality and it is from this standpoint that his criticism has been levelled against the Hīnayānist.

3. *Difference in Ideal*

The ideal of Hīnayāna is Arhatship or Arhantship; the ideal of Mahāyāna is that of the Bodhisattva. To put it in simple English, the ideal of Hīnayāna is individual enlightenment; the ideal cf Mahāyāna is universal enlightenment.

The word 'yāna' is generally translated as way, path or vehicle. In his "Survey of Buddhism", Bhikshu Saṅgharakṣita suggests 'career' for 'yāna'. This seems to be the best English equivalent for 'yāna'.

There were three *yānas* known to Early Buddhism, viz., Śrāvaka-yāna, Pratyekabuddha-yāna and Bodhisattva-yāna. *Śrāvaka* (Pāli-*Sāvaka*) literally means 'hearer'. This name was given to the disciple who having heard i.e, learned the truth from the Buddha or any of his disciples aims at Arhantship. Arhat or Arhant means the status of the holy man who has won enlightenment. The word 'Arhat' means etymologically 'worthy'. Another meaning that is suggested in some Buddhist books is 'one who has slain (*han*) the enemies (*ari*) i. e. the kleśas or defilements.

Pratyekabuddha (Pāli, *Poccekabuddha*) is one who in 'solitary singleness', in independence of all external support, attains Arhatship. The word 'pratyeka' means 'private', 'individual', 'single', 'solitary'. He does not share with others his hard-won knowledge of the means for the attainment of Nirvāṇa. He believes that others too, driven by the stern reality of the miseries of life, may some day take to the holy path, but does not bother to teach or enlighten them.

The above two adepts represent the ideal of individualism. They consider enlightenment as an individual not a social or cosmic achievement.

The Bodhisattva (Pāli, *Boddhisatta*) seeks supreme enlightenment not for himself alone but for all sentient beings. Bodhisattvayāna has for its aim the attainment of Supreme Buddhahood. It is, therefore, also called the Buddhayāna or Tathāgatayāna. The word 'bodhi' means 'perfect wisdom,' or better 'transcendental wisdom', supreme enlightenment. The word 'sattva' means 'essence.' The word 'bodhi' is untranslatable. It is the reflex of the consciousness of Dharmakāya in human beings. A Bodhisattva is one who has the essence or potentiality of transcendental wisdom or supreme enlightenment, who is on the way to the attainment of transcendental wisdom. He is a potential Buddha. His career lasts for aeons of births in each of which he prepares himself for final Buddhahood by the practice of the six perfections and the stages of moral and spiritual discipline (*daśabhūmi*) and lives a life of heroic struggle and unremitting self-sacrifice for the good of all sentient creatures.

Boddhisattva has in him *bodhi-citta* and *praṇidhānabala*. There are two aspects of *bodhi-citta*, viz. *prajñā* (transcendental wisdom) and *Karuṇā* (universal love). *Praṇidhānabala* is the inflexible resolve to save all sentient creatures. These are the three aspects of Dharmakāya (the Absolute Personalized) as reflected in the religious consciousness of Bodhisattva. Prajñā is the highest expression of the cognitive side; *karuṇā* is the highest expression of the emotive side, and *praṇidhānabala* is the highest expression of the volitional side of consciousness. Bodhisattva thus develops all the aspects of consciousness.

Bodhicitta is the most important characteristic of Bodhisattva. On the basis of Nāgārjuna's 'Discourse on the Transcendentality of the Bodhicitta, Suzuki gives a detailed description of *bodhicitta* in his *Outlines of Mahāyāna Buddhism.* It may be summarized thus:

(1) The *bodhicitta* is free from all determinations—the five *skandhas,* the twelve *āyatanas* and the eighteen *dhātus.* It is not particular, but universal.

(2) Love is the essence of the Bodhicitta, therefore, all Bodhisattvas find their *raison d' etre* in this.

(3) The *bodhicitta* abiding in the heart of sameness (*samatā*) creates individual means of salvation (*upāya*).

The Bodhisattva has to pass through ten stages of development (*daśa bhūmis*), viz. (1) *pramuditā* (delight)—which he feels in passing from the narrow ideal of personal Nirvāṇa to the higher ideal of emancipating all sentient creatures from the thraldom of ignorance, (2) *vimalā*—negatively 'freedom from defilement', positively 'purity of heart', (3) *prabhākarī*—the penetrating insight into the impermanence of all things, (4) *arciṣmatī*—In this the Bodhisattva practises passionlessness and detachment and burns the twin coverings (*āvaranas*) of defilement and ignorance (5) *sudurjayā*—In this he develops *samatā*—the spirit of sameness, and enlightenment by means of meditation. (6) *abhimukhī* or Face to Face.—In this the Bodhisattva stands face to face with Reality. He realizes the sameness of all phenomena, (7) *dūraṅgamā* or the far-going.—In this he acquires the knowledge that enables him to adopt any means for his work of salvation. He has won Nirvāṇa, but without entering it, he is busily engaged for the emancipation of all, (8) *acalā* or the immovable.—In this, the Bodhisattva experiences the *anutpattika-dharma-kṣānti* or acquiescence in the unoriginatedness of all phenomena. He knows in detail the evolution and involution of the universe. (9) *Sādhumatī*—In this he acquires comprehensive knowledge, unfathomable by ordinary human intelligence. He knows the desires and thoughts of men and is able to teach them according to their capacities, (10) *dharmameghā*. In this he acquires perfection of contemplation, knows the mystery of existence, and is consecrated as perfect. He attains Buddhahood.

The ideal of Hīnayāna was Arhatship or attainment of personal enlightenment. The ideal of Mahāyāna was Bodhisattvayāna. Śrāvakayāna and Pratyekabuddhayāna, according to Mahāyāna aimed at mere individual enlightenment which was a narrow ideal. Bodhisattvayāna aimed at universal enlightenment. It was the destiny of every individual to become a Buddha. The Bodhisattva ideal of Mahāyāna was higher (*mahā*); that of Hīnayāna was inferior (*hīna*).

The difference in the spiritual ideal of the two is expressed in yet another way. The ideal of Hīnayāna is Nirvāṇa; the ideal of Mahāyāna is Buddhatva, the attainment of Buddhahood. The Mahāyānist does not consider the attainment of Nirvāṇa to be the highest ideal, but the attainment of Buddhatva i.e. *prajñā* (transcendental insight) and *karuṇā* (universal love) to be the highest ideal.

4. *Difference regarding the means for the attainment of Nirvāṇa*

The Hīnayānist believes that by the realization of *pudgala-nairātmya* (not-self or unsubstantiality of the person), one could attain Nirvāṇa.

The Mahāyānist maintains that it is not only by the realization of *pudgala-nairātmya*, but also by the realization of *dharma-nairātmya* (i.e. that all the *dharmas* or elements of existence are unsubstantial, devoid of any independent reality of their own) that one really attains Nirvāṇa.

According to Mahāyāna, the realization of both *pudgala nairātmya* and *dharma-nairātmya* is necessary for the attainment of Nirvāṇa.

5. *Difference regarding the removal of the āvaraṇas or obstacles*

Closely connected with the above is the question of the removal of the *āvaraṇas*.

The Hīnayānist says that man is unable to attain Nirvāṇa, because Reality is hidden by the veil (*āvaraṇa*) of passions like attachment, aversion, delusion (*kleśāvaraṇa*). The *kleśāvaraṇa* acts as an obstacle in the way of the realization of Nirvāṇa. The *kleśāvaraṇa* has, therefore, to be removed before one can attain Nirvāṇa. The *kleśas*, however, depend for their activity on the belief of an identical personal self (*satkāyadṛṣṭi*). It is only by realizing *pudgala-nairātmya* i.e. the non-reality or unsubstantiality of a personal self that the *kleśas* or the obstacles can be removed, and only when the *kleśas* are removed can Nirvāṇa be attained. The removal of *Kleśāvaraṇa* is thus connected with the realization of *pudgala-nairātmya*, The Hīnayānist considers the removal of *kleśāvaraṇa* alone as sufficient for the attainment of Nirvāna.

The Mahāyānist says that Reality is veiled not only by *kleśāvaraṇa* but also by *jñeyāvaraṇa* or the veil that hides true knowledge. The removal, therefore, of *jñeyāvaraṇa* is also necessary. This is possible by the realization of *dharmanairātmya* or *dharmaśūnyatā*, the egolessness and emptiness of all elements of existence.

Just as the removal of *kleśāvaraṇa* is connected with the realization of *pudgala-nairātmya*, so the removal of *jñeyāvaraṇa* is connected with the realization of *dharmanairātmya*.

The Mahāyānist maintains that the removal of *kleśāvaraṇa* alone is not sufficient for the attainment of full freedom; the removal of *jñeyāvaraṇa* is also necessary.

6. *Difference in the Concept of Dharma*

The Hīnayānists believed in certain ultimate reals, called *dharmas*. The word *dharma* in this sense is difficult to translate. It is sometimes translated as 'things'. It should be borne in mind that *dharmas* are not 'things' in the sense of the crude data of common sense. 'Elements of existence', 'ultimate reals'—these are better translations of *dharmas*. Hīnayāna believes that the world is composed of an unceasing flow of certain *ultimate dharmas* which are simple, momentary and impersonal. Most of them are *Saṁskṛta* (*dharmas* with signs), and some are *asaṁskṛta* (dharmas without signs).

According to Mahāyāna, these *dharmas* are not ultimate realities at all, but only mental constructs. Mahāyāna pointed out that even the so-called ultimate *saṁskṛta* and *asaṁskṛta* dharmas are dependent upon conditions and so relative. Being relative, they are *śūnya* (devoid of reality).

7. *Difference in the concept of Buddhology*

The *rūpa-kāya* of the Buddha was simply the visible physical body. Neither Hīnayāna nor Mahāyāna accepted this as the real Buddha.

Earlier Buddhism had also developed the idea of *nirmāṇa-kāya* which was a fictitious body which the Buddha could assume by his yogic power whenever he liked and by means of which he could appear anywhere. There is no difference of view regarding this body also between the Hīnayānist and the Mādhyamika.

The difference lies in the concept of the *dharma-kāya* of the Buddha. The highest conception regarding the *dharma-kāya* reached by Hīnayāna was that it was the sum total of the qualities (*dharmas*) of the Buddha. When a follower takes refuge in the Buddha it is in this Buddha-nature that he takes refuge. He does not take refuge in Gautama Buddha who is dead and gone.

The Mādhyamika developed the concept of *dharmakāya* in a different way.

The concept of *sambhoga-kāya* was the contribution of the Yogācārins. We shall study the concept of these *kāyas* under a separate heading.

8. *Hīnayāna was intellectual, Mahāyāna devotional also*

Hīnayāna was entirely intellectual. The main concern of the Hīnayānist was to follow the eight-fold path chalked out by the Buddha. In Hīnayāna, it was the human aspect of the Buddha which was emphasized.

In Mahāyāna, Buddha was taken as God, as Supreme Reality itself that had descended on the earth in human form for the good of mankind. The concept of God in Buddhism was never as a creator but as Divine Love that out of compassion embodied itself in human form to uplift suffering humanity. He was worshipped with fervent devotion. The devotion of the Mahāyānist gave rise to the art of sculpture and painting. Beautiful statues of the Buddha were carved out, and excellent imaginative pictures representing him and the various aspects of his life were painted. Mahāyāna maintained that the arduous path of *prajñā* (transcendental wisdom) was meant only for the advanced few, for the average man it was devotion to the Buddha which would enable him to attain Nirvāṇa. Buddha was worshipped in the form of Avalokiteśvara, Amitābha and the future Buddha, Maitreya.

9. *Hīnayāna pluralistic, Mahāyāna non-dualistic*

The philosophy of Hīnayāna was one of radical pluralism, that of Mahāyāna was undiluted non-dualism (advaya).

10. *Hīnayāna rationalistic, Mahāyāna mystic*

The approach to truth adopted by Hīnayāna was one of mystically-tinged rationalism, that adopted by Mahāyāna was one of super-rationalism and profound mysticism.

Main Features of Madhyamaka Philosophy

(1) *Śūnya-Śūnyatā*

The most striking feature of Madhyamaka philosophy is its ever-recurring use of *śūnya* and *śūnyatā*. So central is this idea to the system that it is generally known as *Śūnyavāda* i.e., the philosophy that asserts *Śūnya* as the characterization of Reality.

Śūnya is a most perplexing word in Buddhist philosophy, Non-Buddhists have interpreted it only as nihilism. But that is not what it means.

Etymologically it is derived from the root *śvī* which means 'to swell, to expand'. Curiously enough, the word Brahman is derived from the root 'bṛh' or 'bṛṁh' which also means 'to swell to expand'. The Buddha is said to be seated in *Śūnya tattva*, in the *śūnya* principle'. The word *śūnya* seems to have been used in an ontological sense in such contexts. The implication of the etymological signification of the word does not seem to have been fully worked out.

According to some scholars the word *śūnya* has no ontological signification. It has only a soteriological suggestion. But the word *śūnya* has obviously been used also in an ontological sense with an axiological overtone and soteriological background.

In the ontological sense *śūnya* is the void which is also fulness. Because it is nothing in particular, it has the possibility of every thing. It has been identified with Nirvāṇa., with the Absolute, with Paramārtha-sat (the Supreme Reality), with Tattva (Reality). What is the *śūnya-tattva* ? This is what Nāgārjuna has to say:

Aparapratyayaṁ śāntam prapañcair aprapañcitam|
Nirvikalpam anānārtham etattattvasya lakṣaṇam||

(M. K., XVIII, 9)

(1) It is *aparapratyayam.* It is that experience which cannot be imparted to any one by another. It has to be realized by every one for himself.

(2) It is *śāntam* . It is quiescent, unaffected by the empirical mind.

(3) It is *prapañcair aprapañcitam* i.e. inexpressible by the verbalising mind. It is non-determinate.

(4) It is *nirvikalpam* i.e. it is transcendent to discursive thought.

(5) It is *anānārtham.* It is non-dual.

Śūnyatā is an abstract noun derived from *śūnya.* It means deprivation and suggests fulfilment.

The words *Śūnya* and *Śūnyatā* will best be undersood in connexion with *svabhāva. Svabhāva* literally means'own being'. Candrakīrti says that this word has been used in Buddhist philosophy in two ways :

1. The essence or special property of a thing, e.g., 'heat is the *svabhāva* or special property of fire'. *Iha yo dharmo yam padārthaṁ na vyabhicarati, sa tasya svabhāva iti vyapadiśyate, apara-pratibaddhatvāt*" i.e. "In this world an attribute which always accompanies an object, never parts from it, that, not being indissolubly connected with any thing else, is known as the *svabhāva* i. e., special property of that object" (P.P. 105)

2. *Svabhāva* (own-being) as the contrary of *parabhāva* (other-being). Candrakīrti says, *svo bhāvaḥ svabhāva itiyasya padārthasya yadātmīyaṁ rūpaṁ tat tasya svabhāva iti* (P. P. p. 115) "*Svabhāva* is the own being, the very nature of a thing". Nāgārjuna says *akṛtrimaḥ svabhāvo hi nirapekṣaḥ paratra ca* (M. K. 15, 2). "That is really *svabhāva* which is not brought about by anything else, unproduced (*akṛitrimaḥ*), that which is not dependent on, not relative to any thing other than itself, noncontingent, unconditioned (*nirapekṣaḥ paratra ca*)"

The Mādhyamika rejects the first meaning of *svabhāva* and accepts only the second. Candrakīrti says clearly *kṛtrimasya paraśāpekṣasya ca svabhāvatvaṁ neṣṭam.* "We do not accept that as *svabhāva* which is brought about by, contingent on, relative to something else" The first sense is not acceptable, for even the so-called *svabhāva* or essential property of a thing is *kṛtrima* and *sāpekṣa,* contingent and relative. Even the heat which is the special property of fire depends on so many conditions—a match, or a lens, fuel, or the friction of two pieces of wood. It is, therefore, not *svabhāva* in the highest sense of the word. In one word *svabhāva* is the Absolute reality, whereas everything else, all phenomena are *parabhāva* (relative).

The word *Śūnya* has to be understood from two points of view, viz. (1) from the point of view of phenomena or empirical reality, it means *svabhāva-śūnya* i.e. *devoid of svabhāva* or independent, substantial reality of its own; (2) from the point of view of the Absolute, it means *prapañca-śūnya* i.e. devoid of *prapañca* or verbalisation, thought-construction and plurality.

(i) We shall consider the word *Śūnya* in its first signification at first. We have discussed the word *svabhāva* at length so that we may be able to understand clearly the word *śūnya* when used in connexion with phenomenal reality or with *dharmas* (elements of existence). In this context *śūnya* invariably means *svabhāva-śūnya,* i.e. empty or devoid of independent, substantial reality. There is not a single thing in the world which is unconditionally, absolutely real. Everything is related to, contingent upon, conditioned by something else. The long discussion of causality or *pratītya-samutpāda* in Madhyamaka Śāstra is only meant to show that not a single thing in the world exists in its own right, nothing has an independent reality of its own. Everything is conditioned by something (*pratītyasamutpanna*). The world is not Reality : it is a realm of relativity. That is why Nāgārjuna says *yaḥ pratītyasamutpādaḥ śūnyatāṁ tām pracakṣmahe.* "There is no real production : there is only manifestation of a thing contingent on causes and conditions. It is this conditioned co-production that we designate as Śūnyatā." There is no real causal relation between entities; there is only *mutual dependence* between entities which means in other words that entities are devoid of independent self-hood (*svabhāva*). Causal relation, therefore, does not mean a sequence of realities but only a *sequence of appearances*. Every thing in the world is dependent upon the sum-total of its conditions. Things are merely appearances. Hence *pratītya-samutpāda* is equated with *śūnyatā* or relativity. The world is not a conglomeration of things. It is simply process, and things are simply events. A 'thing' *by itself* is 'nothing' at all. This is what is meant by the *śūnyatā* or emptiness of all *dharmas*.

(ii) Now let us see what *Śūnyatā* means from the standpoint of the Absolute. From the standpoint of the Absolute, *śūnyatā* means *prapañcair aprapañcitam* that which is devoid of, completely free of thought-construction, *anānārthām*, that which is devoid of plurality. In other words, *śūnyatā* as applied to *tattva* signifies that it is,

(*a*) in-expressible in human language.

(*b*) that 'is', 'not is', 'both is' and 'not is', 'neither is' nor 'not is'—no thought-category or predicate can be applied to it. It is transcendent to thought.

(*c*) that it is free of plurality, that it is a Whole which cannot be sundered into parts.

To sum up, the import of *śūnyatā* may be understood in six ways. Three of these are given together in 18th verse of Chapter XXIV of the Kārikā :

yaḥ pratītyasamutpādaḥ śūnyatāṁ tām pracakṣmahe|
Sā prajñaptirupādāyā pratipat saiva madhyamā||

"That we call *śūnyatā* which is *pratītyasamutpāda*, *upādāya prajñapti*, *madhyamā pratipat*."

1. In reference to *vyavahāra* or empirical reality, *śūnyatā* means *naiḥsvābhāvya* i.e., devoidness of self-being, of unconditioned nature. In other words, it connotes conditiond co-production or *pratītyasamutpāda*—thorough-going relativity.

2. This idea is conveyed in another way by the term, *upādāyaprajñapti* or "derived name" which means that the presence of a name does not mean the reality of the named. Candrakīrti says, *cakrādīnyupādāya rathāṅgāni rathaḥ prajñāpyate* i.e., a chariot is so named by taking into account its parts like wheel etc; it does not mean that the chariot is something different in its own right *apart* from its constituent parts. This is another instance of relativity.

As relativity, *śūnyatā* also connotes the relative, non-absolute nature of specific views.

3. Śūnyatā exposes the folly of accepting any absolute beginning or total cessation and thus connotes *madhyamā pratipat*—taking things as they are and avoiding the extremes (1) is and (2) is not.

Over and above these three, there are other senses in which the word *śūnyatā* has been used in Madhyamaka philosophy.

4. In reference to *paramārtha* or ultimate reality, *śūnyatā* connotes the non-conceptual nature of the absolute.

5. In reference to the aspirant, *śnūyatā* implies his attitude of *anupalambha* or the skilfulness of non-clinging to the relative as the absolute or to the absolute as something specific.

6. The Mahāprajñā-pāramitā Śāstra brings out another implication of the *śūnyatā* principle, viz; *dharmaiṣaṇā*, the irrepressible longing for the Real, beyond the passing show of mundane life.

Axiological significance of Śūnyatā

Śūnyatā is not merely a word of ontological signification. It has also an axiological implication. Since all empirical things are devoid of substantial reality, therefore they are 'worthless'. It is because of our ignorance that we attach so much value to worldly things. Once *Śūnyatā* is properly understood, the inordinate craving for the mad rush after a thing that :

> 'Like snow upon the Desert's dusty face
> Lighting a little hour or two is gone'

ceases, and we experience the blessing of peace.

Soteriological significance of Śūnyatā

Śūnyatā is not merely an intellectual concept. Its realization is a means in salvation. When rightly grasped, it leads to the negation of the multiplicity of the *dharmas* and to detachment from the 'passing show' of the tempting things of life. Meditation on *Śūnyatā* leads to *prajñā* (transcendental wisdom) which brings about the emancipation of the aspirant from spiritual darkness. Nāgārjuna puts the quintessence of his teachings about *Śūnyatā* in the following verse:

Karmakleśa-kṣayānmokṣaḥ karmakleśā vikalpataḥ||
Te prapañcāt prapañcastu śūnyatāyāṁ nirudhyate||

(M. K. xviii, 5)

"Emancipation is obtained by the dissolution of selfish deeds and passions All selfish deeds and passions are caused by imaginative constructs which value worthless things as full of worth. The *vikalpas* or imaginative constructs are born of *prapañca*, the verbalizing, imaging activity of the mind. This activity of the mind ceases when *Śūnyatā*, emptiness or hollowness of things is realized."

Śūnya as the symbol of the inexpressible

Śūnya is used in Madhyamaka philosophy as a symbol of the inexpressible. In calling Reality *śūnya*, the Mādhyamika only means to say that it is *avācya*, *anabhilāpya* i.e., inexpressible. In the very first verse of *Madhyamaka Kārika*, Nāgārjuna makes the standpoint of *Śūnyavāda* luminously prominent. The standpoint consists of the eight 'Nos'.

Anirodham anutpādam anucchedam aśāśvatam|
Anekārtham anānārtham anāgamam anirgamam.||

It is (1) *anirodham*, beyond destruction, (2) *anutpādam*, beyond production, (3) *anucchedam*, beyond dissolution, (4) *aśāśvatam*, beyond eternity. (5) *anekārtham*—beyond oneness, (6) *anānārtham*—beyond plurality, (7) *anāgamam* beyond ingress (8) *anirgamam*—beyond egress.

In short, Reality is beyond the dichotomies of the intellect. It in inexpressible. The word 'śūnya' (or śūnyatā) has been used in this system, now and then, as indicative of *avācya*, *avyākṛta*.

Śūnyatā not a theory

We have seen that the Mādhyamika uses the dialectic as a criticism of all *dṛṣṭis* (theories) without any theory of his own. By the use of his dialectic, he reaches the conclusion that all the *dharmas* are *śūnya* or *nissvabhāva* i.e. devoid of any independent, substantial reality.

It may be thought that *śūnyatā* itself is a theory. But this would be a misreading of the Mādhyamika's position. *Śūnyatā* is not a theory. It is at once the awareness of the impotence of Reason to realize Truth and the urge to rise to a level higher than Reason in order to realize it. When the thinker lets go his foothold on discursive thought, it is only then that he can mount to something higher.

The purpose of *śūnyatā* is beautifully put by Nāgārjuna in the following verse :

Atra brūmaḥ śūnyatāyāṁ na tvaṁ vetsi prayojanam|
Śūnyatāṁ śūnyatārthaṁ ca tata evaṁ vihanyase||

(M. K. XXIV, 7)

"You do not know the purpose of *śūnyatā*. *Śūnyatā* is not used as a theory just for the sake of *śūnyatā*." In explaining the purpose of *śunyatā*, Candrakīrti says that it is meant to silence the incessant cogitation of the verbalizing mind (*prapañcastu śūnyatāyāṁ nirudhyate*). *Śūnyatā* is taught not for its own sake, but for leading the mind to Reality by restraining its conceptualizing tendency. It is an expression of *aspiration*, not of theory.

Śūnyatā—not nihilism

It is contended by some that *śūnyatā* is sheer negativism. It denounces everything and has no positive suggestion to offer. *Śūnyatā* does not lead us anywhere. It is rank nihilism.

The Madhyamaka dialectic leading to *Śūnyatā* is not mere negativism. It does not simply negate all affirmations about Reality; it also negates all negations about Reality. It says Reality is neither *sat* (existent) nor *asat* (non-existent). It only asserts that the Absolute is inaccessible to thought; it does not say that the Absolute is a non-entity. It only maintains that the Absolute is realized in non-dual, transcendental wisdom. It vehemently pleads for the realization of the absolute Truth. Nāgārjuna says "paramārtham anāgamya nirvāṇaṁ nādhigamyate" i.e., "without realizing the absolute Truth, one cannot attain Nirvāṇa".

The Mādhyamika only negates all views about Reality; it does not negate Reality itself. It cannot, therefore, be called nihilism. As Dr. Mūrti puts it "No-doctrine, about Reality does not mean no Reality doctrine". "*Śūnyatā* is negative only for thought; but in itself it is the non-relational knowledge of the Absolute. It may even be taken as more universal and positive than affirmation" (CPB, p. 160).

Candrakīrti vehemently protests against the Mādhyamika being called nihilist (*nāstika*). He says that the Mādhyamika only points to the relativity of things; and that his doctrine transcends both affirmation and negation (P. P. p., 156-157).

The Kārikā devotes a whole chapter (ch. XXIV) for elucidating its position that *śūnyatā* is not nihilism but only relativity and conditionedness, that it is not a rejection of the world of becoming but an explication of its inner implication viz., that the unconditioned is the ultimate truth of the conditioned. Nāgārjuna puts it beautifully in Kārikā XXIV, 14

Sarvaṁ ca yujyate tasya śūnyatā yasya yujyate||
Sarvaṁ na yujyate tasya śūnyaṁ yasya na yujyate||

"For him who accepts *śūnyatā*, everything stands in its proper place within the harmonious whole, and for him who does not accept śūnyatā, everything is out of joint."

Nāgārjuna only insists that the relative must be taken as the relative and not as the absolute and then there is proper appraisal of values and appreciation of the meaningfulness of life. His so-called negativism is only a therapeutic device.

Śūnyatā—not an end in itself

Nāgārjuna warns that one should not make a fetish of Śūnyatā. It is not an end in itself. It is only a means to lead the mind up to *prajñā* (transcendental insight), and should not be bolstered up as an end in itself. The followning verse of Nāgārjuna expresses this idea bautifully:

Śūnyatā sarvadṛṣṭīnām proktā niḥsaraṇam jinaiḥ|
Yeṣām tu śūnyatā dṛṣṭistān asādhyān babhāṣire||

(M. K. XIII, 8)

"*Śūnyatā* was declared by the Buddha for dispensing with all views or 'isms'. Those who convert *Śūnyatā* itself into another 'ism' are verily beyond hope or help"
Chandrakīrti in commenting on the above refers to a remark of the Buddha about Śūnyatā made to Kāśyapa. The Buddha said to him "O Kāśyapa, it would be better to entertain the

personalistic view (*pudgala dṛṣṭi*) of the magnitude of mount Sumeru than to hug the *Śūnyatā* view of the nihilist (*abhāvābhiniveśikasya*). Him I call incurable who clings to *Śūnyatā* itself as a theory. If a drug administered to a patient were to remove all his disorders but were to foul the stomach itself by remaining in it, would you call the patient cured? Even so, *Śūnyatā* is an antidote against dogmatic views, but if a man were to cling to it for ever as a view in itself, he is doomed."

Elsewhere Buddha is said to have remarked that *Śūnyatā* is to be treated like a ladder for mounting up to the roof of *prajñā*. Once the roof is reached, the ladder should be discarded.

Nāgārjuna, again warns unequivocally in the following verse, against the wrong use of *Śūnyatā*.

Vināśayati durdṛṣṭā śūnyatā mandamedhasam/
Sarpo yathā durgṛhīto vidyā vā duṣprasādhitā//

(M. K. XXIV, 11)

"Just as a snake caught at the wrong end by a dull-witted fellow only kills him or a magic wrongly employed ruins the magician, so too *Śūnyatā* wrongly used by a man who does not understand its implications only ruins him."

Dr. R. H. Robinson sums up the whole issue beautifully in the following words:

"Emptiness (śūnyatā) is not a term outside the expressional system, but is simply the key term within it. Those who would hypostatize emptiness are confusing the symbol system with the fact system." (*Early Mādhyamika in India and China*, p. 49)

Meditation on śūnyatā

It has already been said that *śūnyatā* is not simply an intellectual concept but an aspiration. In order to perfect this aspiration, one has to meditate on twenty varieties of *śūnyatā*. They are too long to be given here.

2. *Prajñāpāramitā*

The second important feature of Mahāyāna Buddhism is the practice of *prajñāpāramitā*.

Meditation on the *śūnyatā* (emptiness) is only a preparation for the spiritual discipline of *prajñāpāramitā*. *Prajñā* is super-rational. It is transcendent insight. *Prajñā* knows reality as it is (*prajñā yathābhūtam artham prajānāti*). Dr. K. V. Ramanan says that *Mahāprajñā pāramitā Śāstra* uses the world *prajñā* in two senses, viz. (1) the eternal *prajñā*, and (2) the *prajñā* that functions along with the five *pāramitās*. The latter is the functional *prajñāpāramitā*, while the former is the substantial or stable *prajñā*. The functional *prajñā* puts an end to the darkness of ignorance and thus the eternal *prajñā* comes to the fore, In the eternal *prajñā*, one cannot find even the distinction of ignorance and knowledge. It is an ever-present luminous knowledge. It is the "eternal light in the heart of man." Particular objects arise and perish, but the light of this *prajñā* keeps for ever shining.

The functional *prajñā* is the act of knowing which consists of analysis, criticism and comprehension. These are only mode of the power of the permanent *prajñā*.

It is only by attaining *prajñā* that we can know Truth. *Prajñā* cannot be attained by the chattering academician 'sicklied over with the pale cast of thought', nor can it be attained simply by putting on the wishing cap. It can be attained only by arduous self-discipline and self-culture. *Prajñāpāramitā* is usually translated as perfection of wisdom, but it really means 'transcendent wisdom' (*prajñā pāramitā*).

There are six spiritual qualities that have to be acquired. Prajñāpāramitā is a blanket term for all these qualities. They are 1. *dāna* (charity) 2. *śīla* (withdrawing from all evil deeds), 3. *kṣānti* (forbearance), 4. *vīrya* (enthusiasm and exertion), 5. *dhyāna* (concentration) 6. *prajñā* (transcendental insight). The first four are moral qualities. Their development prepares one for the practice of *dhyāna*. *Dhyāna* orients the mind towards *prajñā*. After sufficient practice of *dhyāna*, scales fall frcm the eyes and one sees truth face to face (*vipaśyanā*); the chrysalis of the ego is split asunder, and one sees 'the light that never was on sea or land' :

The object of *prajñāpāramitā* is *tathatā*, *dharmadhātu*, *bhūtvkoṭī*

Prajñāpāramitā is the highest kind of knowledge. It is an integral principle which comprehends both the aspects of cognition and emotion and so comprises both truth and universal love. It destroys not only the craving for sense-pleasure but also all desire for power and pelf.

3. *The Ideal of the Bodhisattva*

It has already been said in connexion with the distinction between Hīnayāna and Mahāyāna that the attainment of the status of the Bodhisattva is the ideal of Mahāyāna.

According to the *Mahāprajñāpāramitā-śāstra*, Bodhi means the way of all the Buddhas, and *sattva* means the essence and character of the good *dharma*. The *citta* of the Bodhisattva helps every one to cross the stream of birth and death. Therefore it is the *citta* or the individual that is really the Bodhisattva.

There are three important qualities of the Bodhisattva, viz, the great resolve to save all mankind, the thought that is unshakable, and the effort that knows no set-back.

When an aspirant acquires *anutpattika-dharma-kṣānti* i.e. the capacity to endure and sustain the truth of the unborn *dharma*, then he enters the true status (*nyāma*) of the Bodhisattva. Having entered this status, he is known as *avaivarta*, the irreversible, the unshakable.

When he realizes the *anutpattika-dharma-kṣānti*, he puts an end to the *kleśas* and when he achieves Buddhahood, he puts an end to their residual impressions.

The aspirant evolves to the status of a Bodhisattva by *anuttara pūjā*—a devotional discipline consisting of seven steps, and the practice of the six *prajñāpāramitās*. The highest development of the Bodhisattva consists in acquiring *bodhicitta* which has two aspects, viz. (1) *Śūnyatā* or *prajñā* and, (2) *Karuṇā*. We have already seen what *śūnyatā* or *prajñā* is. *Karuṇā* is usually translated as compassion or commiseration, but it is better to translate it as universal love as Suzuki has done. *Prajñā* or transcendent wisdom and *Karuṇā* or universal love constitute Buddhahood.

4. *Buddhology*

In Hīnayāna, the Buddha was simply a human being who by his own effort became enlightened and divine. In Mahāyāna, it is Divinity itself that incarnates itself in a Buddha and descends to earth to impart the highest teaching about man's destiny as an act of grace.

Mahāyāna evolved the concept of three bodies of the Buddha, viz. (1) *Nirmāṇa-kāya* (2) *Dharma-kāya* and (3) *Sambhoga-kāya*. The *Sambhoga-kāya* or the body of bliss was a concept evolved later by the Yogācārins. The Mādhyamikas speak only of two bodies of the Buddha, viz. *Dharma-kāya* and *Nirmāṇa-kāya*.

Dharma is a most protean word in Buddhism. In the broadest sense it means an impersonal spiritual energy behind and in everything. There are four important senses in which this word has been used in Buddhist philosophy and religion.

(1) *Dharma* in the sense of one ultimate Reality. It is both transcendent and immanent to the world, and also the governing law within it.

(2) *Dharma* in the sense of scripture, doctrine, religion, as the Buddhist *dharma*.

(3) *Dharma* in the sense of righteousness, virtue, piety.

(4) *Dharma* in the sense of "elements of existence." In this sense, it is generally used in plural.

Dharma in the word *Dharma-kāya* is used in the first sense, viz. ultimate Reality. The word *kāya* in this context is not used in the literal sense of body, but in the sense of *āśraya* or substratum, in the sense of unity, organised form. Dharmakāya means 'the principle of cosmic unity'. It is not merely an abstract philosophical concept, but an 'object of the religious consciousness'.

Dharmakāya

Dharma is the essence of being, the ultimate Reality, the Absolute. The *Dharma-kāya* is the essential nature of the Buddha. As Dharmakāya, the Buddha experiences his identity with Dharma or the Absolute and his unity (*samatā*) with all beings. The Dharmakāya is a knowing; loving, willing being, an inexhaustible fountain-head of love and compassion.

When Buddha's disciple, the monk Vakkali was on his death-bed, he expressed his ardent desire to see the Buddha in person. On that occasion, the Buddha remarked "He who sees the *Dhamma* sees Me. He who sees Me sees the *Dhamma*."

This statement of the Buddha gave rise to the conviction that the real Buddha was the *Dharma*, not the historical Gautama known as the Buddha, and thus the idea of *Dharma-kāya* was developed. The Mahāsaṅghikas conceived of Buddha as *lokottara* or *Dharma-kāya* (transcendental) and Śākyamuni only as *Nirmāṇakāya* or a phantom body conjured up by the *Dharma-kāya* for bringing the message of *Dharma* to ignorant humanity.

Dharma-kāya is the essential transcendental aspect of the Buddha. Dharmatā is the ultimate impersonal principle. Dharma-kāya is the ultimate universal person. There is a slight resemblance between the *Brahman* and *Īśvara* of Vedānta and Dharmadhātu and *Dharma-kāya* of the Mādhyamika. *Dharma dhātu* or *tathatā is* like the Vedāntic Brahman and *Dharma-kāya* is something like the Vedāntic *Īśvara*, but there is also a good deal of difference between the two. In Vedānta, *Īśvara* in association with *Māyā* creates, sustains and withdraws the universe. *Dharma-kāya* has no such function. The function of *Dharma-kāya* is to descend out of his deep wisdom and love, to earth as a Buddha in order to teach the *Dharma* and uplift erring humanity. He is Divine and yet not God, for in every system the function of creation of the universe is associated with God. Buddhism does not believe in any such God. Suzuki puts the idea of God in Buddhism in the following words: "Buddhism must not be judged as an atheism which endorses an agnostic, materialistic interpretation of the universe. Far from it, Buddhism outspokenly acknowledges the presence in the world of a reality which transcends the limitations of phenomenality, but which is nevertheless immanent everywhere and manifests itself in its full glory, and in which we live, and move and have our being." (*Outlines of Mahāyāna Buddhism* p. 219)

Dharma-kāya is identified with the Absolute and is also connected with the phenomenal. Therefore it is Dharma-kāya alone that can descend to earth as the saviour of mankind.

Whenever Dharmakāya decides to come down to earth in human form, He conjures up a phantom body called *Nirmāṇa-kāya*. *Nirmāṇa-kāya* is the body assumed by *Dharma-kāya* whenever he decides to come down to earth to save mankind. It is through this that He incarnates in a human form, as a Buddha, as the saviour of mankind. The actual physical body of the Buddha is the *Rūpa-kāya*. It will thus be seen that Buddhism is not a historical religion like official Christianity. The Buddha is not the founder of a religion. He only transmits Dharma which is eternal. There have been many Buddhas before, and there will be many Buddhas in the future.

When a Buddhist takes refuge in the Buddha, it is the eternal *Dharma-kāya Buddha* in whom he takes refuge.

Nirmāṇa-Kāya

It has already been said that *Nirmāṇa-kāya* is a body assumed by the Buddha in order to establish contact with the world in a human form. *Dharma-kāya* is also known as *Svābhāvika-kāya* or the essential, natural *kāya* of the Buddha. The *Nirmāṇakāya* is assumed for the time being for a specific purpose. The *Rūpa-kāya* or the actual physical body of the Buddha is visible to every one. The *Nirmāṇa-kāya* is visible only to adepts.

Significance of the Concept of Madhyamā Pratipad

The Buddha used to say that Truth did not lie in the extreme alternatives but in the middle position (*madhyamā pratipad*). Hīnayānists generally used the concept of *madhyamā pratipad* in the ethical sense, in the sense of neither taking too much food nor too little, neither sleeping too much, nor too little etc.

The Mādhyamikas interpreted *madhyamā pratipad* in a metaphysical sense also. Says Nāgārjuna:

Kātyāyanāvavāde cāstīti nāstīti cobhayam |
Pratiṣiddhaṁ bhagavatā bhāvābhāvavibhāvinā ||

(M. K. XV, 7)

"In the *Kātyāyanāvavāda-sūtra*, the Lord who had the right insight into both *bhāva* (ens) and *abhāva* (non-ens) rejected both the extreme alternatives of 'is' and 'is not.''

In commenting on this, Candrakīrti has quoted the relevant passage in the *Kātyāyanāvavāda-sūtra* which is accepted as an authority by all the Buddhists. In this, Buddha says to Kāśyapa, "O Kāśyapa, 'is' is one extreme alternative, 'not is' is another extreme alternative. That which is the *madhyama* position is intangible, incomparable, without any position, non-appearing, incomprehensible. That is what is meant by *madhyamā pratipat* (the middle position) O Kāśyapa. It is perception of Reality (*bhūta pratyavekṣā*)" (P. P., p. 118) Nāgārjuna takes his stand on this authoritative statement of the Buddha. The word *madhyama* is not to be taken in its literal sense of 'in between' or a 'mean between the two'. As is clear from the adjectives 'intangible, incomparable, incomprehensible etc., *madhyamā pratipat* (the middle position) means that Reality is transcendent to the antinomies of Reason, the dichotomies of thought, and cannot be 'cabined, caged and confined' in the alternatives of 'is' and 'is not'. It is on this basis that Nāgārjuna called his philosophy *madhyamaka* i.e. 'pertaining to the transcendent'.

Extremes become the dead-ends of eternalism and annihilationalism. There are those who cling exclusively to nonbeing and there are others who cling exclusively to being. The great Buddha meant, by his doctrine of *madhyamā pratipat* (Middle way), to drive home the truth that things here are neither absolute being nor absolute non-being, but are arising and perishing, forming continuous becoming, and that Reality is transcendent to thought and cannot be caught up in the dichotomies of the mind.

The Absolute and Phenomena

There are many words used for the Absolute or Reality in Madhyamaka philosophy. *Tathatā* (suchness) *śūnyatā*, *nirvāṇa*, *advaya* (non-dual), *anutpanna* (unproduced), *nirvikalpa* (the realm of non-discrimination), *dharmdhātu* or *dharmatā* (the essence of being, the true nature of Dharma), *anabhilāpya* (the inexpressible) *tattva* (thatness) *niśprapañca* (free of verbalisation and plurality), *yathābhūta* (that which really is), *Satya* (Truth), *bhūtatathatā* or *bhūtatā* (the true reality), *tathāgata-garbha* (the womb of Tathāgatas), *aparapratyaya* (reality which one must realize within oneself), etc. Each word is used from a particular standpoint.

Throughout the *Madhyamaka śāstra*, Nāgārjuna has been at pains to prove that the Absolute is transcendent to both thought and speech. Neither the concept of *bhāva* (ens) nor *abhāva* (non-ens) is applicable to it. Nāgārjuna advances the following reason for the inapplicability of these concepts.

Bhāvastāvad na nirvāṇaṁ jarāmaraṇalakṣaṇam /
Prasajyetāsti bhāvo hi na jarāmaraṇaṁ vinā //

(M. K. XXV 4)

"Nirvāṇa or the Absolute Reality cannot be a *bhāva* or positive ens, for in that case it would be subject to origination, decay, and death; there is no empirical existence which is free from decay and death. If it cannot be *bhāva*, far less can it be *abhāva*, (non-existence), for *abhāva* (non-existence) is only a relative concept (absence of *bhāva*) depending upon the concept of *bhāva*." As Nāgārjuna puts it:

Bhāvasya cedaprasiddhiṛabhāvo naiva siddhyati /
Bhāvasya hyanyathābhāvam abhāvam bruvate janāḥ //

(M. K. XV, 5)

"When *bhāva* itself is proved to be inapplicable to Reality, *abhāva* cannot stand scrutiny, for *abhāva* is known only as the disappearance of *bhāva*."

When the concepts of *bhāva* (empirical existence), and *abhāva* (the negation of *bhāva*) cannot be applied to the Absolute, the question of applying any other concept to it does not arise, for all other concepts depend upon the above two. In one word, the Absolute is transcendent to thought, and because it is transcendent to thought, it is inexpressible.

Nirvṛttamabhidhātavyaṁ nivṛtte cittagocare /
Anutpannāniruddhā hi nirvāṇamiva dharmatā //

(XVIII, 7)

"What cannot be an object of thought cannot, *a fortiori*, be an object of speech. The Absolute as the essence of all being is neither born, nor does it cease to be."

Candrakīrti says, *Paramārtho hi āryāṇām tūṣṇīmbhāvaḥ* (P. P. p. 19) "To the saints, the Absolute is just silence i.e. it is inexpressible".

Phenomena have no independent, substantial reality of their own. Relativity or dependence is the main characteristic of phenomena, and that which is relative is not real in the highest sense of the word. The Absolute is the Reality of the appearances.

The Absolute and the world are not two different sets of reality posited against each other. Phenomena viewed as relative, as governed by causes and conditions constitute the world, and viewed as free of all conditions are the Absolute.

The Absolute is always of uniform nature. Nirvāṇa or the Absolute Reality is not something produced or achieved. Nirvāṇa only means the disappearance of the fabrications of discursive thought.

If the Absolute is beyond all thought and speech, how can the Absolute be described, how can there be any teaching about the Absolute? The answer is—Phenomena do not completely cut us off from Reality. Phenomena are appearances, and appearances point to their Reality. The veil gives a hint of that which is veiled.

Candrakīrti quotes a saying of the Buddha,

Anakṣarasya dharmasya śrutiḥ kā deśanā ca kā |
Śrūyate deśyate cāpi samāropādanakṣaraḥ ||

"How can there be any understanding or teaching of that which is wordless (i.e. inexpressible)? That can be understood and taught only by *samāropa*—an ascribed mark." Phenomena serve as the 'ascribed mark' of Reality. Phenomena are like an envelope that contains within it an invitation from Reality. The superimposed character (*samāropa*) of phenomena veils the noumenon; when that superimposed character is uncovered, when the veil is removed, it only reveals Reality. The philosophy of *Śūnyatā* is meant only to help uncover the veil.

Saṁvṛti and Paramārtha Satya

Are phenomena wholly unreal? Nāgārjuna says they have reality of a sort. They are *saṁvṛti satya*; they are the *appearance* of Reality. Appearance points to that which appears. *Saṁvṛti* is appearance, cover or veil. *Saṁvṛti* or cover is not a mere gossamer floating about in *vacuo*; *saṁvṛti* covers *paramārtha* (absolute reality). Nāgārjuna says:

Dve satye samupāśritya buddhānāṁ dharmadeśanā |
Lokasaṁvṛtisatyaṁ ca satyaṁ ca paramārthataḥ ||

(M. K., XXIV, 8)

"The Buddhas teach the *Dharma* by resorting to two truths, *saṁvṛti-satya* (empirical truth) and *paramārtha-satya* (absolute truth)."

So important is the distinction that Nāgārjuna maintains that no one can understand the teaching of the Buddha who does not know this distinction.

Ye nayor na vijānanti vibhāgaṁ satyayor dvayoḥ |
Te tattvaṁ na vijānanti gambhīraṁ Buddhaśāsane ||

(M. K. XXIV, 9)

"Those who do not know the distinction between these two truths cannot understand the deep significance of the teaching of the Buddha."

Candrakīrti explains *saṁvṛti* in the following way:

Samantādvaraṇam saṁvṛtiḥ. Ajñānaṁ hi samantāt-sarva-padārthatattvāvacchādanāt saṁvṛtirityucyate ||

(P. P. p. 215)

"That which covers all round is *saṁvṛti*. *Saṁvṛti* is *ajñāna* (primal ignorance) which covers the real nature of all things." Phenomena are characterized as *saṁvṛti*, because they throw a veil over Reality. At the same time they serve as a pointer to Reality as their ground. *Saṁvṛti-satya* is *vyāvahārika-satya* .. pragmatic or empirical reality. *Paramārtha-satya* is absolute reality. Two truths—*Saṁvṛti*-and *paramārtha*, however, do not connote two different spheres to which they are applied. The Absolute comprehended through the categories of thought is phenomena and phenomena stripped of these categories are the Absolute.

Candrakīrti mentions three senses of *saṁvṛti*

(1) *Samantāt sarvapadārthatattvāvacchādanāt saṁvṛtiḥ.*

(P. p. p. 215)

Saṁvṛti is that which covers all round the real nature of things. Candrakīrti calls it *ajñāna* (the primal ignorance). *Saṁvṛti* is due to *ajñāna* or *avidyā* and is identical with it. It is the primal ignorance that throws a veil over Reality.

(2) *Parasparasambhavanaṁ vā saṁvṛtiranyonyasamāśrayeṇa*

(P. p. p. 215)

Saṁvṛti is mutual dependence of things or their relativity. In this sense, it is identical with phenomena.

(3) *Saṁvṛtiḥ saṁketo lokavyavahāraḥ. Sa ca abhidhānābhidheya-jñānajñeyādilakṣaṇaḥ.*

(P. p. p. 215)

What is conventionally accepted by people at large is *saṁvrti*.

All these senses are mutually connected. The first one is the primary sense, but each of these senses has an importance from the point of view of empirical reality.

Saṁvrti or pragmatic reality is the means (*upāya*) for reaching

Reality which is the goal (*upeya*). Nāgārjuna expressly mentions the importance of *vyavahāra* or empirical reality in attaining *paramārtha* or absolute reality. Says he:

> *Vyavahāramanāśritya paramārtho na deśyate |*
> *Paramārthamanāgamya nirvāṇaṁ nādhigamyate ||*
>
> (M. K. XXIV, 10)

"Without a recourse to pragmatic reality, the absolute truth cannot be taught. Without knowing the absolute truth, *nirvāṇa* cannot be attained."

Commenting on this, Candrakīrti says:

> *Tasmād nirvāṇādhigamopāyatvād avaśyameva yathāvasthitā saṁvṛtiḥ ādāveva abhyupeyā bhājanam iva salilārthinā ||*
>
> (P. P. P. 216)

"Therefore, inasmuch as *saṁvṛti* as characterized is a means for the attainment of Nirvāṇa, it should, be adopted, just as a pot is to be used by one desirous of water." *Saṁvṛti* is *upāya* (means), *paramārtha* is *upeya* (goal).

There are two kinds of *saṁvṛti*—(i) *loka-saṁvṛti* and (ii) *aloka-saṁvṛti.* (i) *Loka-saṁvṛti* refers to the common empirical objects recognized as real by all as for example, a jar, a piece of cloth etc, (ii) *Aloka saṁvṛti* refers to objects experienced under abnormal conditions. Illusory objects, distorted perceptions caused by diseased or defective sense-organs, dream objects etc. are cases of *aloka-saṁvṛti*. These are *aloka-saṁvṛti*—non-empirical, for they are unreal even for the empirical consciousness.

Prajñākaramati has designated *loka-saṁvṛti* as *tathya-saṁvṛti* (true *saṁvṛti*) and *aloka-saṁvṛti* as *mithyā-saṁvṛti* (false *saṁvṛti*). The former is like the *vyāvahārika sattā*, and the latter like the *prātibhāsika sattā* of the Vedāntists—Just as *aloka-saṁvṛti* is unreal for the empirical consciousness, even so *loka-saṁvṛti* is unreal from the transcendental point of view. *Saṁvṛti* is called *satya* (true or real) by courtesy, for there cannot be degrees in Truth. Paramārtha or the Absolute Reality alone is truly real.

The texts or teachings of the Buddha bearing on *paramārtha satya* or the Absolute Reality are called *nītārtha* (primary or direct) and those bearing on *saṁvṛti-satya* are called *neyārtha* (secondary, indirect) by the Mādhyamika.

Tathatā-Tathāgata

We have seen that *dharma-dhātu* or *dharmatā* or *tathatā* is the word used in Madhyamaka philosophy for the Absolute. Candrakīrti says, *Yā sā dharmāṇāṁ dharmatā nāma saiva tatsvarūpam* (P. P. p. 116). "That which is the essential being of all elements of existence is the nature of Reality." It is *tathatā*, it is Reality such as it is. In the words of Bradley, we can only say *that* it is, not *what* it is. According to Candrakīrti—*tathābhāvo'vikāritvaṁ sadaiva sthāyitā.* (P. P. p. 116) "The thatness of Reality consists in its invariability, in its remaining for ever as it is."

Tathatā is the Truth, but it is impersonal. In order to reveal itself, it requires a medium. Tathāgata is that medium. Tathāgata is the epiphany of Reality. He is Reality personalized. Tathāgata is an amphibious being partaking both of the Absolute and phenomena. He is identical with Tathatā, but embodied in a human form. That is why Tathatā is also called Tathāgatagarbha (the womb of Tathāgata).

The word Tathāgata is interpreted as *tathā+gata* or *tathā+āgata* i.e. 'thus gone' or 'thus come' i.e. as the previous Buddhas have come and gone. This, however, does not throw much light on the concept of Tathāgata. There is one verse in the *Mahābhārata* which, it seems to me, removes completely the obscurity surrounding this word.

> Śakuntānāmivākāśe matsyānāmiva codake /
> Padaṁ yathā na dṛśyate *tathā* jñānavidāṁ *gatiḥ* //
> (*Śāntiparva*, 181, 12)

"Just as the foot-prints of birds flying in the sky and of fish swimming in water may not be seen: *So or thus* is the *going* of those who have realized the Truth."

This very word *tathā-gati* (only a different form of *tathāgata*) is used for those perfect beings whose foot-prints are untraceable. The word 'untraceable' is used for Tathāgata in *Majjhimanikāya*, Vol. I, p. 140, P. T. S. ed. *tathāgatam ananuvejjoti vadāmi* i.e. 'I declare that Tathāgata is *ananuvejja* (skt-*ananuvedya*) i. e. whose track is untraceable, who is above all the dichotomies of thought.' In the *Dhammapada* also, the Buddha has been called *apada* (trackless) in *tam Buddhamananta-*

gocaram apadaṁ kena padena nessatha (verse 179). Again in the verse 254 of the *Dhammapada*, the word Tathāgata has been used in connexion with *ākāse padaṁ natthi*. It appears that Tathāgata only means 'thus gone' 'so gone' i.e. trackless, whose track cannot be traced, by any of the categories of thought.

The *Mahābhārata* is considered by some scholars to be pre-Buddhistic. Whether it is pre-Buddhistic or post-Buddhistic, *tathāgata* seems to have been used for those who had realized Truth and were trackless.

Whatever the origin of the word, the function of Tathāgata is clear. He descends on earth to impart the light of Truth to mankind and departs without any track. He is the embodiment of Tathatā. When the Buddha is called *Tathāgata*, his individual personality is ignored; he is treated as a 'type' that appears from time to time in the world. He is the earthly manifestation of *Dharma*. The *Tathāgata* who has gone beyond all plurality and categories of thought (*sarvaprapañca-atīta*) can be said to be neither permanent nor impermanent. He is untraceable. Permanent and impermanent can be applied only where there is duality, not in the case of the non-dual. And because *Tathatā* is the same in all manifestation, therefore all beings are potential *Tathāgatas*. It is the *Tathāgata* within us who makes us long for *Nirvāṇa* and ultimately sets us free.

Śūnyatā and *Karuṇā* are the essential characteristics of *Tathāgata*. *Śūnyatā* in this context means *prajñā* (transcendental insight). Having *Śūnyatā* or *prajñā*, Tathāgata is identical with *Tathatā* or *Śūnya*. Having *karuṇā*, he is the saviour of all sentient beings.

The true being of the Tathāgata which is also the true being of all is not conceivable. In his ultimate nature, the Tathāgata is "deep, immeasurable, unfathomable."

The *dharmas* or elements of existence are indeterminable, because they are conditioned, because they are relative. The Tathāgata is indeterminable in a different sense. The Tathāgata is indeterminable, because, in his ultimate nature, he is not conditionally born. The indeterminability of the ultimate nature really means 'the inapplicability of the ways of concepts.' Nāgārjuna puts it beautifully in the Kārikā:

Prapañcayanti ye Buddham prapañcātītam avyayam |
Te prapañcahatāḥ sarve na paśyanti Tathāgatam || (XXII, 15)

"Those who describe the Buddha who is transcendent to thought and word and is not subject to birth and death in terms of conceptual categories are all victims of *prapañca* (the verbalising mind) and are thus unable to see the Tathāgata in his real nature."

Candrakīrti quotes a verse from *Vajracchedikā* (verse 43) :

Dharmato Buddhā draṣṭavyā dharmakāyā hi nāyakāḥ |
Dharmatā cāpyavijñeyā na sā śakyā vijānitum ||

(P. P., p. 195)

"The Buddhas are to be seen in their real *dharma*-nature, for these supreme guides (of humanity) have the *dharma*-nature in their core. But the essence of *dharma* is transcendent to thought and cannot be grasped by ideation."

The *tathatā* or the unconditioned Reality is not another entity *apart* from the conditioned. The unconditioned is the ground of the conditioned. To think that the determinate things are ultimate and self-existent in their distinct natures is to commit the error of eternalism śāśvata-vāda), and to think that the indeterminate or the unconditioned is wholly exclusive of the determinate is to commit the error of negativism.

The *Mahāprajñāpāramitā Śāstra* distinguishes three kinds of *tathatā* or essential nature. The first consists of the specific, distinct nature of every thing, the second of the non-ultimacy of the specific natures of things, of the conditionedness or relativity of all things that are determinate, and the third of the ultimate reality of every thing. Actually, however, the first two are called *tathatā* only by courtesy. It is only the ultimate, unconditioned nature of all that appears which is *tathatā* in the highest sense.

Tathatā or the "true nature' of things at the different levels, viz., mundane or appearance and transmundane or Reality is also called *dharmatā* at the two different levels.

DHARMADHĀTU AND BHŪTAKOṬI

Tathatā or Reality is also called Nirvāṇa or *dharmatā* or *dharmadhātu*. The word *dhātu* in this context means the inmost nature, the ultimate essence.

The *tathatā* or *dharmadhātu* is both transcendent and immanent. It is transcendent as ultimate Reality, but it is present in every one as his inmost ground and essence.

Bhūtakoṭi refers to the skilful penetration of the mind into the *dharmadhātu.* The word 'bhūta' means the unconditioned reality, the *dharmadhātu*: The word 'Koṭi' means the skill to reach the limit or the end ; it signifies realization. Bhūtakoṭi is also called *anutpādakoṭi*, which means the end beyond birth and death.

All things mentally analysed and tracked to their source are seen to enter the *anutpādadharma*, the *dharmadhātu.* This entering of all things into the unconditioned Reality is known as *anutpādakoṭi*, *anutpāda* signifies Nirvāṇa which is beyond birth and death. In the *dharmadhātu*, all beings are transformed into the dharma nature.

Prajñāpāramitā is equated with *dharmadhātu. Advaya— the non-dual* or *undivided.*

According to Madhyamaka philosophy, Reality is non-dual. The essential conditionedness of entities, when properly understood, reveals the unconditioned as not only as their ground but also as the ultimate reality of the conditioned entities themselves. In fact, the conditioned and the unconditioned are not two, not separate. This is only a relative distinction, not an absolute division. That is why Nāgārjuna says, "What from one point of view is *saṁsāra* is from another point of view Nirvāṇa itself "

(XXV, 20)

We have seen the main features of Madhyamaka philosophy. It is both philosophy and mysticism. By its dialectic, its critical probe (*prasaṅgāpādana*) into all the categories of thought, it relentlessly exposes the pretensions of Reason to know Truth. The hour of Reason's despair, however, becomes the hour of Truth. The seeker now turns to meditation on the various forms of *śūnyatā*, and the practice of *prajñāpāramitās.* By moral and yogic practices, he is prepared to receive the Truth. In the final stage of *Prajñā*, the wheels of imagination are stopped, the discursive mind is stilled, and in that silence Reality (*bhūta-tathatā*) stoops to kiss the eye of the aspirant; he receives the accolade of *prajñā* and becomes the knight-errant of Truth. There is no greater certainty than that of the mystic and equally there is no greater impotence laid upon him in giving expression to the Truth which he has received on that dizzy summit of experience. It is an experience of a different dimension-spaceless, timeless, *nirvikalpa* (beyond the province of thought and speech) Hence it cannot be expressed in any human language. The question is put at the logical level of Reason; the answer is found at the supralogical, suprarational level of *prajñā* which one can mount to only by a life of moral and spiritual discipline. The Madhyamaka system is neither scepticism nor agnosticism. It is an open invitation to every one to see Reality face to face.

We saw at the outset that the ideal of Mahāyāna is the Bodhisattva. We shall conclude this brief summary of Madhyamaka system with the following words of Saṅgharakshita: "Buddhism may be compared to a tree. Buddha's transcendental realization is the root. The basic Buddhism is the trunk, the distinctive Mahāyāna doctrines the branches, and the schools and sub-schools of the Mahāyāna the flowers. Now the function of flowers, however beautiful, is to produce fruit. Philosophy, to be more than mere barren speculation, must find its reason and its fulfilment in a way of life; thought should lead to action. Doctrine gives birth to Method. The Bodhisattva ideal is the perfectly ripened fruit of the whole vast tree of Buddhism. Just as the fruit encloses the seed, so within the Bodhisattva Ideal are recombined all the different and sometimes seemingly divergent elements of Mahāyāna" (*A Survey of Buddhism*, p. 432).

THE CONCEPTION OF BUDDHIST NIRVĀṆA
ANALYSIS OF CONTENTS

I-II Preliminary

Before the rise of Buddhism, there was a variety of views about the survival of the individual after death. Materialists denied survival of the individual after death in any form. Some adherents of the sacrificial religion believed in a blissful existence in paradise. Some believed that the individual would enjoy supreme bliss by the dissolution of its personality in an impersonal all-embracing Absolute. Some believed in an eternal individual soul which would return to its original condition of a pure spirit after many rebirths.

Buddha adopted a middle course. He agreed with the Eternalists that there was an accumulation of merit through a series of progressive rebirths, but he denied that there was any eternal spiritual principle. He did not believe in any permanent substance. He considered the world-process to be an appearance of discrete evanescent elements. His was a system of radical Pluralism.

Buddha had reduced Reality to discrete elements of matter and mind without any permanent substance or a permanent personality. Therefore it became difficult for him to explain moral law without a personality on whom the law would be binding or salvation without the existence of some one who would reach that goal.

Buddha attempted to solve the problem by emphasizing the attainment of "quiescence" as the highest bliss. According to him, the goal of man was to escape from the movement of phenomenal life into absolute quiescence in which all mental activity was stilled for ever. The name for this quiescence was Nirvāṇa. The term was pre-Buddhistic used in the sense of the dissolution of the personal in the universal whole (brahma-nirvāṇa). The means of attaining this was *Yoga*.

According to some scholars early Buddhism was merely Yoga, and lack of permanent individual, Nirvāṇa etc. were invented by later Buddhism. These scholars interpret Yoga as vulgar magic. Yoga is, however, not magic but a well-developed technique of concentration.

Yoga brings about a 'condition of quiescence.' A personality (*pudgala*) which, in other systems, is considered to be a permanent spiritual principle (*ātmā*), is according to Buddhism, only a bundle of elements or forces (*Saṁskāra-Samūha*) and a stream of thought (*santāna*). It contains nothing permanent, or substantial; it is *anātma*. Some of the elements are constant, some appear only under certain conditions.

Among the constantly present elements, there are two precious ones, viz., *prajñā* or the faculty of appreciative analysis and *samādhi* or the faculty of concentration. When fully developed, *prajñā* becomes transcendent wisdom (*prajñā amalā*). Life in ordinary men is controlled by ignorance (*avidyā*) which is not a constant faculty and can be eliminated (*prahīṇa*).

The moral progress of man is the outcome of a struggle, in man between the good (*kuśala*) and the evil (*akuśala*) inclination. The presence of defiling ignorance (*avidyā*) together with its disturbing qualities (*kleśas*) makes the whole stream of thought (*santāna*) impure.

The disturbing or defiling faculties (*kleśas*) *are* divided into two classes, (1) those that can be remedied by insight (*dṛṣṭiheya*) and (2) those that can be remedied only by concentrated attention (*bhāvanā-heya*). In the path of Nirvāṇa, *bhāvanā* is the most decisive step. It can transport the individual into a higher realm of existence.

Existence is divided into two distinct spheres—the mystic world or *samāpatti* , and the gross world of carnal desire or *kāma-dhātu*. The latter includes hells, earth and the heavens where gods are living and enjoying themselves in a human way.

The mystic worlds are further divided into two classes—those in which the denizens possess ethereal bodies, and those in which they do not possess any physical bodies. The purely spiritual realms (*arūpa-dhātu*) are four. Their denizens are engrossed in contemplation (*samāpatti*) out of the three incentives of human action on earth, viz., wealth, love and duty (*artha-kāma-dharma*), the last alone continues its unimpeded sway in the mystic's world.

III. *Mystic Intuition (Yogi-Pratyakṣa)*

It is contended both in Hīnayāna and Mahāyāna that in a mystic trance, the mystic sees in a moment the construction of both the gross and the mystic worlds as vividly as if they were an experience of direct sense-perception. But the picture given by Hīnayāna and Mahāyāna mystics is entirely different. The Hīnayāna mystic views the universe as an infinite continuity of single moments in gradual evolution towards 'Final Extinction.' The Mahāyāna mystic sees another picture corresponding to the theoretical teaching of that system.

The preparation for salvation consists of (1) a preliminary course of acquiring moral qualities (*sambhāra mārga*), (2) a subsequent course of training (*prayoga mārga*), (3) insight into essential truths (*dṛṣṭi mārga*). *Dṛṣṭi mārga* means insight into the four truths of the saint (*Catvāri āryasatyāni*), viz., (1) phenomenal existence (*duḥkha*), (2) its driving force (*samudaya*), (3) its extinction (*nirodha*), and (4) the means for the final extinction (*nirodha-mārga*).

In Hīnayāna, the process of illumination is described in two aspects (1) that of feeling (2) and that of knowledge. The feeling is one of satisfaction (*kṣānti ruci*). This is followed by knowledge or intuition which means the vision of the elements of existence (*dharma-jñāna*).

In later times when the study of Abhidharma was superseded by that of logic and epistemology, direct cognition was defined as containing no synthetic thought (*kalpanāpoḍha*). The four truths were at first ascertained by sound logic (*pramāṇena viniṣcita*), and then suddenly perceived as vividly as a grain of corn on the palm of the hand. In Mahāyāna, the preparation consisted in a course of negative dialectic after which the intuition of the transcendental truth, springs up as an inward conviction (*pratyātma-vedya*).

Buddhist yoga was an inseparable part of the belief in a pluralistic universe of separate elements (*dharmas*) gradually evolving towards extinction. All yoga practices which did not have this philosophical aim were condemned by the Buddha.

All the systems of philosophy in India excepting *Mīmāṁsā* believed in yoga as a means for 'transition out of the phenomenal into the absolute.'

IV. Buddha's Belief in Personal Immortality

'Immortal' is one of the epithets used for Nirvāṇa. Does immortality connote blissful existence among the forefathers in heaven? or does it connote the paradise of Amitābha? The epithet 'Nirvāṇa' does not mean any of these things. Nirvāṇa is 'beyond all imaginable spheres; it is the absolute limit.' It simply means changeless, lifeless, deathless condition; it connotes a state in which there is neither birth nor death. "People enter paradise by being re-born in it; they disappear for ever in Nirvāṇa by being extinct."

V. Was Buddha An Agnostic?

Buddha maintained a studied silence regarding some fundamental metaphysical questions e.g., 'Is the world beginningless or has it a beginning, is it finite or infinite; what is the condition of the saint after death or what is the nature of the Absolute?' Buddha either did not answer such questions at all or declared them as futile.

Scholars like N. de la Vallee Poussin and B. Keith interpret his silence as due to ignorance, but the fact is that fundamental reality cannot be explained in terms of the discursive intellect. Buddha maintained that the very effort of the intellect to confine truth to a simple 'either-or' to extremes is bound to prove futile, the truth lies in the middle path. It cannot be described in terms of the human language which is the product of analytical intellect. It is 'unspeakable' 'indefinable'. Non-duality is above words.

VI. The Position Of The Later Schools Of Hīnayāna

Scholars like N. de la Vallee Poussin divide the history of Buddhism into three main periods, viz., a period of primitive faith, a period of confused ideology and a period of scholasticism. Such scholars have only attempted to construct the history of Buddhism on lines parallel to the Western Church.

Such a division of Buddhism is artificial. It is preferable to keep to the broad divisions of Buddhism into early or Hīnayāna and later or Mahāyāna and the Sautrāntikas as a transitional school.

Scholasticism is used in two senses, viz., (1) philosophy in the service of religion, (2) excessive subtlety and artificiality in philosophical constructions. Scholasticism in Buddhism is to be taken in the second sense. The Vaibhāṣikas were scholastic in this sense. The Sautrāntikas were in favour of simplification.

Mahāyāna may be assigned to the 1st Century A. D. and the decline of Hīnayāna in the North to the 5th Century A. D. The Sautrāntikas occupied an intermediate position between the extreme Mahāyānists and the "schoolmen". Finally they coalesced with the Mahāyānists forming the school of Yogācāra-Sautrāntika.

The Vaibhāṣikas considered Nirvāṇa to be something real (*vastu*); the Mahāyānists and the Sautrāntikas maintained that it was only nominal; it was nothing real by itself, it was merely the cessation of all personal life.

Poussin has given interesting details of the controversy regarding Nirvāṇa, but he has missed the meaning of the controversy. The Vaibhāṣikas did not maintain that Nirvāṇa was a kind of paradise as Poussin seems to think, but that the annihilation of all life (*nirodha*) the essence of Nirvāṇa was a reality (*nirodha-satya, vastu*) i.e. 'a materialistic lifeless reality'. The Sautrāntikas adhere to the Mahāyāna conception which consists in identifying Nirvāṇa with the living world itself. They deny the reality of that materialistic kind of Nirvāṇa which was maintained by the Vaibhāṣikas.

VII. The Double Character Of The Absolute

Nirvāṇa may be said to be the equivalent of the Absolute. With regard to Nirvāṇa, there are two diametrically opposed views both in Brāhminical and Buddhist philosophies.

Nirvāṇa is considered to be either eternal annihilation or eternal life. The various views may be represented clearly in the following tabular form:

Schools	*Views*
Early Nyāya-Vaiśeṣika	In Mukti, there is mere *sat* or existence without *cit* or consciousness.

Early Buddhism and the Vaibhāsika school	Nirvāṇa is a reality (*dharma, vastu*) but without any consciousness (*yasmin sati cetaso vimokṣaḥ*)
Vedānta, Sāṅkhya and Yoga	Nirvāṇa is eternal life.
Hīnayāna	Supreme Buddha has no body.
Mahāyāna and Sautrāntikas	Buddha has a glorious, all-embracing cosmic body (*dharma-kāya*)
Early schools of Hīnayāna and the Vaibhāṣikas	Both Saṁsāra and Nirvāṇa are real separately.
Mādhyamika	Both Saṁsāra and Nirvāṇa are separately unreal.
Sautrāntika	Saṁsāra is real; Nirvāṇa is separately unreal.
Yogācāra or Vijñānavāda	Saṁsāra is unreal; Nirvāṇa in real.

VIII. The Vaibhāṣikas

They may be considered to be the representatives of the Sarvāstivādins or Early Buddhism in general. Their views may be summed up in the following words. Existence has a dual aspect, viz. (1) transient and phenomenal, (2) eternal and absolute. The phenomenal aspect may be analysed into matter, mind, and forces, the eternal into Space and Nirvāṇa.

There are two sets of elements of the phenomenal life, viz. (1) the one representing their everlasting nature (*dharma-svabhāva*), (2) the other representing their momentary manifestation in actual life (*dharma-lakṣaṇa*). When all manifestations are stopped and all forces become extinct, only lifeless residue remains. This is similar to the undifferentiated Prakṛti of Sāṅkhya. It must, however, be remembered that the Sāṅkhyas admitted both eternal Matter and eternal Souls, but the Buddhists denied Soul.

The Vaibhāṣika maintains that Nirvāṇa is an entity (*dharma*) which remains when consciousness becomes extinct.

IX. The Sautrāntikas

According to the Sautrāntikas, Nirvāṇa was the absolute end of all manifestation known to us, the end of passion and life (*Kleśa-Janmanoḥ kṣayaḥ*), without any positive counterpart. They denied any residue or substance in which life was extinguished. In other words, like all the Mahāyānists, they denied materialistic Nirvāṇa.

They neither admitted the monistic spiritual principle (*ālaya-vijñāna*) of the idealistic Mahāyānists, nor the principle of relativity (śūnya-vāda) of the Mādhyamikas.

It appears from the works of the famous Sautrāntika, Vasumitra that according to this school, there were two kinds of elements (*skandha*)—those which were subject to total extinction, and a subtle consciousness which survived after Nirvāṇa,and of which the former were but a manifestation.

X. The Yogācāras

This was an idealistic school founded by Āryāsaṅga in the 4th, 5th Century A. D.

The Yogācāra School is divided into two : (1) Āryāsaṅga and his followers, (2) Dignāga and his followers. According to Āryāsaṅga, *ālaya-vijñāna* is a store-consciousness in which the seeds (*bīja*) of all future ideas and the traces of all past deeds are stored up. It is not the Absolute. It belongs to the phenomenal part of existence, because all the results of *karma* are stored therein.

From their predecessors, the Mādhyamikas, the Yogācāras adopted the theory of the relativity and consequent unreality, (*śūnyatā-niḥsvabhāvatā*) of all individual existence, of all plurality, with the difference that they introduced different degrees of this unreality.

According to this school, individual ideas were unreal, since they were merged in the unique reality (*pariniṣpanna*) of the Absolute (*tathatā—dharmatā*). This was called their unreality in the absolute sense (*paramārtha niḥsvabhāvatva*). The Absolute was immanent in the phenomenal world, neither different, nor non-different (*nānya, nānanya*). It was a pure consciousness, undifferentiated into subject and object (*grāhya-*

grāhaka-rahita). It is identified with the cosmic body (dharmakāya) of the Buddha.

Both Vasubandhu and Asaṅga ultimately adopted the idealistic view, according to which all separate elements were relative, not real in themselves, but real only when regarded *sub specie aeternitatis*.

Hīnayāna regarded both Saṁsāra and Nirvāṇa as realities, Yogic power achieved the transition from Saṁsāra into Nirvāṇa.

According to Mahāyāna, the Absolute was immanent in the world. So there was no need to convert the *saṁskṛtadharmas* into *asaṁskṛta-dharmas*. There was only a change of aspect when Nirvāṇa was attained.

The Yogi viewed every separate object as unreal separately, but real *sub specie aeternitatis*.

Dignāga analysed reality into the concrete and the individual (*svalakṣaṇa*), a point-instant (*kṣaṇa*) in which existence and cognition, object and subject coalesce.

XI. The Mādhyamikas

The Mādhyamika system of philosophy and dialectics is the main foundation of the Mahāyāna religion. The Mahāyāna religion differs from early Buddhism in many respects and has several points of contact with Brāhminical religion.

The Mādhyamika system of philosophy is represented as extreme nihilism. Kumārila, Vācaspatimiśra and Śaṅkara have all condemned it as downright nihilism. Japanese scholars have, however, never committed the mistake of regarding its philosophy as nihilism or pure negativism.

XII. The Doctrine of Causality in The Hīnayāna

Hīnayāna contains an analysis of existence into its component elements, and establishes a certain number of ultimate data. It transforms soul into a stream of continuously flowing discrete moments of *vijñāna*, *vedanā*, *saṁjñā*, *saṁskāra* etc. Matter (*rūpa*) is also considered to be a flow of momentary flashes without any continuant stuff. It admits only the reality of sense data and the elements of mind.

Its conception of causality, viz., *pratītya-samutpāda* is in consonance with its conception of reality which could neither move nor change, but could only appear and disappear. *Pratītyasamutpāda* can hardly be called causation in the sense in which it is usually understood. It really means dependently co-ordinated-origination or dependent existence. According to it, every momentary entity springs into existence in co-ordination with other moments. Its formula is *asmin sati idam bhavati* there being this, there appears that ! According to this, there could be neither *causa materialis* nor *causa efficiens*. An entity is not really produced, it is simply co-ordinated.

Apart from the momentary entities called *nāmarūpa*, Hīnayāna believes in two unchanging entities viz. space and Nirvāṇa. It considers both Saṁsāra and Nirvāṇa, as realities, somehow interconnected in a whole.

XIII. *The Doctrine Modified in Mahāyāna*

The main distinctions between Hīnayāna and Mahāyāna are the following:

(1) According to Mahāyāna, the Real was that which possessed a reality of its own (*sva-bhāva*), which was not produced by causes (*akṛtaka* = *asaṁskṛta*), which was not dependent upon anything else (*paratra nirapekṣa*).

(2) In Hīnayāna, the elements, although interdependent (*saṁskṛta* = *pratītyasamutpanna*), were real (*vastu*). In Mahāyāna, all elements, because *interdependent*, were unreal (*śūnya* = *svabhāva-śūnya*).

(3) In Hīnayāna, every whole (*rāśi* = *avayaviṇ*) is regarded as a nominal existence (*prajñaptisat*) and only the parts or ultimate elements (*dharma*) are real (*vastu*). In Mahāyāna, all parts or elements are unreal (*śūnya*) and only the whole of all wholes (*dharmatā* = *dharmakāya*) is real.

According to Mahāyāna, Reality (*tattva*) is 'uncognisable from without, quiescent, undifferentiated in words, unrealisable in concepts, non-plural'.

(4) In Hīnayāna, the individual (*pudgala*), the self (*ātmā*) was resolved in its component elements (*skandha—āyatana—dhātavaḥ* = *anātma*) ; there were no real personalities (*pudgala-nairātmya*), but a congeries of flashing forces (*saṁskāra-samūha*).

In Mahāyāna we have, on the other hand, a denial of real elements (*dharma-nairātmya*), and an assertion of the absolute Whole (*dharma-kāya*).

In Hīnayāna, we have a radical pluralism; in Mahāyāna, we have a radical monism.

XIV The Doctrine of Relativity

Mahāyāna gives a new interpretation of *pratītya-samutpāda.* It maintains that whatsoever is dependent or relative cannot be considered as ultimate reality.

The central conception in Early Buddhism is a plurality of ultimate elements (*dharmas*). The central conception of Mahāyāna is their relativity (*śūnyatā*). The word *śūnya* can best be translated by 'relative or contingent' and the term *śūnyatā* by 'relativity or contingency'. The entire Mahāyāna literature goes to show that the term *śūnya* is a synonym of dependent existence (*pratītyasamutpāda*) and means not something 'void', but something 'devoid' of independent reality (*svabhāva-śūnya*). Śūnya has two implications, viz., (1) that nothing short of the whole possesses independent reality (2) and that the whole forbids every formulation by concept or speech (*niṣprapañca*). Concept or speech (*vikalpa*) can give us only a distorted view of reality; it can never seize it.

XV. The Real Eternal Buddha

Mahāyāna does not believe in the Hīnayānistic conception of Buddha having a real existence of his own. According to Mahāyāna, Buddha is above every possible determination (*niṣprapañca*). The real Buddha must be perceived directly by intuition. Those who dichotomise him as eternal or non-eternal, existent or non-existent, relative or non-relative, omniscient or non-omniscient are misled by words. Buddha must be regarded as the cosmical order (*dharmatā*); his Body is the Cosmos. It is impossible to know the essence of the Cosmos conceptually.

XVI. The New Conception of Nirvāṇa

Early Buddhism and Vaibhāṣikas regarded Space and

Nirvāṇa as ultimate realities on the ground that they possessed a character (*dharma*), a reality (*vastu*), an individuality (*svalakṣaṇa*), an existence of their own (*svabhāva*). These contentions were rejected by the Sautrāntika on the ground that they did not possess any such reality.

The Mādhyamikas also rejected those contentions because of their new definition of reality (*anapekṣaḥ svabhāvaḥ*). The Mādhyamika's conception of Relativity (*śūnyatā*) covered everything, the conditional as well as the eternal elements of the Vaibhāṣikas. The new interpretation of the principle of Relativity (*pratītya-samutpāda*) made the Hīnayānistic Absolute also relative, and according to Mahāyāna, whatever was relative was false, transient and illusory.

The unique reality, according to Mahāyāna, cannot be characterised in words (*anirvacanīya*), but a hint of it may be found in the following descriptions. It is the Whole of all wholes; it is the element of all elements (*dharmāṇāṁ dharmatā* or *dharma-dhātu*), as their relativity (*śūnyatā*), as 'thisness' (*idantā*), as 'suchness' (*tathatā*) as the suchness of existence (*bhūta-tathatā*), as the matrix of the Lord (*tathāgata-garbha*) and as Buddha's Cosmic Body (*dharma-kāya*). In the last conception, Buddhism becomes at once pantheistic and theistic, or as Prof. Anesaki puts it, *Cosmotheistic.*

The great Mahāyānist, Nāgārjuna gives a new orientation to Nirvāṇa. The Vaibhāṣika maintained that Nirvāṇa was something real (*dharma*) in which consciousness and life were extinct for ever: the Sautrāntika believed that it was the simple cessation of the world process. In both cases, something real was assumed to exist before Nirvāṇa and to disappear afterwards. This made Nirvāṇa a product of causes (*saṁskṛta*). Nāgārjuna asserted that there was not a shade of difference between the Absolute and the Phenomenal, between *Nirvāṇa* and *Śaṁsāra.* The universe viewed as a whole is the Absolute, viewed as a process, it is the phenomenal.

XVII. *Is Relativity Itself Relative?*

The main problem for Mahāyāna is—"Is Relativity itself relative?" Obviously the concept of Relativity depends upon its opposite—the Non-relative. It should be borne in mind that the principle of Relativity is invoked to destroy all theories and to replace them by direct mystic intuition, not by a new theory. Candrakīrti, the commentator on Nāgārjuna's *Madhyamaka-śāstra* puts it beautifully. "Relativity is here the common characteristic of all the elements (*dharma*) of existence. That is our view. But since there is no element which would be non-relative, Relativity itself, for want of those objects with which it could be contrasted, becomes as inane as a mirage, as a garland of flowers in the sky."

Relativity (śūnyatā) may be used to understand that all existence is relative and when that is understood, the theory of Relativity should be discarded.

Middle path in Early Buddhism meant middle course between materialism *ucchedavāda* and the doctrine of Eternal Soul (*śāśvatavāda*). In Mahāyāna, Middle path comes to mean Relativity.

XVII. Parallel Developments in Buddhism and Brāhmanism

Just as Mahāyāna moved towards radical Monism, even so Brāhmanism moved towards radical Monism. It is most probable that Mahāyāna is indebted to some Upaniṣadic influence. Gauḍapāda and Śaṅkara have been, in their turn, influenced by the dialectic of Nāgārjuna.

XIX. European Parallels

To characterize Nāgārjuna as a 'nihilist' as some scholars have done would be misleading, for his condemnation of Logic is only one part, and not the principal one, of his Philosophy.

Prof. Keith and Prof. M. Walleser suppose that Nāgārjuna denies even the empirical reality of the world., this is because they have missed the positive counterpart of his negativism, the identity of *Dharma-kāya* and *Brahman*. Nāgārjuna's philosophy was certainly opposed to rationalism, European or Indian, which believes that Reality could be known by logical reason.

Prof. H. Jacobi has suggested a comparison between Zeno of Eleia and Nāgārjuna. The similarity was not limited only to their dialectic. Nāgārjuna's philosophy points to a Whole which, when characterized in limited particulars leads to the antinomy of reason. Particulars are merely relative (Śūnya). Zeno also devised his "sophisms" to prove the impossibility of motion, and to lead the thinker to Parmenides' conception of the world as a motionless whole.

There are remarkable coincidences between Nāgārjuna's negativism and Bradley's condemnation of the concepts of things and qualities, relations, space and time, change, causation, motion, the self etc. Bradley may be characterized as genuine Mādhyamika.

A similarity may be found between Hegel's dialectic method and that of Nāgārjuna. Hegel challenges common sense to point some object which is certainly known for what it is, and solves the question by stating that all we know of the object is its "thisness", all its remaining contents being merely relation. This is also the meaning of *tathatā* or "suchness", and, as we have seen *śūnyatā* only means Relativity. Both philosophers assure us that Negativity (*śūnyatā*) is the soul of the Universe. Reducing the world of fact to a realm of universal relativity implies that everything cognisable is transient and illusory.

A similarity may also be noticed between the Mahāyānist conception of Buddha's Cosmical Body as the unique substance and Spinoza's conception of God as the only substance.

It will be seen, therefore, that it will not be correct to characterize Nāgārjuna as a "Nihilist". All that Nāgārjuna was at pains to show was that logic was incapable of giving us an idea of the Absolute, and that we can have a knowledge of the Absolute only by direct mystic intuition.

XX. The Position of Nyāya-Vaiśeṣika

In the conception of *Mokṣa* of Nyāya-Vaiśeṣika a similarity to the Buddhist conception of Nirvāṇa may be noticed. The highest goal of life, according to Nyāya-Vaiśeṣika, is *Mokṣa* or *Apavarga* in which there is neither consciousness as we know it here down on Earth nor bliss. Vātsyāyana, the great commentator on the Nyāya-sūtras says that such a goal could hardly be acceptable to the average man. He puts the aversion of the average man to such a goal in the following words.—"Is it possible that an enlightened man should favour a final Release in which there is neither bliss nor consciousness ?" And he answers the question by a counter-question—"Is it possible that an enlightened man should not favour the idea of a final Release where all turmoil of life is stopped for ever and where there is no consciousness about it?"

The goal of Indian philosophical systems is *Mokṣa* or Nirvāṇa. They start with the conception of whole (*sarvam*) which is divided into phenomenal life and the Absolute (Saṁsāra and Nirvāṇa). The phenomenal part is further analysed into its actual condition (*duḥkha*), its driving force (*duḥkha-samudaya*), its extinction (*nirodha*), and the means for acquiring this extinction (*nirodha-mārga*). It is not only Buddhism which preaches these four truths. This scheme is accepted by almost all the Indian philosophical systems.

Both in Nyāya-Vaiśeṣika and Buddhism, phenomenal life is designated as *duḥkha.* It is wrong to translate it as suffering, misery or pain, since it covers such items as inanimate matter, the five objects of sense etc.

In both the systems, the analysis of existence into its elements is undertaken in order to determine the means by which all the forces of life must be brought to a standstill.

There is another general feature of practically all the systems of Indian philosophy. They believe in a central force which keeps life going in all the worlds. This general force (*karma*) is resolved into special ones called delusion, desire and aversion. They produce germs of future action which bring about the continuation of phenomenal life. The decisive and final step which stops empirical life for ever, and transforms the individual into the Absolute is *Yoga.*

The Nyāya-Vaiśeṣika system assumes a limited number of substances with their changing qualities. In this system, the soul of the individual is an eternal substance; it is ubiquitous and conterminous with space. Knowledge is produced in it by contact with *buddhi* or the internal organ. By the power of Yoga, *buddhi* is kept back from all contact with the soul. No consciousness is then produced; all phenomenal life is annihilated, but the substance of the soul reverts in *Mokṣa* (liberation) to its original and natural condition (*svarūpāvasthā*).

There is a controversy between the Nyāya-Vaiśeṣika systems and Vedānta regarding the condition of the liberated soul.

The Vaiśeṣikas maintain that it is a cessation of all life, just as there is cessation of fire when all fuel is exhausted. According to them, there is no eternal bliss and eternal consciousness in *mokṣa* as Vedānta maintains. Since all objects of knowledge have disappeared for ever in *mokṣa*, if there is any joy in that condition, it would be joy without anything to be enjoyed; if there is any knowledge in that condition, it would be knowledge without knowing anything. Such feeling and such knowledge would be as good as non-existent (*sthitopy asthitān na viśiṣyate*).

The only meaning of *Mokṣa* or *Nirvāṇa* according to Nyāya-Vaiśeṣika is the annihilation of phenomenal life. This closely resembles the conception of Nirvāṇa of the Vaibhāṣika school of Buddhism. The Nirvāṇa of the Mahāyānists and the Sautrāntikas, however, resembles the conception of *Mokṣa* entertained by the Vedāntists.

XXI. Conclusion

The following stages may be marked in the Buddhist conception of the Absolute.

(1) In the 6th century B. C. there was a great effervescence of philosophical thought among the non-brāhmanical classes in India. Buddha at that time proposed a system denying the existence of eternal soul and reducing phenomenal existence to a congeries of separate elements, evolving gradually towards final extinction.

(2) Only some schools remained faithful to this ideal of lifeless Nirvāṇa and an extinct Buddha.

(3) In the 1st century A. D. Buddha was converted into a superhuman, living principle. This system of thought was probably influenced by the Upaniṣads. Buddha now became converted into a full-blown Brahman and its personification was worshipped under the name of a Cosmical Body (*dharmakāya*), Samantabhadra, Vairocana and others.

(4) The Mahāsaṁghikas and Vātsīputrīyas assumed a kind of consciousness surviving in Nirvāṇa.

(5) The philosophical doctrine of the old school stuck to the conception of separate elements of matter, mind and forces, and investigated the method of their gradual extinction in the Absolute.

(6) The Sautrāntikas cut down the list of artificially constructed elements, cut down Nirvāṇa itself as a separate entity, and thus constituted a transition towards Mahāyāna.

(7) The philosophy of the new religion is an adaptation of Vedānta. It became monistic.

(8) This monistic philosophy was divided into two different schools. One school known as Vijñānavāda maintained that there was store-consciousness (*ālaya-vijñāna*) of which all phenomenal life was a manifestation. This school made a good deal of contribution to Logic. The other school denied the possibility of cognising the Absolute by logical methods. It declared all plurality to be an illusion, and nothing short of the Whole to be Reality which could be known only in mystic intuition.

(9) The transitional Sautrāntika school merged in the 5th Century A. D. in the idealistic school of Mahāyāna and produced philosophers like Dignāga and Dharmakīrti. According to it, Nirvāṇa was a pure spiritual principle in which subject and object coalesced, and the force of transcendental illusion (*vāsanā*), producing the phenomenal world disappeared.

(10) In the 7th century A. D., the relativistic school (*śūnyavāda*) of early Mahāyāna received a fresh impetus.

(11) The Vijñānavāda and Śūnyavāda now influenced Vedānta which adapted its methods for its own purpose.

A TREATISE ON RELATIVITY

By

Nāgārjuna

Prefatory

Nāgārjuna has written three works on Buddhist Theory of Relativity (Śūnyatā), viz. *Madhyamaka Śāstra*, *Yuktiṣaṣṭikā* and *Śūnyatā-saptati*

The first work is divided into 27 chapters. It is his main work. It calls into question the various concepts of philosophy accepted by Hīnayāna and other systems, and proves that they are all relative, and that Reality cannot be established intellectually. It indirectly establishes Non-dualism (*advaita*).

Nāgārjuna is also the author of *Vigraha-Vyāvartinī* (The Refutation of Contests). It is doubtful whether some other works attributed to him were really written by him. It is also doubtful whether Nāgārjuna, the metallurgist-chemist, and Nāgārjuna, the philosopher are the same person. His pupil and successor, Āryadeva wrote *Catuḥśataka*, and *Hastavālaprakaraṇa*. Both flourished in the 2nd century A. D. and both belonged to South India.

In the 5th Century A. D., the brothers Asaṅga and Vasubandhu developed the idealistic school of Mahāyāna, known as Vijñānavāda or Yogācāra.

The Śūnyavāda school of Mahāyāna is divided into two—(1) that of Nāgārjuna and his followers that totally condemned Logic for understanding the Absolute and (2) that of Bhavya and his followers who advocated independent arguments to support the tenets of Nāgārjuna. The first is known as Mādhyamika-Prāsaṅgika, the second is known as Mādhyamika-Svātantrika.

In the 7th century A. D. arose Candrakīrti who, by his learned commentary on Nāgārjuna's *Madhyamaka Śāstra* cast the Svātantrika school into the shade and firmly established the Prāsaṅgika school.

The following periods may be marked in the development of the philosophy of Mahāyāna:

(1) 1st century A. D.—The rise of Mahāyāna—*Ālaya-Vijñāna* and *tathatā* admitted by Aśvaghoṣa.

(2) 2nd century A. D.—The theory of Universal Relativity (*Śūnyatā*) formulated by Nāgārjuna and Āryadeva.

(3) 3rd and 4th century—No particular philosophical activity.

(4) 5th century—The idealistic interpretation of Asaṅga and Vasubandhu.

(5) 6th century A. D.—A split in the Śūnyavāda school between the Mādhyamika—Prāsaṅgika and the Mādhyamika Svātantrika.

(6) 7th century A. D.—Final establishment of the Mādhyamika-Prāsaṅgika school by Candrakīrti.

EXAMINATION OF CAUSALITY

I. Preliminary

What is the subject-matter of this work ? Nāgārjuna gives a hint of it in the prayer given in the beginning of the work. It is the Principle of Relativity (*pratītyasamutpāda* or *Śūnyatā* or *anta-dvaya-rahitatva*)—the principle that nothing (in the Universe) can disappear or arise, or has an end or is eternal or is identical with itself, nor is there anything differentiated (in itself) and that there is no motion, whether towards us or away from us. In one word, everything is relative.

The aim of this work is Nirvāṇa which may be characterised as the bliss of the quiescence of all plurality.

The universe of apparent plurality is governed by the principle of Relativity or *pratītya-samutpāda*.

II. The Meaning of Pratītya-samutpāda

'Pratītya' is formed by the affix *prati* (towards) and the root '*i*' (moving, approaching). The affix modifies the meaning of a verb. Therefore *pratītya* here means 'reaching' in the sense of 'dependent' or 'relative'. The word *samutpāda* means 'appearance, manifestation'. The whole word *pratītya-samutpāda*, therefore, means in this system 'the manifestation of separate entities as relative to their causes and conditions' (*hetu-pratyayāpekṣo bhāvānām utpādaḥ pratītyasamutpādārthaḥ*)

III. The Meaning of this Term in Hīnayāna

Śrīlābha and other Hīnayānists explain *pratītya-samutpāda* in a somewhat different way. They say that *itya* is a *taddhita* or a derivative derived from the noun *iti* which means disappearance. *itya*, therefore, means 'fit to disappear'. The affix *prati* is used in the sense of *vīpsā* i.e. repetition implying continuous or successive action. Thus according to them *pratītyasamutpāda* means *prati prati ityānāṁ vināśināṁ samūtpādaḥ* i.e. appearance of everything bound to disappear i.e., everything momentary. So their explanation comes to this—The evanescent momentary things appear.

IV. The Hīnayānist Interpretation Rejected

The Hīnayānist interpretation may do in a passage of the Scripture like the following:

Pratītyasamutpādaṁ Bhikṣavo deśayiṣyāmai i.e. "O Bhikṣus, I shall teach you *pratītyasamutpāda*", but in a passage like the following, the Hīnayānist interpretation will utterly fail—*Cakṣuḥ pratītya rūpāṇi ca utpadyate cakṣurvijñānam* i.e. "visual consciousness appears when coordinated with the faculty of vision and colour."

But the interpretation which we propose viz. 'appearances coordinated with conditions, appearances relative to conditions' applies in all cases.

V. The Opinion of Bhāvaviveka Refuted

Bhāvaviveka misquotes the opinion of Mahāyānists, and then on the basis of that misquotation alleges that the Mahāyānists mean by 'prati' *vīpsā* or generalisation. This is wrong. The Mahāyānists, as we have already pointed out, mean by *pratītya-samutpāda* 'relative existence' 'appearance relatively to conditions' and this applies both to generalisation and single cases.

VI. Bhāvaviveka's Criticism Unsound

Bhāvaviveka interprets the explanation *Pratītya prāpya* literally as 'reaching' and then criticises by saying that there are no two things here reaching each other. But his criticism is not to the point, for *prāpya* in this context means *apekṣya* i. e. relatively 'being dependent'.

VII. The Definition of the Term By Bhāvaviveka

Bhāvaviveka interprets *pratītyasamutpāda* in the following way, 'if this is, that appears'. It is not right to treat it as a disjunctive judgment. Although *pratītya-samutpāda* consists of two words, it is not right to suppose that each refers to a different object.

Bhāvaviveka again treats *pratītyasamutpāda* as a conventional expression (*rūḍhi*). This too is not right.

At last Bhāvaviveka explains *pratītyasamutpāda* as 'this being, that becomes.' In this way, he ultimately accepts our explanation.

VIII. The Principle of Relativity : The Law of All Pluralistic Existence

By the doctrine of *pratītya-samutpāda*, Buddha teaches that all entities in life are relative. Nothing disappears, and nothing new appears.

The essence of Relativity is Nirvāṇa, the Quiescence of Plurality, for which there are no words.

The doctrine of Relativity is the Central teaching of Buddha.

IX. Causality Denied

Causation which is imagined in other systems (as a real production) appears either as a new manifestation of the same (continuant) stuff, or as an effect of separate factors, or as a result of both or as proceeding at random. Nāgārjuna maintains that none of these theories is right.

X. Identity of Cause and Effect Denied

Buddhapālita rightly says that entities do not arise out of their own selves, since such origination would serve no purpose, and since an absurd consequence will follow that everything is eternally arising.

XI. Bhāvaviveka Assails The Comment of Buddhapālita.

Bhāvaviveka has raised an objection against the above interpretation of Buddhapālita, saying that his comment misses the mark, because

(1) neither a reason nor an example is given,
(2) objections are left unanswered,
(3) it is a mere *deduction ad absurdum*.

XII. The First objection of Bhāvaviveka Answered

In saying that the cause is the self, you seemingly maintain that one's own self is once more produced. There is no sense in a new production of what already exists, and there would be infinite regress. But according to the Mādhyamika method of dialectics, a reason with an example is not needed. He is interested only in showing the absurdity of conflicting views.

XIII. The Second Point of Bhāvaviveka Rejected

The accusations of the opponent (viz. Sāṅkhya) were absolutely out of place. It was, therefore, not incumbent upon Buddhapālita to refute them. So Bhāvaviveka's assertion that 'objections are left unanswered' is irrelevant.

XIV. The Mādhyamika Method Explained

Bhāvaviveka says that Buddhapālita has given no valid argument to prove his thesis. Bhāvaviveka does not realize that the method of the Mādhyamika is different. He does not vindicate any assertion in order to convince his opponent. It is enough for him if he shows that his opponent is not capable of establishing his thesis.

XV. Buddhapālita's Comment Vindicated from the Standpoint of Formal Logic.

On close consideration, it will be found that Buddhapālita has actually given an independent argument to prove his thesis. It stands thus:

Entities do not arise out of themselves.

Because such origination would serve no purpose. Here the word 'such' refers to a new origination of something by itself (already) existing.

This argument may be expanded in the following way:

Thesis—An entity does not require a second production.
Reason—Because it exists.
Example—Just as a jar.

Major premise—Whatsoever exists does not require to be produced once more.

Bhāvaviveka is, therefore, not right in saying that Buddhapālita has given no independent argument to prove his thesis.

XVI. *The Answer of The Sāṅkhya Virtually Repudiated By Buddhapālita*

Buddhapālita has clearly shown that in the case of a manifested jar, it would be absurd to maintain the identity of cause and effect. Regarding a non-manifested jar, it is all the more clear that it cannot be produced, for it has been shown that entities do not arise of their own self.

It is clear, therefore, that Buddhapālita has pointed out the contradictions in the Sāṅkhya theory of causality by an independent argument.

XVII. *Some Minor Points Explained*

The argument against the Sāṅkhya may have also been formulated by Buddhapālita in another way, viz.,

Thesis—All physical entities do not arise out of themselves.

Reason—Because they always exist in their own essence.

Example—Just as the eternal spirit does.

It might be said that the Sāṅkhya is not affected by the denial of origination, for he maintains that causality consists in a new manifestation of an existing stuff. But origination also means manifestation, for both origination and manifestation have the common feature of representing something that was formerly unperceived and became perceived after.

XVIII. *The Third Stricture of Bhāvaviveka Answered. The Denial of one View does not imply the Acceptance of the contrary.*

It is wrong on the part of Bhāvaviveka to suggest that the repudiation of the Sāṅkhya theory of causation by a mere *reductio ad absurdum* involves acceptance of the opposite theory, viz., that cause and effect represent two different substances.

The only result of our deduction is to repudiate the theory of our opponent. It is not at all implied that we accept the converse of the theory.

XIX. Examination of Bhāvaviveka's Formal Argument Against The Sāṅkhya.

Bhāvaviveka has composed the following syllogism to combat the Sāṅkhya theory of Causality.

Thesis—Mental phenomena, if considered from the transcendental standpoint, are no new productions of the same substance.

Reason—Because they exist.

Example—Just as the conscious principle of the Sāṅkhya which is an eternal unchanging entity.

Major Premise—Whatsoever already exists is not a new self-production.

In this syllogism, what is the use of the qualification 'from the transcendental standpoint?'. We deny the identity of cause and effect from the phenomenal point of view also.

Therefore the formal argument of Bhāvaviveka is faulty.

XX. Bhavāviveka's Argument Assailed From The Standpoint of Formal Logic.

From the standpoint of formal logic, Bhāvaviveka's argument contains either *pakṣadoṣa* (faulty thesis), since it will refer to something, i.e. transcendental reality of mental phenomena which he himself does not accept as real or *āśraya asiddha hetu dosa* (faulty reason) which will then refer to something equally unreal.

The argument is wrong, either from the standpoint of its author for whom separate mental phenomena are not real, or from the standpoint of those to whom it is addressed, because they do not admit any difference between phenomenal and absolute reality.

XXI. Another Attempt of Bhāvaviveka to Vindicate His Argument.

Bhāvaviveka says that the fallacy pointed out in his argument will not be correct, since he is taking the syllogism in question as referring in general terms to the relation between a fact (e.g. mental phenomena) and one of its characteristics (viz., existence) without taking into consideration the special theories about the nature of mental phenomena or the essence of existence.

As in the case of the evanescent character of sound, only the relation of this characteristic to the characterized substratum in general terms is taken into account, even so in the present case, the mere fact that there is some substratum (called sensations), should be taken in general, without entering into details whether it be a phenomenal or absolute existence.

Bhāvaviveka's argument is not sound, for in the present case it is just the existence of such a general substratum that is denied. It is denied even by Bhāvaviveka himself. His aim is to deny Causality. In denying every causality, he is, at the same time, denying its substratum (thing), the substance of the thing produced, converging it in a thing which oweṣ its existence to merc illusion.

Since for the transcendentalist, in what he considers to be absolutely real, there is no room for non-reality, Bhāvaviveka's syllogism would be meaningless. He takes the phenomenal visual sensations and other mental phenomena as a minor term (the subject of his deduction). He thus cannot escape the criticism that his thesis is logically impossible, since it refers to a non-entity, or that his middle term is contradictory, since it appertains to an unreal substratum. The syllogism would be equivalent to the assertion that *non-existing* things do not arise out of themselves, *because they exist.*

XXII. Bhāvaviveka Also Avails Himself of the Argument That for the Monist All Individual Existence is Unreal

When the Hīnayānist maintains that 'causes and conditions which produce mental phenomena really exist, Bhāvaviveka assails his argument on the ground that if the word 'cause' in the above statement is taken in the phenomenal sense, the reason has no ultimate reality, if it is taken in the transcendental sense, then as Nāgārjuna has poined out there is altogether no efficient causality.

By adopting this line of argument, Bhāvaviveka has himself admitted the unreality of every reason from the transcendental standpoint.

In certain other syllogisms given by Bhāvaviveka, the middle term is faulty.

In another case, Bhāvaviveka admits that the transcendentalist has to forego usual logical methods.

In certain other syllogisms adduced by Bhāvaviveka, one may notice the unreality of the reasons.

XXIII. Another Formal Error in the Syllogism of Bhāvaviveka

The reason, viz., "because the mental phenomena exist" is uncertain from the standpoint of the Sāṅkhya.

XXIV. The Mādhyamika Repudiates His Opponent on Principles Admitted By Him

It may be objected that all the arguments of the Mādhyamika will also be wrong, because the reasons adduced by him will either be non-entities themselves, or they will represent something pertaining to a non-entity.

The Mādhyamika says in reply that he does not resort to direct proof by syllogism. His arguments are advanced on the basis of the principles admitted by his opponents and they are meant only to repudiate the tenets of his opponents.

XXV. Logical Refutation on The Basis of Facts Admitted By Only One Party

If logical refutation is to be done on principles admitted by only one party, it must be on the basis of the principles admitted by yourself, not on the basis of principles admitted by your opponent.

XXVI. Denial of Causality Through A Separate Substance

Entities do not arise out of something different from them. Because they do not pre-exist in something else, they cannot be produced out of it.

Buddhapālita rightly says that entities cannot arise out of something different from them, since it would follow that every thing could then arise out of anything.

Bhāvaviveka assails this by saying that it is mere *deductio ad absurdum* but we have shown above that a *deductio ad absurdum* is a valid proof.

XXVII. Combined Causality, Denied

Nor do entities arise out of both continuant stuff and separate factors, since all the incongruity attaching to each of these hypotheses separately will be applicable to their combination.

XXVIII. No Pluralistic Universe Without Causation

As Buddhapālita has said the entities of this world cannot arise without any cause, since everything would then be possible at any time, and in any place.

Bhāvaviveka's criticism of this point is entirely trivial.

XXIX. Causality Through The Will of God

Nor can God be said to be the cause of this world, for God also is to be included in one of the alternatives already discussed and dismissed.

Therefore the doctrine of Dependent Origination (or Relativity) with its characteristics of no real origination etc. is established.

XXX. Mahāyāna And Hīnayāna Contrasted

The Hīnayānist says that if the principle of Dependent origination is to be interpreted only as a principle of Relativity, and not real Causality, how are the deliverances of Buddha to be explained, for they assume Causality.

Buddha says that the forces of life are influenced in this world by illusion and desire. When these are suppressed in Nīrvāṇa, they become extinct. This suggests the reality of the force of illusion and of Nirvāṇa.

Similarly there are other utterances of Buddha which go to show that he believed in real Causality.

The Mahāyānist replies that it is for this very reason that Nāgārjuna has composed this Treatise on Relativity in order to show the real and conventional meaning of the scriptures. All the utterances of Buddha mentioning the principle of Dependent Origination do not refer to the pure essence of the objects which reveals itself when the darkness of our ignorance is dispelled.

There are other utterances of Buddha which refer to absolute reality, e.g.,

"The permanent Reality, Brethren, is Nirvāṇa. All the combined forces of phenomenal life are illusion" etc.

XXXI. The Direct And Indirect Meaning of Buddha's Words

It must be borne in mind that certain words of the Buddha are *nītārtha* i.e. they have a direct meaning, and certain words are *neyārtha* i.e. they have only indirect or conventional meaning.

In general terms, it must be said that those discourses which have been delivered in order to teach the path of salvation (*mārgāvatārāya*) are *neyārtha** (conventional), those which are delivered in order to teach the final result (*phalāvatārāya*) are also *neyārtha** (metaphorical or conventional); those discourses which specify the entrance into that kind of final Deliverance which is Relativity, where there is no separate object, no profound meditation, no volition, no birth, no causation, no existence, no Ego, no living creature, no individual soul, no personality, and no lord are *nītārtha* (having direct meaning).

This is why in order to show that the doctrine which admits causality is wrong, Nāgārjuna has undertaken to consider the doctrine of *pratītya-samutpāda* or Dependent Origination.

XXXII. How Is The Moral Law To Be Vindicated in An Unreal World?

If there is no real causation, and the plurality of the

* Stcherbatsky considers the discourses delivered to teach the final result to be *nītārtha*. The text published by the Mithilā Vidyāpīṭha calls this also *neyārtha*. Probably Stcherbatsky had a different reading before him.

elements of life is a mere illusion, it will follow that wicked actions do not exist and so the moral law will become useless in an unreal world.

The answer is that so long as one is steeped in the world of duality, in illusion, the moral law has its usefulness. Once one has risen above duality, above the pairs of opposites, above illusion, he does not need to be regulated by a law.

Illusion is a condition of complete error in regard to all elements of existence. So long as illusion is not perceived as illusion, it becomes reality to us.

Hell and heaven are the product of imagination. Just as in sleep we dream that we are suffering from the horrors of hell, but on awakening find that there was no hell, even so illusion is like the state of sleep, and in that condition we experience all the suffering; but once we are awakened to reality, there is no suffering whatsoever.

The separate entities of the phenomenal world have no real independent existence of their own. To people who are misled by their own subjective illusions, they become a source of moral defilement.

XXXIII. The Twelve Membered Causal Series Refers to The Phenomenal World

The Hīnayānist objects that if there is no causation, how is the causal series taught by Buddha to be understood? The reply of the Mādhyamika is that it is the phenomenal point of view (*saṁvṛti*); it is not absolute reality (*tattvam*). Phenomenalism is only the fact of Universal Relativity (*Pratītya-samutpādamātram*).

XXXIV. Controversy About the Validity of Logic.

Logician—You cannot assert that the separate entities are not caused. If you have the right to say that all elements of existence are uncaused, others have a right to maintain that whatsoever exists has a cause.

Mādhyamika—Ours is a system of Universal Relativity. There is no room in it for an assertive judgment.

Logician—But your proposition, viz., 'entities arise neither out of themselves, nor out of something different, nor out of both, nor at random, looks like a definite assertion.

Mādhyamika—This statement of ours appears decisive to simple people who interpret everything according to arguments familiar to them., but not to saints who can intuit absolute reality.

Logician—Do saints believe in no argument?

Mādhyamika—Saints remain silent about the Absolute.

Logician—If saints do not use arguments how do they convey their idea of the Absolute to simple folk?

Mādhyamika—Saints do not use their own arguments. They just use the arguments that appeal to simple folk and convey the truth by methods which simple folk can understand.

Logician—But causality exists because such is our direct experience.

Mādhyamika—But a man suffering from ophthalmia has the direct experience of a double moon. Even so the direct experience of a man suffering from ignorance is misleading.

It has been proved by the negative method that entities of the phenomenal world have never originated. It will now be shown in the light of Relativity that particular characteristics of the so-called real entities are not real.

XXXV. Controversy with The Buddhist Logician Continued

The Buddhist Epistemologists maintain that they are only giving a scientific description of what just happens in common life, in regard to the sources of knowledge and their respective objects; they do not consider their transcendental reality. The Naiyāyikas have given wrong definitions. Therefore they consider it their duty to give the right ones.

The Mādhyamika replies that Nāgārjuna in his "Repudiation of Contests" rightly says that if every cognition of an object depends on reliable sources of knowledge, and these sources being objects cognised by us in their turn depend on other sources of knowledge, we shall be landed into a *regressus ad infinitum.*

XXVI. Critique of the Notion of An Absolute Particular Point-instant

The Logician says that by essence we need not mean a

characteristic but the object characterized. The Mādhyamika replies that firstly this is not the commonly accepted notion of essence. Secondly, if it is suggested that the point-instant is characterized by our awareness of it, then it would mean that the single point-instant contains a double aspect—the thing characterized and its characteristic. There will then be a double particular essence, one of which will be the thing characterized and the other will be the characteristic. If our awareness of the point-instant represents its characteristic, the thing characterized i.e. the objective side of the relation will represent something different from its characteristic. If it is maintained that this second aspect is in its turn also a thing characterized, it will then require some other thing as a characteristic. This will lead to *regressus ad infinitum*.

XXXVII. Introspection

The Logician says that the consciousness which represents our awareness of a point-instant is apprehended by introspection. It thus contains inherent objectivity and immanent cognizability.

The Mādhyamika says that the theory of Introspection has already been refuted in Mādhyamakāvatāra. Consciousness arises when there is an object. Does it mean that consciousness is one thing and the object another or that they are identical? In the first case, we shall have a double consciousness. If they are identical, it is not possible to cognize consciousness through consciousness. Consciousness cannot know itself as an object.

XXXVIII. The Discussion About The Point-instant Resumed

The Mādhyamika puts a further question. Is in the thing which is its own essence any difference between the essence and the thing possessing that essence or is there none? In the first case, the essence will be different from the thing, and it will cease to be its essence, and the thing being detached from its essence will just be nothing.

If the thing and its essence are identical, the thing characterized ceases to be characterized.

The Logician says that just as Mādhyamika asserts that ultimate reality is unspeakable, even so it can be said that the relation between the thing characterized and its characteristic is unspeakable.

The Mādhyamika says that unspeakability cannot apply to a dichotomy like "this is the characteristic; this is the thing characterized." It has been proved that both the alternatives taken independently are unreal.

XXXIX. Is There A Cogniser ?

The question now is whether there is a cognizing agent. The Logician says that he does not admit the reality of a cognizing soul, but the element of pure sensation may be considered as an agent.

The Mādhyamika says that even pure sensation cannot be taken as an agent, for the function of pure sensation is to indicate the mere presence of something.

XL. Vindication of Phenomenal Reality

The gist of the long argument in this section is the following:

The Logician maintains that there is such a thing as *svalakṣaṇa* or the thing-in-itself which does not involve any possessive relation, but is only a conventional verbal expression as in 'the head of Rāhu'. Just as in this expression, the head is not something separate from Rāhu and possessed by him, but Rāhu is nothing else except the head itself; even so we can say that "solidity is the exclusive essence (*svalakṣaṇa*) of solid bodies."

The Mādhyamika says that the cases are not similar. In the first case (viz, head of Rāhu), it is only a conventional way of speech. In the latter case, there cannot be solid bodies apart from the sense-datum of resistance (*kāthinyādi*). There is no substance in solid bodies over and above the quality of resistance. Substance and quality are merely correlative terms. The substance has no separate, independent existence apart from the quality. In the example viz. head of Rāhu, there is no mutual interdependence of two phenomenal realities. Therefore this example cannot be applied to substance and quality.

The thing-in-itself (*svalakṣaṇa*) is no exception to the law of Universal Relativity. The phenomenal is real only in the sense of relative reality.

XLI. *The Definition of Sense Perception*

Dignāga and his followers define perception as *Kalpanāpoḍha* i.e. pure passive sensation free from any constructive thought. The Mādhyamika criticizes this definition on the ground that this is mere abstraction. In actual concrete perception, there is always an element of thought. Therefore from the phenomenal point of view the common-sense view of perception (as that which is present to the senses) is the correct one.

XLII. *The Hīnayāna Theory of Causation Examined*

The Hīnayānist says that out of the four-cornered dialectic of the Mahāyānist, he agrees with three, viz. (1) that entities cannot arise out of themselves (*na svata utpattiḥ*), (2) that they cannot arise out of both sources (*na dvābhyām utpattiḥ*) i.e. out of pre-existing stuff and separate agents.) (3) that they cannot come into being at random i.e. without any cause (*na ahetutaḥ*). but he says he cannot concur in the fourth alternative viz., that they cannot arise out of something separate from them (*na parata utpattiḥ*).

The Hīnayānist avers that the Buddha himself said that existing things are produced by causes, and that the causes are different from the things produced. There are only four conditions or *pratyayas* which bring about anything viz., (1) its cause or *hetu* (2) its objective condition or *ālambana* the immediately foregoing condition for the production of the result *samanantara* and (4) the decisive or predominant condition which is efficient to bring about the result or *adhipatipratyaya*. There is no fifth condition like God, Time etc. Entities arise under these conditions which are not identical with the thing produced.

The Mādhyamika says that entities are also not produced out of conditions which are separate from them (*na parata utpattiḥ*). If the produced entities had any pre-existence in the causes and conditions which are separate from them, then alone could they appear out of them, but they are not perceived to be pre-existing. Therefore the conditions of an entity do not contain any real existence of the result. If the effect is different from the cause, there would be lack of relation between the two. In that case, anything may produce anything whatsoever.

XLIII *The Existence of Separate Energies Denied*

There are some philosophers who maintain that entities may not be produced out of other entities, called causes; they may originate through special energies. For instance the organ of vision, colours etc. may not be producing visual sensation; there may be some energy inherent in them that may be producing this sensation. Similar is the case with physical energy e.g. heat producing cooked rice.

The Mādhyamika says that the plea of energy also will not do. If the supposed energy appears when the sensation already exists, it is useless. Nor can the existence of an energy be assumed in the causes previous to the sensation produced, for the energy cannot take shape as long as the result is absent. Nor can the existence of an energy be possible at the moment of production, for a thing is either produced or not produced. There is no existence between these two moments. Therefore, no such energy productive of effects exists.

XLIV. *Causation Is Not Co-ordination*

The Hīnayānist says that whether causes possess energy or not, the fact remains that entities, such as sensation, arise in co-ordination with other entities, e.g. the organ of vision. This is all that is meant by saying that the existence of an organ of vision etc. are the conditions under which a visual sensation etc. can arise.

Nāgārjuna says that upto the moment when the socalled result, e.g., visual sensation arises, the organ of vision etc. will be only non-causes, and nothing can be produced out of non-causes.

Nāgārjuna urges a further argument. An organ of vision

etc. is supposed to be the cause of visual sensation etc., but the question that arises is—whether there are causes of existing sensation or of a sensation not yet existing. If a sensation is already existing, it is useless to assume some cause producing it. If it is non-existing, how can it have a cause ? If it is said that it is called cause in anticipation, for the present it is only a latent force, the reply of the Mādhyamika is that the assumption of latent energy has already been examined and shown to be hollow.

XLV. *The Cause-Condition*

Nāgārjuna is now examining the four cause-factors of the Hīnayānist. The first is the *hetu-pratyaya* or cause-condition.

The Hīnayānist says that the notion of a cause-condition (*hetu-pratyaya*) is very well established. It is agreed on all hands that a cause-condition is that which produces or effects something. Therefore cause must be accepted.

The Mādhyamika says that the existent (Ens) is not produced, because it exists. The non-existent (non-Ens) cannot be produced, because it does not exist. The two together cannot be produced because they are mutually contradictory. Since there is no production of effects, there is no sense in accepting causes.

XLVI. *The Object—A Condition of Mental Phenomena*

The second condition-factor of the Hīnayānist is *ālambana pratyaya* or objective counterpart. Nāgārjuna says that pure, indefinite sensation (*citta*), and definite mental phenomena (*Caitta*) are said to have an objective counterpart or objective condition (of the mental element). The question is whether the objective condition is assumed for sensation already existing or for sensation not yet produced. If the sensation is already existing, the objective condition is useless. If the sensation is not yet existing, it would be absurd to imagine that it combines with an object.

It may be asked how is it then that a sensation or mental phenomenon refers to an object. Nāgārjuna replies that this is only *sāṁvṛta* or empirical, not *pāramārthika* or absolute.

XLVII. *The Cause Materialis Denied*

The third condition-factor of the Hīnayānist is *samanantara pratyaya* or the disappearance of the immediately preceding condition.

It is maintained by the Hīnayānist that the disappearance of the immediately preceding condition is the cause of the following effect, e.g., when the seed is destroyed i.e. when the seed as seed disappears then does the sprout appear. Nāgārjuna says that if the seed disappears, it becomes non-existent. How then can a non-existent factor be the cause of anything whatsoever ?

XLVIII. *The Special Cause Also Denied*

The fourth condition factor of the Hīnayānist is *adhipati pratyaya* or predominant or special condition.

According to Hīnayāna, an *adhipati pratyaya* or predominant condition is that special factor which being present, the effect inevitably follows.

The Hīnayānist says that it is a matter of common knowledge that a piece of cloth is produced out of threads, so the existence of threads is a necessary condition for the existence of a piece of cloth.

The Mahāyānist says that the cloth exists neither in the threads, nor in the weaver's brush, nor in his loom, nor in the shuttle, nor in the pins nor other causes taken singly, and from a plurality of causes, a plurality of effects would be expected. Since the cloth does not exist in any one of its parts singly, it does not exist in all of them taken together. Since there is no such thing as an effect in the strict sense of the word, the existence of causes as separate entities cannot be admitted.

The Hīnayānist says that the result is not something outside its causes; the presence of the whole complex of the causes of a given event is equivalent to the production of the event.

The Mādhyamika says that the so-called causes are themselves not independent realities. They have no *svabhāva* 'own being' or independent realities.

So there is no such thing as a cause-possessing result.

The Hīnayānist says that it is admitted by all that there

is regularity in the world according to which certain facts are co-ordinated and others are not so co-ordinated. The cloth is co-ordinated with threads, and the mat is co-ordinated with straw, not with threads.

The Mahāyānist says that from the transcendental point of view, neither the event, nor the cause has an independent reality of its own. All things in the world are only relative.

CHAPTER XXV

Examination of Nirvāṇa

I. The Hīnayānistic Nirvāṇa Rejected

According to Hīnayāna, personalities that have lived a pure life and have acquired knowledge of the elements of existence as taught by the Buddha can attain Nirvāṇa. There are two kinds of Nirvāṇa—(1) Sopādhiśeṣa Nirvāṇa—Nirvāṇa in lifetime in which the residual substratum of the five *upādānaskandhas* remains and (2) Nirupādhiśeṣa Nirvāṇa—without any residue.

These two kinds of Nirvāṇa are possible only when there is *nirodha* or suppression of (1) *kleśa* (defilements, obstructions) in the *sopādhiśeṣa* Nirvāṇa and of (2) *skandhas* (groups of elements making a personality) in the *nirupādhiśeṣa* Nirvāṇa. If everything is *śūnya* (devoid of independent reality), there would be neither *kleśa* nor *skandha* by whose Suppression Nirvāṇa may be attained.

The Mādhyamika says that if the *kleśas* and *skandhas* are absolutely real, if they have an "own-being" (*svabhāva*) of their own, then their "own-being" (*svabhāva*) cannot disappear. If they cannot disappear, how can there be Nirvāṇa on the Hīnayānistic assumption?

The Mādhyamika does not advance a conception of Nirvāṇa consisting in the annihilation of the elements. Hence this incongruity cannot apply in his case.

II. *The Mahāyānistic Nirvāṇa*

According to the Mādhyamika, Nirvāṇa is that indefinable

essence which can neither be extinguished as e.g. a desire, nor which can be attained as, e.g. a reward for renunciation, nor which can be annihilated, as, e. g. all the active elements of life, nor which is eternal, as e.g. an absolute principle, which cannot really disappear, nor which can be produced. Nirvāṇa really means the Quiescence of all plurality (*Prapañcopaśama*)

Suppression of desire or the elements of existence etc. is simply a false construction of our imagination. It is really the suppression of the false construction of our imagination which is Nirvāṇa.

Desire, illusion etc. have no real existence in the absolute sense even in the phenomenal condition of life.

III. *Nirvāṇa Not An Ens* (*a particular existing entity*)

There are people who imagine that Nirvāṇa is a particular kind of. existence. (*bhāva*).

Nāgārjuna says that Nirvāṇa is not a partioular kind of existence (*bhāva*). Every existence is invariably connected with decay and death. If Nirvāṇa is a *bhāva* (an existing entity) that would also be subject tc decay and death.

All particular *bhāvas* (existing entities) are produced. If Nirvāṇa is a *bhāva*, that would also be produced. All are agreed that Nirvāṇa is not a particular kind of production.

IV. *Nirvāṇa is not Non-Ens* (*non-existing entity*)

It may be said that if Nirvāṇa is not an Ens, it must be a non-Ens (*abhāva*), for it consists in the fact that the defiling elements (*kleśas*) and their consequence, the individual existence is stopped.

Nāgārjuna says that this is impossible. If it is maintained that Nirvāṇa is the absence of defiling elements and individual existence, then the impermanence of the defiling elements and personal existence would attach to Nirvāṇa. It would follow that impermanence is Nirvāṇa.

Again if Nirvāṇa is considered to be a non-Ens (*abhāva*) it cannot be independent, for every non-Ens (*abhāva*) is dependent on its positive counter-part (*bhāva*).

V. *Nirvāṇa Is The World Viewed Sub specie Aeternitatis*

The phenomenal world consists of birth and death, appearance and disappearance. All the so-called entities of the phenomenal world are either dependent upon conditions (i.e. they are relatively real) just as long is real relatively to short or they are produced, just as the sprout is produced by the seed. In both cases when the continuity of birth has ceased, it is called Nirvāṇa. This cessation of phenomenal life is one view of Nirvāṇa. The Mādhyamika says that mere cessation of aspect can neither be considered as an Ens (*bhāva*), nor a non-Ens (*abhāva*). So Nirvāṇa is neither an Ens nor a non-Ens.

A second view of Nirvāṇa is the following. Some followers of the Buddha e.g. Sarvāstivādins maintain that in the universe, there is no abiding central principle, that the world-process consists in the procession of co-ordinated energies. When all causal laws cease to operate, when all energies are extinct, there is Nirvāṇa.

There is a third view of Nirvāṇa like that of the Vātsīputrīyas which maintains that there is a central principle termed 'personality' (*pudgala*) which passes from one existence into another. It is neither momentary nor eternal. It goes on evolving. When the evolution of this principle stops, it is said to have entered Nirvāṇa.

Regarding the second and third view also, the Mādhyamika says that whether it be co-ordinated energies or some central principle, called "personality", the mere fact of their evolution being stopped can neither be characterized as an Ens, nor a non-Ens.

Nirvāṇa (Absolute) and Saṃsāra (phenomenal world) are not two separate realities, nor two states of the same reality. The Absolute viewed through thought-forms is the phenomenal world; the phenomenal world free of the thought-forms is Nirvāṇa or the Absolute. Nirvāṇa or the Absolute is the phenomenal world viewed *sub specie aeternitatis*:

VI. *Nirvāna Is Not Both Ens And Non-Ens together*

Some, as for example the Vaibhāṣikas assume a double character in Nirvāṇa. It is a non-Ens (*abhāva*) insofar as the defiling elements (*kleśas*) and the elements of existence are extinct in it, and in itself this lifeless condition is an Ens (*bhāva*). So it is both an Ens and a non-Ens together.

The Mādhyamika says that this double character is impossible. A final Deliverance (from phenomenal life), and the energies (of phenomenal life) cannot be the same.

If Nirvāṇa were both Ens and non-Ens, it would be relative to the totality of causes and conditions. It would thus not be the Absolute. Both Ens (*bhāva*) and non-Ens (*abhāva*) are relative to each other. Nirvāṇa is not within the realm of relativity. It is uncaused.

Again since Ens and non-Ens are mutually incompatible like light and darkness, Nirvāṇa cannot be both Ens and non-Ens.

VII. *Nor Is Nirvāṇa A negation of Both Ens And Non-Ens Together*

Some say that Nirvāṇa is neither an Ens nor a non-Ens. No one knows what a real Ens or non-Ens is. Therefore their negation is absurd.

VIII. *The Real Buddha, What?*

Just as all the alternatives of the four-cornered dialectic are inapplicable to Nirvāṇa, even so they are inapplicable to the Buddha.

IX. *Ultimate Identity of The Phenomenal And The Absolute*

Ultimately there is no difference between the phenomenal and the Absolute. The phenomenal in essence being nothing but the Absolute, it is impossible to imagine either its beginning or its end.

X. *The Antinomies*

All the theories about these questions are inconsistent. They are mere antinomies of reason. The phenomenal and the Absolute are merged quiescent in the unity of the Whole. None of the alternatives of the four-cornered dialectic has ultimate reality. Every thing is "relative". Therefore questions about the finite and the infinite, identity and difference, eternity and non-eternity are meaningless.

XI. *Conclusion.*

Our bliss consists in the cessation of all conceptualization about Reality, in the quiescence of plurality. The Buddha really did not preach any doctrine about separate elements.

I. PRELIMINARY

Although a hundred years have elapsed since the scientific study of Buddhism has been initiated in Europe, we are nevertheless still in the dark about the fundamental teachings of this religion and its philosophy. Certainly no other religion has proved so refractory to clear formulation. We are confronted with an intricate terminology about whose meaning a variety of interpretation is current and which is often declared to be untranslatable or incomprehensible. In despair, some scholars were led to the conclusion that a religion or a philosophical system in India is not what it is in Europe; it is not a clear-cut construction of consistent speculation. It is always vaguely indefinite, a display of dreamy thoughts about whose meaning their authors themselves are not quite sure.[1] In a recent work M. de la Vallèe Poussin[2] has undertaken to reconsider the question about the meaning of the Buddhist ideal of Nirvāṇa, and he warns us from the outset that we have not to expect something very illuminating from the Indian sources.[3] Formerly, he confesses, the idea of Nirvāṇa seemed to him vague enough, but recently he has completely changed his opinion upon this subject and thinks that even the hazy speculations which he was trying to disentangle are but later additions, that at the beginning Nirvāṇa meant a simple faith in soul's immortality, its blissful survival in a paradise, a faith emerging from practices of obscure magic.

In the following pages we will try to test the arguments by which this new interpretation is supported, and append some considerations about the vicissitudes of this Buddhist conception

1. The late Professor G. Bühler gathered from a long intercourse with Indian pandits in their own country a quite different impression. He used to repeat to his pupils when perplexed by some difficult texts, "was ein Brahmane gemacht hat, das muss heraus", for very often it is something simple and clear, but expressed in a technical scientific terminology.

2. Etudes sur l'histoire des Religions, 5. Nirvāṇa par Louis de la Vallee Poussin, Paris, 1925.

3. Op. cit., p. XI-XII.

of the Absolute and the changes which, in our opinion, it underwent during the first thousand years of its history.

II. BUDDHISM AND YOGA

In the VI-V century B.C., at the time immediately preceding the rise of Buddhism, India was seething with philosophic speculation. A great variety of views and systems was springing up and actively propagated among the different classes of its population.[1] Materialistic doctrines, denying every survival of the individual after death and every retribution for his moral or immoral deeds were widely spread. The orthodox Brahmanical community was also divided. A part of it stuck to the old sacrificial religion which promised to its votaries the reward of a blissful existence in a celestial paradise. Another part of it favoured, from an early date, a monistic view of the universe, and interpreted the reward of supreme bliss as the dissolution of the personality in an impersonal all-embracing Absolute. Later on, some Brahmanical circles developed the idea of an eternal individual soul[2] which after having been bound up in many existences would return to its genuine condition of a pure spirit as a reward for accumulated merit.

Between the materialists who denied retribution and the eternalists who imagined a return to a pure spiritual condition, Buddha took a middle course. From the eternalists he borrowed the doctrine of a gradual accumulation of spiritual merit through a series of progressing existences, but he was averse to their doctrine of an eternal spiritual principle.

As far as we can understand his philosophic position, it seems that he was deeply impressed by the contradiction of assuming an eternal, pure, spiritual principle which, for incomprehensible reasons, must have been polluted by all the filth of mundane existence in order, later on, to revert to its original purity. He was thus led to a denial of every permanent principle. Matter and mind appeared to him as split in an infinite process of evanescent elements (Dharmas), the only

1. This period coincides with a period of philosophic activity in China and in Greece; cf. P. Masson Oursel; La Philosophie Comparee, p. 56.

2. Cp. H. Jacobi. Die Ind. Philosophie in Das Licht des Ostens, p. 150 f.

ultimate realities, besides space and annihilation. The conception of an impersonal world-process was probably prepared by the idea of an impersonal unique substance of the world, as developed in the Upaniṣads. The analysis of the world into its elements of matter and mind was probably, to a certain extent, prepared by the work of the Sāṅkhya school. The originality of Buddha's position consisted in denying substantiality altogether, and converting the world-process in a concerted appearance of discrete evanescent elements. Forsaking the monism and the dualism of the Sāṅkhyas, he established a system of the most radical pluralism. That the essence and the starting point of Buddhism were speculative appears very clearly, if we give credit to the records about the other wandering teachers who were the contemporaries of Buddha and often engaged in controversies with him. The questions at issue between them were of a speculative nature. Ethical questions, the explanation of retribution, were predominant, but they always were narrowly linked together with some system of ontology and some doctrine of a final release.[1]

If we make an effort wholly to realise the position of a philosopher to whom the universe presented itself as an infinite process of separate elements of matter and mind, appearing and disappearing, without any real personalities, nor any permanent substances, and if we bear in mind that this philosopher was eagerly seeking for a theoretical basis on which to establish morality, we must confess that for our habits of thought his position was not an easy one. Striving to escape the contradiction of eternality, of monism and of Materialism he was landed in what, from our standpoint, was a fresh contradiction, the contradiction of a mere law without a personality on whom this law would be binding, and of a salvation without altogether the existence of somebody entitled to reach that goal which, we, more or less generally, understand under salvation.

We will better understand the solution at which Buddha arrived, if we take into account a specific Indian habit of mind, its idea of quiescence as the only real bliss which life can afford. The Buddhist saint (*ārya*) regards the life of the worldling as an

1. Cf. the information about the wandering teachers collected by B. C. Law, Historical Gleanings, ch. II and III (Calcutta, 1922).

unhappy existence of constant turmoil. His aim is to escape from the movement of phenomenal life into a state of absolute quiescence, a condition in which all emotion and all concrete thought is stopped for ever. The means of attaining this quiescence is profound meditation (*yoga*), the technique of which was developed in India at a very early date.

The picture of the universe which suggested itself to the mental eye of the Buddha, represented thus an infinite number of separate evanescent entities in a state of beginningless commotion, but gradually steering to quiescence and to an absolute annihilation of all life, when all its elements have been, one after another, brought to a standstill. This ideal received a multitude of designations among whom the name of Nirvāṇa was the most appropriate to express annihilation. The term was probably pre-Buddhistic and was formerly applied to the Brahmanical ideal of the dissolution of the individual in the universal whole (*brahma-nirvāṇa*).[1]

The reward for a virtuous life and a strict observance of all religious duties consisted for the orthodox Brahmin in a blissful survival in heaven. For the Brahmanical monist it consisted in being merged in the impersonal absolute. The Buddhist could promise nothing else than quiescence of life and its final annihilation, a result which, taken by itself, was not very remote from what was offered by simple materialism. The latter promised annihilation after every life. Buddha promised likewise annihilation but after a long series of efforts in virtue and concentrated meditation. This result could not but strike as strange, not to European scholars alone. Although the denial of a soul as a separate substance is quite familiar to them, yet they were not prepared to find it clearly stated at so early a date, in so remote a country and not in a system of scepticism, but in a religion. Numerous were also the Indian voices which protested against such radical denial of personal identity.

1. Cf. the information by E. Senart in Album Kern, p. 104, and J. Dahlman, in Nirvāṇa (Berlin 1896) and in Die Sāṁkhya Philosophie (Berlin 1902). Senart's characteristic "un simple equivalent de brahma" is right, as will be seen, in respect of the Mahāyānistic Nirvāṇa only.

In the Buddhist community itself, it provoked opposition which grew ever stronger and resulted 500 years after the demise of the master, in what may be called a quite new religion, reposing on a quite different philosophic foundation.

The apparent contradictions of early Buddhism have been variously explained. It was assumed either that Buddha did not care for speculation or that he, like many other founders of religion, was incapable of clear logical thinking. We are now presented with an attempt to reconstruct a kind of Buddhism which had no speculative tendencies at all and to ascribe the philosophic part of it to a later date to which the final constitution of Pali canon belongs.

It is thus assumed that there has been a primitive Buddhism, very much different, even, as it would seem, quite contrary to what later on finds its expression in the Pali canon. Pessimism, nihilism, soul-denial, psychology without a soul, annihilation as ultimate end, all these features that mark out Buddhism among other religions, Indian as well as non-Indian, did not exist.[1] It was the Buddhism of Buddha himself which was so radically different from anything that appeared later, in historical times, as Buddhism. The consequence of the hypothesis of a simple creed preceding historical Buddhism, is an attempt to interpret the latter in the light of the former.

But if all, or almost all, the doctrines contained in our oldest documents are later inventions, what is it then that Buddha has taught and what in the III and II century B.C.—for this is probably the date which is assigned to the Pali canon in its final form was superseded by another, reconstructed, Buddhism. We have a definite answer. It is Yoga. This only partly solves the difficulty, because if we are asked what Yoga is, we are told that one feels uneasy when asked such a question, "*arien de plus malaise.*" Nevertheless, on the next page, we are informed that Yoga is nothing but vulgar magic and thaumaturgy coupled with hypnotic practices. This would mean that Buddha was not a follower of some philosophic system in the genre of Patañjali's where the psychology of trance played a conspicuous part for the solution of definite problems, but that he was an ordinary magician who certainly did not think of

1. pp. 17, 27, 32-34, 46, 52, 115-116, 125, 129, 132, etc.

denying the existence of a soul, or of establishing a psychology without a soul, or of being a pessimist. Not only is it asserted that *yoga* practices existed in India previously to the rise of Buddhism—this, of course, is very probable—but it looks as though the authors were prepared to maintain that Buddhism itself, the genuine Buddhism of Buddha, nay that even the Pali canon, contains nothing but obscure thaumaturgy.[1] How else could one understand the following very explicit deliverances? "The *yoga* out of which Buddhism was produced had no speculative tendencies" (p. 53), i.e. it was "a technical routine in itself quite foreign to every moral, religious or philosophic view" (p. 12).[2] It was, in a word, magic and thaumaturgy. "In this condition", i.e., in the condition of a *yoga* without speculative tendencies, "has the Buddhism of the Hīnayāna remained, beginning from the *Mahāvagga* up to Buddhaghoṣa, viz. it was a *yoga* almost without any alloy" (p. 53).[3]

---

1. A similar tendency is displayed in another recent book, A. B. Keith, Buddhist Philosophy in India and Ceylon (Oxford, 1923). Buddhism is here represented as a product of a "barbarous age" (p. 267), Buddha as a "magician of a trivial and vulgar kind" (p. 29) Buddhist philosophical conceptions as lacking "both system and maturity, a fact historically reflected in the Negativism of the Mahāyāna" (p. 4).

2. Similar opinions were expressed by H. Beck, "Der ganze Buddhismusist durch und durch nichts als Yoga," (Buddhismus, II, p. 11) Ed. Lehmna (Buddhismus p. 49) N. Soderblom (La vie future, p. 397 f.), Fr. Heiler (Die Buddhistiche Versenkung, p. 7 et passim). They are all more or less mystics. They imagine to have found in Buddhism something congenial with their own emotions. Buddhist mysticism is for them hardly distinguishable from Christian devotion, (cp. Heiler, op. cit., p. 51 f., p. 61 f., p. 66). The identification of Buddhism and Yoga by M. de la V. P. seems to be inspired by quite different feelings; he therefore converts Buddhism into magic or sorcery.

3. M. de la Vallee Poussin tries to impress on his readers that he finds himself in agreement with M. E. Senart, as far as I can see, with but little foundation. The origin of Buddhism was formerly sought in some kind of Upaniṣad ideology or some Sāṅkhya ideas. M. Senart has shown (R.H.R. mt. 42, p. 345) that the coincidences with the *yoga* of Patañjali are much more numerous and striking. Although this work is now proved (by H. Jacobi, see, J.A.O.S., 31, I ff.) to be much later than M. Senart assumed and, in some points, at least, had itself been influenced by Buddhism, nevertheless the coincidences pointed out by M. Senart are solid facts which nobody is likely to deny. They can be now supplemented; in that sense

Here we beg leave to remark that the case of Indian philosophy would really be a desperate one if a conception so familiar in it, so fundamental, so thoroughly developed in every possible detail, a conception to which a whole system is specially devoted, were something vague and undefinable. Yoga is defined as concentrated thought (*samādhi*) or fixing the attention on a single point (*ekāgratā*) and doing it persistently (*punaḥ punaḥ cetasi niveśanam*). It is synonymous with *dhyāna* and *samāpatti* which mean the same.[1] According to a peculiarity of the Sanskrit language all these terms can be used in an objective sense (*karma-sādhana*), in an instrumental sense (*karaṇa-sādhana*) or in a locative sense (*adhikaraṇa-sādhana*).[2] Yoga and *samādhi* thus mean either the concentrated thought itself, as a psychical condition, or this same thought, as the method through which the condition has been created, or as the place where it has been produced. It is usual to apply in the latter sense, as a designation of the mystic worlds, where the denizens are eternally merged in trance, the term *samāpatti*. It is applicable to all the eight planes of mystic existence, of whom the denizens are, so to say, born mystics. In this sense the term is contrasted with the worlds

---

the yoga ideas have found their way into many other Indian systems as well. Senart's main result (ibid. p. 364) I understand to refer to pre-Buddhistic conditions.

1. The subtle difference between these terms assumed in Y. S. II 29 and III 2-4, 11, rendered by Prof. J.H. Woods as "singleness of intent, contemplation and concentration," as well as the definition of *yoga* as the "restriction of the fluctuations of the mind stuff" ibid. I 2 are a peculiarity of that system. Prof. M. Anesaki and Prof. J. Takakusu, ERE S. V. *dhyāna*, assumed that *samādhi* is the result, arhatship, and *dhyāna* one of the means. But that is against Ab. Kośabh. ad VIII. 1, where *samāpatti-dhyāna* "concentration" is distinguished from *upapatti-dhyāna* "existence in a mystic world". That *samādhi* has also a general meaning is clear from its position among the *citta mahā bhūmikas* where it is defined as *citta ekāgratā*, cf. my Central Conception, p. 100. When concentrated meditation here on earth is contrasted with a birth in an imagined higher world of eternal trance the terms *samāpatti* and *upapatti* are respectively used, the first is explained, as *samā-patti* smoms par. hjug-pa, cf. below the opinion of Śrīlābha, p. 14.

2. Much of the confusion wrought by the inadequate translation of the term *saṁskāra* is likewise due to a failure of realising its double character, it either means a force, *saṁskriyate anena saṁskāraḥ sam-bhūya-kāri*, or it means an element, *saṁskriyate etad, saṁskṛtadharma*.

of gross bodies and carnal desire (*kāma-dhātu*) where the denizens possess thoughts non-concentrated, disturbed. This is its more general acceptation. In a more special sense it is applicable to the four highest planes of existence alone, the immaterial worlds (*arūpa-dhātu*), It then is contrasted with the four lower mystic worlds which are specially called the four *dhyānas*. The word *samādhi* has also a general and a special sense. It can mean the usual faculty of concentrated attention, or it may mean cultivated, developed concentration. It then becomes a mystical power which can transfer the meditator into higher worlds and change life altogether. Yoga is usually applied in the latter kind of connotation, but it would not be inconsistent with the spirit of Sanskrit language to use it in all the three senses : (*yujyate etaditi yogaḥ, yujyate anena iti yogaḥ, yujyate asminn iti yogaḥ*) A complaint, if any, can be only about the detailed and subtle precision with which this notion is analysed, not about its vagueness. For supernatural power the term *ṛddhi* is used. But, of course, when concentration is supposed to produce supernatural mystic powers, then, by a metaphor, the former may be mentioned instead of the latter. The context will always indicate to the careful reader what is the meaning intended.

Very far from being vulgar magic and thaumaturgy, the Buddhist teaching about Yoga contains the following philosophic construction which, in my opinion, the historian of philosophy can neither disregard nor fail to appreciate.

Its fundamental idea consists in the fact that concentrated meditation induces a condition of quiescence. The meditative man is the opposite of the active man. Life is then dissected in its active elements (*saṁskāras*) with a view to their being reduced one after the other to final quiescence and extinction.

A personality (*pudgala*), in which other systems imagine the presence of a permanent spiritual principle, a soul (*ātmā*), is in reality a bundle of elements or forces (*saṁskāra-samūha*) and a stream of thought (*santāna*). It contains nothing permanent or substantial: it is *anātma*. This means that, according to the general idea of radical pluralism, the spiritual part of an individual consists of separate elements (*dharma*), just as its physical frame consists of atoms.[1] Although separate, these elements are linked together by causal laws (*hetu-pratyaya*). Some of them always appear simultaneously, they are satellites (*sahabhū*). Or they follow one another in consecutive-moments, they are then homogeneous (*niṣyanda-phala*): they constitute chains of moments (*kṣaṇa-santāna*). The law of causation is, therefore, called the law of dependently-together-origination (*pratītya-sam-utpāda*). The number of psychical elements (*arūpiṇo-dharmāḥ*) at every given moment of an individual life is variable. It may be very considerable, because undeveloped; dormant faculties are also reckoned as actually present. This circumstance has even provoked gibes from the side of Sautrāntikas in regard to the impossibility of an actual co-existence of so huge a quantity of separate elements at a single moment. However some of them are constant, always present every moment, others appear only under certain conditions. Faculties of ten different kinds[2] are supposed always to be present. They are termed the general faculties (*citta-mahā-bhūmika*). Among them we find the faculty of concentration, *samādhi* or *yoga*. They are morally indifferent. To them are added either a certain number of faculties morally good, or a certain number of faculties morally evil. But not only do the elements which combine in one moment vary in number, they can vary also in intensity (*utkarṣa*). In a certain individual,[3] at a certain time, a certain element may predominate, while in another individual or at another time in the same individual another element may reach prominence.[4]

1. The theory of separate elements (*dharma*) is expounded in detail by Prof. O. Rosenberg, 'Problems of Buddhist Philosophy' [now translated into German from Russian by his widow (Heideberg 1924) and also by myself in my 'Central Conception of Buddhism' (London 1923). R.A.S.].

2. Yaśomitra, ad. Ab. Kośa II. 40, computes that, if in the first moment 27 *dharmas* are present, there will be 486 elements in the sixth one, and so on, *iti ananta-dravyā (Prāṇinaḥ) pratisantāna-śarīrakṣaṇe bhavanti*. If these elements were resistent stuff, says Vasubandhu, there would be not enough room for them in the whole universe.

3. Cf. the tables appended to my 'Central Conception', p. 100.

4. We accordingly say "I remember", "I wish", but this does not mean that at the moment when I wish I do not think, or that in the moment when I remember I do not wish. All mind is regarded consisting at every moment of an assemblage of mental atoms, faculties (*saṁskāra*), elements (*dharma*).

Among the constantly present elements, there are two exceedingly precious ones which, when given the proper opportunity of full development become predominant and change the character of the individual and his moral value altogether. They are the faculty of appreciative analysis (*prajñā*) and the faculty of concentrating our thoughts upon the single point to the exclusion of all other disturbing considerations and occurrences, it is just *samādhi* or *yoga*. These elements may be quite undeveloped and insignificant. *Prajñā* is then called *mati*, but it is the same faculty. When fully developed it becomes transcendent wisdom (*prajñā amalā*). Life in ordinary men is controlled by ignorance (*avidyā*) which is the reverse of *prajñā*, but not its mere absence. It is a separate element which can be and, in every ordinary man really is, present at the same time with his dormant faculty of wisdom. But it is not a constant faculty; it can be suppressed (*prahīṇa*) and thrown out of the mental stream altogether which then becomes purified or saintly (*ārya*).

Now, the moral law or moral progress or moral education of mankind is conceived as a struggle within the stream (*santāna*) between the good (*kuśala*), the noble faculties of man and his bad (*akuśala*) defiling inclinations. Since the elements are *ex hypothesi* separate and momentary, they cannot really influence one another. Nevertheless the presence of defiling ignorance and other disturbing qualities makes the whole stream impure. All the elements are then impure, even the central element, bare consciousness, or pure sensation (*vijñāna*), becomes affected (*kliṣṭa, sāsrava*). A special law of causation (*sarvatraga*-hetu) is imagined to account for the fact that the elements of the stream are either all of them pure in the saint, or all impure (*kliṣṭa*) in the ordinary man.[1]

It is part of the system; it is also a deep belief in all Buddhist countries that the noble and sublime faculties will finally, in the long run, triumph. The defiling faculties (*kleśa*) are divided into two classes, so far as one class can be remedied by insight so to say, by reason, and the other by concentrated attention only. The first are called *dṛṣṭi-heya*, the other *bhāvanā-heya*.[2]

1. Ab. Kośa, II 54, 57; IV. 12,
2. Ibid. I. 40.

It is of course a natural, and even a trivial, fact that some of our shortcomings and vices can be eradicated by knowledge, and others by concentrated attention only. But the faculty of concentration, if fully developed, has a greater force.[1] It then becomes a mystic power. It can stop life altogether. In the path of salvation, it is the last and most decisive step. It can also transfer the individual into a higher plane of existence. He is then reborn or transferred into the realm of ethereal (*accha, bhāsvara*)[2] bodies, into the sphere of purified matter (*rūpudhātu*), or into the still higher regions of pure spirits (*arūpa-dhātu*).

Here we forsake the ground of reality and enter into the worlds of the mystic. From this point of view, existence is divided into three different spheres. The division is in reality bipartite, into the mystic worlds (*samā-patti*) and into the non-mystic ones, i.e. our gross worlds of carnal desire, (*kāma-dhātu*). The latter includes the hells, earth and the lower heavens, where the gods are living and enjoying themselves in a very human way. The position which is assigned to the gods in this sphere is very characteristic for the Buddhist as well as for the Jaina religions. These gods are not superior beings in a moral sense. For the sake of moral progress and salvation, the condition of man is preferable. Speaking technically, the gods of the *kāma-dhātu* represent assemblages of elements of all the 18 categories (*dhātu*). Not a single of them is brought to a standstill by yoga. They are full of passions and are superior to man by their power, but not by their conduct.[3] The mystic worlds are further divided into two classes, those in which the denizens possess ethereal bodies and those in which they have no physical frame. The faculty of concentration (*samādhi*,

1. When *samādhi* has reached full development, it becomes the predominant element in the bundle of elements (*saṁskārasamañha*) which make up an individual. The single term *samādhi* may then be used for this element together with its satellites, it then becomes synonymous with the individual or his 5 *skandhas*, cp. Ab. Kośabh ad VIII. 1. The same applies to the developed *prajñā*.

2. Cp. Ab. Kośabh, ad II. 12.

3. The higher planes of these carnal gods, however, are morally purer than the lower ones; they gradually approach to the still higher moral standard of the worlds of trance, cp. Ab. Kośa. III. 70.

yoga) has here attained predominance; it has become the central element; the others are their satellites. Imagination has built up above the heavens of the carnal gods a series of mystic worlds. They correspond exactly to the degrees of trance which are gradually reached or supposed to be reached, by the mystic. The purely spiritual realms (*arūpa-dhātu*) are four. Their denizens are merged in contemplation (*samāpatti*) of some unique idea, either the idea of the infinity of space, or of the infinity of thought, or of the void, or in a dreamy semi-conscious state. Their condition is nearly catalepsy, a state where consciousness is quite arrested. The worlds of ethereal bodies are also four in number, exactly corresponding to the initial four degrees of trance (*dhyāna*) and are accordingly designated as the worlds of the first, the second, the third and the fourth *dhyāna*.

Our material frame consists of elements of 18 kinds, but four of them are in abeyance in the worlds of ethereal bodies. The sense-data of smell and taste and the corresponding two sets of sensations do not exist. It is because these beings do not want any hard food, no food which is taken piecemeal, chewed and swallowed.[1] Their nutrition is spiritual. Here imagination evidently is founded upon the fact that the mystic, when deeply engaged in meditation, forgets all about his meals. Therefore, olfactory and gustatory sense-data lose their *raison d'etre*. They are by the mystic power of yoga extinct altogether. But the physical organs, the nose and the tongue remain, because, their absence would make the body ugly. All the bodies are beautiful, none is mutilated. Their faculties of sight and audition are unlimited; they possess *divya-cakṣuḥ* and *divya-śrotram*.[2] Their tactile sensations are the same as the characteristic agreeable feeling of bodily ease and lightness (*prasrabdhi*) which produces levitation in the mystic. Their movements are, therefore, extremely swift and dexterous. But the faculties of smelling and taste are absent altogether, because their food is immaterial. They have no need for clothes,[3] they are born with a light ethereal covering that lasts all their very long life through. Neither do they want any dwellings. Every new born finds a

1. Ab. Kośa. I 30, III, 39.
2. They have, as a monk in Mongolia expressed himself in a conversation with me, telescopes and telephones.
3. Ab. Kośa, III. 70.

house provided for him by *karma*, i.e. by nature. The phenomenon of sex is spiritualised. The bodies are without the members of physical procreation. This does not make them mutilated. Gross sexual passion does not exist at all. But total indifference does neither exist. The feelings are delicate. The birth of a new being is quite free from all pain and filth. The new born child does not come out of the matrix of a female, it is apparitional (*upapāduka*). Those who happen to be nearest to the place of his birth are his parents.[1] No government,[2] of course, is needed in such a community, because there are no crimes, no gross passions. Total absence of passion would mean total absence of volitions, and this, according to the Indian conceptions, would stop life altogether; it would be Nirvāṇa. But all the feelings have a mild form. The feeling of hatred (*pratigha*) is totally absent. Other feelings are veiled indifference (*nivṛta-avyākṛta*).[3]

The imagination of the man who has drawn this picture, whether it be Buddha or another, seems to have been guided by the idea that manual work is the curse of humanity. Therefore a state is imagined where there is no need for it, because food, clothes and homes are naturally provided. The other debasing feature of mankind, the gross sexuality of love, is quite absent. Thus from the three incentives of human action on earth, wealth, love and duty (*artha-kāma-dharma*) the last alone continues its unimpeded sway in the mystic world. However, there is no absolute equality between the denizens. There are lofty and ordinary characters. The quality of being a "worldling" (*pṛthag-jana*) can occasionally appear in these regions. At least some of the schools are quarrelling about this question.[4]

1. Ab. Kośa. III. 71.

2. Ibid. III. 98.

3. A full account of the Buddhist heavens and their denizens is given in Prof. H. Kirfel, Die Kosmographie der Inder (Bonn, 1920), p. 190 ff, but their connection with the degrees of absorption in yoga-meditation is mentioned only in regard to the 4 *sampattis* on p. 198. Cp. also B. C. Law, Heaven and Hell (Calcutta 1925).

4. The Vātsīputrīyas explained the fact that a person having reached in a higher world the condition of a Saint (*ārya*) could sometimes nevertheless fall back into ordinary humanity and become again a common worldling, by the circumstance that some element of this common world-

The details of this picture have given rise to a great deal of controversy, and even now we can come across Buddhist monks who will, with extraordinary vivacity, debate some of the moot points.

The Abhidharma discusses the question whether in order to possess all supernatural powers existing in the mystic worlds it is a necessary condition to be born in them or whether it is possible to possess them even while living here on earth, in the realm of gross bodies. We find the following answer[1] :

> There are beings living here on earth in the realm of gross bodies (*kāma-dhātu*), and there are others living in the first, second and higher worlds of ethereal bodies (*prathama-dhyānādi*). They are all possessors of a body, of a faculty of vision and of corresponding visible objects. Is it a necessary rule, that body, sight and object should all belong to the same plane of existence or are such beings possible whose sight and objects are those of another world than their body ? We answer, that different combinations of each element are possible.
>
> "If a being is born on earth and he contemplates surrounding objects with his usual sense of vision all the three elements will belong to the same sphere. But if this very man will acquire that mystical power of vision, which is characteristic of the first world of trance, then the combination will change. The body and the surrounding objects will remain the same as before, but the faculty of vision and the corresponding sensations will be those which are characteristic of the first world of trance. If, in addition to that, he will attain a degree of mystic concentration where all objects are changed, then the body remaining on earth, his faculty of vision, his visual sensations and his external world will all be those of the mystic...... This being, still remaining in the plane of gross bodies, may acquire the faculty of vision characteristic of the second and higher worlds. Corresponding combinations will then arise which can easily be imagined

liness (*pṛthagjanatva*) was left dormant in him, it had not been quite eradicated at the time when he became a saint, cp. Ab. Kośabh. I 40. II 40.

1. Condensed from Ab. Kośabh, pp. 88. 14-90-7 (B.B.XX), cp. M. de la V. P's translation, pp. 93. ff.

by the analogy of what has been stated....Further if a denizen of the first mystic world would contemplate the surrounding objects with his own faculty of vision, then all the elements will belong to his own plane of existence. But if he will look down upon the plane of existence below him, then his body, his sight and his sensations will remain his own, though his objects will belong to another plane. The denizen of the first mystic world may acquire the sight-power characteristic of the second mystic world, and so on. The corresponding combinations may easily be imagined.

"However, there is a limitation. The faculty of vision cannot be that of a lower plane than the body, (there can be no ethereal bodies with a gross faculty of vision), but there can be a gross body with a mystic power of vision. Ordinary men with an ordinary power of vision do not perceive the higher worlds, but the denizens of the higher worlds might perceive what is going on in the gross worlds, if they care to. The organ of vision, connected with a certain body, can appertain either to its own plane of existence, or to a higher one; it can never descend to a lower plane. But the visible objects and visual sensations either belong to the same plane as the body or to a lower one, never to a higher one. The same refers to the faculty of audition. As to the faculties of touch, smell and taste, they always belong to the same plane of existence as that of their body.

These speculations help us to understand the Buddhist denial of personal identity. The separate elements combining in a personality may even be such as normally belong to different planes of existence. Determined by actual observation these elements, by an effort of imagination, are transferred to a higher plane where they continue to combine under changed circumstances according to the same laws of evolution, *elan vital* or *karma*, which were settled by the analysis of actual facts. The work of philosophy here resembles a mathematical computation. Being given a certain change in the axiom of existence, e.g. the necessity of food, clothing and homes being in abeyance, what will be the consequent changes in all the formulas of personal existence? This is also clearly seen out of the following discussion in the Abhidharma.[1]

"It has been determined that 18 kinds (*dhātu*) of elements are cooperating in making up life in all the three spheres of existence.[2] It is then asked how many cooperate in the whole worlds of gross bodies, how many in the worlds of ethereal bodies, and how many in the spiritual worlds. It is answered—18 in the first, 14 in the second and 3 in the last. All the 18 elements combine in creating life in the sphere of gross bodies. "They combine" means that they are inseparable from it, they constitute this world. In the plane of ethereal bodies, the fragrant and savoury stuff, as well as the corresponding sensations (*vijñāna*) are excluded. They represent physical food (*kavalī-kāra-āhāra*). But ethereal bodies belong to beings who can live without such food; they have no desire for it. The olfactory and gustatory sensations are thus absent, because their objects—that physical food which contains the fragrant and savoury stuff—do not exist.

"Objection: But in this case neither the resistant stuff would exist in these worlds, since it is also a part of the nutriment stuff?

"Answer: That part of it alone exists which is not nutriment.

Objection: The fragrant and the savoury stuffs are in the same condition (a part of them is not nutriment)?

"Answer: The resistant stuff is necessary as a support for the sense faculties, as a support for the bodies and as clothes for them. But for the fragrant and savoury stuffs there is no necessity, because there is no physical food. Therefore, since the instinct for such food is absent, neither do the corresponding stuffs exist (i.e. they are not produced by *karma*). The case of resistant stuff is different.

"Opinion of Śrīlābha: If some body here (on earth) by concentrated meditation reaches ecstasy, he con-

---

1. Condensed from Ab. Kośabh. bh., pp. 52. 2-53.8 (B.B.XX). Cp. M. de la V. P.'s translation p. 54 ff.
2. Cp. the tables in Central Conception, p. 97.

tinues to see colours, to hear sounds and his sense of touch is agreeably effected by some special tangible stuff which is produced simultaneously with the production in him of a high degree of levitation (*prasrabdhī*), but odours and tastes are in abeyance. For this reason, when beings are reborn in these worlds of trance, the first three sense data exist, but smells and tastes are absent."

It is seen out of this passage that the conditions of life in the sphere of ethereal bodies are imagined by transferring personal mystic experiences into a separate plane of existence.

A very interesting discussion then follows about that driving force of nature called *karma* which, in this connection, corresponds to our conception of evolution, or *elan vital.*[1]

It produces, according to a regular plan and answering to necessities, all the varieties of life in the plane of gross bodies and *mutatis mutandis* in the imagined planes of existences constructed according to mystic experiences.

Such is the theory of Yoga in Hīnayāna. It is quite different in Mahāyāna where the philosophic foundation is different. All the devices which are employed for helping the mind to concentrate upon a single point are more or less the same in all philosophic systems. There is absolutely nothing Buddhistic in them.[2] The psychological fact of concentration which is at

1. What confusion arises from a wrong translation of the term *karma* appears clearly from M. de la V. P.'s translation of this passage, Ab. Kośa II 30, p. 56. "Quelle est la cause de la naissance d'un organe, sinon un certain acte aommande par un dèsir relatif a cet organe". This can only mean that there has been once upon a time, a man who evidently did not possess this organ, or did possess no organ s at all, but he manifested a desire to possess some and committed an action in consequence. After that all men, who peacefully existed withou t any organs at all, suddenly acquired them. No wonder that Indian philosophy, when presented in such a garb, ceases to be attractive. About *karma* in Buddhism cp. O. Rosenberg, Problems, XVI.

2. Fr. Heiler, op. cit. p. 47, following Prof. Rhys Davids, thinks that (brahmanical) yoga is predominantly physical and hypnotic, whereas the Buddhist method of meditation is intellectual and moral. I would not venture to endorse this opinion. In this respect the difference, if any, is negligible. Heiler evidently overlooks, in his Buddhist fervour, the devotion to God (*īśvarapraṇidhāna*) of the brahmanical Yogī. The process of moral purification of the latter is very vividly described by Prof. S.N.

the bottom of them is a very simple one.[1] When carried on systematically they induce special mystic states of mind. Patañjali has given their explanation according to the principles of Sāṅkhya philosophy. In Hīnayāna Buddhism, they are explained in a manner fitting the system of radical pluralism, i.e. that theory of separate elements (*dharma*) which has been established with a view to their gradual extinction in Nirvāṇa. Very characteristic for Buddhism is the system of heavens or paradises in which, at their middle and highest stages, imaginary beings are lodged, who are also called gods, but are nothing but born mystics, beings in whom the condition of trance is a natural one. This distinguishes Buddhism from all other religions and philosophical systems.[2] It is also inseparable from the conception of the Hīnayānist Nirvāṇa, or the so-called Nirvāṇa of the Śrāvakas. According to the teaching of some schools the highest cataleptic states of trance are eternal (asaṁskṛta), i.e. they do not differ from Nirvāṇa.[3] But, according to the majority of schools, Nirvāṇa is beyond even that. It is the absolute limit of life, the extinction even of this kind of the thinnest vestige of consciousness which is still left in the highest of all imaginable worlds of cataleptic trance.

III. MYSTIC INTUITION (YOGA-PRATYAKṢA)

Apart from the above described general function of Yoga, there is another special kind of it, the subjective counterpart

---

Dasgupta, The Study of Patañjali, p. 142 ff. (Calcutta, 1920) and his other works.

1. The late Prof. O. Rosenberg has himself practised some yoga-meditation in a Zen Monastery in Japan. He used to compare the agreeable feeling of ease which he then experienced to the effect produced by music, especially when executed personally. Attention is then fixed and a light feeling of ecstasy makes you forget all troubles of life. The warlike Samurai before going to war used to go through a course of yoga-experiences in some Zen monastery, and this had the most beneficial influence upon their moral condition in strengthening their courage and endurance.

2. It is interesting to note that the gods of Epicurus are also quiescent, inactive and also possess ethereal bodies of a special atomic structure.

3. Cp. Kathā-vatthu, VI 4. The yogācāras likewise reckon catalepsy among the *asaṁskṛta* elements.

of the first. It then appears as the mystic intuition of the true condition of the universe. The Buddhist saint is supposed, in a moment of mystic illumination, suddenly to perceive the whole construction, with its gross and mystic worlds, as vividly as if it were a direct sense perception. As a psychological process, it is equally taught in Hīnayāna and in Mahāyāna, but its content, the picture which reveals itself at this moment, is quite different in both systems. It corresponds to their theoretical parts, to the system of pluralism which is taught in Hīnayāna and to the monist view which is the central conception of Mahāyāna, as will be seen later on. For, although a sudden illumination, it does not come without preparation. The future saint has gone through a long course of moral training and he has carefully studied all the details of the philosophic construction, when in the moment of sudden illumination what he had before tried to understand only theoretically, comes up before him with the vivacity of living reality. Beginning with this moment he is a saint, all his habits of thought are changed. He directly views the universe as an infinite continuity of single moments in gradual evolution towards final extinction. In Mahāyāna, the Bodhisattva sees directly or feels inwardly, quite another picture, corresponding to the theoretical teaching of that religion. The path towards salvation is therefore divided in a preliminary path of accumulating merit (*sambhāra-mārga*), in a subsequent course of training (*prayoga-mārga*) and in the path of illumination (*dṛṣṭi-mārga*).[1] The latter is momentary. It is technically called perception of the four truths, such perception being the exclusive property of the saint (ārya). Therefore, they are called the four truths of the Saint (*āryasya satyāni*). They express the general view that there is a phenomenal existence (*duḥkha*), its driving force (*samudaya*), there will be final extinction (*nirodha*), and there is a path towards it (*mārga*). In this general

1. Mrs. C. Rhys Davids (Dhamma-saṅgaṇī Transl., p. 256, n. 2) calls it a "mental awakening", "intellectual conversion", "a certain vantage-point for mind and heart from which the Promised Land of Nirvāṇa was caught sight of, and the fact of impermanence first discerned", "Under the fact of impermanence" the theory of the impermanent *dharmas* must be evidently understood. A poetical description of *dṛṣṭi-mārga*, which is the same as *srotāpattiphala*, is found in D. N. I. 76 ff.

form the four truths are accepted by all Indian systems.[1] There is absolutely nothing Buddhistic in them. Their meaning changes according to the content which is put into them, according to what is understood under phenomenal life (*duḥkha*)[2] and under extinction (*nirvāṇa*). Within the pale of Buddhism, these conceptions have, at a certain date, undergone a radical change. In early Buddhism they correspond to a pluralistic universe, in Mahāyāna to a monistic one.[3]

In Hīnayāna, the process of illumination is described as a double moment, it consists in a moment of feeling and a moment of knowledge. The feeling is satisfaction (*kṣānti-ruci*), after which in the next following moment comes intuition, the vision of the elements of existence (*dharma-jñāna*). The intuition refers at first to the surrounding gross world, and then, as is always the case, it is transferred to the imagined worlds of trance (*anvaya-jñāna*). Thus in sixteen consecutive moments[4] the intuition of the future saint has run through the whole universe, its real and imaginary worlds, and has viewed them in the light of four stages of their evolution towards quiescence. The supreme moment of illumination is the central point of the teaching about the path of salvation. An enormous literature, especially in Mahāyāna, is devoted to this conception of mystic intuition[5].

When in later times the study of Abhidharma has been superseded by the study of logic and epistemology, the mystic perception of the saint has retained its place among the different categories of direct cognition which were then established.

---

1. About the "four truths" in Nyāya-Vaiśeṣika see below.

2. It is *saṁskāra-duḥkhatā* or *pariṇāma-dhuḥkhātā* the counterpart of *asaṁskṛta=nirodha*, cp. Ab. Kośabh. VI. 3. This kind of *duḥkha* is much nearer to our ordinary conception of joy, than of suffering.

3. In Nyāya-Vaiśeṣika the *yogin* perceives at that moment of illumination the atoms and all categories directly, cp. Praśastap., p. 187.7.

4. About the 16 moments cp. Ab. Kośa, VI. 18, 25 ff. and M. de la V. Vp. in his edition of Madhy. vi, p. 497 n. 4.

5. The text book for the study of this part of Mahāyāna is the Abhisamayālaṅkāra of Maitreya-Asaṅga, of which 21 Indian commentaries alone existed besides a huge indigenous Tibetan literature. Among the seat of the "yellow caps" the chief commentary studied is the Lam-rim-chen-po-by the great Tson-kh-pa, partly translated into Russian by G. Tsibikoff.

Direct cognition was then defined as containing no synthetic thought (*kalpanāpoḍha*). It was pure sensation which could apprehend an indefinite moment of sensation only. The four truths, i.e. ontology, were at first studied and ascertained by sound logic (*pramāṇena viniścita*) and then suddenly perceived as vividly as a grain of corn on the palm of the hand[1]. The number of moments was then reduced to three. In the Madhyamaka system, where logic was denied altogether, the preparation consisted in a course of negative dialectic, after which the intuition of the transcendental truth springs up as an inward conviction (*pratyātma-vedya*).[2] In both the philosophic systems which are represented in Buddhism—the pluralism of the Hīnayāna and the monism of Mahāyāna—there is a course of preparation and meditation and a moment of sudden illumination.[3]

If we now try to answer the question about the age and the history of this Buddhist doctrine of Yoga, we must, first of all wholly appreciate the fact that it is an inseparable, inherent part of the pluralistic universe of separate elements (*dharma*) gradually evolving towards extinction.[4] The possibility is

1. Cp. Nyāya-bindu and ṭikā, p. 11 (B.B. VII).

2. Madhy. vi. p. 493-11

3. According to H. Bergson (De l'intuition philosophique) every great philosopher has once had a vision of the universe to which he then remains faithful the rest of his life in a series of attempts to formulate it ever clearer and clearer. This will then be the *dṛṣṭi-mārga* of that philosopher. In the life of Kant, it will be the time when after the year of literary activity and meditation, the central conception of the Critique of Pure Reason revealed itself to him and he then wrote, "das Jar 69 gab mir grosses Licht." The rest of his life was indeed spent in repeated attempts at a clear formulation of that vision. The preceding study and meditation were, so to say, his *sambhāra* and *prayogamārga*.

4. It has been supposed that the four *dhyānas* are of an earlier date than the four *samāpattis*, cp. Heiler, op. cit, p. 43 ff. The conception of ethereal existences in the Rūpa dhātu as consisting of 14 *dhātus* only, because they did not want any physical food is evidently a rationalisation of the myth about the descent of man from one of the Buddhist mystic worlds where the denizens fed on *samādhi*, cp. D. N. III. 84 ff. The full theory probably existed already at the time of the formation of the Pali Canon.

not excluded, as we have stated elsewhere,[1] that the germ of this theory is older than Buddha himself. In any case there is no historically authenticated Buddhism without this theory, without the mystic worlds and its inherent part, the philosophic and moral aim; all sorcery and thaumaturgy, the Brahmanical sacrifices not excepted, were strongly condemned by Buddha. They were considered as one of the cardinal sins.[2] The details of the condition in the worlds of the mystic and the degrees of mystic concentration have always given opportunities to much scholastic controversy between the schools. We can safely assert that within the pale of Hīnayāna Buddhism there is no place for trivial sorcery.[3]

The psychology of trance is indeed a characteristic feature of many Indian systems, not of Buddhism alone. It appears almost inevitably in that part of every Indian system which is called "the path" (*mārga*) in which the means of a transition out of the phenomenal world into the Absolute are considered. With the exception of the orthodox Mīmāṁsakas and the materialists, every system in this part, but not in others, contains a certain amount of mysticism. The Jainas had their teaching about Yoga. Even the realistic and theistic Naiyāyikas, when feeling it difficult to explain the transition into the Absolute, i.e., from *saṁsāra* into *nirvāṇa*, have recourse not to God, but to Yoga.[4] However, just as the European mind is not altogether and always free from mysticism, so is the Indian mind not

1. Central Conception, p. 65 ff.

2. Cp. the article on Buddhist Magic in ERE where mysticism, magic and popular superstition are not sufficiently distinguished. In the Brahmajālasutta, D. N. I. 9 ff., we have a long list of superstitions and magical practices, all strongly condemned.

3. If every supernatural world or power, imagined by the mystic is represented as magic, then of course Hīnayāna will be full of magic, but Christianity, especially that which believes in miracles, will neither escape a similar reproach. The *ṛddhis* and *abhijñās* should, therefore, be more properly characterised as mystical imagined powers, with the proviso that "of the reality or unreality of the mystic's world we know nothing" (B. Russell, External World, 1922, p. 20) Very interesting are the explanations, and a certain vindication, of the Buddhist supernatural cognitions and powers by Fr. Heiler, op. cit. pp. 33 ff.

4. About the place Yoga occupies in the system of Nyāya Vaiśeṣika see below.

at all necessarily subject to it. Not to speak about numerous materialistic doctrines, the orthodox Mīmāṁsakas themselves held about Yoga an opinion which probably represents just what all of us, so far as we are not mystics, think about it, viz. that Yoga is sheer imagination, just as any other ordinary fantasticism.[1] Considering that the Mīmāṁsakas are the oldest philosophical system in India whose roots go down into the Vedic age, we at once can measure the exact value of the "historical method" which finds it highly improbable that in India, at the time of Buddha, nothing but vulgar magic and thaumaturgy could exist.

It is the common lot of every philosophy or religion to reach a point where further explanation becomes impossible. A higher and mystical principle is then invoked, because the usual methods have failed to give satisfaction. With Descartes and Leibnitz it is God, with many Indian systems, it is Yoga as a mystical power. An appeal to this power plays a considerable part in Buddhism, but not otherwise.

IV. BUDDHA'S BELIEF IN PERSONAL IMMORTALITY

Additional arguments in favour of an unphilosophic primitive Buddhism are derived from the occurrence in the Pali Canon of the word "immortal" among the epithets of Nirvāṇa, the interpretation of the passages where Buddha is reported to have given no answer at all when questioned about Nirvāṇa, the occurrence in later literature of the term reality (*vastu*) in connection with Nirvāṇa.

A short examination of the value of these additional arguments will not be out of place.

The practical as well as the theoretical part of Buddhism converge towards the idea of an extinction of all the active forces of life in the Absolute. This Absolute, Nirvāṇa, accordingly receives in emotional passages an overwhelming-mass of *epitheta ornantia* among which the term "place of immortality" occurs several times. But what is this immortality? Is it the immortality of Vedic times? The blissful existence among

1. Cf. Ślokavārt., on pratyakṣasūtra, 32.

the forefathers in heaven?[1] Or is this hypothetical immortality, something like the paradise of Amitābha? Or something like the paradise of later Viṣṇuism? Not the slightest indication. Because indeed the word occurs only as an epithet of Nirvāṇa—annihilation. There is no deficiency, as we have seen, of paradises in the Buddhistic outlook. But Nirvāṇa is beyond all imaginable spheres, it is the absolute limit. The words "immortal place" simply means changeless, lifeless and deathless condition, for it is explained as meaning a place where there is neither birth (i.e. rebirth) nor death (i.e. repeated death).[2] People enter paradise by being reborn in it, they disappear forever in Nirvāṇa by being extinct.

V. WAS BUDDHA AN AGNOSTIC?

Another additional argument is drawn out of a new interpretation of very well-known passages in the Canon where Buddha is reported to have answered a series of metaphysical questions by sheer silence. It is literally an argument *a silentio*. Considering these questions more closely, we see that they are metaphysical questions, such as: is the world beginningless or has it a beginning, is it finite or infinite, what is the condition

---

1. M. dela V. P. evidently thinks that all religious developments start with an idea of a surviving immortal soul, a theory that has been exploded as far as Indian religions are concerned. Dr. Paul Tuxen in the Det Klg. Danske Videnskabernes selskab Hist-phil. Meddleseer, II 5 Forestillingen om Sjaelen i Rigveda, has proved that such an idea is quite absent from the Ṛgveda. In the oldest Upaniṣads the surviving *homunculus* is represented as a congeries of 5 elements which dissolve at death and then a new combination of them springs into being. It is not impossible to see in them the forerunners of the Buddhist 5 skandhas. The idea of a soul, in our acceptation of the term, appears in the metrical Upaniṣads and is contemporaneous with the rise of Sāṅkhya and Jainism, probably also with some kind of pre-Buddhistic Buddhism, cf. H. Jacobi, Gottesidee, p. 7 ff. and my Central Conception, p. 65 ff.

2. The epithet "place of immortality" is also used in connection with Nirvāṇa in Brahmanical systems which adopt a lifeless Nirvāṇa, cf. Vātsyāyana, (ed. Vizian) p. 30. It means a place where there is no death, it does not mean a place where there is eternal life. It is likewise called a place where there is no birth, *na jayati, na jīyati, na mīyati te amatam ti vuceati* (Comm. Khuddaka, p. 180) just as birth always means rebirth, death means reiterated death, cf. Oldenberg, Buddha, p. 46.

of the saint after death, this last question meaning, what is the nature of the Absolute? When these questions were addressed to Buddha on a certain occasion by a certain interlocutor, it happened that either no answer at all was forthcoming, or it was declared that the questions were futile. Scholars, Indian and European, ancient and modern, did not find much difficulty in harmonizing this occasional "agnosticism" with the main lines of the teachings of the Pali Canon. So scholars went all the length of comparing these reserved questions with a series of topics declared insoluble in modern critical philosophy. There is indeed some similarity.[1]

However M. de la Vallee Poussin explains Buddha's silence by his incapacity in the philosophical field. He did not know what to answer![2] He was prepared to answer the question of the existence of an eternal soul in the affirmative if his interlocutor preferred so, if not, he did not mind denying it (p. 119). This is confirmed by a reference to Kumāralābha who is quoted by Vasubandhu in the course of a very long discussion about the cardinal tenet of all Buddhists, the "personalists" (*pudgala-vādins*) not excluded, i.e. the non-existence of a substantial soul. This tenet is discussed here in a masterly way with perfect clearness and every possible detail.[3] Buddha denies an eternal soul as against the eternalist, but maintains moral responsibility as against the materialist. Both extremes are declared to be follies against which the doctrine of Buddha is directed. He has sought and found a "middle path" which evades the dangers of both extremes. How then could such a categorical denial and emphatic protest against two extremes be turned into a connivance in them? This is as much a riddle as the conversion of the Pali Canon into a manual of thaumaturgy. It would be interesting to know when did Buddha "teach to some persons the existence of self" (p. 119), i.e., a full blown *ātmavāda* or *satkāyadṛṣṭi*?

1. They are questions which "human reason in its natural progress must necessarily encounter", (Kant, Critique of Pure Reason, transl. by Max Muller, p. 340) Sp. O. Franke, Kant u. die altindische Philosophie, in "Zur Erinnerung an Emanuel Kant" (Halle, 1904), p. 137-8.

2. The same explanation is given by A. B. Keith, op. cit. p. 63

3. Translated by M. de la V. P. in the 1st volume of his Abhidharma-kośa, pp. 128 ff. and by me in the Bulletin de l'Academie des Sciences de Russie, 1919, pp. 823 ff.

In many systems, ancient and modern, eastern and western, the reality in itself, the pith of reality, is declared to be something incognisable. It is, therefore, quite natural to find in the *sūtra* literature, where the style of popular discourses is adopted, the device of impressing upon the audience the mystic-character of the Absolute by silence. The Mahāyāna *sūtras* do not tarry in characterising it as "unspeakable", "unknowable", "undefinable" etc. A long discussion about the essence of the absolute is given in the *Vimalakīrti-sūtra*. The question is tackled from different sides, and when Vimalakīrti is at length asked to summarise, he remains silent, whereupon Bodhisattva Mañjuśrī exclaims, "Well done. Well done, non-duality is truly above words !".[1]

Nor is this feature limited to Buddhist literature. The Vedāntins resorted to the same device when wishing to bring home the transcendental character of their *advaita-brahma*. Śaṅkara reports a case when the question about the essence of *Brahma* was reiterated three times without eliciting any answer.[2] At last, when it was asked, "Why don't you answer ?" the reply was, "I do answer (sc. by silence), but you do not understand me". Is it permissible to draw the conclusion that Vimalakīrti and those men to whom Saṅkarācārya refers had themselves no reasoned opinion about the Absolute or that they were quite indifferent and prepared to answer just as the questioner preferred, in the affirmative or in the negative ?[3]

VI. THE POSITION OF THE LATER SCHOOLS OF THE HĪNAYĀNA

M. de la Vallée Poussin insists that in order to escape obscurity we must construct an outline ("un schéma d'ensemble) of the history of Buddhism, that this outline must harmonize

---

1. Cf. Suzuki, Mahāyāna, p. 106-7
2. Ad. V. S. III. 2. 17
3. Vasubandhu (Ab. Kośa. V 22) reports that it was a rule of dialectics at the time of Buddha to answer by silence these questions which were wrongly formulated, e.g., all questions regarding the properties of non-existing thing. Prof. H. Oldenberg rightly remarks on another occasion, Upaniṣaden, p. 133 "Die eigenste Sprache dieser Mystik, wie aller Mystik, ist Schweigen."

with the general conception we have about the history of ancient India,[1] and that questions of detail become at once settled, if tehy find their place in this historical outline (p. XX). This scheme seems to be the following one. There was in the beginning a simple faith in soul and immortality and a primitive teaching of an indefinite character, mainly of obscure magic. After that a mixed period supervened when this simple creed was contaminated with confused ideology, and this allows us to ask the question whether Buddhism at that period was not agnosis. At last Buddhism received a superstructure of inane scholasticism and we have a scholastic period in Buddhism, just as we have one in mediaeval Europe.

Primitive faith, a period of agnosticism and a period of scholasticism,—we at once see wherefrom the scheme is borrowed. It is an attempt to construct the history of Buddhism on parallel lines with the history of the Western Church.

What the primitive faith and the supposed agnosticism represent we have already seen.

Now what is scholasticism? It is either (1) philosophy in the service of religion or (2) excessive subtlety and artificiality in philosophical constructions. Buddhism, early or canonic, is contrasted with Buddhism later or scholastic (p. 46).[2] This leads to the supposition that the school, e.g. of the Vaibhāṣikas represented in its teaching something substantially different from the early canonical schools. But as a matter of fact, the Vaibhāṣikas are only the continuators of one of the oldest schools, the Sarvāstivādins. They derive their name from the title of a huge commentary upon the canonical work of this school and follow in philosophy generally the same lines as did the original school. Quite different is the position of the second school, the Sautrāntikas. It is really a new school, a precursor or contemporary of that momentous change which

1 This general conception of the history of India is apparently mentioned as implying the opinion of the author about the social milieu (p. 107) in which nothing but obscure magic could possibly originate, an opinion fully shared by Prof. Keith. It would be interesting to know the opinion of both these authors about the milieu in which the grammar of Pāṇini, this one of the greatest productions of the human mind, originated!

2. But on p. 128 M. de la Vallee Poussin mentions the "nihilistic seholasticism" as the scholasticism of the canon.

splits the history of Buddhism into two quite distinct periods. It is, therefore, preferable to keep to the broad lines of the old division of Buddhism into early or Hīnayāna and later or the Mahāyāna, and to admit the existence of a transitional school in the Sautrāntikas.[1]

We readily think that there was a considerable growth of scholasticism in early Buddhism, but it is scholasticism in the second sense. Since the simple faith in immortality never existed, it is impossible to speak of its being blurred or contaminated by scholasticism. Early Buddhism started from a sound philosophical idea of ultimate realities (*dharmas*). Some of these elements are highly artificial constructions. Early Buddhists and their continuators, the Vaibhāṣikas, have paid a heavy tribute to that innate tendency of the human mind to infer difference of things from a difference of words. The Sautrāntikas most decidedly opposed this tendency, they sharply distinguished nominal realities (*prajñaptisat*) from ultimate data. They accordingly mercilessly cut down the lists of elements adopted in the schools of early Buddhism and by the Vaibhāṣikas. They thus reduced them exclusively to a list comprising sense data and the primitive data of mind. It is, therefore, quite wrong to throw them into the same bag with the Vaibhāṣikas. They are, if anything, anti-scholastic. Their role may be usefully compared with that of Occam's Razor in European philosophy. They even can be more properly called a critical school, a name which their continuators, the Yogācāra-Sautrāntika school, fully deserves. But these already belong to the Mahāyāna. If we roughly assign the beginning of Mahāyāna to the I century A.D. and the decline of Hīnayāna in the North to the V century, we shall have about five hundred years when both these tendencies kept the field. The Sautrāntikas apparently began by taking an intermediate position between the extreme Mahāyānists[2] and the

---

1. Another transitional school between Hīnayāna and Mahāyāna is the so-called Satya-siddhi school of Harivarman known only from Chinese sources, cf. Yamakami Sogen, Systems of Buddhist Thought, p. 172 ff. (Calcutta, 1912), O. Rosenberg, Problems, p. 274.

2. This Vasubandhu himself hints, cf. my Soul Theory, p. 852 and M. de la V. p.'s transl. IX P. 273. Vasubandhu who himself favoured

"school men". Then the battle that raged during 500 years was coming to its end, they coalesced with the Mahāyānists who had won the battle and formed with them the hybrid school of Yogācāra-Sautrāntika. Among the ultimate realities of the earlier lists which were declared by the new movement, i.e. by both the Mahāyānists and the Sautrāntikas, to be nominal we find Nirvāṇa (*nirodha*).

It was known long ago that the Vaibhāṣika and the Sautrāntika schools were engaged in a dispute regarding the nature of Nirvāṇa. The first maintained that it was something real (*vastu*), the second objected that it was nothing real by itself, that it was merely the cessation of all personal life. The exact meaning of this issue could, of course, be fully appreciated only if the complicated arguments of both contending schools would have been known. Our information about the Vaibhāṣikas is much more ample now, and we can present in detail the argumentation which led to the tenet of Nirvāṇa as a reality. About the other school, the Sautrāntikas, our information is still indirect. The works of the early Sautrāntikas, Kumāralābha, Śrīlābha, Mahābhadanta, Vasumitra and others are still inaccessible. Vasubhandhu can be taken as the exponent of the latest phase of this school, when it was about to coalesce with the Mahāyānists. However, enough is known to allow a definite conclusion about their supposed "denial" of Nirvāṇa and the meaning of their answer to the Vaibhāṣikas.

M. de la Vallee Poussin thinks that his hypothesis about a pre-canonic Buddhism, consisting of a simple faith in immortality and yoga practices, as well as his interpretation of the passages where Buddha is reported to have answered some metaphysical questions by silence—that both these hypotheses are fully borne out by the position which the later schools take regarding Nirvāṇa (p. 132). When it is called a "reality" he declares it to be a confirmation of the existence (some 500 years ago) of that simple faith in immortality which, by a similar method, he has discovered in early Buddhism. We find in his

this school, as well as his pupil and continuator Dignāga, are already Mahāyānists and have partly adopted Vijñānavāda views. They call themselves Vijñānvādins although in the cardinal point of absolute reality they partly adhere to the Sautrāntika view (cf. Nyāyabinduṭīkāṭipp. ed. B. B. p. 19).

book (pp. 136-148) many interesting details about the battle that raged between the two schools in the V century A.D., but unfortunately the meaning of the controversy has entirely escaped his attention, since it is *exactly the reverse* of what he assumes it to be. The Vaibhāṣikas did not maintain that Nirvāṇa was a kind of paradise, but that the annihilation of all life (*nirodha*), the essence of Nirvāṇa was a reality (*nirodha-satya*, *vastu*), i.e. a materialistic lifeless reality. The Sautrāntikas, on the other hand, admit the existence of Buddha's Cosmical Body (*dharmakāyo*), i.e. they adhere to the Mahāyāna conception which consists in identifying Nirvāṇa with the living world itself. Therefore, just like the Mahāyānists, they deny the reality of Nirvāṇa *as a separate element* which transcends the living world. It is a denial of the reality of that materialistic kind of annihilation which was favoured by the Vaibhāṣikas.

VII. THE DOUBLE CHARACTER OF THE ABSOLUTE

With regard to Nirvāṇa the Absolute, Indian philosophy, just as, in a broader sense, the philosophy of mankind, is divided between two diametrically opposed solutions. The absolute end is either eternal death, or it is eternal life.[1] The first is materialism, the second some kind of idealism. Both theories are represented in India, in Buddhism as well as in Brāhmanism. The theory of eternal death is represented, on the Buddhism side, by early Buddhism and the Vaibhāṣikas, on the Brahmanical side, as will be seen later on, by the early Nyāya-Vaiśeṣika. The theory of eternal life is represented in the Buddhist side by the Mahāyāna and its precursors, on the Brahmanical side by the Vedānta, Sāṅkhya, Yoga and the later Naiyāyikas. Nirvāṇa is a reality (*dharma*, *vastu*) in the sense of a materialistic, lifeless (*yasmin sati cetaso vimokṣaḥ*, *acetanaḥ*)[2] reality in the majority

1. I find in modern popular works pertaining to biology the conception of a lifeless Nirvāṇa and the term itself applied to describe that condition of the universe which will obtain when all energies will be exhausted (entropy). There is assumed a biological "Lusttrieb" and a "Todestrieb", the first would correspond *to heyopādeya-hānopādāna*, the second to *sarvaṁ heyam* or *sarvaṁ duḥkham*, cp. Sigm. Freud, Jenseits des Lustprincips (Vienna 1925), pp. 52, 80.

2. Cp. Madhy. vi, p. 525.9. cp. transl. in the Appendix.

of the schools of early Buddhism and in the Vaibhāṣika school. They are also atheists and treat their Buddha as essentially human.[1] Such reality is denied by all those schools which adhere to the conception of a divine Buddha, i.e. by the Mahāyānists and their precursors in the Hīnayāna. The conception of Buddha's Cosmical Body (*dharma-kāya*) is shared by all the schools of Mahāyāna and by the intermediate school of the Sautrāntikas. According to the modern Mongol's way of expressing it, in Hīnayāna the supreme Buddha (*burhan-bagshi*) has no body, in the Mahāyāna and with the Sautrāntikas he has a Body, and a better one (than before becoming Buddha), a glorious, all-embracing Body.

As regards the reality or ideality of Nirvāṇa the relative position of the contending schools may be roughly represented in the following schematic way :—

Vaibhāṣika and early schools—both saṁsāra and nirvāṇa real.

Mādhyamika—both saṁsāra and nirvāṇa unreal (sc. separately unreal).

Sautrāntika—saṁsāra real, nirvāṇa unreal (sc. separately unreal.) Yogācāra or Vijñānavāda—saṁsāra unreal, nīrvāṇa real). The meaning of this scheme will emerge from the arguments advanced by each of the schools.

VIII. THE VAIBHĀṢIKAS

As mentioned above, they are the continuators of the early school of the Sarvāstivādins and may be here treated as the representatives of early Buddhism in general. Their tenets which concern us at this place are the following ones. Existence is of a double kind, either transient and phenomenal, or eternal and absolute. Both parts are then analysed into their elements, classified as elements of matter, mind and forces for the phenomenal part, and as space and Nirvāṇa for the eternal one. The elements of phenomenal life are divided into past, present and future, and are all conceived as realities; the past and the future

---

1. This, of course, does not mean that exceptional, supernatural powers were not ascribed to him, but he belonged to the *manuṣyaloka*.

ones are as real as the present ones. This leads to the construction of two sets of elements, the one representing their everlasting nature (*dharma-svabhāva*), the other their momentary manifestation in actual life (*dharma lakṣaṇa*).[1] It is clear that this theory brings the Sarvāstivādin very near to the Sāṅkhya system which assumes an eternal matter and its momentary manifestations.[2] Therefore, students are specially warned not to confound both doctrines, and not to overlook their difference.[3] When all manifestations are stopped, all forces extinct, only lifeless residue remains. It is impersonal, eternal death, and it is a separate element, a reality, the reality of the elements in their lifeless condition. This reality is very similar to the reality of the Sāṅkhya's undifferentiated matter (*prakṛti*), it is eternal, absolute death.[4] The Sāṅkhyas were dualists, and admitted besides eternal matter eternal souls, but the latter, as is well-known, the Buddhists very energetically denied. Candrakīrti refers to the Vaibhāṣika view in the following way: "If Nirvāṇa is a reality *per se* (*bhāva*), it cannot be a simple extinction. Of course, it has been declared that consciousness is extinct (*vimokṣa*) in nirvāṇa, just as a light becomes extinct (when fuel is exhausted,) but for us extinct life is not an entity (*bhāva*)." To this (the Vaibhāṣikas) answer "You must not understand nirvāṇa to be the extinction of passion (and of life), but you must say that the entity (*dharma*) called nirvāṇa is the thing *in which* passion and life are extinct. The extinction of light is a mere example, and it must be interpreted as pointing to that (inanimate) thing which remains when consciousness is extinct".[5]

---

1. This theory of the double set of elements is very clearly analysed by O. Rosenberg in his Problems, cf. IX and XVIII. Had M. de la V. P. devoted to this book all the attention it deserves he never would have maintained that the Nirvāṇa of the Vaibhāṣikas is a paradise. Judging by his sweeping and unfair remark on p. XXI he has entirely mis-understood this remarkable book.

2. Cf. Ab. Kośa, V 25, and my Central Conception p. 89.

3. When pressed to give details about this lifeless condition of *dharma-svabhāva* the Vaibhāṣikas confess their ignorance, ibid, p. 75 and 90.

4. Or something quite undefinable, *niḥsattāsattaṁ niḥsadasad nirasad avyaktam aliṅgam pradhānam*, Y. S. Vyāsa II 19.

5. *Yasmin sati cetaso vimokṣo* (=*nirodho*) *bhavati*, ibid. 525. 9., cp. translation in the Append.

We need not insist that the school was atheistic and genuinely denied the reality of a substantial soul, whereas the Mahāsāṁghikas, Vātsīputrīyas, Sautrāntikas and Mahāyānists denied it one way and admitted it in another. The state of Nirvāṇa, as imagined by the Vaibhāṣikas, affords some points of similarity with that state of the universe which modern science imagines will exist when all energies will be worked out, they will exist, since energy itself (sc. *dharma-svabhāva*) is eternal, but they will not work. A condition in which all energies are extinct cannot be spiritual.[1]

Of course simple materialism goes under the name of *ucchedavāda*, against which Buddha is reported to have made an emphatic protest. But simple materialism in India, as elsewhere, is nirvāṇa at death (*dehochedo mokṣaḥ*)[2] without retribution for one's deeds in future life. The complicated system of worlds imagined by Buddha, through which the elements composing individual existences are gradually, one after the other, reduced to a state of quiescence and extinction, until in final nirvāṇa all are extinct—is nothing but the realisation of the moral law. The worlds are "produced" by *karma*, which corresponds to a conception of evolution going on under the influence of an accumulation of moral merit.[3] Simple materialism leaves no room for the working of this law. But neither does, according to Buddha, an eternal spiritual principle leave room for it. The moral law conduces through a very long process of evolution the living world into a state of final quiescence where there is no life, but something lifeless, inanimate.[4] In this sense, the Vaibhāṣika outlook resembles the materialism of modern science.[5]

---

1. European mystics, of course, put all the variety of the Indian speculations about Nirvāṇa into the same bag and declare that negative for our reason, it is emotionally very positive indeed, "dem Gefühl nach ein Positivum stärkster Form", cf. Heiler, op. cit. p. 41, following R. Otto, Das Heilige.

2. Sarvadarś., p. 3 (B. Ind.).

3. Cp. O. Rosenberg, Problems XVI.

4. All the references adduced by M. de la V. P. from Saṅghabhadra and Ab. Kośa. II, 55 only assert that nirvāṇa, according to the Vaibhāṣikas, was a *vastu*, but not that it was living or spiritual.

5. Prof. M. Anesaki, Nichiren (Cambridge, 1916) p. 137 ff. evidently alludes to the Vaibhāṣikas when asserting that Buddhism includes a mate-

IX. THE SAUTRĀNTIKAS

This school, as mentioned above, had quite different tendencies. They denied that the past and future elements really existed in the same sense as the present ones did. They took much more natural view. The past is what did exist, and the future is what will exist after not having existed. They consequently rejected the double set of elements, the eternal essence and the manifestations, and admitted the reality of these manifestations alone. Nirvāṇa was the absolute end of the manifestations, the end of passion and life (*kleśa-janmanoḥ kṣayaḥ*), without any counterpart. It decidedly insisted upon the fact that nirvāṇa means only the end of the process of life, without any lifeless substance (*dharma*) as the residue or the substratum *in which* life has been extinguished. Nirvāṇa thus loses its materialistic character. The denial of the Sautrāntikas is no denial of Nirvāṇa in general, not a denial of an idealistic absolute. There is no Buddhism possible without Nirvāṇa, since without Nirvāṇa means without a Buddha. But the Sautrāntikas denied the materialistic Nirvāṇa, just as all the Mahāyānists did.

The original works of the Sautrāntika school, as mentioned above, are not yet accessible. The school probably contained a great variety of philosophical constructions. The later Sautrāntikas coalesced with the Mahāyānists and formed the hybrid schools of the Sautrāntika-Yogācāra and Mādhyamika-Sautrāntikas.[1] This fact alone proves that on the vital questions of Nirvāṇa and Buddha they closely adhered to later Buddhism and can be characterised as a transitional school. From Tibetan sources[2] we know that they admitted the doctrine of

rialistic school, or a school which its opponents characterised as materialistic. As a curiosity it may be added that when the educational authorities of the newly founded republic of Buriats in Transbaikalia started an anti-religious propaganda, they first of all assailed the doctrine of transmigration in its popular form and insisted on the fact that modern science favours a materialistic view of the universe. The Buddhist monks, who are Mahāyānists, retorted in a pamphlet in which they developed the view that materialism is not unknown to them, since the Vaibhāṣikas maintained that after Nirvāṇa, every life ceases forever.

1. Wassilief, Buddhism, pp. 321 ff.
2. Ibid. p. 286.

dharmakāya, i.e., of a divine Buddha, and this solves the question, because this dogma is the common characteristic of all the schools of the Mahāyāna. They differed from the latter in that they admitted the reality of the phenomenal world which with them included only sense-data, consciousness and volition. The momentary flashes to which these entities were reduced were nevertheless conceived as real, not illusions, and their total extinction in Nirvāṇa was maintained. They neither admitted the monistic spiritual principle (*ālaya-vijñāna*) of the idealistic Mahāyānists, nor the principle of relativity (*śūnyavāda*) of the Mādhyamikas. What their line of argument was we know from the work of Vasumitra upon the early schools.[1] The author was himself a Sautrāntika and closes his work with an enumeration of their principal tenets, such tenets as were shared by all the adherents of the school. We find here (under No. 3) their tenet that there are two kinds of elements (*skandhas*). Besides those which are subject to total extinction at the time of Nirvāṇa, there is a subtle consciousness which survives after Nirvāṇa and of which the former are but a manifestation.[2] We have here the germ of the *ālaya-vijñāna* of the Yogācāras. If later on the Sautrāntikas objected to this tenet, they probably did it only because, in the Yogācāra system, it involved the illusory character of the external world, whereas the Sautrāntikas stuck to its reality. Most probably they were in this point only the continuators of the Mahāsāṁghikas, i.e. they adhered to that tendency which at an early date manifested itself among the schools of the Hīnayāna and represented a protest against the treatment of Buddha as essentially human and against the theory of his total disappearance in a materialistic Nirvāṇa. Since every school of the Mahāyāna interpreted *dharmakāya* according to their own ideas in philosophy, the Sautrāntikas likewise interpreted it as a personification of their subtle consciousness.[3]

---

1. Samaya-bheda-uparacana-cakra, transl. for the first time by Wassilief in his Buddhism. A new English translation with copious and very instructive notes by J. Masuda appeared in Asia Major, II. 1, pp. 1-78.

2. This is also known from Tibetan sources, cf. Wassilief op. cit., p. 273.

3. It thus appears that Prof. H. Kern, Manual, p. 123, was right in maintaining that "among old sects the Mahāsāṁghikas entertained views

X. THE YOGĀCĀRAS

This was an idealisic school founded by Āryasaṅga in the IV-V Century A.D.

Idealistic views (*vijñāna-vāda*) have appeared in the history of Buddhistic philosophy several times and at different places. We have, first of all, canonical works like the *Laṅkāvatārasūtra* and others, which are written in imitation of the Upaniṣads, in a style intentionally averse to precision.[1] And then we have the three systems of Aśvaghoṣa, Āryasaṅga and Dignāga. As Mahāyānists, they are all monists and believers in the Cosmical Body of the Buddha. But in the process of realisation of this unique substance they all admit the existence of one initial or

---

agreeing with the Mahāyāna". It is also clear that the Vātsīputrīyas (Vajjiputtakas) established their *pudgalavāda* with no other aim than that of supporting the doctrine of a supernatural, surviving Buddha from the philosophical side. Indirectly this proves how philosophic the genuine primitive Buddha must have been. The very character of the argument of the Vātsīputrīyas in favour of the *pudgala* is suggestive. It was neither a *dharma*—this they could not maintain, so fresh was its categorical denial by the Master in memory—but neither was it something different from a *dharma*. It was already inexpressible at that time. Had not the denial of the *ātmā* been so categorical, the Vātsīputrīyas would have certainly invented another, and not so twisted an argument in support of their belief in a supernatural Buddha. Cf. Ab. Kośa, IX and my Soul Theory. p. 830.

1. In the Laṅkāvatāra, pp. 182-86 (ed. Tokyo 1924) more than 20 different opinions about Nirvāṇa are mentioned. The first evidently alludes to the opinion of the Hīnayānists and the last looks like the opinions of the Yogācāras. All are rejected on the score that Nirvāṇa is undefinable. It is the Mādhyamika view. But the majority of the solutions there mentioned evidently never existed, and those that existed are so formulated that it is difficult to recognise them. It is a fanciful literary composition, Āryadeva's comment transl. by G. Tucci, T'oung Pao XXV, p. 16 ff., looks like forgery by some incompetent pandit. The Tibetan Bstan-ḥgyur, as already noticed by Wassilief, is also full of forged tracts ascribed to Aśvaghoṣa, Nāgārjuna and Āryadeva. The last solution, p. 184, 1. 15 ff., which in the sūtra is evidently mentioned *pour la bonne bouche* is not to be discovered at all in the enumeration of the comment. It has not escaped the perspicacity of E. Burnouf, Introduction. (2) p. 462, that this last solution, although seemingly rejected, was the one favoured by the author. I find no mention of E. Burnouf's translation and comment in the article of G. Tucci.

store-consciousness *ālaya-vijñāna* in addition to that indefinite[1] consciousness (*citta = manas = vijñāna*) which was admitted in the Hīnayāna, and they all deny the reality of the external world. They thus reduce all the elements (*dharma*) of Hīnayāna to modes of one single conscious principle. Aśvaghoṣa's system[2] is in all essential points the same as the Mādhyamika's, but it accepts the theory of an "All-conserving mind" (*ālaya-vijñāna*), as a stage in the evolution of "Suchness (*tathatā*) in which consciousness is awakened".[3]

The Yogācāra school is divided into the ancient one, or the followers of Āryasaṅga, and the new one, or the followers of Dignāga. The first[4] established their idealistic views on a new interpretation of the old Abhidharma. Āryasaṅga himself composed a Mahāyānistic Abhidharma,[5] where the number of elements (*dharma*) is increased from 75 to 100. The *ālaya-vijñāna* is here a new element, a store-house, a real granary, where the seeds (*bīja*) of all future ideas and the traces of all past deeds are stored up. However, it is not the Absolute. It belongs to the phenomenal part of existence because all the results (*vipāka*)[6] of *karma* are there stored up. This store-consciousness in this system occupies a position analogous to the primitive matter (*pradhāna*)[7] of the Sāṃkhya school. All individual objects and ideas are regarded as its modifications (*pariṇāma*) by the Sāṃkhya. The Yogācāras

1. That *vijñāna-skandha* is nothing else than *nirvikalpakaṁ jñānam* and *saṁjñā skandha* nothing else than *savikalpakaṁ jñānam* as stated in my Central Conception, pp. 18-19, is now corroborated by Udayana, Pariśuddhi, p. 213-14 (B.I.)

2. Whether this Aśvaghoṣa, a Mahāyānist, is the same as the author of Buddhacarita has been doubted. About this system cp. Suzuki, Discourse on the Awakening of the Faith (Chicago, 1900) and Yamakami Sogen, Systems of Buddhist Thought, p. 252 ff. (Calcutta, 1912).

3. Suzuki, Op., cit. p. 151.

4. A clear exposition of Āryasaṅga's system is to be found in the Triṁśikā of Vasubandhu with a comment by Sthiramati, ed. by Sylvain Lévi (Paris 1925). Cp. Yamakami Sogen, op. cit. 210 ff. Cp. A.B. Keith, Buddhist Phil., p. 242 ff. where all the literature is indicated. A still earlier (third) school of that name is mentioned, cf. Wossilief, Dharmatā, p. 76.

5. Abhidharma-samuccaya, Bṣtan-hgyur, Mdo, vol. 32.

6. Cp. Triṁśikā, p. 18.21.

7. Ibid. p. 36.9.

likewise regard all separate ideas as modifications of their store-consciousness. This represents a disguised return from the theory of a stream of thought to the doctrine of a substantial soul[1]. In the stream of thought, every preceding moment of the consciousness is the cause of the next following one. This relation called *samanantara-pratydya* is now replaced by the relation of the store-consciousness (*ālaya*) to its modifications (*pariṇāma*).[2]

But in the Sāṁkhya system both the Primitive Matter and its modifications were realities. The Yogācāras regarded both as unreal. From their predecessors, the Mādhyamikas, they adopted the theory of the relativity and consequent unreality (*śūnyatā-niḥsvabhāvatā*) of all individual existence,[3] of all plurality, with the difference that they introduced different degrees of this unreality. First of all, individual ideas were unreal because they were logical constructions (*parikalpita*) without any adequate reality corresponding to them in the external world. This was called their essential unreality (*lakṣaṇa-niḥsvabhāvatā*). They were nevertheless contingently real (*paratantra*)[4] in the sense that they obeyed to causal laws (*pratītya-samutpāda*).[5] This was called their causal unreality or relativity (*utpattiniḥsvabhāvatā*). They were at least unreal individually as far as they were merged in the unique reality (*pariniṣpanna*) of the Absolute (*tathatā-dharmatā*). This was called their absolute unreality (*paramārtha-niḥsvabhāvatā*)[6] as individual entities. It was the same as their reality in the Absolute, their reality, so to say, *sub specie aeternitatis*. The Absolute thus became immanent in the phenomenal world, it was neither different, nor nondifferent (*nānya nānanya*).[7] As an assemblage of individual ideas

1. Cp. my Central Conception, 35.

2. Triṁśikā, p. 34.5 ff. This is Sthiramati's view about *ālaya*. Other views were entertained by Nanda, Dignāga and Dharmapāla. Cp. Schiefner, Tāranātha, p. 301.

3. Ibid. p. 41-2.

4. Triṁśikā p. 41.14.

5. Ibid. p. 41-18 cp. p. 16.16. vijñānam pratitya-samutpannatvād dravyato'sti.

6. Ibid. p. 41. 23-4.

7. Ibid. p. 40.6.

it was different, but viewed as an organic whole it became identical. It was a spiritual Absolute (*citta-dharmatā*),[1] pure consciousness, undifferentiated into subject and object (*grāhya-grāhakarahita*).[2] It is the essence of Reality (*dharma dhātu*) and it is, therefore, identified with the Cosmical Body (*dharma-kāya*) of the Buddha.[3] All the numerous synonyms which are used to characterise this conception in other schools can be applied to it.[4] The yogin in his mystic intuition is supposed to possess a direct cognition of this undifferentiated pure consciousness (*advayalakṣaṇaṁ vijñapti-mātram*).[5]

In the closing chapter of his Abhidharmakośa, Vasubandhu mentions the Mahāyānist view that all separate elements, the *dharmas* of the Hīnayāna, have no ultimate reality.[6] At that time he rejects this view, but later on, near to the close of his long life, he changes his standpoint, and accepts the idealistic theory of his elder brother Asaṅga. Asaṅga himself seems also to have, at a certain period of his life, fluctuated between the two main lines in which Mahāyāna was split.[7] But at the end of their career both brothers definitely settled in the conviction that the Universe was a logical construction,[8] that all its separate elements were relative, not real, in themselves, but that they possessed another reality, the *parinispanna*, a reality in the Absolute; they were real when regarded *sub specte aeternitatis*. The Theory of Salvation, of this transition from saṁsāra into nirvāṇa, out of the phenomenal world into the Absolute—this greatest puzzle of the Indian mind—underwent a complete change as a consequence of the change in the ontological view. In Hīnayāna where, as we have seen, both *saṁsāra* and *nirvāṇa*

1. Triṁśikā, p. 42. 16.
2. Ibid. p. 40. 4.
3. Ibid. p. 43. 25.
4. Ibid. p. 41. 26.
5. Ibid. p. 42. 20.
6. Cp. the translation of M. de la V. P., IX p. 273 and my Soul Theory. p. 858.
7. According to the Tibetans, among the 5 works of Maitreya-Asaṅga some are written from the Yogācāra standpoint, some from Mādhyamika-svātantrika and one from the Mādhyamika-prāsaṅgika view.
8. Triṁśikā, XVII, *sarvam vijñaptimātrakam*, and Sthiramati remarks p. 35, that *sarvam* includes both the phenomenal world and the Absolute, *sarvam iti traidhātukam asaṁskṛtaṁ ca*.

were considered as realities, the mystic power of yoga was called upon to achieve the transition out of the one into the other. Actual experience of trance in meditation suggested to the Buddhist philosophers that *yoga* was capable of arresting some functions of the senses and of the intellect. And since the world was analysed in bits of senses and sense data, it seemed only logical to admit that yoga could achieve the task of arresting the life of the universe forever.

The great change produced by the Mahāyāna consisted in the view that the Absolute was immanent in the World. There was consequently no need of converting the elements of the phenomenal world into eternal elements, the *saṁskṛta-dharmas* into *asaṁskṛta-dharmas*, the *saṁsāra* into *nirvāṇa*. The change consisted in the change of aspect. The mystic power of *yoga* was now invoked not in order to produce a real change in the constitution of the Universe but in order to replace the wrong ideas of unsophisticated humanity by an intuition of what was absolutely real. To the *yogī*, the world appeared in a quite different aspect, he viewed every separate object as unreal separately, but real *sub specie aeternitatis* For him the elements (*dharmas*) of the Universe needed no conversion into eternal ones, they were themselves eternally "quiescent".

The Hīnayānistic conception of separate elements (*dharmas*) which were active in phenomenal life and quiescent (*śānta*) or extinct (*niruddha*), in Nirvāṇa was, according to the Yogācāras, contrary to reason. If they were real they could not disappear totally. They were, accordingly, declared to have been always quiescent, quiescent or extinct from the outset (*ādi-śānta*).[1] To regard them as active, in the transcendental sense, is an illusion. In that sense, it can be asserted, that *nirvāṇa* is real and *saṁsāra* unreal.

1. Cf. Mahāyānasūtrālaṁkāra, ed. Sylvain Lévi (Paris 1907), XI 51 trsl. ibid. (Paris 1911) "ils (les *dharma*) sont originellement en Paix et en etat de Pari-Nirvāṇa". Cf. St. Schayer. Die Erlosungslehren der Yogācāras nach dem Sūtrālaṁkāra des Asaṅga, Z. fur Indologie, II, 1. p. 99 ff. The idea that all elements are originally quiescent (śānta=nirvṛta) sc. eternally extinct, an idea leading to the theory of everything being real *sub specie aeternitatis* is likewise expressed by Nāgārjuna, Madhy. s., VII, 16—*Pratītya yad yad bhavati tat tac chāntaṁ svabhāvataḥ*.

In the system of Dignāga, the old Abhidharma is forsaken altogether and replaced by logic and epistemology. Dignāga started with the reform of the Brahmanical logic (nyāya) and adapted it to Buddhist ideas. His analysis of cognition resulted in the conception of an extreme concrete and individual (*svalakṣaṇa*), the root, or, so to say, the differential of cognition, a point-instant (*kṣaṇa*) in which existence and cognition, object and subject, coalesce.[1] The conception of this idealistic school regarding Nirvāṇa may be gathered from the closing words of Dharmakīrti in his "Examination of Solipsism".[2] The question is asked how is the omniscience of Buddhas to be understood, of the Buddhas which are the personification of pure consciousness undifferentiated into subject and object, and it is answered that the "penetration of the Buddhas into every existing object is something inconceivable, it is in every respect beyond what we may express in speech or cognise in concepts."

XI. THE MĀDHYAMIKAS

This system of philosophy and dialectics is the foundation of the Mahāyāna religion. Although other systems—the realism of the Sarvāstivādins and the idealism of the Yogācāras—are also studied in the monastic schools of the countries where this religion flourishes, nevertheless the Mādhyamika system is generally regarded as the true background of the religious feelings of its votaries. For it must be allowed that the Mahāyāna is a truly new religion, so radically different from Early Buddhism that it exhibits as many points of contact with later Brahmanical religions as with its own predecessor. Prof. O. Rosenberg calls it a separate "church" and compares its position with the Roman Catholicism *versus* Protestantism.[3] The difference is even more radical, since the new religion was obliged to produce a new canon of Scriptures.

---

1. A very interesting and rather subtle discussion between Candrakīrti and Dignāga about the point-instant in which existence and cognition are supposed to coalesce is found in M. vr. p. 59. ff., transl. in the Appendix. Cp. my Buddhist Logic and Epistemology, ch. VII.
2. Saṁtānāntarasiddhi, edited by me in the B.B. and translated into Russian in the series.
3. O. Rosenberg, Probleme der B. Philosophic, XIX.

It never has been fully realised what a radical revolution had transformed the Buddhist church when the new spirit which however was for a long time lurking in it arrived at full conclusion in the first centuries A.C. When we see an atheistic, soul-denying philosophic teaching of a path to personal Final Deliverance, consisting in an absolute extinction of life, and a simple worship of the memory of its human founder,—when we see it superseded by a magnificent High Church with a Supreme God, surrounded by a numerous pantheon and a host of Saints, a religion highly devotional, highly ceremonious and clerical, with an ideal of Universal Salvation of all living creatures, a Salvation by the divine grace of Buddhas and the Bodhisattvas, a Salvation not in annihilation, but in eternal life,—we are fully justified in maintaining that the history of religions has scarcely witnessed such a break between new and old[1] within the pale of what nevertheless continues to claim common descent from the same religious founder.[2] Yet the philosophical system which is the foundation of this new religion is usually represented as the extreme expression and the logical consequence of that pessimism and skepticism by which

1. Very characteristic is also the fact that Buddhist art of the ancient period represented Buddha by an empty place or a symbol which later on is replaced by a divine figure of the Apollo type. Notwithstanding Prof. Grunwedel's contrary view (Buddhistiche Kunst, 1st ed. p. 68) the only explanation seems to be that the total disappearance of Buddha in Nirvāṇa was thus given pictorial expression.

2. The two churches co-existed peacefully in the same monasteries, because the Buddhists very wisely always made allowance for human nature which sometimes feels inclination towards a simple rationalistic Low Church and sometimes is attracted towards a devotional and magnificent High Church. They divided humanity in families (gotra) of which some by nature belonged to the low-church family (Hīnayāna= hīnādhimukti) and others to the high church family. We must imagine the process by which some originally Hīnayānistic monasteries gradually turned Mahāyānistic as a process of aggrandisement. The educational Buddhist monasteries, which are comparable to mediaeval universities, were aggrandised by the addition of a new college which received its own temple and body of monks studying a new special literature and conducting a special worship. In present days we can witness in Transbaikalia the addition of monks, a special literature and a special worship. The different types of Buddhist monasteries are described by B. Baradiin in a very instructive work now published at Verchne-Oudingsk. It was accessible to me in MSS during my visit to that town in 1925.

Early Buddhism is supposed to have been inspired. It is characterised as "complete and pure nihilism", as the "legitimate logical outcome of the principles underlying ancient Buddhism".[1] It is accused of teaching that "all our ideas are based upon a non-entity or upon the void".[2] It is represented as a "negativism which radically empties existence up to the last consequences of negation",[3] a doctrine whose conception of reality was one of "absolute nothingness",[4] The Madhyamikas are called the most radical Nihilists that ever existed.[5] When compared with Vedānta, it has been asserted that negation has a positive counterpart in that system, whereas there is none in the Mādhyamika. Negation in the latter is represented as its "exclusive ultimate end (Selbstzweck).[6]

The opponents of Mahāyāna in India describe it much in the same manner. Thus Kumārila accuses the Mādhyamikas not only of denying the existence of external objects, but of deny-

---

1. H. Kern, Manual, p. 126; a Barth Quarante ans, I p. 108; M. de la Vallee Poussin, Bouddhisme, p. 186.

2. H. Jacobi, A. O. J. m XXXI p. 1.

3. M. Walleser, Die B. Phil II. p. III Der altere Vedānta, p 44.

4. A.B. Keith, op. cit., pp. 237, 239, 247, 261 etc. Prof. Keith's exposition contains (p. 259) what, in my opinion, is the right view, viz, that Nāgārjuna's real object was to show that the intellect "condemns itself as inadequate just as it finds hopeless antinomies in the world of experience." As prof. Keith very well knows, Nāgārjuna is not the only philosopher who adhered to such a line of arguing, very celebrated men have done that. Why then should Nāgārjuna's main conceptions be "difficult and obscure" (ibid).? He also hits the right mark when he points to a primitive, non-differentiated reality, identified with Buddha's Cosmical Body (dharmakāya), as the central conception of Mahāyāna. He even finds (ibid. p. 225) much more reality and activity in this conception than in the absolute of the Vedānta with which it is so strikingly similar. How are these views to harmonize with the conflicting opinions of the same author e.g. p. 261 where it is asserted that for Nāgārjuna the world was "absolute nothingness", that it was "utterly unreal" I am at a loss to explain. Or does prof. Keith suppose that Nāgārjuna did not admit the doctrine of Dharmakāya, or that, having admitted it, he did not fully realise its consequences, or that "the positive side of the Mahāyāna" (p. 257) is a later development out of its negative side?

5. I. Wach, Mahāyāna, p. 58.

6. M. Walleser, Der altere Vedānta, p. 42 "Sekbstaweck is explicitly denied by Nāgārjuna, XXIV, 7 and many other places.

ing the reality of our ideas as well.[1] Vācaspatimiśra is full of respect towards Buddhist logicians, but for the Mādhyamikas he has only remarks of extreme contempt; he calls them fools,[2] and accuses them of reducing cognition to nothing.[3] Śaṅkara accuses them of disregarding all logic and refuses to enter in a controversy with them. The position of Śaṅkara is interesting because, at heart, he is in full agreement with the Mādhyamikas, at least in the main lines since both maintain the reality of the One-without a-second, and the mirage of the manifold. But Śaṅkara, as an ardent hater of Buddhism, would never confess that. He, therefore, treats the Mādhyamika, with great contempt, but not on the score of a "denial of the existence of our ideas", or of maintaining "absolute nothingness", but on the charge that the Mādhyamika denies the possibility of cognising the absolute by logical methods (pramāṇa). Vācaspatimiśra in the Bhāmatī rightly interprets this point as referring to the opinion of the Mādhyamikas that the logic is incapable of solving the question about what existence or non-existence really is. This opinion Śaṅkara himself, as is well-known, shares. He does not accept the authority of logic as a means of cognising the Absolute, but he deems it a privilege of the Vedānta to fare without logic, since he has Revelation to fall back upon. From all his opponents he requires strict logical methods.[4] It must be added that the Japanese scholars, Suzuki,

---

1. Ślokavārttika, Nirālambanavāda, 14. In fact, the Mādhyamikas denied the validity of the pramāṇas and maintained that external and internal were correlative terms which are meaningless beyond this correlation, see below. p. 42.

2. devānām-priya, cf. Tātp-ṭīkā, p. 341.23. 469.9.

3. Ibid. ad N. S. IV. 1. 28 sarva-śūnyatve khyātur abhāvāt khyāter abhāvaḥ. Vācaspati knows that they deny abhāva just as much, and in the same sense, as they deny bhāva, cf. Bhāmatī ad. V. S. II 2. 32. na ca nistattvataiva tatvaṁ bhāvānām, tathā sati hi tattvābhāvaḥ syāt, so'pi ca vicāram nāsahata ity uktam bhavadbhiḥ. He also knows that to transform every thing into abhāva is tantamount to endowing non-reality with reality, to have a vigrahavān abhāvaḥ, ibid. 389. 22. But this does not prevent him from repeating popular accusations.

4. Cf. Deussen, System des Vedānta p. 99; Śaṅkara ad. V. S. II. 2. 38. The Mādhyamika denies the validity of logic. i.e. of discursive conceptual thought, to establish the ultimate truth. On the charge that in doing so he himself resorts to some logic, he replies that the logic of common life is

Anesaki, Yamakami Sogan and others who have a direct knowledge of what Mahāyāna is have never committed the mistake of regarding its philosophy as nihilism or pure negativism.

We will now shortly refer to the main lines of the philosophy of the Hīnayāna in order better to show the radical change produced by the spirit of Mahāyāna and thus to elicit the aim of its philosophy.

XII. THE DOCTRINE OF CAUSALITY IN THE HĪNAYĀNA

In a previous work[1] we have characterised Early Buddhism (Hīnayāna) as a system of metaphysics which contained an analysis of existence into its component parts, and established a certain number of ultimate data (dharma). Every combination of these data was then declared to represent a nominal, not an ultimate reality. A substantial Soul was thus transformed into a stream of continuously flowing discrete moments of sensation or pure consciousness (vijñāna), accompanied by moments of feeling, of ideation, volition (vedanā-saṁjñā-saṁskāra) etc. Matter (rūpa) was conceived on the same

sufficient for showing that all systems contradict one another and that our fundamental conceptions do not resist scrutiny, cf. Vācaspati, Tātparya-ṭīkā, p. 249—avicārita-siddhaiḥ pramāṇair itareṣām prāmāṇyam pratiṣidhyate. This is exactly the standpoint which is developed with such infinite subtlety and ingenuity by Śrīharṣa in his Khaṇḍana-khaṇḍa-khādya where he openly confesses that there is but little difference between Buddhism and Vedānta, a circumstance which Śaṅkara carefully conceals. But in later works, e.g., Vedānta-paribhāṣā, or Nyāyamakaranda, different pramāṇas are established as proofs for the existence of brahman. When commenting upon the V. S. II. 2. 28. Śaṅkara, in combating Buddhist idealism resorts to arguments of which he himself does not believe a word, since they are arguments which the most genuine realist would use. He thus argues not *svamatena*, but *paramatam āśritya*, a method very much in vogue among Indian pandits. Deussen's interpretation of this point, op. cit. p. 260, as intended to vindicate vyavahāra satya is a misunderstanding, since the Buddhist never denied the vyavahāra or saṁvṛtti. Against M. Sallewer's (Der altere Vedānta, p. 43) opinion that the objectivity of our ideas themselves is meant, it must be pointed out that the Buddhists did not deny the jñānākāra, and Śaṅkara clearly states that external objects, not ideas are meant—tasmād arthajñānayor bhedaḥ.

1. The Central Conception of Buddhism.

pattern, as a flow of momentary flashes without any continuant stuff, but characterised by impenetrability, and representing the senses (āyatana 1-5) and sense data (āyatana 7-11). The world was thus transformed into a cinema. The categories of substance, quality and motion—for momentary flashes could possess no motion—were denied but the reality of sense data and of the elements of mind, was admitted. All these elementary data were conceived as obeying causal laws. But the conception of causality was adapted to the character of these entities which could neither change nor move, but could only appear and disappear. Causation was called dependently-coordinated-origination (pratītya-samutpāda), or dependent existence. The meaning of it was that every momentary entity sprang into existence, or flashed up, in coordination with other moments. Its formula was "if there is this, there appears that."[1] Causality was thus assumed to exist between moments only, the appearance of every moment being coordinated with the appearance of a number of other moments. Strictly speaking it was no causality at all, no question of one thing *producing* the other. There could be neither *a causa efficiens*, since one momentary entity, disappearing as it did at once, could not influence any other entity. So the formula was supplemented by another one "not from itself (causa materialis), not from something foreign (causa efficiens), nor a combination of both does an entity spring up",[2] it is coordinated, it is not really produced".[3] Apart from these momentary entities[4] the system admitted eternal

1. The same formula in the Pali Canon (Majjh. II. 28. etc.) in the Ab. Kośa, III 18 and 28 and Madhy. vi., p.10. In the latter instance asmin sati idam bhavati, hrasve dīrgham yathā sati, the formula clearly refers to coordination, not to causation.

2. Samy. II 113 and Madhy. Kar. I. 1. XII. 1.

3. Madhy. vi. p. 7—tat tat prāpya yad utpannaṁ notpannaṁ tat svabhāvataḥ; ibid. p. 375-6—paramārthato' tyantānut-pādatvāt sarvadharmāṇāṁ.

4. If I am not very much mistaken, this view of causality viz. that there is, properly speaking, no real causality, that this notion should be cancelled altogether and replaced by a law of coordination between point-instants, is not quite a stranger to modern science and philosophy, cf. B. Russell, On the Notion of Cause, in Mysticism and Logic., p. 194. The Buddhist conception of causality would thus be something similar to the

unchanging elements, Space and Nirvāṇa, the latter representing some indefinite essence (*dharma-svabhāva*), of these forces which were active in phenomenal life, but are now extinct and converted into eternal death. Thus both the phenomenal world and this kind of an Absolute, both *saṁsāra* and *nirvāṇa*, were conceived as realities, somehow interconnected, linked together in a whole (sarvam), but in an ideal whole, having as a combination of elements, only nominal existence.[1]

XIII. THIS DOCTRINE MODIFIED IN MAHĀYĀNA

Now, the Mādhyamika system started with an entirely different conception of reality. Real was what possessed a reality of its own (sva-bhāva), what was not produced by causes (*akṛtaka = asaṁskṛta*), what was not dependent upon anything else (*paratra nirapekṣa*).[2] In Hīnayāna, the elements, although interdependent (*saṁskṛta = pratītyasamutpanna*), were real (*vastu*). In Mahāyāna all elements, *because interdependent*, were unreal (*śūnya = svabhāva-śūnya*).[3] In Hīnayāna, every whole (*rāśi = avayavin*) is regarded as a nominal existence (*prajñaptisat*) and only the parts or ultimate elements (*dharma*) are real (*vastu*). In Mahāyāna, all parts or elements are unreal (*śūnya*), and only the whole, i.e. the

---

conception of a function in mathematics, "funktionelle Abhangigkit", such a view of causality as was entertained in Europe by D'Alembert, Comte, Claude Bernard, Avenarius, E. Mach and others, cp. the references on Eister, Handworterbuch der Philosophie, p. 338. We hope to devote before long a special article to this question.

1. Cp. my Central Conceptions, p. 6 and below p. 54 n. 6.

2. Madhy. Kār. XV. In the sequel, the references with *Roman* figures will refer to chapter and kārikā of Nāgārjuna's Madhyamaka Śāstra, and the references in Arabic figures to Candrakīrti's comment B.B. IV.

3. It is clear that we have here that conception of a substance independently existing which is well known to the students of European philosophy. Cp. Spinoza's definition of substance as "quod in se est et per se concipitur". This conception resulted either in establishing the theory of a harmonia generaliter stablits in order to explain the interdependence of the monads, or to the view that there is only one unique substance. The latter view is taken in Mahāyāna, the former in Hīnayāna, where the harmony between monads is established by karma as a special force (saṁskāra).

whole of the wholes (*dharmatā = dharma-kāya*), is real. The definition of reality (tattva) in Mahāyāna is the following one—"uncognisable from without, quiescent, undifferentiated in words, unrealisable in concepts, non-plural—this is the essence of reality".[1] A dependent existence is no real existence, just as borrowed money is no real wealth.[2] The theory that all real existence can last only for a moment, since two moments implied already a synthesis, was abandoned, and the conception of a momentary entity (kṣaṇa), so characteristic for other schools of Buddhist thought was given up,[3] as unwarranted (asiddha), not capable of resisting critique.[4] In Hīnayāna, the individual (*pudgala*), the Self (*ātmā*) was resolved in its component elements (*skandha-āyatana-dhātavaḥ = anātma*), there were no real personalities (*pudgala-nairātmya*), but a congeries of flashing forces (*saṁskāra-samūha*). In Mahāyāna we have, on the contrary, a denial of real elements (*dharma-nairātmya*), and an assertion of the whole, in the sense of the Absolute Whole (*dharma-kāya*).[5] In Hīnayāna, in a word, we have a radical pluralism, converted in Mahāyāna in as radical a Monism.

XIV. THE DOCTRINE OF RELATIVITY

In Mahāyāna, we are thus faced by a new interpretation of the old Buddhist principle of the dependently-coordinated-

1. Ibid. XVIII. 9.
2. Ibid. p. 263. 3. Kālika-āyācitakam.
3. Ibid. p. 173-9, 545-13 147.4.
4. Ibid. p. 547.1.
5. Although the Hīnayānist presses to the utmost the reality of the elements (dharma) alone, nevertheless the importance of the whole is foreshadowed in the conception of *sarvam* (cp. below p. 54), as well as in the conception of a general Causality. Under the name of kāraṇa-hetu, a kind of causality is asserted through which every moment of reality is conditioned by nothing short of the state of the whole Universe. This is expressed in the following way, (Ab. Kośa II 50), svato'nye (sarve dharmāḥ) kāraṇa-hetuḥ, i.e. an element or a moment cannot be its own cause, but all the other elements, i.e. the whole Universe, are in some, direct or indirect, causal relation with it. Since the three times (adhvan), i.e. all the future and all the past moments are included in the conception "all the elements", sarve dharmāḥ, it is clear that although the world appeared in Hīnayāna as validly analyzable into bits, the idea of it as a logical continuum was foreshadowed. In Mahāyāna, it became definitely asserted.

existence of the elements (*dharmāṇām pratītya-sam-utpāda*). It is now being declared that whatsoever is dependent or relative cannot be considered as an ultimate reality, and this feature is then pressed to its last extreme. In Hīnayāna, existence was bifurcated in conditioned and unconditioned (*saṁskṛta* and *asaṁskṛta*), both being realities. Neither of them is now considered as ultimately real, and both are brought under the higher unity of Relativity. The central conception in Early Buddhism is the idea of a plurality of ultimate elements (*dharmas*). The central conception of Mahāyāna is their relativity (*śūnyatā*). The Buddhists themselves contended that the idea of ultimate elements (*skandha-āyatana-dhātavaḥ*), of their interdependence (*pratītya-samutpāda*) and of the "Four Truths of the Saint" are admitted in both Hīnayāna and Mahāyāna. But in the first they are referred to the reality of separate elements, and in the second they are interpreted as meaning their relativity, or non-reality[1].

Since we used the term "relative" to describe the fact that a thing can be identified only by mentioning its relations to something else, and becomes meaningless without these relations, implying at the same time that the thing in question is unreal, we safely, for want of a better solution, can translate the word *śūnya* by relative or contingent, and the term *śūnyatā* by relativity or contingency.[2] This is in any case better than to

---

1. The germ of the idea that the elements of existence, because interdependent, are not real can be found in some passages of the Pāli Canon. This Candrakīrti himself admits (Mādhy. avat. p. 22 15ffB. B IX). But it does not in the least interfere with the fact that Hīnayāṇa is a system of radical pluralism, all *dharmas*, even Nirvāṇa, are *vastu*, whereas Mahāyānism is a monistic system (*advaya-niṣprapañca*). It is quite impossible to maintain that Hīnayāna is an *advaita*-system. But if the Mādhyamika system is characterised as negativism, and everything negative is thrown into the same bag, then it is not difficult to discover in Majjh. N.1.1, a full blown *prajñā-pāramitā*, and to maintain that "es ist ein Irrtum anozunchmen, in alten Buddhismus seietwas anderes als Negativissmus gelehrt worden", as prof. B. Otto Franke has done, cp. *Ernst Kuhn Memorial Volume*, p. 332ff. (Munchen 1916). It is also difficult to say what the contention of M. de la V. P. that "there is a great deal of Mādhyamika philosophy in the Pāli Canon" (E R E VIII. p. 334) exactly means.

2. The notion of Relativity is thus taken in a generalised sense, just as Aristotle himself uses it in the *Metaphysica*, where he treats Ad aliquid,

translate it by 'void' which signification the term has in common life, but not as a technical term in philosophy. That the term *śūnya* is in Mahāyāna a synonym of dependent existence (*pratītya-samutpāda*) and means not something void, but something "devoid" of independent reality (*svabhāva-śūnya*), with the implication that nothing short of the whole possesses independent reality, and with the further implication that the whole forbids every formulation by concept or speech (*niṣprapañca*), since they can only bifurcate (*vikalpa*) reality and never directly seize it—this is attested by an over-whelming mass of evidence in all the Mahāyāna literature[1]. That this term never meant a mathematical void or simple non-existence is most emphatically insisted upon. Those who suppose that *śūnya* means void are declared to have misunderstood the term, they have not understood the purpose for which the term has been introduced[2]. "We are relativists, we are not negativists" insists Candrakīrti[3]. The text book of the Madhyamaka school opens by something like a hymn in honour of Dependent Origination or Relativity. It can be renderd thus:

The perfect Buddha, the Foremost of all
Teachers I salute !
He has proclaimed the principle of Relativity,
The principle that nothing (in the Universe)
can disappear,
Nor can anything new appear,
Nothing has an end,

---

not as one among the distinct categories, but as implicated with all the categories (cp. G. Grote, *Aristotle*, ed. Bain. p. 88) and although he does not maintain that the relative is unreal, yet he declares it to be Ens in the lowest degree (ibid. p. 85). The question whether Ens is itself relative he leaves unsolved.

1. Ibid. 491. 1.—*niravaśeṣa-prapañca-upaśamārthaṁ śūnyatā upadiśyate*; *XXIV*, 18—*yaḥ pratītya-samutpādaḥ śūnyatāṁ tām pracakṣmahe*; *p*. 503, 12-*yo'yam pratītya-samutpādo hetupratyayān apekṣya rūpa-vijñānādīnām prādur-bhāvaḥ sa svabhāvena anutpadaḥ*......*sā śūnyatā*; *p*. 504, 3—*yaḥ*, *pratītya-adhīnaḥ sa śūnya uktaḥ*; 403, 1-*aśūnyam—apratītya-samut-pannam*; *p*. 591, 6—*iha sarva-bhāvānām—pratītya-samutpannatvācchūnyatvaṁ sakalena śāstreṇa pratipāditam etc*. *etc*.
2. Ibid. XXIV. 7 p. 490 11 *na cābi śūnyatāyāṁ yat prayojanaṁ tad vijānāsi*.
3. Ibid. 368. 7

Nor is there anything eternal,
Nothing is identical (with itself),
Nor is there anything differentiated,
Nothing moves, neither hither, nor thither.
It is (*Nirvāṇa*), the blissful quiescence,
Of every (possible) Plurality[1].

XV. THE REAL ETERNAL BUDDHA COGNISED IN MYSTIC INTUITION

Applying this method to the Hīnayānist conception of an extinct Buddha, representing nevertheless an eternal lifeless substance (*svabhāva* or *dharma*), Nāgārjuna flatly denies the reality of the latter, notwithstanding all the reverential feelings which the idea must have evoked. Buddha is conceived in the Hīnayāna as the ultimate goal of the world's progress, realised in a continuous stream of existences (*bhāva-saṁtati*)[2]. He can really exist so far as this progress really exists: but an independent existence of both is impossible, because, being interdependent, they are correlative and hence not absolutely real. Just as a man suffering from an eye-disease perceives a double moon in the sky, does the inveterate ignorance of mankind dichotomise every reality. Only ignorance[3] can imagine that the Hīnayānist Buddha has real existence of his own[4]. Never did the Buddhas declare that either they themselves or their elements really did exist.[5] But, of course, for the unsophisticated simple man the Hīnayānistic Buddha is not devoid of any existence. Not being able to withstand the lion's roar of Relativity,[6] the Hīnayānist, the man of a poor enthusiasm,[7] runs away, like an antelope into the dark forest of Realism. But the Mahāyānist's denial does not mean that

1. M. vr. p. 11. 13.
2. Ibid. p. 432 ff.
3. Ibid. p. 432. 10.
4. The Hīnayānistic Buddha is not real, he has no *svabhāva*, cp. XXVII 2. 4, 16, but the Mahāyānistic one has a svabhāva. The synonym of *dharma-kāya* is *svabhāva-kāya*.
5. Ibid. p. 443. 2 cf. XXV 24.
6. Ibid. 442. 13
7. *Svādhimukti-daridra*, ibid. p. 443. 1

every hope of salvation must be given up[1] because that Buddha who is above every possible determination (*niṣprapañca*) is not denied.[2] The Mahāyānist, when maintaining that the Buddha, as conceived in Hīnayāna, is not absolutely real (*niḥsvabhāva*), if he wishes to state the whole truth (*aviparītārtha*), must confess[3] that he cannot even assert so much. Strictly speaking he can assert neither that the Buddha is relational, nor non-relational, nor both at once, nor neither.[4] Such characteristics are also conventional (*prajñapti*). They are imputed characteristics (*āropitavyavahāraḥ*).[5] The real Buddha must be perceived directly by intuition. The reserved questions, the impossibility of answering whether the world is finite or infinite, and whether the Buddha survives after Nirvāṇa are referred just to this impossibility of whatsoever determination.[6] If you insist that there is a Buddha, you must concede that after Nirvāṇa there is none.[7] But if you realise the relativity of the conception, never will the question about his existence occur to you Buddha is merged quiescent in nature and beyond every possible determination.[8] Those who proceed to dichotomise him as eternal or non-eternal, existent or non-existent, relative or non-relative, omniscient or non-omniscient are all misled by words.[9] They have no direct intuition (*na paśyanti*) of the Absolute Buddha.[10] Just as a man who is blind from birth cannot see the sun,[11] so are men in the throes of conventional conceptions; they do not perceive the Buddha directly, but wish to detail (*prapañcayanti*) him conceptually. Only by them can He not be seen directly (*aparokṣa-vartin*)[12]. Buddha must

1. Ibid. p. 442. 13
2. Ibid. p. 443. 11
3 Ibid. p. 443. 13.
4 Ibid. p. XXII. 11
5. Ibid. p. 444. 4.
6. Ibid. p. XXII. 12
7. Ibid. p. XXII. 14.
8. Ibid. p. 448. 1
9. Ibid. p. XXII. 15.
10. Ibid. p. 448. 10.
11. Ibid. p. 448. 10.
12. Ibid. p. 448. 9. Such a definition of sense perception, *pratyakṣam aparokṣam* (sc. *artha*, not *jñāna*) is opposed by Candrakīrti to the definition of Dignāga *pratyakṣam kalpanāpoḍham*, cp. M. vr. p. 71. 10. It has been later

be regarded as the cosmical order (*dharmataḥ*), his Body is the cosmos (*dharmatā*). The essence of the cosmos is incognisable, it is impossible to know what it is conceptually.[1] The reality of Buddha is the reality of the universe, and as far as the Buddha has no separate reality (*niḥsvabhāva*), neither the Universe has any, apart from him. All the elements of existence, when sifted through the principle of Relativity, become resplendent.[2] All the millions of existences (*bhūtakoṭi*) must be regarded as the body of the Buddha manifested in them. This is Relativity, the climax of wisdom (*prajñāpāramitā*).[3]

XVI. THE NEW CONCEPTION OF NIRVĀṆA

Space and that kind of eternal death which was termed Nirvāṇa were entered in the list of ultimate realities by the Schools-Early Buddhism and the Vaibhāṣikas, on the score that they possessed a character (*dharma*), a reality (*vastu*), an individuality (*svalakṣaṇa*) an existence (*bhāva*) of their own (*sva-bhāva*), since they fitted into the current definition of reality, (*sva-bhāva-dhāraṇād dharmāḥ*). They were cancelled by the Sautrāntikas on the consideration that they did not possess any such separate reality. They also were cancelled by the Mādhyamikas in consequence of the new definition of reality (*anapekṣaḥ svabhāvaḥ*). This new weapon proved much more efficacious than the Occam's Razor of the Sautrāntika, especially as it was wielded by the Mādhyamika with unflinching resolve. His conception of Relativity (*śūnyatā*) covered everything, all the conditional as well as the eternal elements of the Vaibhāṣika list. Indeed the idea of an Absolute becomes meaningless, if there is nothing to set against it[4]. It then loses every individuality or reality (*sva-bhāva*). And *vice versa* the phenomenal

---

accepted by the Vedāntins (cp. Vedāntaparibhāṣā) and others; Brahma, the Absolute, is then declared to be cognised by sense-perception, by *pratyakṣa*.

1. Ibid. p. 448, 15.

2. *Prakṛti-prabhāsvarāḥ sarvadharmāḥ prajñāpāramitā-pariśuddhyā*. Ibid. p. 444. 9.

3. *Tathāgata-kāyo bhūta-koṭi-prabhāvito draṣṭavyo yad uta prajñā-pāramitā*. Aṣṭas. 94—14.

4. Ibid. VII. 33.

ceases to be phenomenal if there is nothing non-phenomenal with which it is contrasted. With the new interpretation of the principle of Relativity (*pratītya-samutpādaśūnya*) the Hīnayānic Absolute becomes just as relative as all other ultimates of this system.

Very far-reaching consequences had inevitably arisen from this newly adopted principle. The whole edifice of early Buddhism was undermined and smashed. The Nirvāṇa of the Hīnayānists, their Buddha, their ontology and moral philosophy, their conceptions of reality and causation were abandoned, together with the idea of the ultimate reality of the senses and sense data (*rūpa*), of the mind (*citta-caitta*), and of all their elements of matter, mind and forces. "Nowhere and never" says Candrakīrti, "have Buddhas preached the reality of the soul or of these Hīnayānistic elements."[1] All the constructions so laboriously built up by the schools of Early Buddhism had to be relinquished with the only exception of the principle of dependently-coordinated-existence (*pratītya-samutpāda*) in its new interpretation as Relativity (*śūnyatā*). The textbook of the School devotes a chapter to every conspicuous item of the constructions of Early Buddhism, and destroys it by the same weapon, for whatsoever is relative is false, transient and illusory.

The fortunes of Mahāyāna were greatly assisted by the wonderful style in which Nāgārjuna couched his celebrated aphorisms. Notwithstanding the somewhat monotonous method by which he applies to all the conceptions of Hīnayāna the same destructive dialectics, he never ceases to be interesting, bold, baffling, sometimes seemingly arrogant. And this method of endless repetition of the same idea, although in different connections, impresses the student with the overwhelming, all-embracing importance of the principle of Relativity. In their Tibetan garb, owing to the monosyllabic precision of this wonderful language, the aphorisms become, if possible, still more eloquent than in the original, and are, up to the present day, studied in the monastic schools, and repeated by the monks with rapturous admiration. Sometimes terror is inspired by this insistent and obstinate denial of all, even the most revered and cherished notions of the Hīnayānist. "What are we

1. Ibid. p. 443. 2.

to do, exclaims Āryadeva, the next best Founder of the doctrine, "nothing at all exists"[1] "Even the name of the doctrine inspires terror"[2].

However, it is only the Hīnayānist and all pluralists in general that need to be afraid of Nāgārjuna's dialectics[3]. He does not assail, but extols the idea of the cosmical body of Buddha. He extols the principle of Relativity, and destroys through it every plurality, only in order to clear up the ground and establish on it the unique, undefinable (*anirvacanīya*) essence of being, the one-without-a-second. According to the principle of monistic philosophy, consistently applied, all other entities have only a second hand, contingent reality; they are borrowed cash.

This unique reality, although declared to be uncharacterisable (*anirvacanīya*), has been variously characterised as the "element of the elements" (*dharmāṇām dharmatā*) or (*dharma-dhātu*), as their relativity (*śūnyatā*), as "thisness" (*idaṁtā*)as, their "relation to thisness" (*idaṁpratyayatā*) as "suchness" (*tathatā*), as the "suchness of existence" (*bhūta-tathatā*) as the matrix of the Lord (*tathāgata-garbha*), and lastly as the "cosmical body of the Lord", as Buddha's *Dharmakāya*[4]. In this last attribution, the unique essence of the universe becomes personified and worshipped under the names of Vairocana, Amitābha, the Goddess Tārā and others, as a supreme God. Buddhism becomes at once pantheistic and theistic, or as prof. M. Anesaki prefers to put it, cosmotheistic[5].

---

1. P. L. Vaidya, *Catuḥśataka* (Paris, 1923). Kar. 184.

2. Ibid. Kar. 289

3. Prof. H. Kern, *Manual*, p.127 seems also to have been terror-stricken. He exclaims, what sounds like genuine solicitude, "there is no birth, there is no Nirvāṇa ! etc." and for this disaster he makes responsible "the principles underlying ancient Buddhism."

4. The terms *prajñā-pāramitā* and *abhisamaya*, when used in an objective sense (*karma-sādhana*), mean the same. The Yogācāras would add as synonymous *citta-dharmatā, vijñaptimātratā, pariniṣpannatā*. cp. *Triṁśikā, p.* 42

5. In a very interesting book prof. M. Aneseki, *Buddhist Art in its relation to Buddhist Ideals*, (Boston and New York, 1915) shows how the perfection of that Japanese art which has evoked the admiration of the world is due to the influence of Mahāyāna ideals, to this genuine feeling of communion with the eternal, all-pervading principle of life, the *Dharmakāya* realised by the artist in mystic intuition in every flower, every plant and

Buddha and Nirvāṇa are different names for the same thing. But Nāgārjuna treats the same thing under four or five different headings, his object being to show that whatever be the verbal designation (*prapañca = vāk*)[1], from whatever side the problem of the absolute be tackled, the result is the same.[2] If the phenomenal world is not real, neither can it have a real end[3]. To suppose that the phenomenal world really existed before Nirvāṇa, in order to be changed so as not to exist after Nirvāṇa, is an illusion which must be given up and the sooner it is given up the better[4]. Whether we take the Vaibhāṣika view and maintain that Nirvāṇa is something real (*dharma*) in which consciousness and life are extinct for ever[5], or if we, with the Sautrāntika, admit that it is the simple cessation of the world process,[6] in both cases something real is assumed to exist before Nirvāṇa and to disappear afterwards. This makes Nirvāṇa not only relative, but a product of causes (*saṁskṛta*)[7]. In full accordance with the idea of a monistic universe, it is now asserted that there is not a shade of difference between the Absolute and the phenomenal, between *nirvāṇa* and *saṁsāra*[8]. The universe as a whole is the Absolute, viewed as a process it is the phenomenal, Nagārjuna declares[9]

"ya ājavaṁjavībhāva upādāya pratītya vā /
so pratītyānupādāya nirvāṇam upadiśyate."//

This may be rendered thus—"Having regard to causes or conditions (constituting all phenomena) we call this world a phenomenal world. This same world, when causes or conditions are disregarded, (i.e. the world as a whole, *sub specie aeternitatis*) is called the Absolute."

---

every living creature he was painting. Is it not strange that the philosophy which establishes these ideals has been so utterly misunderstood by European scholarship?

1. M. vr. 373.9
2. Ibid. p. 175
3. Ibid. XXVI. 1
4. Ibid. p. 522. 6
5. Ibid. p. 225. 10
6. *Kleśa-janmanor abhāvaḥ*, ibid. p. 527. 7
7. Ibid. XXV. 5, 13
8. Ibid. XXV. 20.
9. Ibid. XXV. 9

XVII. IS RELATIVITY ITSELF RELATIVE? CONDEMNATION OF ALL LOGIC FOR THE COGNITION OF THE ABSOLUTE

But the principle of Relativity (*śūnyatā*) did not prove an entirely safe foundation for the New Buddhism. A danger lurked in it which was likely to bring the whole construction in jeopardy. Just as the Absolute of early Buddhism could not escape from the fate of being declared relative, so was Relativity itself relative[1]; it clearly depended upon its opposite, the non-relative, and without this contrast it was likely to lose every meaning. Nāgārjuna did not shrink before this danger and faced it with the same audacious spirit as he was wont to do. This principle, the pivot of the system, is called upon in order to destroy all theories and to replace them, as we have seen above, by direct mystic intuition, not in order to replace it by a new theory. As a theory it is just as bad as the old ones, it is even much worse. "If something non-relative," says Nāgārjuna,[2] "did really exist, we would then likewise admit the existence of the relative, but there is absolutely nothing non-relative: how then can we admit the existence of the relative (or the truth of Relativity)." "Relativity", explains Candrakīrti "is here the common characteristic of all the elements (*dharmas*) of existence. That is our view. But since there is no element which would be non-relative, Relativity itself, for want of those objects with which it could be contrasted, becomes as inane as a mirage, as a garland of flowers in the sky." Does this mean that Relativity should be rejected? No, "because the Buddhas have taught that to realise the relativity of all artificial conceptions is the only way to get rid of them. But if people then begin tocling to this very concept of

---

1. I find the question whether Relativity is itself relative mentioned by B. Russell. (*A B C of Relativity*, p. 14) and declined with the remark that it is absurd. Nevertheless the question exists and cannot be dismissed on such grounds, the more so by an author from whom we learn that whosoever wishes to become a philosopher must learn not to be frightened by absurdities." (*Problems of Philosophy*, London, 1921, p. 31)

2. Ibid. XIII. 7

Relativity, they must be called irreclaimable."[1] "It is," explains Candrakīrti[2] "as if somebody said, "I have nothing to sell you", and would receive the answer, "All right, just sell me this your absence of goods for sale."

We read in the Ratnakūṭa,[3] "I declare those are often, and many times rotten who having conceived relativity, cling to it (as a new theory)...... It is much better to cling to the false idea of a really existing personality (*pudgala*), though it is a blunder of Himalayan dimensions, than to cling to this doctrine of relativity which (in this case would be) a doctrine of the void (*abhāva*)......It is as if a doctor[4] administered a powerful remedy which would remove all the ailments of the patient, but could not afterwards be expelled from the abdomen. Do you think that the patient would be really cured? No, he would suffer even much more than he did suffer before."

The characterisation of reality as Relativity is resorted to *in extremis* for want of any other expedient. It is a verbal characterisation, it takes into account the necessities of speech (*śabdam upādāya prajñaptiḥ*)[5]. The Sautrāntika made use of the conception of a nominal entity (*prajñaptisat*), as has been mentioned above, when combating the artificial constructions of early Buddhism. This conception was extended by the Mahāyānists so as to cover all elements without exception. Sense data, consciousness, feeling, volitions were declared by the Sautrāntika as ultimate realities. But Nāgārjuna did not spare them. They became all relative and nominal, and relativity itself was but a nominal "middle path" of approaching reality. Middle path meant in early Buddhism steering beween materialism (*ucchedavāda*) and the doctrine of an eternal soul (*śāśvatavāda*). Its positive content was the doctrine of separate elements (*dharma*). In Mahāyāna this term changes its meaning and becomes synonymous with Relativity (*śūnyatā*). Relativity is the middle path[6].

1. Ibid. XIII. 8
2. Ibid. p. 247. 6
3. Ibid. p. 248. 7
4. Ibid. p. 248. 11
5. Ibid. XXIV. 18. XXII. 11, p. 215. 1,2 86. 1
6. Ibid. XXIV. 18. Therefore Madhyamaka-śāstra must be translated "A Treatise on Relativity."

XIX. PARALLEL DEVELOPMENTS IN BUDDHISM AND BRAHMANISM

That the evolution from Hīnayāna to Mahāyāna ran parallel with the movement which in other Indian religions at the same epoch led to the establishing of their pantheons, and their supreme deities of Śiva and Viṣṇu, is quite obvious. The Brāhmaṇical religions were likewise founded on a background of pantheism, on monism with the Śaivists, and as omewhat mitigated one with the Vaiṣṇavites. Both tendencies represented old traditions based on explicit, though contradictory, utterances of the Upaniṣads. That the Mahāyāna is indebted to some Aupaniṣada influence is most probable. That Gauḍapāda and Śaṅkarahave been, in their turn, influenced by the dialectic of Nāgārjuna can hardly be denied. But it is at present impossible to elicit something definite aboutthe strength of these influences, their time and their place. A Mahāyānistic tendency seems to have manifested itself very early in the Buddhist schools. Part of the community was not satisfied to see in Buddha an essentially human nature, and felt restive before the idea of his total disappearance in Nirvāṇa Some centuries later this tendency reaches full conclusion and a great man, Nāgārjuna, gives lustre and popularity to a new church. Its philosophy made volte-face from pluralism to monism.

XIX. EUROPEAN PARALLELS

To assign to Nāgārjuna his place among the great philosophers of humanity is not so much the task of the Indianist, as of the historian of general philosophy. But until the texts are made accessible in translations, intelligible to him, we cannot expect him to guide us.[1] The Indologist finds himself obliged tentatively to do it himself in comparing the ideas he comes across in India with what may be found similar in the vast field of European philosophy. In characterising the Indian

1. The two translations by Prof. M. Walleser, Die Mittlere Lehre, (Heidelberg 1911 and 1912) are extremely useful for the study of the texts, they would have been still more useful if comparative indices were added to them. But being literal we doubt they could convey any definite impression on the mind of a philosopher.

philosopher as "nihilist", rationalist, pantheist or realist some comparison is already involved. If A. Barth, E. Senart and others have protested against premature and misleading comparisons, it is only because they were inclined to find between the Indian philosopher and his European associate more points of divergence than of similarity, but to find divergence means already to compare. To characterise Nāgārjuna as a "nihilist", means to make a misleading comparison, since his condemnation of logic is only one part, and not the principal one, of his philosophy. In order to understand a philosopher there is no better method than the one proposed and so brilliantly applied by H. Bergson, i.e. to dissect him in different parts which by themselves will not be the philosopher in question, but which summarised will help us to understand him.[1]

Upon the Indian side we must first of all point to the almost absolute identity with Vedānta, as a probable consequence of his indebtedness to Aupaniṣada tradition. If Prof. A. B. Keith and Prof. M. Walleser suppose that Nāgārjuna stops at negation, or denies even the empirical reality of this world, it is only because his real aim, the positive counterpart of his negativism, the identity of *dharmakāya* and *Brahma*, has escaped their attention. It follows from this identity that all the points of contact which Prof. Deussen has really found, or imagined to have found, between Schopenhauer and Vedānta, will equally apply to Nāgārjuna. This philosophy was most decidedly opposed to rationalism, to those systems, modern or ancient, Indian or European, which asserted the capacity of human reason to cognise things as they really are. He even presses this incapacity to the utmost and challenges the claims of logic with greater emphasis than any philosopher ever has done. Other remarkable parallelisms may be pointed out which refer to the step taken by Nāgārjuna from pluralism to monism. Whether the systems operated with the conception of an independent substance and assumed the existence of separate, though harmonising, monads, or assumed a perpetual stream of passing events, the next step is to imagine one all-embracing indivisible substance. This, as we have seen, is the position of Mahāyāna versus Hīnayāna. It has been paralleled in Greece by the

1. De l' intuition philosophique de Metaph. 1911

position of Parmenides versus Heraclitus. The step was repeated in modern German philosophy. Prof. H. Jacobi has already suggested[1] a comparison between Zeno of Eleia and Nāgārjuna. We may add that the similarity was not limited to their dialectics. Zeno, as is now known, devised the celebrated "sophisms" in order to prove the impossibility of motion, and in support of Parmenides' conception of the world as one motionless whole.[2]

Very remarkable are then the coincidences between Nāgārjuna's negativism and the condemnation by Mr. Bradley of almost every conception of the every day world, things and qualities, relations, space and time, change, causation, motion, the self. From the Indian standpoint Bradley can be characterised as a genuine Mādhyamika. But above all this parallelism we may perhaps find a still greater family likeness between the dialectical method of Hegel and Nāgārjuna's dialectics. Hegel in his *Phenomenologie des Geistes*[3] challenged common sense to point out some object which is certainly known for what, in our experience, it is, and solves the question by stating that all we really know of the object is its "thisness", all its remaining content is relation. This is the exact meaning of the *tathatā*, or of "suchness", of the Mahāyānist, and Relativity, as we have seen, is the exact meaning of the term *śūnyatā*. We further see the full application of the method which maintains that we can truly define an object only by taking explicit account of other objects, with which it is contrasted, that apart from this contrast the object becomes "devoid" of any content, and both the opposites coalesce in some higher unity which embraces them both. The facts are knowable only as interrelated and the universal law of Relativity is all that is properly meant by reality. Both philosophers assure us that negativity (*śūnyatā*) is the soul of the universe, "Negativitat ist die Seele der Wekt." Reducing the world of fact to a realm of universal relativity implies that every thing cognisable is false, transient and illusory but that the constitution of the real world depends upon this very fact. Even sensations and sense data (*rūpa*)[4] which first

1. A. O. J. XXI. 1, p. 1
2. Cf. Bertrand Russell, External World, p. 167. ff.
3. For the English Phrasing of Hegel's principles I am indebted to Baldwin's dictionary.
4. Ibid. IV. 1

appeared as ultimate realities are gradually discovered to stand in relations without which they prove to be meaningless. Relativity, or negativity, is really the Soul of the universe.

Some more points of similarity will be easily detected between Nāgārjuna and every monistic philosophy, the more so between him and those philosophers who, like Nacolaus Cusanus, G. Bruno and others, insist upon the negative method of cognising the Absolute. It will hardly be denied that the Mahāyānist conception of Buddha's cosmic body as the unique substance is very similar to Spinoza's conception of God as the only substance, *Deus sive substantia*, *Deus sive natura*. Although Spinoza's *intuitus* of everything particular *sub specie aeternitatis* is supposed to be a rational capacity of the intellect and Nāgārjuna's intuition is mystic, nevertheless both lead to the same result.

These several points of similarity should, as a matter of course, be taken for what they are worth. For one thing, they might preclude the characteristic of a 'nihilist' to be applied to Nāgārjuna. The chief divergence between him and his European colleagues in monism is that he did not believe in logic, at least for the ultimate aim of cognising what reality in itself is. Hegel and Bradley seem to believe in the efficiency of their logic. It did not occur to them that their logic would sublate itself if applied to their own results. Nāgārjuna was fully aware of this fact. Therefore abandoning logic altogether he betook himself to direct mystic intuition of the Absolute, the One-without-a-Second. This step, or jump, from condemned logic to direct intuition, has been made by many philosophers and in our own days it has a very eloquent exponent in the person of M. H. Bergson.

XX. THE POSITION OF NYĀYA-VAIŚEṢIKA

The estrangement which befell many scholars at the idea of annihilation as the ultimate goal of a religion would perhaps never have been so strong if it had been known that Buddhism was by no means the only Indian system which had arrived at such conclusions. Besides a series of systems of a decidedly materialistic tinge, the orthodox Nyāya-Vaiśeṣika system adhered to the conception of an absolutely lifeless Nirvāṇa.[1] This annihilation of all life is here called final deliverance (*mokṣa*) or Absolute End (*apavarga*) and is characterised as a kind of "super bliss", (*niḥśreyasa*).[2] "Is it possible", asks Vātsyāyana, "that an enlightened man should favour a final Release in which there is neither bliss nor consciousness ?" And he should not favour the idea of a final Release where all turmoil of life is stopped for ever and where there is no consciousness about it. "This release," he says, "is tranquillity where everything is given up, everything has ceased to exist, and therefore a great deal of depression, horror, and sin are extinct."[3] Jayanta exclaims likewise, "Is it possible that reasonable men should make efforts in order to reduce themselves to a stonelike (inanimate) condition ?" and gives the same reply.[4]

All Indian philosophical systems are professed to be doctrines of salvation. They, therefore, start from the conception of a whole (*sarvam*) which is then split into two halves, phenomenal life and the Absolute (*saṁsāra* and *nirvāṇa*). The phenomenal part is further divided into an analysis of its actual condition (*duḥkha*), its driving forces (*duḥkha-samudāya*) their gradual extinction (*nirodha*) and the way to achieve this extinction. When this extinction *nirodha* is reached, life merges into the Absolute about whose essence a variety of constructions exists. These four topics, the four "noble truths" as the term has been very inadequately translated and represented as a fundamental principle of Buddhism, contain in reality

1. Cf. S. N. Dasgupta's *History of Indian Philosophy*, *p*. 362 ff.
2. *Nyāyasūtra* 1, 1, 2 and 22.
3. *Nyāyabhāṣya* p. 9 (Vizian)
4. *Nyāyamañjarī*, p. 509 (Vizian)
5. That *sarvam*, in its technical sense, does not include nirvāṇa, as M. de la Vallee Poussin asserts, op cit. p. 139, is quite wrong. *Sarvam* means *sarvaṃ jñeyam* which is but another name for the 12 *āyatanas* (corresponding to the 12 *prameyas* of *Nyāyasūtra* 1, 1, 9. Nirvāṇa is included in *āyatana* No. 12. 'dhamma' cf. My *Central Conception* appendix II, p. 106z the elements E 2-3. This is also clear from *Saṁyutta* IV 15 where *sabba* is used in its technical sense, *sabba-vaggo, sabbaṃ vo bhikkhave dessissāmi*. The passage in *Majjhima* N.13 contains no statement about this topic at all. The classification of the elements into I 2 *āyatanas* and into 16 *dhātus* includes nirvāṇa, the one into *skandhas* (with classification) does not, cp. also *Triṁśikā*, p. 36, *sarvam iti traidhātukam asaṁskṛtam ca*.

no doctrine at all.[1] It is only a scheme for philosophical constructions and is accepted as such by all Indian systems without exception. They cover, indeed, the Indian conception of philosophy. Uddyotakara says, "these are the four topics which are investigated by every philosopher in every system of metaphysics."[2] Accordingly every philosophical system must contain an analysis of the elements of life, a doctrine about its driving forces, a doctrine of the Absolute and a doctrine about the method to be followed in order to escape out of phenomenal life and become merged in the Absolute. Phenomenal life receives in the Nyāya-Vaiśeṣika system the designation of *duḥkha,* just as in Buddhism. It is very inadequate to translate this term by suffering, misery, pain etc., since it covers such items as inanimate matter, the five objects of sense, colours, sounds, tastes and tactile phenomena[3]. These are not

---

1. This clearly appears from the fact that the 'truths" are explicitly admitted in the Sāṁkhya, Yoga, Nyāya, and Vaiśeṣika systems and implicitly in all the others. Within the pale of Buddhism they cover two opposite theories, the *dharma=pudgala-nairātmya* theory of the Hīnayāna and the *śūnyatā=dharma-nairātmya* theory of Mahāyāna. They are a classification of the elements in four stages as viewed by the Saint, the ārya, cf., *Madh. vṛtti* p. 127, *āryāṇām eva tat satyam,* and *Ab. Kośa,* VI, 2 and the tables appended to my *Central Conception.* The editors of the P.T.S. Pali Dict. think that ārya has a "racial" meaning, *ārya-pudgala* would then mean, not the same as *anāsravadharmaḥ* or *mārga-satya,* but something like "a noble gentleman", ; but T. W. Rhys Davids rightly translates it *Arhat* in D. N. 1.37, cf. *Dialogues* 1.51

2. *Nyāyavārt,* ed. B. I. p.13 *etāni catvāry arthapadāni sarvāsu adhyātmavidyāsu sarvācāryair varṇyanta iti.*

3. Vātsyāyana says that *duḥkha* means *janma,* (ad N. S., 1. 1. 22) and Vācaspati explains, *duḥkhaśabdena sarve śarīrādaya ucyante,* and warns against confounding it with suffering, *mukhyam eva duḥkham iti bhramo mā bhūt*; the same is pressed by Jayanta, *na ca mukhyameva duḥkham bādhanāsvabhāvam avamṛśyate kim tu tatsādhanaṁ tadanuṣaktaṁ ca sarvam eva. Nyāyamañjarī.* Vizian p. 506 and *Madhyavṛtti,* p. 127. *iha hi pañcopādāna-skandha duḥkham iti ucyate.* Exactly the same definition in *Saṁyutta N.,* III, 47. It is a technical term the equivalent of the first *ārya-satya* and of the *sāsrava-dharmāḥ*; "suffering" is *duḥkhavedanā,* a quite different thing, it has another place in the system under *vedanā-skandha.* cf. Ab. Kośa VI. To confound them is a mistake just as to confound *rūpa-āyatana* with *rūpa-skandha* (the latter includes 10 *āyatanas,* or the 3 *dhātus,* or the 6 *indriyas* with the 22 *indriyas,* or the 75 *dharmas,* etc. the 18 dhātus. Cf M. C. Rhys David B. *Psych.* p. 83.

the objects to which the term suffering can be safely applied in our language, if we are to escape confusion. Bliss itself is entered into the classification of existence (*duḥkha*) as one of its 21 items. And this is quite natural because there is no eternal bliss neither in early Buddhism nor in Nyāya-Vaiśeṣika, if the "super-bliss" of disappearing into an eternal senseless condition be excepted. The classification into 21 items is but a slight modification of the Buddhist classification into 16 component parts of existence (*dhātu*)[1]. One reason why this term has been chosen as a designation of phenomenal life is that philosophy seeks a way out of it. Philosophy is the science of the Absolute, of Nirvāṇa. For every philosopher, all phenomenal life is something that must be shunned, it is *heya*. The analysis of existence into its elements, as has been stated above, is undertaken in order to determine the means by which all the forces of life must gradually, one after the other, be brought to a standstill.

It is likewise a general feature of all Indian systems that they assume the existence of a central force which keeps life going in this world, nay in all the imaginable worlds. This general force (*karma*) is resolved into the special ones, termed illusion, desire and aversion. They produce germs of future actions and until they are neutralized by corresponding methods, they will always produce a continuation of life. Illusion is neutralised by philosophic insight, but the decisive and final step which stops empirical life for ever and transfers the individual into the Absolute is achieved by Yoga, i.e. by that mystical power which is produced by absorption in intense concentrated meditation. These conceptions represent a characteristic Indian habit of thought. We meet them everywhere. Their origin is certainly not to be sought for in the Yoga system of Patañjali which has been proved to be a very late production about 800 years later than the origin of Buddhism. Their most primitive and crude form appears in the Jaina system. The defiling elements of illusion, desire, aversion etc. are here represented as a kind of subtle matter which through the pores of the skin flows into the body and fills it up like absorbed medicine or like a bag

---

1 Another classification of every cognizable thing into 12 *prameyas* cf. *Nyāyasūtra*, I. I. 9. corresponds, to a certain extent to the *Buddhi* classification into 12 *āyatanas*.

filled with sand.[1] By taking vows, by ascetic and meditative practices, the entrance into the body is shut up, the inflow ceases, and the individual becomes purified. In all other systems this process is spiritualized, and instead of an "inflow" of defiling matter we have an "influence" (*āsrava*) of defiling psychical elements which is being stopped by insight and meditation. All elements of existence are in the Buddhist system, as mentioned above, divided in such as can be extinguished by philosophic knowledge, and such as can be extinguished by mystical absorption only. The first class includes wrong views, under which item the naive realism of ordinary men is understood. Desire, passion and even the physical elements of matter can be extinguished for ever only by the force of absorption[2]. Although the Nyāya-Vaiśeṣika system favours a naively realistic view of the universe, it has no other means of reaching Nirvāṇa than the mystical power of Yoga. "The details about this matter," says Vātsyāyana, "will be found in special yoga manuals"[3]. Any question about the efficiency of this method is answered by stating that the power of Yoga is unlimited. The Nyāyasūtras mention a characteristic objection from some sceptic mind[4]. A man, says he, may be intensely absorbed in meditation, so as to forget everything which exists about him. He

1 Cf. *Tattvārthādhigamasūtra*, VI. 2 ff, VIII. 2 transl. by H. Jacobi. Z.D.M.G. LX Cf. also the detailed and very clear exposition of the complicated Jaina theory in H.V. Glassenapp, *Der Jaininsmus* (Berlin 1925) p. 158 f. The passions are imagined as a kind of tar by which the fluent matter is glued with the soul, ibid. VI. 5.

2 *Samudaya-satya* (*-heya-hetuh*) consists in Nyāya just as in Buddhism of *avidyā-tṛṣṇe*, cf. *Nyāyavārt*, p. 4.1.13, It is specified that these elements are also included in *duḥkha* (i.e. in the *upādānaskandhas*)—*taddhetus ca duḥkham uktam*, ibid. Their respective antidotes (i.e. *mārga*) consist on both sides of *prajñā* and *Samādhi*, Vats; Sūtra, V. 17-18 Prajñā is characterised as *dharma-praviveka* (cf. Vātśyāyana ad VI 2.417 which corresponds to the Buddhist *dharma-pravicaya* (Abh. Kośa).

3 *Nyāyabhāṣya* ad IV 2.46. Although the *prasaṅkhyāna* is analogous to *prati-saṅkhyā-nirodha* of the Buddhists, its procedure is different. By the unlimited mystic power of Yoga innumerable "magic bodies" *nirmāṇa-kāya*, must be created at once, to atone in them for endless former deeds and thus to reach Final Extinction, Cf. *Tātparyaṭīkā*, *p*. 6. This Prof. A.B. Keith (Indian Logic and Atomism, p. 260) calls "vulgar thaumaturgy". According to such phrasing Dr. H. Beck, who interprets even the knowledge of *duḥakha-satya* as a vision of ethereal bodies (Buddhismus 2 II, p. 89 f.), would be called a magician. Usually these men are called mystics.

4 IV. 2. 39-44.

may retire into a lonely place, a forest, a cave, a sandy beach, and there practise meditation until every perception of the external world has ceased. Nevertheless when external phenomena of exceptional force, as e.g. a thunder storm overcomes him, he will awake out of the most intense meditation. Why could not the same happen to him in the moment he is about to attain Final Release, if this is to be attained by such meditation? The objection is answered by pointing to the mystical power of trance which stops all energies of life for ever. After that no living bodies, no feeling and no cognitions can exist.

We thus see that an appeal to the mystical power of yoga is a common feature of many Indian philosophical systems. It is needed to fill up the place of the four main subjects which are another general feature of the Indian systems. The originality of each system lies in its Ontology, its theory of cognition, its conception of the Absolute, and the details of its construction of a path leading to final release. The Nyāya-Vaiśeṣika system assumes a limited number of substances with their changing qualities. The soul of the individual is here represented as an eternal substance, it is ubiquitous and coterminous with space. Knowledge is produced in it by a special contact with an internal organ of physical nature. When the body is removed from one place to another, feelings and ideas are produced in a new part of this same motionless[2] substance by its occasional contact with the internal organ which follows the movement of the body. Soul is thus a semi-material ubiquitous substance similar to space and time which in this system are equally conceived as separate ubiquitous substances. This construction facilitates the transition out of phenomenal life with its feelings and cognitions into the Absolute, which is the Absolutely senseless and lifeless state of this very substance. By the power of absorption the internal organ is kept back from all contact with the soul and the senses. No consciousness is then produced., all life is annihilated but the substance of the soul reverts in Nirvāṇa to its original and natural condition (*svarūpāvasthā*). The Nyāya and Vaiśeṣika were at an early date engaged in a controversy

1 Faddegon, *Vaiśeṣika System*, p.272-3 thinks that this Soul was imagined "as really moving." This is quite impossible since it represents a unity and is omnipresent (*vibhu*, *parama-mahat*, ibid. VII. 1.22) Cf. also *Nyāyabindutīkā* ed. B. B. p. 65 *niṣkriyaś cātmā...sarvagataḥ*.

with the Vedāntins about the condition of the liberated soul. The Vaiśeṣikas maintained that it was simply a cessation of all life, just as a cessation of fire when all fuel is exhausted[1]. What is this internal bliss and what is this eternal consciousness, they ask, which constitute the essence of the eternal spiritual principle according to the Vedāntins? Since all objects of knowledge have entirely disappeared for ever in Nirvāṇa, it is a joy without something to be enjoyed, and it is knowledge without knowing anything. Such feeling and such knowledge, even if they existed, would be as good as if they never existed at all (*sthitopy asthitān na viśiṣyate*)[2]. "But then," asks an objector, "your soul would be as lifeless as a stone?[3] The Vaiśeṣika concedes the argument, although he seems to prefer, as a sort of image médiatrice, the comparison with space.[4] A question is next asked which gives expression to that feeling of estrangement which is so strong when we think of annihilation as an ultimate goal. "No wise men will ever strive to attain final deliverance (*mokṣa—nirvāṇa*) if, after all consciousness and life have been annihilated, it becomes similar to a piece of rock (*śilā-śakala-kalpa*) if it is indistinguishable from a stone (*pāṣāṇa-nirviśeṣaḥ*),[5] if it is inanimate (*jaḍa*)" "But, says the author, wise men do not exert themselves for bliss alone. Experience shows that they also exert themselves to escape pain, as when they, e.g., "avoid being stung by thorns."[6] Phenomenal life being here comparable to pain, the result is that the annihilation of it alone is the ultimate aim of man on earth. This ultimate annihilation and this lifeless substance receive the epithet of the place of Immortality (*amṛtyu-padam*),[7] the same epithet which final annihilation receives in early

1 In his vindication of a substantial Soul Faddegon op, cit, apparently assumes that the Vaiśeṣikas imagined the soul as a conscious substance, just as the Sāṅkhyas and the Vedāntins did. But the consciousness (*buddhi*) is in that system only a *guṇa* of the *ātman*, it appears occasionally through a special contact. The soul in itself (*svarūpāvasthāyām*) has neither consciousness, nor feeling.

2 *Nyāyakandalī*, p. 286 (Vizian, cf. *Nyāyamañjarī*, 510. 1. 12-3.

3 Ibid. That the pure essence of a Soul, or of the substance that produces consciousness is itself as lifeless (*jaḍa*), as a stone, seems to be here an extreme consequence drawn by the objector, the comparison with space as an ubiquitous substance is more adequate.

4 Cf. *Vaiś. sūtra*, VII. 1.22. *Bhāsarvajña's Nyāyasāra*, p. 39, (B. Ind. 1910).

5 Cf. *Nyāyamañjarī*, p. 508 f. and *Nyāyatātparyadīpikā*, p. 282 (ibid).) cp. *Naiṣadhīya* XVI, 75 *muktaye yaḥ śilātvāya śāstramūce......Gotamam*.

6 *Nyāyasāra*, p. 40.

7 *Nyāyabhāṣya*, p. 30. Cf. likewise pp. 31-34. where the controversy with Vedānta is already in full swing.

Buddhism. Its eternal unchanging character is thereby emphasized.

Nor was this analogy between the theories of the Buddhists and the Naiyāyikas ignored by the latter. We find in the *Nyāyamañjarī* of Jayanta the following very characteristic deliverance "By nirvāṇa and similar expressions the Buddhists mean the absolute end (*apavarga*) which is either (in Hīnayāna) the annihilation of the flow of consciousness, or (in Mahāyāna) a flow of pure (objectless) consciousness. (The first) solution—annihilation—is even more pitiful than the condition to which soul is reduced in nirvāṇa according to the Naiyāyikas, since it does not leave to the soul even a stonelike condition. But in one point we agree with the Buddhists, viz. that there is a difference between the essence of the soul by itself and the form in which it appears in its reciprocal action with other objects. A constant change of (this substantial) soul (as maintained by the Buddhists) is absolutely inconceivable; it must be rejected as impossible, just as (the converse theory of the Buddhist about the sound, viz.) that sound is a substance (sc. atomic)".

The Nirvāṇa of the old[1] Nyāya-Vaiśeṣika school is thus lifeless and similar to the Nirvāṇa of the Vaibhāṣika-Buddhists. On the other hand, the Nirvāṇa of the Mahāyānists, to which the Sautrāntikas adhered, has the same pantheistic character as the Nirvāṇa of the Vedāntins.

XXI. CONCLUSION

The probable theory of the Buddhist conception of the Absolute is, therefore, the following one.

1. In the VI century B.C. there was a great effervescence of philosophical thought among the non-brahmancial classes of

---

1 In later theistic Nyāya final deliverance is reached by the direct contemplation of God, and the condition of the liberated Soul is defined as blissful, cf. *Nyāyasāra*, p. 40 and *Nyāyatātparya dīpikā*, p. 293. Both the Vaiśeṣika and the Naiyāyika systems were originally atheistic, cf. H. Jacobi *Die Gottesidee bei den Indern*, (Bonn 1923), p. 47 ff. and Faddegon, op. cit. p. 165 and 354. That the idea of an eternal God could not easily tally with the system if seen from the embarrassment to decide whether it should be classed as a *muktātman* or not. The question is solved, in agreement with *Yogasūtra* I. 24 b admitting that the quality of consciousness, which is only accidental in Souls, becomes eternal in God, cf. *Nyāyakandalī*, 58 (Vizian) and *Nyāyavārttika*, p. 469. Both theistic and atheistic Naiyāyikas existed at Srīharṣa's time, cf. *Naiṣadhīya* XVII 75 and 77.

India, and a way out of phenomenal life was ardently sought for, the majority of the solutions having a materialistic tinge. Buddha at that time proposed, or accepted, a system denying the existence of an eternal soul, and reducing phenomenal existence to a congeries of separate elements evolving gradually towards final extinction.

2. To this ideal of a lifeless Nirvāṇa and an extinct Buddha some schools remained alone faithful. A tendency to convert Buddha into a superhuman, eternally living principle manifested itself early among his followers and led to a schism.

3. This tendency gradually developed until in the I century A.D. it ended into the production of a luxuriant growth of a new canonical literature. It then adopted, probably borrwoing from some Aupaniṣad school, the Brahmanical ideas of a pantheistic Absolute, of a spiritual and monistic character. After this Buddhistic adaptation of the Vedānta, Buddha was converted into a full blown Brahman and its personification worshipped under the names of a Cosmical Body (*dharmakāya*), Samantabhadra, Vairocana and others.

4. The philosophical doctrine of the old church stuck to the central conception of separate elements of matter, mind and forces, composed lists of them with a view to investigate the method of their gradual extinction in the Absolute.

5. Among the early schools the Mahāsāṁghikas, Vātsiputrīyas and others already assumed a kind of consciousness surviving in Nirvāṇa.

6. They were followed by a school with critical tendencies, the Sautrāntikas, which cut down the list of artificially constructed elements, cut down Nirvāṇa itself as a separate entity and transferred the Absolute into the living world, thus constituting a transition to Mahāyāna.

7. The philosophy of the new religion is an adaptation of the Vedānta system. It forsook the pluralistic principle altogether and became emphatically monistic.

8. It then took a double course. It either assumed the existence of a store-consciousness of which all phenomenal life was but a manifestation. This school is the sequel of cultivated logic. The other school denied the possibility of cognising the Absolute by logical methods; it declared all plurality to be an

illusion, and nothing short of the whole to be the reality directly cognised in mystic intuition.

9. The transitional school of the Sautrāntikas coalesced in the V century A.D. with the idealistic school of the Mahāyāna and produced India's greatest philosophers Dignāga and Dharmakīrti. With regard to Nirvāṇa, it assumed the existence of a pure spiritual principle, in which object and subject coalesced, and, along with it, a force of transcendental illusion (*vāsanā*) producing the phenomenal world.

10. Contemporaneously with this highest development of Buddhist philosophy, in the VII century A.D., the relativist school of early Mahāyāna received a fresh impulse and a revival of popularity. This led to the formation of new hybrid schools.

11. The very high perfection to which the philosophy was brought by both the idealistic and relativistic schools of Buddhism could not but influence all philosophical systems of India, and we see in the next period the old Vedānta remodelled and equipped with fresh arguments by an adaptation to it of the methods elaborated in the Vijñānavāda and Śūnyavāda schools of Buddhism.

APPENDIX

NĀGĀRJUNA'S TREATISE ON RELATIVITY

Chapters I and XXV

PREFATORY

Nāgārjuna is the author of three different works upon the Buddhist Theory of Relativity (śūnyatā), a fundamental (mūla), complete work, Madhyamaka-Śāstra, and two short summaries—Yukti-ṣaṣṭikā and Śūnyatā-saptati.

The complete work contains about 400 aphorisms divided into 27 chapters. The first chapter is devoted to a critique of the conception of Causality. It reduces our every-day conception of it and all realistic theories *ad absurdum* and thus indirectly establishes Monism (advaita). The rest of the work is filled with the application of this result to every separate item of the Hīnayānist philosophical system[1]. Nāgārjuna is also

1 The following is the list of subjects treated, ch. I on Causality. II on Motion, III on the sense-faculties, (indriya), IV on the elements of existence (skandha) V, on the component elements (dhātu) of an individual, VI on Passions (rāga), VII on momentariness (saṁskṛta=trilakṣaṇī) VIII on Agent and Action (Karma-kāraka), IX on the unreality of the preceding moment (pūrva), X on the relation of fire and fuel, XI on the Infinite (pūrvāparakoṭi), XII on the unreality of all the phenomenal world (duḥkha=pañcopādānaskandha,) XIII on the unreality of all the forces (asaṁskāra) of life, XIV on the unreality of relations (saṁsarga), XV on the notion of Essentia (svabhāva), XVI on Bondage and Deliver-

the author of two short tracts dealing with the method of negative dialectics adopted by him. One of them, "The Refutation of contests" "vigrahavyāvartanī" is very often quoted.

Whether he is the author of numerous other works which go under his name, and whether he is the same personality as the celebrated metallurgist, chemist and alchemist Nāgārjuna is very doubtful[1]. His pupil and successor Āryadeva, a Ceylonese by birth, has composed an independent treatise about the same subject, also in 400 aphorisms, but following another, more systematic, arrangement.

About the date of both these authors there is till now no absolute certainty, but the II century A.D. is generally accepted as most probable. Although both were born in the South, the scene of their activity is Northern India, during the best time of Kushan empire.

---

ance, XVII on Karma and its results, XVIII on the doctrine of a Soul (ātman), XIX on the notions of origin and end (saṁbhāra-vibhava), XX on time, XXI on the notion of a totality of causes (sāmagrī), XXII on the reality of Buddha, XXIII on logical incongruity (viparyāsa), XXIV on the "Four Truths", XXV on Nirvāṇa, XXVI on the Twelve Stages (nidāna) in the development of an individual life, XXVII on false dogma (dṛṣṭi).

1 There is an old tradition according to which the authentical works of Nāgārjuna are six, but there is no agreement about how this number is composed. Generally admitted are (1) Mūla-madhyamaka-Śāstra, also called Prajñā-mūla, 8 celebrated men have commented upon it, Nāgārjuna himself, Buddhapālita, Bhavya, Candrakīrti, Devaśarmā, Guṇaśri, Guṇamati and Sthiramati. (2) Yukti-ṣaṣtikā, a very condensed statement of the theory, its composition, Wassilieff thinks, possibly preceded the compostion of the main work, (3) Śūnyatā-saptati, a short poem on Relativity with the author's own comment, (4) Vigraha-vyāvartanī, also with comment, a work on logic already mentioning the four pramāṇas of the Naiyāyikas, (5) Vaidalyasūtra and prakaraṇa, self defence of Nāgārjuna against the charge of perverting logic. The sixth is according to Bu-ston a work which is not translated Tha-snad-grub-na, "A vindication of empirical Reality." However, others reckon, instead of it, Akutobhaya, a comment upon the mūla-kārikās. But Wassiflieff remarks (in his "Review of the Mādhyamika literature" Mss musei As. Petrop.) that "the authenticity of this work was doubted even by the credulous Tibetans". Candrakīrti evidently held that Nāgārjuna did not write any comment upon the mūla-kārikās, cf. text, p. 25-6, but Avalokitavrata, commenting upon Prajñā-pradīpa calls it rān-ḥgrel. Besides these works the Bstan-hgyur contains (1) Mahāyāna-viṁśikā, in 20 verses, (2) Akṣara-śataka, in 3 lines and (3) Pratītya-samutpādahṛdaya, in 5 lines, renewed attempts to express with utmost shortness the main conception of a monistic (aikyam) motionless Universe. They probably are spurious.

After that, there was a break in the development of the Madhyamaka philosophy. During two centuries we hear of no prominent personalities and no works dealing with it. It seems as though it were partly fallen into oblivion. It is impossible otherwise to explain the total silence of Buddhaghoṣa about it.

During the next period, the golden age of Indian civilization, the age of the Gupta empire in Northern India, the brothers Asaṅga and Vasubandhu appear in the V century as the champions of a somewhat modified Monism which receives in their hands an idealistic interpretation.

The scene of the development of the Madhyamaka philosophy after that shifts to the South. We witness there in the VI century A.D. a powerful revival of the genuine, uncompromising Relativisim of Nāgārjuna. Contemporaneously with the pupils of Vasubandhu, Sthiramati and Dignāga, two very celebrated men, who were working, the one of Vallabhi in Surat, the other mainly in Orissa, two equally celebrated champions of the Madhyamaka system, the Masters (ācārya) Buddhapālita and Bhavya or Bhāvaviveka,[1] appear in the South. The Mahāyāna Monism becomes now definitely split into the idealistic school in the North, the Yogācāras, and the relativistic one in the South. The latter is again divided into the followers of Buddhapālita and the followers of Bhavya.

The condemnation of all logic for the cognition of the Absolute was final in the first of these schools, it admitted no bona-fide argument at all, but undertook it only to show hopeless inconsistency in whatever logical argument would be produced by its opponents. This school received the name of Mādhyamika-Prāsaṅgika. The other school, the followers of Bhavya thought it necessary to supplement the short rules of Nāgārjuna by independent (svatantra) arguments constructed in accordance with the rules of logic. This school received the name of Mādhyamika-Svātantrika. Bhavya is a very subtle logician. He perhaps, more than any other one, deserves to be compared with Zeno of Eleia. Some of his baffling sophisms made his name celebrated in the Buddhist world. His school had success and was more numerous than the school of Buddhapālita in the

1 Perhaps Bhavyaviveka=legs-ldan-hbyed.

beginning. But in the VII century A.D. the Master Candrakīrti appears as a mighty champion of the purely negative method of establishing Monism. He succeeds in driving Bhāvaviveka's school into the shade and finally settles that form of the Madhyamaka System which is now studied in all monastic schools of Tibet Mongolia where it is considered to represent the true philosophical basis of Mahāyāna Buddhism.

We can thus establish the following periods in the development of the philosophy of the Mahāyāna.

(1) I century A.D. the rise of Mahāyāna, ālayavijñāna and tathatā both admitted by Aśvaghoṣa.

(2) II century, the theory of Universal Relativity (śūnyatā) formulated by Nāgārjuna and Āryadeva.

(3) III and IV centuries a gap.

(4) V century, the idealistic interpretation of Asaṅga and Vasubandhu.

(5) VI century, a split between the idealistic and relativistic schools, Sthiramati and Dignāga as representing the first, Buddhapālita and Bhāvaviveka the second.

(6) VII century, final establishment of the Madhyamaka system in its extreme form by Candrakīrti.

We now give the translation of the first chapter of the treatise of Nāgārjuna with Candrakīrti's comment.[1] All the protagonists of the development just sketched together with some representatives of the Brahmanical systems will be here seen at work. From the rest of the work the chapter about Nirvāṇa has been chosen as an illustration of the method which is in turn applied to every philosophic conception.

In our translation we have endeavoured to avoid, as far as possible, literal renderings when they convey no clear meaning, in order to escape what M.A. Barth has called "traductions infideles a force d'etre literales." Sanskrit scientific works are not supposed to be read, but to be studied, their style is laconic and their technical terms suggestive of a wide

---

1 Candrakīrti has given to his comment the title of "The Clearworded" (prasanna-padā) probably not without some dose of irony, since, as Prof. Wassilieff attests, its extreme dialectical subtlety, especially in the first chapter, is equalled by no other work in the whole domain of Northern Buddhist literature.

connotation. Their translation, in order to be comprehensible should be, to a certain extent, an explanation. The literal rendering, when, needed is given in a footnote. The Sanskrit text has been edited by M.de la Vallee Poussin in the Bibliotheca Buddhica. The division into small sections has been introduced by the translator in order to facilitate a *vue d'ensemble.*

DEDICATION

The Perfect Buddha,
The foremost of all Teachers I salute.
He has proclaimed
The principle of Universal Relativity,
'Tis like blissful (Nirvāṇa),
Quiescence of Plurality.
There is nothing disappears,
Nor anything appears,
Nothing has an end.
Nor is there anything eternal,
Nothing is identical with itself,
Nor is there anything differentiated,
Nothing moves,
Neither hither nor thither.

CHAPTER I

EXAMINATION OF CAUSALITY

I

There absolutely are no things,
Nowhere and none, that arise (anew),
Neither out of themselves, nor out of non-self,
Nor out of both, nor at random.

II

Four can be the conditions
(Of everything produced),
Its cause, its object, its foregoing moment,
Its most decisive factor.

III

In these conditions we can find
No self-existence of the entities.
Where the self-existence is deficient,
Relational existence also lacks.

IV

No energies in causes,
Nor energies outside them.
No causes without energies,
Nor causes that possess them.

V

Let those facts be causes
With which coordinated other facts arise,
Non-causes will they be,
So far the other facts have not arisen.

VI

Neither non-Ens nor Ens
Can have a cause.
If non-Ens, whose the cause ?
If Ens, what for the cause ?

VII

Neither an Ens nor a non-Ens,
Nor any Ens-non-Ens.
No element is really turned out.
How can we then assume
The possibility of a producing cause?

VIII

A mental Ens is reckoned as an element,
Separately from its objective (counterpart).
Now, if it (begins) by having no objective-counterpart.
How can it get one afterwards?

IX

If (separate) elements do not exist,
Nor is it possible for them to disappear.
The moment which immediately precedes.
Is thus impossible. And if 'tis gone,
How can it be a cause?

X

If entities are relative,
They have no real existence.
The (formula) "this being, that appears"
Then loses every meaning.

XI

Neither in any of the single causes
Nor in all of them together
Does the (supposed) result reside.
How can you out of them extract
What in them never did exist?

XII

Supposing from these causes does appear
What never did exist in them,
Out of non-causes then
Why does not appear?

XIII

The result is cause-possessor,
But causes are not even self-possessors.
How can result be cause-possessor,
If of non-self-possessors it be a result ?

XIV

There is, therefore, no cause-possessor,
Nor is there an effect without a cause.
If altogether no effect arises,
(How can we then distinguish)
Between the causes and non-causes ?

Finished the Examination of Causality, the first chapter of the Treatise on Relativity.

CHAPTER XXV

EXAMINATION OF NIRVĀṆA

I

If everything is relative,
No (real) origination, no (real) annihilation,
How is Nirvāṇa, then conceived?
Through what deliverance, through what annihilation?

II

Should every thing be real in substance,
No (new) creation, no (new) destruction,
How should Nirvāṇa then be reached?
Through what deliverance, through what annihilation?

III

What neither is released, nor is it ever reached,
What neither is annihilation, nor is it eternality,
What never disappears, nor has it been created,
This is Nirvāna. It escapes precision.

IV

Nirvāṇa, first of all, is not a kind of Ens,
It would then have decay and death.
There altogether is no Ens.
Which is not subject to decay and death.

V

If Nirvāṇa is Ens,
It is produced by causes,
Nowhere and none the entity exists
Which would not be produced by causes.

VI

If Nirvāṇa is Ens,
How can it lack substratum,
There whatsoever is no Ens
Without any substratum.

VII

If Nirvāṇa is not an Ens,
Will it be then a non-Ens?
Wherever there is found no Ens,
There is neither a (corresponding) non-Ens.

VIII

Now, if Nirvāṇa is a non-Ens,
How can it then be independent?
For sure, an independent non-Ens
Is nowhere to be found.

IX

Coordinated here or caused are (separate) things,
We call this world Phenomenal;
But just the same is called Nirvāṇa,
When from causality abstracted.

X

The Buddha has declared
That Ens and non-Ens should both be rejected.
Neither as Ens nor as a non-Ens
Nirvāṇa therefore is conceived.

XI

If Nirvāṇa were both Ens and non-Ens,
Final Deliverance would be also both,
Reality and unreality together,
This never could be possible.

XII

If Nirvāṇa were both Ens and non-Ens,
Nirvāṇa could not be uncaused.
Indeed the Ens and the non-Ens
Are both dependent on causation.

XIII

How can Nirvāṇa represent
An Ens and a non-Ens together?
Nirvāṇa is indeed uncaused,
Both Ens and non-Ens are productions.

XIV

How can Nirvāṇa represent
(The place of Ens and non-Ens together—
As light and darkness in one spot)
They cannot be simultaneously present.

XV

If it were clear, indeed,
What an Ens means, and what a non-Ens,
We could then understand the doctrine.
About Nirvāṇa being neither Ens nor non-Ens.

XVI

If Nirvāṇa is neither Ens nor non-Ens,
No one can really understand
This doctrine which proclaims at once
Negation of them both together.

XVII

What is the Buddha after Nirvāṇa ?
Does he exist or does he not exist,
Or both, or neither ?
We never will conceive it.

XVIII

What is the Buddha then at life time ?
Does he exist, or does he not exist,
Or both, or neither ?
We never will conceive it.

XIX

There is no difference at all
Between Nirvāṇa and Saṁsāra,
There is no difference at all
Between Saṁsāra and Nirvāṇa.

XX

What makes the limit of Nirvāṇa
Is also then the limit of Saṁsāra.
Between the two we cannot find
The slightest shade of difference.

XXI

(Insoluble are antinomic) views
Regarding what exists beyond Nirvāṇa,
Regarding what the end of this world is,
Regarding its beginning.

XXII

Since everything is relative (we do not know),
What is finite and what is infinite,
What means finite and infinite at once,
What means negation of both issues ?

XXIII

What is identity, and what is difference ?
What is eternity what non-eternity,
What means eternity and non-eternity together,
What means negation of both issues ?

XXIV

The bliss consists in the cessation of all thought,
In the quiescence of Plurality.
No (separate) Reality was preached at all,
Nowhere and none by Buddha.

Finished the Examination of Nirvāṇa, the twenty-fifth Chapter of the Treatise on Relativity.

THE CLEARWORDED

A Comment Upon

NĀGĀRJUNA'S TREATISE ON RELATIVITY

by

CANDRAKĪRTI

THE CLEARWORDED

DEDICATION

To that Nāgārjuna I bow who has done away all recourse to the abode of Duality.[1] 2.3.

Who has emerged out of the ocean-like (all-embracing) Spirit of the Supreme Buddha.[2] 1.3.

---

1 The method of adopting a middle course (madhyamā pratipad) between the two opposite extremes from which the Mādhyamika school has received its name is differently applied in Hīnayāna e.g., S.N. III. 135. It is there a term designating the central conception of Hīnayāna, a middle course between "everything exists and nothing exists," meaning that a limited catalogue of ultimate elements (dharma) exists in interdependence (pratītya samutpāda). In Mahāyāna, it is synonymous with the central conception of the Mādhyamikas and means their idea of Relativity of Negativity (madhyamā pratipad-śūnyatā-pratītya-samutpāda)cp. XXIV 19. The ff. terms are declared by Candrakīrti p. 504.13 to be viśeṣa-saṁjñas i.e., different manners of expressing the same idea, anta-dvaya-rahitatva-sarvasvabhāvānutpatti-pratītya-samutpāda-śūnyatā- upādāya-prajñapti-madhyamā pratipad. As usual the first word of the work is significant, it refers to its main idea. The translation of madhyamaka-śāstra as The Doctrine of the Middle Path (Die Mittlere Lehre) is ambiguous since there are different middle paths.

2 Sambuddha-dhī-sāgara refers evidently to the doctrine of dharma-kāya.

Who mercifully has explained the deeper meaning of the treasury[1] of the religion, according to his own conceptions of it. 1.4.

Whose philosophic fire consumes even now the fuel of opposed systems and burns down the darkness in the heart of simple mankind. 1.5.

Whose words, containing imcomparable knowledge, (like) a host of arrows, completely destroy the army of our foes (and deliver us from the bonds of phenomenal) existence. 2.1.

Whose words assume the majesty of rule over the denizens of all the three spheres of existence[2], the Buddhist converts and the gods. 2.2.

Having made my salutation to that Nāgārjuna, I am proposing to write an explanation of his aphorism in clear sentences containing the right explanation unobscured by the fires of dialectics.[3]

1 Read kośasya with the Tib.

2 i.e.—the world of carnal desire (kāma-dhātu), the heavens of ethereal beings (rūpa-dhātu) and the heavens of pure spirits (arūpa-dhātu).

3 This is a jeer at Bhāvaviveka who is called a champion of logic (tārkika). It does not mean that dialectical subtleties will be avoided, but that all arguments will be indirect. The word tarkānala evidently alludes to Tarkajvāla the title of Bhāvaviveka's work.

CHAPTER FIRST

EXAMINATION OF CAUSALITY

I. PRELIMINARY

The treatise which will be here expounded is that which begins with the statement "there is neither a causa materialis, nor a causa efficiens, nor are the things of the Universe a product of the combination of both these causes."[1] The question now arises how does this doctrine affect (us), what is its subject matter and what its aim. The connection of the treatise with us[2] is the following one. (In a previous work), "Introduction to the Madhyamaka System"[3], we have made it clear that in order to attain the supreme knowledge of the Buddha, the first step to be taken is an initial vow of devoting oneself to the Final Deliverance of all living creatures, (this vow harmonising with a monistic view of the Universe, and inspired by a feeling of Great Commiseration.)[4] Our revered Master Nāgārjuna was himself wholly equipped with the (true) unflinching method of (our monistic system revealed in the predication about) the "Climax of Wisdom"[5], and he graciously has condescended to lay it down in a treatise for the enlightenment of others.

(Indeed a philosophic treatise should contain a doctrine of Salvation, it then "rules and it saves"). "It rules over all our enemies, our passions. It saves us from the misery and from

---

1 Lit., p. 2.5. "not from self, not from other, not from both". cp. infra, p. 93.

2 'Sambandha' discussed at the beginning of every scientific work means usually its relation to the subject matter, Nyāya-bindu, p. 2.15 (B.B.) Here it refers to the importance of the work for the Salvation of mankind.

3 Mādhyamika-avatāra. The Tib. transl. ed by de la Vallee Poussin in B.B. IX and partly translated in the Mus on 1907, 1910 and 1911.

4 The Mahāyānistic Great Commiseration (mahākaruṇā) differs from the Hīnayānistic one; it agrees with monism. This means that the Mahāyānist strives for the weal of all living beings, cp. Suzuki Mahāyāna. p. 292 ff. Madhy. av. p. 6.9 ff. The Tibetans make a distinction between the Mahāyānistic conception thugs-rje-chen-po and the Hīnayānistic one, snin-rje-chen-po; in Sanskrit the same word is used.

5 prajñā-pāramitā; one of its synonyms is śūnyatā.

phenomenal existence (altogether). Those two advantages are not to be found in other philosophic doctrines".

(Therefore the teaching of Nāgārjuna should appeal to every one).

(What is the subject matter)

The master himself (discloses it in his initial prayer). He hints at the idea which will be developed during the whole treatise and at its aim. He tries to impress upon us that it will be a grand and fundamental treatise,[1] because it will present this idea in a thorough[2] and unflinching manner. Since this central idea of the whole treatise cannot be separated from the Mahāyānist's conception of the Buddha.,[3] Nāgārjuna in making his initial salutation to him, the Supreme Teacher, alludes to the cause that induced him to compose this treatise and says :

> (Buddha has proclaimed) the monistic Principle of Relativity[4], the principle that nothing in the Universe can disappear, nor can anything new arise, nothing has an end, nor is there anything differentiated in itself, there is no motion, neither towards us, nor from us, etc. etc. everything is relative.

The subject matter, the central idea of the treatise is the monistic principle of Relativity characterised by these eight negative characteristics, nothing disappears, etc. The aim of the treatise is indicated in the same salutation. It is Final Deliverance, Nirvāṇa, which is characterised as the bliss of Quiescence of every Plurality.[5]

The salutation itself is expressed by the words "I praise this highest of all Teachers".

---

1 māhātmyam sc. śāstrasya. The ideal scientific work for India is the Grammar of Pāṇini with the Mahābhāṣya of Patañjali. A mahāśāstra is a śāstra, possessing māhātmya i.e. treating the subject with the thoroughness exhibited by both these authors in their great work.

2 sam-prakāśana—samyak prakāśana.

3 Buddha's Cosmical Body dharma-kāya, is the unique transcendental essence of the Universe and it is synonymous with śūnyatā, cp. de la V. P. the three Bodies, J.R.A.S., p. 952.

4 pratītya-samutpāda-śūnyatā-antadvaya-rahitatva.

5 On Mahāyānistic Nirvāṇa see above and Suzuki, op. cit. p.339. ff. m S. Schayer, Die Mahayanistichen Erlohsungslehren (Munchen 1921).

This is first of all, the general meaning of the first two stanzas. We are now going on to give in detail the meaning of every word.

"To disappear" means to be evanescent. The split (of all existence into discrete) point-instants is here meant.

(Nothing new can arise), to "arise" means cutting off the stream of (consecutive point-instants)[1].

"Eternal" means perpetual, existing, through all times.

(Non-identical) Being identical means not being separate, not being discrete.

(Non-differentiated) Differentiated means being different, i.e. discrete.

"Motion hither", means the motion of distant objects into a near remote place.

II. THE MEANING OF PRATĪTYA SAMUTPĀDA ACCORDING TO THE AUTHOR

The first part of the term consists of the gerund of the root 'i' and the preposition 'prati'. The root 'i' means motion, the preposition 'prati' means 'reaching'. But the preposition (when added to a verbal root) modifies its meaning. It has been said that "the meaning of the verbal root is changed by the preposition as if it were violently dragged into another place just as the sweet waters of the Ganges (change their savour when reaching) the waters of the ocean". Therefore the word pratītya, being a gerund, means "reaching" in the sense of being dependent (or relative). The word samutpāda means appearance, manifestation. It comes from the verbal root 'pad' which with the preposition 'samut' has this meaning. Thus the term pratītya-samutpāda (in our system) conveys the idea of a manifestation of (separate) entities as relative to their causes and conditions.[2]

---

1 prabandha-kṣaṇa-santāna.

2 hetu-pratyaya-apekṣa.

III. THE MEANING OF THIS TERM IN HĪNAYĀNA

Others, (Śrīlābha and other Hīnayānists),[1] maintain that pratītya-samutpāda means (appearance and immediate) disappearance of everything. The verb 'i' means to go, to disappear; 'itya' is the participle, meaning "fit to disappear." The preposition 'prati' generalises. 'Pratītya' is thus (not a gerund), but a derivative noun (meaning that everything is momentary). The evanescent momentary things appear—that is their explanation.

IV. THE HĪNAYĀNIST INTERPRETATION REJECTED

This interpretation fits very well such passages of the Scripture as the following one, "O Brethren, I will teach you the Dependent Origination (of everything). Those who will get an insight into it, will have grasped the teaching of the Buddha, etc". The sense of generalisation and the suggested grammatical composition of the term can be accounted for. But in other passages there is altogether no generalisation,[2] because a single particular case is directly referred to e.g., in the following words, "visual consciousness appears when co-ordinated with the faculty of vision and a patch of colour". In this expression "in co-ordination with the faculty of vision" the word "in co-ordina-

---

1 In the sūtras of the Hīnayāna the term applied to the doctrine about the twelve consecutive degrees in the development of an individual life (sc. of the skandhas), from prenatal forces saṁskāra up to the continuation of life, after death (jāti). But this, according to the 'abhidharma', is only a special case of the general law of inter-dependence as a synonym of all saṁskṛta-dharmas, cp. my Central Conception p. 28. The formula of this interdependence "this being, that becomes, from this arises that" has then been criticised, because the generalized formula, since it refers to all elements, to those also that exist simultaneously, the meaning of a consecution will not be quite correct. Therefore Śrīlābha proposed his interpretation, according to which the first part of the term is a participle, not a gerund and does not imply consecution, but simultaneity and evanescence. Cp. Ab. Kośa-bhāṣya, and III. 28. In this treatise pratītya-samutpāda is treated in the first chapter, the 12 nidānas quite separately in the 26th.

2 This is the same criticism which is already mentioned by Vasubandhu, op. cit. ad III. 29.

tion" takes into account the one single flash[1] of consciousness, produced also from one single moment of the faculty of vision. There is no generalisation.

But the interpretation which we propose applies in both cases. The meaning of relativity applies when the word 'pratītya' does not refer to a single case. It then means relative existence in general, origination relatively to something else. It also can be applied when a particular single occasion is referred to, for in that case we interpret it as meaning "with reference to the faculty of vision, in co-ordination with this faculty, having regard for this faculty,—visual consciousness appears".

If we take the word 'itya' as a derivative adjective, then the above sentence "visual consciousness arises in co-ordination with the faculty of vision and some colours" will altogether change its meaning. This word, if not a gerund and when not the first part of a compound, must appear in its inflected form (pratītyam).[2] The meaning of the sentence would then be the following one, "all visual consciousness is evanescent (pratītyam) in regard to the faculty of vision and the colours"[3]. This is impossible, therefore it must be taken as a gerund and indeclinable. We will then get for the whole term the meaning of dependent origination, or relative, unreal existence.

V. THE OPINION OF BHĀVAVIVEKA

Now, another author, Bhāvaviveka, dealing with this topic begins by quoting opposed opinions and then goes on to refute them. He quotes in the following way: "One party The Mahāyānist Buddhapālita, explains the term 'pratītya-samutpāda' as meaning "manifestation, dependent on every cause", or relative existence". They assume that the preposition 'prati' has a generalising sense, the verbal root 'i' the sense of relativity, the word samutpāda the sense of existence or origination. Another party the Hīnayānist Śrīlābha, maintains that 'pratītyasamutpāda' means the appearance of all immediately disappearing things".[4]

1 eka-vijñānotpatti.
2 pratītya-samutpādaḥ pratītyasya (kṣaṇikasya) samutpādaḥ.
3 Lit. "eye-evanescent sensation and colours".
4 Lit. p. 7. 6-8. 1 "But one who quotes the explanation of others thus,

First of all, we notice here a remarkable incapacity of quoting foreign opinions with anything like precision. How is that? Because that party which interprets the word 'pratītya' as indicating relativity, does not give to the preposition 'prati' a generalising sense, nor does it give to the verb 'i' by itself, the meaning of being relative. It on the contrary explains the preposition 'prati' as meaning relativity, and then takes the whole composite word 'pratītya' as meaning likewise relativity.[1]

Now, if we take pratītya-samutpāda as meaning "relative existence" then it will cover both cases, where the generalised meaning is wanted and where a single case is meant. When it takes into account all possible things then the generalised meaning is applied in the following way, "in every case, dependent upon a corresponding complex of causes and conditions, something exists, i.e. it arises, in coordination with them".[2] But when a single thing is referred to, then there is no need for applying the generalising meaning, we then understand it to mean that, e.g. some visual consciousness has arisen, in coordination with some momentary flash of the faculty of vision and some colour. But the Master Bhāvaviveka maintaining that we assume generalisation in all cases has betrayed his incompetence to quote the opinion which he combats.

VI. BHĀVAVIVEKA'S CRITICISM OF BUDDHAPĀLITA'S COMMENT

The following criticism of our definition by Bhāvaviveka is likewise unfounded. He thinks that our interpretation of the sentence "visual consciousness arises when co-ordinated with the sense of vision and some colour" is wrong, because we have

---

since the preposition means generalisation, it means 'reaching' and the word *samutpāda* means 'becoming', with reference to such and such cause reaching, becoming, thus one party; in every case origination of evanescent things is pratītya-samutpāda, thus the other party......".

1 But they never have given to the root the meaning of *prāpti* as imputed. p. 7-6.

2 This is also mentioned by Vasubandhu loco. cit. and Yaśomitra, as the interpretation of Śrīlābha. The interpretation pratītya-prāpya is also criticised in the Ab. Kośaḥ. ad III. 20, but on different grounds. It is supposed to suggest a consecution of elements, and to leave out of account the interdependence of simultaneously existing elements.

expressed this inter-dependence by the word "reaching", pratītya-prāpya, one thing springs up when "reaching" the other. "There are here (says he) no two things 'reaching one another'. We cannot understand this criticism. What is the reason adduced? He says that if one thing is not attained, not "reached", how is the other to originate? There is no argument. It is mere begging the question.[1] But perhaps his real argument is the following one. Consciousness being mental and the sense of vision physical, the first cannot be reached by the second. Experience teaches that only material things can be reached by the sense of vision. But this is a trivial objection. The term reaching is used in Scripture when the attaining of spiritual aims is in question, e.g., "this recluse has reached the goal". Others reject the criticism upon the score that reaching is synonymous with being dependent. Our common Master Nāgārjuna has himself used it in this sense (in his Yukti-ṣaṣṭikā) "if something springs up after having reached this or that, (i.e., if something is dependent upon this and that), it is not really produced *by these conditions*".

VII. THE DEFINITION OF THE TERM BY BHĀVAVIVEKA

As to the opinion pleaded by Bhāvaviveka himself it is also not quite correct. Indeed he gives the term pratītya-samutpāda the meaning of "of being relative to something else" in the sense of a disjunctive judgment), "if this is, that appears" "because this has appeared, that will appear[2]. Although the word "dependent origination" consists of two words, it is not right to suppose that each refers to a different object[3]. The parts are only mentioned with a view to etymological explanation.

1 Lit. p. 9.10.9.1. "And this is wrong on the part of Bhāvaviveka. He says, and moreover it is not right to maintain that in the relation to reaching the eye and the colours, visual sensation arises, because two things (reaching one another are here) impossible." Just as the incriminated fault is nonsense. Why ; Because how is it that one thing will arise when the other is not attained, not reached.? these words of Bh. are a bare postulate without any argument". On p. 9.1 read with the Mss. Katham anava (ga) te 'prāpte sambhavaḥ', and on p. 8.10 preferably etaccayuktam.

2 Bhāvaviveka here partly returns to the interpretation already contained in the Hīnayāna sūtras (e.g. M.N. III 63), but of course its meaning is quite changed. Formerly it referred to real elements (dharmas), now it means śūnyatā, or unreal dharmas—

3 The difficulty arising from the interpretation of the term as involving a disjunctive sentence is also mentioned by Vasubandhu, op. cit. ad III 28.

Bhāvaviveka further says, "pratītya-samutpāda" is thus named without any regard to its being composed of two words, we can take it as a conventional expression for Relativity just as the expression "the forest ornament" is used to designate something utterly useless, without any connection either with forest or with ornament.

This also misses the mark, since our Master admits the term to have a meaning which harmonises with the meaning of its parts. Indeed he says, "whatsoever appears as relative to this and that is not really existent".

At last Bhāvaviveka explains the term to mean (mere Relativity), "this being, that becomes, e.g. as far as there is something short, there is also something long". Does he not admit exactly (not independently, but) as far as it is coordinated to the short, as relative to the short, as dependent upon the short. Thus Bhāvaviveka rejects with one hand what he accepts with the other. This is not right, but we will not insist upon this point.

VIII. THE PRINCIPLE OF RELATIVITY THE LAW OF ALL PLURALISTIC EXISTENCE

Thus it is that Buddha wished to put in a strong light[1] (the principle of Relativity), i.e. the fact that entities are produced only in the sense of being co-ordinated.[2] He, therefore, maintains that nothing is produced at random, neither from a unique cause, nor from a variety of causes; he denies that they are identical with their causes, that they are different from them, or that they are both (partly identical and partly non-identical). By this negative method he discloses the true relative character of all the relative entities of everyday life.[3] This is the relative existence or dependent origination, because nothing really new is produced. From the transcendentalist's point of view, it is a

1 paridīpayata-parito dīpayata.

2 hetu-pratyaya-apekṣa.

3 pratītya-samutpāda is here synonymous with śūnyatā-anta dvaya-rahitatva—advaita, and although it is the contrary of saṁvṛtti, it is here called saṁvṛttaḥ pratītya-samut-pādaḥ meaning, that pratītya-samutpannatva or advaita or śūnyatā is the real condition which is covered or hidden behind the phenomenal world, the saṁvṛtti. (It is a karmasādhana i.e., saṁvṛyate etad iti saṁvṛta, not a karaṇa-sādhana, i.e. not saṁvṛiyate anena.)

condition where nothing disappears, nor something new appears etc., and in which there is no motion.[1] It is a condition characterised by the eight above mentioned characteristics, nothing disappears etc.[2] The whole of this treatise is intended by its author to prove that the condition of interdependence or the principle of Relativity does not allow for something in the Universe to disappear, nor for something new to appear.

The principle of Relativity being the central law of all existence can be characterised by an infinite number of finite characteristics,[3] but only eight have been selected, because they are predominant in the sense of having given opportunities for discussion.

---

1 The ārya or ārya-pudgala is the Buddhist Saint who has entered the path of Salvation, has become srota-āpanna, has reached insight (dṛṣṭi-mārga) of reality as it reveals itself to the philosopher. In Hīnayāna, it is the man who has acquired the intellectual habit of seeing everywhere only separate, discrete, evanescent elements (dharmatā-anātma). He has got rid of the impression of stability which the world produces upon the ordinary man. In Mahāyāna, as is seen from this passage, it is the man who has acquired a monistic view of the Universe, he has cognised the pratītya-samutpāda as śūnyatā-dharma-nairātmya. From the phrasing of this and many other passages, it clearly appears that the Mahāyānistic Saint, the ārya and the Bodhisattva, possesses in addition to his moral achievement his Mahāyānistic bodhi-citta-utpāda, the practice of the pāramitās, the attainment of bhūmis and the Mahāyānistic Great Commiseration, as a foundation of all this, a monistic view of the Universe, acquired by yogi-pratyakṣa. It constitutes the omniscience, sarvajñatā, of the Bodhisattva which together with the sarva-ākāra-jñatā of the Buddha is the main idea of the abhisamaya or prajñapāramitā in Aryasanga's interpretation. This sarvajñatā is accordingly very different from our conception of Omniscience. We find a very interesting exposition of these topics in Vācaspati Miśra's Nyāyakaṇikā, the sarvajña-vāda begins p.110-16 (Reprint from the Pandit), the Buddhist yogipratyakṣa p., 147 ff the brahmanical yogiabhimata-sarvajña, refutation sva-matena Naiyāyika-abhimata-yogi-pratyakṣa.

2 Lit. p. 10.12.11.2 "By this negation the concealed essence of the covered entities is disclosed as it exists. And now just this concealed pratītya-samutpāda is characterised by eight characteristics, non-disappearance etc., Since, as it has not been produced in its own essence, there is in it with reference to the ārya, no disappearance, up to "there is no motion out."

3 Cp. Spinoza's idea that the essentia Dei is equal to infinite number of finite attributes or modes. Here we have exactly the same thought expressed by the Indian Monist, viz. (Buddha-dharma-kāyasys-śūnyatāyāḥ) anantaviśeṣna-sambhave...

It is also called Nirvāṇa, the Quiescence or equalisation of all plurality, because when it is critically realised[1] there is for the philosopher[2] absolutely no differentiation of existence to which our words[3] and concepts could be applied. That very essence of Relativity is called Nirvāṇa the Quiescence of Plurality, for which there are no words.

Thoughts and feelings[4] do not arise in this (undifferentiated whole), there is no subject and no object of knowledge, there is consequently no turmoil like birth, old age and death, there is eternal bliss.[5]

Since the principle of Dependent Origination as it is here defined (as meaning the Relativity of existence) represents the direct object of the process of instruction, it is in the dedicatory verses alluded to as the object of Buddha's teaching:—

The perfect Buddha,
The foremost of all Teachers I salute,
He has proclaimed
The principle of (Universal) Relativity.
'This like blissful Nirvāṇa,
Quiescence of Plurality.
There nothing disappears,
Nor anything appears,
Nothing has an end,
Nor is anything eternal,
Nothing is identical (with itself),
Nor is there anything differentiated,
Nothing moves,
Neither hither, nor thither.

---

1 yathāvasthita...darśana.

2 āryāṇām, p. 90, no 4.

3 prapañco vākca. M. vr, p. 373-9 the reality is niṣprapañca-anirvacanīya, but of course, not only words, concepts are also meant.

4 citta-caittāh.

5 This idea of bliss as equivalent to absence of suffering is the same as in the Nyāya system, p. 54 ff. It coincides with the Vedānta idea by the conception of all plurality-being merged in a unique all-embracing substance. It is also a spiritual substance because dharma-kāya is spiritual (jñāna). According to Deussen, System des Vedānta, p. 228-9 ānanda with Śaṅkara also means Freiheit von biden, cp. ibid. p.150. Nevertheless the Buddhists would probably not characterise their śūnyatā as ānanda which carries a flavour of worldliness.

Buddha alone has rightly taught the doctrine of Relativity, because he has conceived it in the manner here described. Our Master Nāgārjuna having, realised that tall divergent doctrines are nothing but foolish talk (as compared with this doctrine of Buddha) gives expression to his deep feeling of devotion and praises the Buddha by inserting the characteristic. He is the foremost of all Teachers.

IX. CAUSALITY DENIED

In such a Universe nothing can disappear. The denial of extinction comes first. This is to illustrate the fact that it is not in every respect established that every thing must first appear and then disappear. Indeed it will be stated below:—

If birth comes first,
Decay and death comes later,
We will then have a birth
Without decay and death,
And what is born will be immortal.

Therefore there is no hard and fast rule that everything must first appear and then disappear. The author now intends to explain the principle of that Relativity which implies the denial of extinction and other characteristics. But he thinks it more convenient to begin with the denial of origination, i.e. of causality, because the denial of extinction etc. will become after that an easy task.

Causation which is imagined in other systems as a real production appears either as a new manifestation of the same continuant stuff, or as an influence of separate factors, or as the result of both a continuant stuff and separate factors, or as proceeding at random without any regulation. The author decides that one of these theories is in the right.

Never at all nowhere and none
Are the things that arise
Out of self, of non-self, or both,
Or at random

(The meaning of the words is here the following one, "At all" means at any time, "Somewhere" means the place, it is equivalent to 'in what-ever-place', "something" means the objects situated on the place, it is equivalent to some things. All this is denied—never, nowhere, and none. The meaning is the following one. Never, nowhere and nothing is found which is produced out of its own self. And in the same way the three next predicates, out of non-self, out of both, without a cause must be interpreted.

It can be objected that an undesirable consequence[1] will follow, (if we lay stress upon the negation and maintain that entities do) not at all arise out of themselves. It will follow that they arise out of some non-self, (i.e. out of the factors separate from them). No, this will not follow, since only a simple negation is expressed,[2] (without any implied affirmation of the contrary). Production out of something separate will likewise be denied.

X. IDENTITY OF CAUSE AND EFFECT DENIED

The argument against self-origination, (i.e. against the preexistence of the effect in its material cause) must be constructed upon the same lines which we have sketched in our "Introduction to the Madhyamaka system".

We find there the following statement.[3]

Thus,

No real advantage (will accrue)
If something will be born (that already exists).
If (something really) does exist,
Its own repeated birth is quite a nonsense.

The Master Buddhapālita makes the following comment. "Entities do not arise out of their own self, since each origination would serve no purpose, and because the quite absurd consequence[4] would follow that everything is eternally arising. Indeed if things exist, there is no need to produce them once more, and supposing an existing thing could be (once more) produced, never would it be non-nascent".

---

1 prasaṅga.
2 prasajya-pratiṣedha.
3 M. av. (B.B.) IX. vi. 8.
4 atiprasaṅga-

XI. BHĀVAVIVEKA ASSAILS THE COMMENT OF BUDDHAPĀLITA

Some philosophers viz. Bhāvaviveka have raised objections against this interpretation of Buddhapālita. His comment, (they maintain) misses the mark, because,

(1) neither a reason nor an example is given,

(2) objections are left unanswered,

(3) it is a mere deduction *ad absurdum*,[1] (consequently) in contrast (with the denial) expressed, a contra-thesis and a contra-reason will emerge (by implication). It will then follow that entities are produced out of something essentially separate from them, since this will serve a purpose, and since this will prevent eternal new production of the same already existing thing.[2]

XII. THE FIRST OBJECTION OF BHĀVAVIVEKA ANSWERED

We consider all this attack to be ill founded. For what reason? Regarding the first objection, viz. that no independent reason and no example are given, we answer that this is not to the point. Why, because the position is the following one. An opposing party (the Sāṅkhya System) advocates the identity of cause and effect,[3] and is invited to explain, what may be the use of causation in regard to something already existent. In saying that the self is the cause, you seemingly maintain that one's own self is once more produced. Now, we do not understand the meaning of a new production of what already exists. Moreover, we see the danger of an infinite regress. The newly produced thing will be as long as it exists again and again produced and so on *ad infinitum*.[4]

---

1 prasaṅga-vākya.

2 Lit., p. 15. 1-2. "Through an obversion of the subject stated, when the contrary subject, as a predicate and its appurtenance, will emerge, it will be a contradiction with the adopted principle, viz. entities have arisen from something extraneous, since their birth is useful and since their birth shall have an end," (sādhyapakṣa; taddharma-pakṣa-dharma, vyakti-arthāpatti, kṛtāntasiddhānta.)

3 (svata utpattiḥ, satkāryam.)

4 It would be similar to the Hīnayānist and Yogācāras' view 'sarvaṁ kṣaṇikam'.

But you, (the Sāṅkhya) do not really mean to maintain that an existing thing is once more produced, neither do you admit an infinite series[1] of self-productions. It follows that your theory of a substantial identity between cause and effect is absurd[2] and, expressed as it is, it runs against your own intentions.

Now, (you think) that if (the Sāṅkhya) our opponent, is assailed merely in this way, he will not yield (to our onslaught), and an (other) reason with example is needed in order to make it (more) efficacious. But if you have detected a self-contradiction (in the argument of your) opponent[3] and he nevertheless persists (in his errors) neither will he be reduced to silence by new arguments and examples, for his obstinacy is due to his impudence and it is not worth our while to carry on a disputation with a fool.

The Master, Bhāvaviveka betrays indeed a certain bias for syllogistic reasoning. He would like a syllogism to be introduced at the wrong place. But according to the Mādhyamika method of dialectics an independent argument is never needed. This method consists in producing a contrathesis and then balancing two conflicting views without admitting either of them. It has been said by Āryadeva,

If I neither admit a thing's reality,
Nor unreality, nor both (at once),
Then, to confute me
A long time will be needed.[4]

In the "Repudiation of Conflicts", (the manual of Nāgārjuna), it is likewise stated,

When I have theses (of my own to prove),
I can commit mistakes just for the sake (of proving)
But I have none, I cannot be accused
(Of being inconsistent).
If I did (really) cognise some (separate) things,

1 anavasthā.

2 nirupapattika.

3 The Sāṅkhya admits both utpāda and svata, i.e., he admits that *tad eva utpadyate*, but he does not wish it to be an absolute identity, thus he is in conflict with himself, there is sva-upagamavirodha.

4 Lit. p.16. 4.5. "who has no thesis, is, is-not is is-not, his confutation even long it is impossible to tell" Cp. Catuḥśataka, XVI. 25.

I could then make an affirmation or a denial
Upon the basis of these things perceived or (inferred)[1]
But these (separate) things do not exist for me.[2]
Therefore I cannot be assailed on such a basis.

XIII. THE SECOND POINT OF BHĀVAVIVEKA VIZ. THAT THE ANSWER OF THE SĀṄKHYA IS LEFT UNNOTICED BY BUDDHAPĀLITA, REJECTED

Thus it is that since the Mādhyamika is not obliged to have an argument of his own in which he believes, why do you require Buddhapālita to confute the Sāṅkhya by an independent argument, like the one produced by yourself, viz. that "the mind and the sense faculties[3] are not necessarily[4] identical with their cause? The Sāṅkhya, indeed, has responded to this argument in the following way.

"What is the meaning of your argument? Do you deny an identity between cause and effect because an effect is really a new manifestation of the same matter, or because you deny the identity of matter itself?[5] If it is the first, then you bring against us a point which we never doubted, (we agree that the effect is a new manifestation of a continuant stuff). If it is the second, then it is you, Buddhapālita, who are contradicting yourself,[6]

---

1 Adi. in 16-10 refers to probably anumāna.

2 i.e., for the Monist.

3 adhyātmika-āyatana are the six subjective bases of our cognitions. i.e., for sense faculties and pure, undifferentiated consciousness (vijñāna), cp. My Central Conception. p. 7. All mental phenomena are, according to the Sāṅkhya System, essentially physical, products of the evolution of Matter and, in this sense, they are identical with their cause or, as this is here expressed, produced out of their own self, out of the same substance. Bhāvaviveka sets forth against this theory a regular syllogism, which will be analysed by Candrakīrti in the sequel, p. 25.

4 From the Tib. nes-te, cp. M. vr, p. 17.4.

5 Lit. p. 17.1., 18.1 "What is here the meaning of the thesis? It is 'from self' as containing the result of 'from self' as being the cause. If (from the self) as being the cause it is contradiction, since everything having origination originates as being necessarily existent as a cause".

6 Buddhapālita first accuses the Sāṅkhya of self-contradiction by imputing to him the idea that an already existing thing is once more produced, although it already exists. The Sāṅkhya answers by accusing Buddhapālita of self-contradiction on the score that a Monist must admit the identity of cause and effect. The Vedānta, indeed, admits satkārya-vāda.

not I, because even you, the Monist, must agree that every product necessarily preexists in its cause.[1]

(To this retort of the Sāṅkhya, Bhāvaviveka requires that Buddhapālita should give a reply). But how can we (Mādhyamikas who do not believe in logic altogether) produce an argument[2] like the one produced by Bhāvaviveka about the transcendental reality of all mental phenomena ? This argument the Sāṅkhya could indeed declare either trivial, because he never doubted it, or self contradicting because it really implies the identity of cause and effect. Why should we bother about imputed irrelevance or this imputed self-contradiction ? Therefore, since these accusations of the opponent are absolutely out

1 The Sāṅkhya maintains that, since Matter is eternal everything is identical with it as far as it is an impermanent manifestation of this permanent Matter. He does not deny the evolution of this Matter into different forms. The objection of Buddhapālita is unfair, because the Sāṅkhya never denied the variety of the manifestations. If *nasvataḥ=na-Kāraṇātmakaṃ* this will contradict the principle of *satkāryavāda*, =therefore, na svataḥ if na kāryātmakam, the Sāṅkhya will agree, he will say sarvam kāraṇātmakaṃ vidyate, kāryātmakam (kāryam-āvirbhāvaḥ) na vidyate, kāraṇe nāsti vivādaḥ, kāraṇaṁ sat, kārye tu mahān vivādaḥ. The Vaiśeṣika maintains that in the effect even the stuff is different, although related by samavāyi-kāraṇa. The Hīnayānist Buddhist deniest he existence of a continual stuff altogether. The Mādhyamika's intention is to show the hopeless mutual contradictions of all these views and thus indirectly to establish Monism. By leaving the main issue, the difference between origination and manifestation, intentionally in the dark, by taking the expressions svata utpādaḥ "origination out of one's own self," satkārya "preexistence of the result" literally Buddhapālita secures a dialectical triumph. Bhāvaviveka wishes to improve the position of the Mādhyamika by producing a sound argument.

2 This argument of Bhāvaviveka is given below, text, p. 26.1. For the Sāṅkhya, all mental phenomena and the intellect are of a physical nature, but an eternal, unchanging, motionless Spiritual Principle is reflected in them. Bhāvaviveka, as a monist, assimilates all mental phenomena, from the transcendental point of view, to this eternal unique principle. The Sāṅkhya replies that this is not a refutation, but a corroboration of an identity between cause and effect, and that it is a self-contradiction, since it at the same time denies and accepts this identity. For Buddhapālita, it is enough to point to the contradiction between utpāda and vidyamānatva, he, from his transcendental point of view, neither believes in the one, nor in the other. Cp. p. 105. Art. XVIII.

of place, it was not incumbent upon our revered Buddhapālita to refute them[1].

XIV. THE MĀDHYAMIKA METHOD EXPLAINED

But perhaps we must understand Bhāvaviveka to mean the following thing. Since the Mādhyamika does not admit any valid reason, thesis or example, and cannot produce any independent argument, let us concede that he is incapable of proving what he would like to prove, viz. that there is no real causation out of the same stuff. We also admit that it is impossible for him to combat the tenet of the opponent by an argument based upon facts the reality of which both parties admit.

However in accusing your opponent of contradiction, you must yourself take your stand upon an argument which, in your own opinion[2], would be free of those logical errors to which a thesis, a reason or an example is liable. But Buddhapālita has given no reason and no examples, neither has he shown his capacity of avoiding the logical errors pointed out by the Sāṅkhya. Therefore, the accusation that he has proved nothing by his deduction *ad absurdum* stands.

To this we answer : this is not right. Why ? Because of the following considerations. Certainly, when some one is vindicating an assertion, he is desirous to convince other people, just as he is convinced himself. He must prove to his opponent the validity of that very argument by which he himself has arrived at the right conclusion.

It is indeed a general rule that the opponent should be at length induced to agree with that very line of argument which the respondent himself has set forth in order to prove his own

1 Lit. 18. 1-3. "How can we have a reason, because they exist,—a reason that would either be a proof of the proved or a contradiction, for the refutation of whose proving the proved or its contradictory character we should take pains ? Therefore, since he is quite unaffected by the accusations pronounced by the opponent, revered Buddhapālita is not obliged to expatiate upon their refutation. If we accept the Sanskrit, not the Tibetan, text of the last sentence sc. omitting na and the a of prasaṅga, it will mean, "therefore revered Buddhapālita is obliged to expatiate upon a refutation of them only when he himself is affected by the accusations of the opponent".

2 svataḥ eva.

thesis. But the case of the Mādhyamika is quite different. He does not vindicate any assertion in order to convince his opponent. He has no *bona fide* reasons and examples of which he himself is convinced. He sets forth a thesis of his own and undertakes to prove it only so far as it runs parallel and destroys the argument of his opponent.

He thus brings assertions which cannot be proved.[1] He is in conflict even with himself. He certainly cannot convince his opponent of (this imagined thesis).

But can there be a more eloquent refutation of an opponent than the proof that he is not capable of establishing his own thesis? Is there really any necessity to produce new counter arguments?[2]

XV. BUDDHAPĀLITA'S COMMENT VINDICATED FROM THE STANDPOINT OF FORMAL LOGIC

However if you insist that this must be necessarily done and require that the contradiction in the tenet of the opponent should be disclosed by an independent argument, we maintain that Buddhapālita has done it. If you ask, how is that? We answer: he has said,

Entities do not arise out of themselves,

Because such origination would serve no purpose,

Here the word "such" refers to a new origination of something by itself already existing.

The following words contain a comment upon this short statement.[3] "If something already exists in its own real individuality, it does not need to be produced once more." This sentence points to the example,[4] i.e., an analogous case admitted by the opponent where both the reason and the predicate coexist

1 nirupapattika-pakṣa.

2 anumāna-bādha.

3 read. p. 203. tasya grahṇaka-vākyasya. What a grahaṇaka vākyam is appears clearly from Tātparyaṭīkā, p. 145. 16 and an overwhelming multitude of similar phrasing in all Nyāya literature. The argument is first stated laconically. (grahaṇaka) and then developed (vivaraṇa).

4 The example is always a very important part of the Indian syllogism, parārthānumāna. It points to the particular facts on which the general rule or the major premise is established. Apart from such formal syllogism, Indian logic knows a simple inference from one particular to another one, svārthānumāna, it is a simple inference by analogy which is considered as representing the essence of thought or of synthesis in general.

e.g., an existing jar. The reason is indicated by the words "existing in its own individuality", and the predicate is indicated by the words "because such origination would serve no purpose." We thus shall have the following regular syllogism—

Thesis: An entity does not require a second production.

Reason: Because it exists.

Example: Just as a jar.

Major premise: Whatsoever exists does not require to be produced once more.

We can indeed express a syllogism in two different ways, e.g., we can express it thus:—

Thesis: The word is not an eternal substance[1].

Reason: Because it is produced.

Major premise: Whatsoever is produced is not eternal.

But we can put it also in another way :—

Major premise: Whatsoever is produced is known to be non-eternal.

Example: As for example, a jar.

Minor premise: The word is produced.

Conclusion: Therefore, being produced, it is not eternal.

In this instance the reason (middle term) reveals itself in the minor premise, "the word is produced", where the application of the middle term to the minor is indicated.

This is (just what Buddhapālita has done) in the present case. (He has said),

Entities do not arise of their own self,

Since the production of what already exists is not needed.

He might have put the same argument in another form:—

Major premise: Whatsoever already exists does not want to be produced.

Example: As e.g., this jar standing before us.

Minor premise: It already exists.

Conclusion: It needs no second production.

---

1 The school of the Mīmāṁsakas imagined that the word was an eternal transcendental substance, somewhat similar to the Platonic idea. The uttered word was then only its particular manifestation. The logicians and all other schools of philosophy denied the existence of the eternal word on the score that the word which we know from experience is an impermanent production. To illustrate the rules of logic this example is as popular in the whole East, as the deduction of Socrates' mortality is the current example of the first form of the syllogism in the West.

The jar in its (potential) condition in a lump of clay is an example (by contrast)[1], since it needs to be really produced. But if you mean the jar which already exists by itself, such a jar is not produced once more. Thus it is that the reason (i.e. the middle term in Buddhapālita's syllogism) is the fact of direct individual existence, a fact which precludes a second origination of the existent; it is expressed (in the minor premise, the so-called) application[2] of the middle term to the minor, and thus it is that Buddhapālita has really elicited in the argument of the Sāṅkhya a contradiction. He has done it just by an independent argument of his own. How is it then that you accuse him of giving neither a reason, nor an example ?

XVI. THE ANSWER OF THE SĀṄKHYA VIRTUALLY REPUDIATED BY BUDDHAPĀLITA

We have thus shown that the accusation of Buddhapālita for not having produced a regular syllogism with a reason and example is not sound. But only not this. Equally unfounded is the accusation of not having repudiated the double stricture of the opponent, (sc. The Sāṅkhya, who accuses him either of telling nothing new, of contradicting himself). (Virtually he has repudiated the Sāṅkhya also). How is that ? The Sāṅkhya maintains that if our denial of identity between cause and effect only means that the effect is a new manifestation of the same stuff, tnis he has himself always admitted. Yes, but the Sāṅkhya never admitted that causation consists in a manifested jar, a jar standing before us, being once more manifested and it is just manifested jar, in its ready form,[3] that we take as an example when we prove the absurdity of the idea of an identity between cause and effect.

Regarding the non-manifested jar, the jar in its potential condition[4] as a lump of clay, it is clear *a fortiori*,[5] from our point of view it cannot be produced. How is it then possible to accuse

1 Instead of reading, 'tathā ca' it would be preferable to read 'na tu', but 'tathā ca' is also possible,since a vaidharmyadṛṣṭānta is also sometimes introduced in this way. After avasthāyāṃ a *cheda* must be inserted.

2 upanayana.

3 Lit. "because its form or essence, rūpa-svarūpa is established as an example", cp. the Tib. transl.

4 śakti-rūpāpanna.

5 viśiṣṭa-sādhya, a qualified predicate, a predicate *a fotrori*; anabhivyakta-rūpa-anutpatti-kāraṇa-rūpa,-kāryasya anutpattiparatā anutpattiḥ.

our thesis of falling in with the Sāṅkhya view[1], and how is it possible to accuse our argument of being self-contradictory ?[2]

To summarize our opinion, Buddhapālita has pointed out the contradiction in the Sāṅkhya theory of causality not only by a deduction *ad absurdum*, but also by an independent argument. Nevertheless the faults imputed to him do not exist. It is, therefore, impossible to maintain that he has not answered the accusations of the Sāṅkhya. The whole onslaught (of Bhāvaviveka) is therefore absolute nonsense.

XVII. SOME MINOR POINTS EXPLAINED

It might be objected that the example of a jar is not convincing enough. The rule may apply for the production of a jar out of clay, and not apply to the production of a piece of cloth out of threads ? No, because we say a jar etc. By the etc., the inclusion of every possible object which can originate is indicated. There is not the slightest possibility to doubt (that the rule might not apply to a cloth etc.).

The argument (against the Sāṅkhya) may have also been formulated (by Buddhapālita) in another way, viz.

Thesis: All physical entities do not arise out of themselves.

Reason: Because they always exist in their own essence, (i.e., because Matter is eternal).

Example—Just as the (eternal) Spirit does.

The Sāṅkhya who advocates the identity of cause and effect must accept this argument for that very reason that he advocates this identity which is here exemplified by his changeless Spirit. This example of the spirit whose eternal identity the Sāṅkhya admits may have also been quoted by Buddhapālita in order to combat the Sāṅkhya view[3].

---

1 Lit. the objection of a faulty thesis of the proved.

2 Lit. "Therefore if there is also an objection (codanā) of contradiction by a self-argument (-svānumānena, i.e., even admitting that Buddhapālita has produced a real argument, since the faults as they have been depicted do not exist, the non-refutation of the faults mentioned by the opponent is quite impossible. Thus this critique is quite incongruous. This should be well known".

3 Lit. "Or else the following other way of formulation. Entities which are not Spirit, i.e. are physical, for the advocate of self origination, for that very reason, do not originate out of themselves, because they exist in their own self, just as the individual Soul. Thus this example can be quoted".

It might be maintained that the Sāṅkhya is not affected by this denial of origination. He vindicates the theory that causality consists in a new manifestation of an existing stuff. However the term origination may also have the meaning of manifestation.

Indeed both origination and manifestation have the common feature of representing something that was formerly unperceived and became perceived after. Therefore, a new manifestation can also be called a new origination.

It then becomes impossible for the Sāṅkhya to maintain that he is not affected by the denial of an identity between a cause and its effect.[1]

It may be asked, how is it possible to deduce all these considerations of detail out of the short statement of Buddhapālita, since he does not mention them? We answer. His words are full of profound meaning. In a concise manner they include the above-mentioned details. When analysed they reveal their own self in these details. We do not invent something that is not included in them.[2]

XVIII. THE THIRD STRICTURE OF BHĀVAVIVEKA ANSWERED. THE DENIAL OF ONE VIEW DOES NOT IMPLY THE ACCEPTANCE OF THE OTHER

Bhāvaviveka maintains that the repudiation of the Sāṅkhya theory of causation by a mere deduction involves acceptance of the opposite theory, viz. that cause and effect represent two different substances. This is wrong. Because the converse theory will be again charged to the same account of the same

1 Lit. "Although the denial of origination does not repudiate the maintainer of manifestation, nevertheless by using the word origination in the sense of manifestation, since by the similarity of non-perception before and perception after just a manifestation is expressed by the word origination, the denial is not non-repudiatory."

2 Lit. "How is again this detailed analysis (vyastavicāra) attained without an expression of the meaning as it is here told? If this is asked, then this is answered. These sentences, full of meaning, are very much significant, they turn out (pravṛttāni) as summarising the meaning as it has been told and, being commented upon, they give birth to their own self, the meaning as is here told, thus nothing is imagined which is not really assumed."

opponent, not to our account[1] since we have declared that we have no theory of our own. We, therefore, cannot be accused of contradicting our own principles. But if the many objections that have been already raised against the opponent accrue by charging to his account the counterpart of our deduction, we really will only welcome it.[2]

The Master Buddhapālita is a faithful adherent of the method of Nāgārjuna. How can we possibly pronounce something inadvertently[3] that would give an opportunity to his opponent? When a philosopher who denies the reality of single objects, deduces *ad absurdum* the conception of their reality,[4] how can he be charged with the counterpart of this deduction? Our words are not policemen? They cannot deprive us of our liberty. Words possess a power to express something, but they are controlled by the intention[5] of the speaker. Therefore the only result of our deduction is to repudiate the theory of our opponent. Our acceptance of the converse theory is not at all therewith implied.[6]

Our common Master Nāgārjuna, when combating opposed opinions, has very often had recourse just to a deduction *ad absurdum*, without ever admitting its positive counterpart.

E.G. :

We find nothing (called empty) Space,
Before its essence has (here) been determined.
If it would previously to this determination preexist,
It would be Space without an essence.[7]
Supposing all the causes of some matter taken off,
And we would call it matter nonetheless,
It would be matter without causes.
But nowhere without causes any matter does exist.[8]

---

1 Both *prasaṅga* and *tad-viparyaya* are used together to prove the same thesis in, e.g. Sarvadarś., p. 21. (Poona 1924)

2 Lit. "And the more faults of the opponent are deduced through a deduction of the contrary of (his, Sc. Buddhapālita's) deduction, the more desirable will it indeed be for us."

3 sāvakāśam.

4 Lit. deduces *ad absurdum* "the maintainer of reality", the realist (sa-svabhāva-vādin).

5 We would expect either *vivakṣayā* or *vivakṣām anu vidhīyante*.

6 Lit. "There is no accepted deduction (arthāpatti) being the contrary of the unacceptable deduction (prasaṅga)."

7 M. s., VI. It does not follow that Nāgārjuna admits the existence of a real space.

8 M. s. IV 2.

This does not at all imply that Nāgārjuna admitted the existence of caused matter.

Another example:

Nirvāṇa is no separate entity,
Or else it would be subject to decay and death.
There is no separate entity
That never would decay and never die.[1]

Bhavaviveka: But these are aphorisms[2]. The sentences of our Master contain profound intentions. They can be variously tackled[3] and give rise to a variety of syllogistic formulation.

Answer: Why, to be sure, should not the comment of Buddhapālita which does not contain any syllogistic formulation be accepted just in this sense, as the only faithful rendering of Nāgārjuna's intention.

Bhāvaviveka: It is the business[4] of the writers of detailed commentaries to make detailed statements about the syllogistic formulations implied in the aphorisms.

Answer: This is not always the case. Our Master has written a commentary upon his own manual of dialectics, "The Repudiation of Contests," but he did not indulge in it in syllogistic formulations. You are, indeed, merely parading your cleverness in the science of dialectics. Although you pretend to be an adherent of the Mādhyamika system, you nevertheless compose independent syllogistic arguments. But for such a logician, as you would like to appear, the Mādhyamika method is only a very great encumbrance.[5]

It makes him pile up mistake upon mistake.[6]

How is that?

---

1 M. s., XXV. 4. If the converse conception be that of a Nirvāṇa immanent in the world and eternal, Nāgārjuna admits it. Cp. ibid XXV 9.

2 artha-vākya

3 parikalpyante.

4 or method, nyāya,

5 This statement can be interpreted as an indirect indication that Candrakīrti knew nothing about a commentary written upon the Mūlakārikas by Nāgārjuna himself. It would follow that the work called Akutobhaya is a forgery as suggested by Wassilieff.

6. Lit., "Merely through the desire of displaying one's own proficiency in the science of dialectics, the use of independent syllogisms (prayogavākya), although having accepted the Mādhyamika system, is an indirect indication (upalakṣyate) of such a logician who is in a very high degree the receptacle of an assemblage of many mistakes"

XIX. EXAMINATION OF BHĀVAVIVEKA'S FORMAL ARGUMENT AGAINST THE SĀṄKHYA

To combat the Sāṅkhya theory of Causality you have composed the following syllogism.

Thesis: Mental phenomena,[1] if considered from the transcendental standpoint of the Monist, are no new productions out of the same substance.

Reason: Because they exist.

Example: Just as the Conscious Principle of the Sāṅkhya which is an eternal unchanging entity.

Major premise: Whatsoever already exists is not a new self-production.

Now, in this syllogism, so formulated by you, what is the use of the qualification "from the transcendental standpoint of the Monist?"[2]

Bhāvaviveka: If we take our stand on phenomenal reality we cannot deny origination of mental phenomena. If this were denied, it would follow that the contrast which we assume between the absolute thing in itself and phenomenal reality does not exist[3].

Answer: This is not right, because we deny the identity of cause and effect[4] from the phenomenal point of view also. It is corroborated by the following words of the Scripture[5].

"This sprout which springs up from a seed is not produced out of itself, neither is it produced out of nonself, nor out of both, nor without a cause. It is neither created by God[6], nor by Time, nor from the Atoms, nor from Primitive Matter[7], nor by Nature"[8]. Here is another text. "The sprout does not belong to the seed, neither is the seed identical with the sprout, nor is it non-identical. It is a manifestation of that unique Reality[9]

---

1 ādhyātmikāny āyatanāni.

2 Lit. "Here the syllogism which has been thus stated, as absolute reality the internal bases do not arise out of self, since they exist, just as consciousness, what for again in it the qualification "as absolute reality" has been assumed?"

3 Lit. "And if denied the admitted repudiation (bādha), of the phenomenal by the absolute would not be entailed (read prasaṅgāt)".

4 svata utpatti.

5 From Sālistamba-sūtra, cf. Śikṣāsamuccaya, p. 219. 10 ff.

6 Īśvara

7 prakṛti.

8 svabhāva.

9 dharmatā.

which neither can be determined as annihilation[1], nor as one of the eternal principles"[2].

And in this treatise the author will make the following statement.:

Whatever relativity does exist
Is really not what it appears to be.
But neither is it something else.
Therefore it neither has an end,
Nor has it a beginning[3].

Bhāvaviveka: The qualification ("from the standpoint of transcendental reality") has been introduced into the above syllogism in consideration of the opinion held by the opponent.

Answer: This is a wrong method, because we do not admit his construction[4], even from the point of view of phenomenal reality[5]. Non-Buddhists are absolutely lacking the right understanding of the division between both realities, the transcendental and phenomenal one. It is, therefore, much better to repudiate them, from both these standpoints. I would think it a great advantage. The above qualification is thus out of place, even if it is introduced in order to distinguish the view taken by the author from the view of the opponent or from the ideas of simple people.

As to simple people they do not understand what self-origination means. For them also the qualification is useless. Unsophisticated people simply admit that an effect is produced by a cause. They do not enter into such considerations as to whether the effect is identical with the cause or not.

Our Master Nāgārjuna has really established the same thing viz. that we must avail ourselves of the every day idea of causality without any hope to explain it metaphysically. It is, therefore, clear that the qualification is absolutely senseless.

---

1 uccheda.

2 Such as god, time, atom, matter, nature, etc. all with capitals.

3 M. s. XVII, 10 pratītya-śūnya-śāśvata—"beginning" cp. XXV. 21 cf. Kant's solution of the first antinomy, viz. that the world is neither finite, nor infinite because "a phenomenon does not exist by itself". op, cit. p. 410 ff.

4 vyavasthā.

5 It is not right to maintain that the Sāṅkhya's view of phenomenal reality is admissible with the qualification that from the transcendental point of view it will be an illusion.

XX. BHĀVAVIVEKA'S ARGUMENT ASSAILED FROM THE STANDPOINT OF FORMAL LOGIC

However let us agree and admit that the qualification might have been introduced in order to intimate that phenomenal causality is not denied. The syllogism of Bhāvaviveka will then nevertheless be formally deficient, since its example, the Spirit, and its reason, the fact of "the existence" of mental phenomena, will both be ultimately unreal. We will then have either the logical error of a faulty thesis, since it will refer to something (sc. the mental phenomena) which the author of the syllogism himself, from his own monistic point of view does not accept as real,[1] or we shall have the logical error of a faulty reason,[2] (viz. the fact of the existence or reality of mental phenomena) which will then refer to something equally unreal.

Indeed (Bhāvaviveka) himself being a Mādhyamika does not admit the transcendental reality of separate mental phenomena[3] and at the same time he composes a syllogism about this very non-existing thing.

Bhāvaviveka: This does not matter, since we admit the phenomenal reality of the sense of vision etc.

Answer: But then, what is qualified by the words "from the transcendental standpoint"?

Bhāvaviveka: If considered from the transcendental point of view the existence[4] of the phenomenal sense faculties[5] and of empirical consciousness[6] is not real.

The qualification is introduced in order to specify the kind of causality which is denied.

Answer: Then you ought to have expressed yourself otherwise. You ought to have spoken exactly thus: "the supposed phenomenal reality of the sense-faculties etc. is no reality in the

---

1 This *pakṣa doṣa* would be probably classified by Dignāga as *anumāna-nirākṛta*, cp Nyāyabindu, p. 59. 1 (B. B.) VII.

2 About the *āśaya-asiddha hetu-doṣa*, cf. Nyāyabindu, p. 46.16. The logic of Dignāga forbids deductions from facts which the author of the syllogism, from his own point of view, does not admit as real. cp. ibid, p. 63.13 f.

3 Lit. "of the basis of the sense of vision (*cakṣu-āyatana*) and other subjective basis of cognition i.e. *ādhyātmika-āyatana*."

4 *utpatti*.

5 *cakṣurādi*.

6 *citta* (=*manas*=*vijñāna*) is indicated among *cakṣurādi* as *āyatana* cf. My Central Conception., p. 96.

transcendental sense." But your expression is different[1]. However, even supposing you had expressed yourself properly, nevertheless you would not have escaped the logical error of a faulty thesis since it would then have referred to empirical sensations, i.e., something quite unknown to your opponent[2]. For the Sāṅkhya indeed all sensations are absolutely real. He has altogether no nominal (or empirical) realities.

Thus it is that the argument is wrong either from the standpoint of its author, for whom the separate mental phenomena are not real, or from the standpoint of those to whom it is addressed, because they do not admit any difference between phenomenal and absolute reality.[3]

XXI. ANOTHER ATTEMPT OF BHĀVAVIVEKA TO VINDICATE HIS ARGUMENT

But be that as the case may, we may envisage the syllogism in question as referring in general terms just to the relation between a fact, (the mental phenomena) and one of its characteristics, viz., existence, without enlarging upon the special theories which might be entertained by both parties about the nature of mental phenomena or the essence of existence. E.g., when it is inferred that words are non-eternal the general relation of this characteristic to the characterized fact is alone referred to. Indeed the work of inference would become quite impossible, if the special view entertained in different systems

1 The expression that "from the transcendental standpoint the sensations do not arise out of themselves" can be understood as meaning the transcendental sensations are not identical with their causes. But transcendental sensations do not exist from the monist's point of view. Hence for him it will be a syllogism composed about a non-existing thing.

2 Lit., p. 28. 1-3 "And even if told, since the opponents admit exclusively a really existing faculty of vision etc., and do not admit nominal realities, it will be a faulty thesis whose substratum will be unreal for the opponent. Thus it is not right.

3 According to the logic of Dignāga, a discussion must start from facts admitted by both parties, cp. Nyāyabindu, p. 62.3. Sensations real in the absolute sense do not exist for the Monist. The difference of sensations empirically real is unknown to the Sāṅkhya, for him all sensations are real. Hence, accordingly as we take it, the syllogism of Bhāvaviveka will refer either to something not admitted by the respondent himself, or to something not admitted by his opponent.

were to be taken into account. There are no two systems which agree on the question about the nature of sound. If we admit with the Hīnayāna Buddhist that sound is a secondary thing or element of matter, dependent upon the four universal elements[1], this will not be admitted by his opponent the Vaiśeṣika, because he, on the contrary, maintains that the sound is a quality of ether, it is not a substance. This again the Buddhist does not admit on his own behalf. Similarly when the Vaiśeṣika undertakes it to prove that the word is non-eternal, he can be asked whether he means the word as a physical product, or the word as a manifestation of an eternally existing substance. The first is not admitted by his opponent the Mīmāṁsaka who postulates the existence of a special eternal substance of which the spoken words are nothing but separate manifestations. The second is not accepted by the Vaiśeṣika himself.

The same applies *mutatis mutandis* to every philosophic issue. If you admit that the destruction of an object must have a cause, this will not be accepted by Buddhist on his own behalf, since he maintains that every existence consists of discrete moments which are evanescent by themselves, without a cause.[2] But if he alludes to uncaused invisible destruction going on at every moment this will not be admitted by his opponent, the Vaiśeṣika.

Therefore, just as in the case of the evanescent character of the sound, only the relation of this characteristic to the characterized substratum, in general terms, is taken into account, just so in the present instance, the mere fact that there is some substratum called sensations, should be taken in general[3], without entering into details, whether it be a phenomenal or an absolute existence.

Answer : This is not so, since in the present case, it is just the existence of such a general substratum that is denied. It is denied by no one else than Bhāvaviveka himself. His avowed aim is here to deny Causality. However, just in denying every causality, he at the same time *eo ipso* denies its substratum, the caused thing, the substance of the thing produced, converting it into a thing which owes its existence to a mere illusion. Illusion and reality are indeed opposites. The

1 Cp. My Central Conception.
2 *yathā-sambhavam*.
3 Cp. Nyāyabindu, p. 33.6 ff.

pluriverse as it appears before the unsophisticated eyes of mankind is either logically inconsistent or it is a reality[1].

If it is logically inconsistent[2], and if this plurality which is not the real condition of the universe is wrongly apprehended by us as real, if it is a false impression in the mind of the perceiver[3], then there is in this plurality not the slightest bit of what is absolutely real[4]. But if there is no transcendental illusion, if it is not a mirage[5], if we perceive a real[6] pluriverse, not the one constructed by our imagination, then there is not the slightest vestige of something unreal in pluralism, nothing at all to justify the claim that a phenomenal reality has been established by us[7].

---

1 We find here an eloquent expression of that genuine conviction very much spread, even in our days, among the pandits of India who have studied the various systems of their country that Monism is superior to all other systems by the fact of reaching the limit of all philosophic construction. The realism of Nyāya-Vaiśeṣika and Mīmāṁsā, the dualism of the Sāṅkhya, the radical pluralism of Hīnayāna Buddhist all were engaged in constructing a skeleton of the Universe out of a limited number of ultimate data and have then stopped before them, refusing to go deeper into them and to reduce them to their still deeper root. Should they have embarked on a further analysis of those ultimate principles at which they had arrived they would have inevitably landed in Monism. Only in Monism does philosophic analysis reach its real limit, *yathā yathā vicāryate tathā tathā brahmaṇy eva ekasmin sarvam paryavasyati.* In modern philosophy, as far as I am aware, a similar view has been taken by Ladd, Introd. to Philos. p. 403.

2 *viparyāsa.*

3 Lit., "Like non-existing hair etc. by the ophthalmic."

4 *sad-bhūta-padārtha-leśa, a hint at Dignāga's kṣaṇa=svalakṣaṇa=parmārtha* and at his claim to have vindicated phenomenal reality, cp. below. text p. 66 ff.

5 Lit., "like real hair etc. by the non-ophthalmic".

6 Read *bhūtam,* instead of *abhūtam.*

7 Lit., p. 30. 1.5 Because just when the denial of origination is here intended to be a charateristic to be established, just then the negation of the characterised, of its substratum, which has reached its own existence only through an illusion, is admitted just by himself. Different are indeed illusion and non-illusion. Therefore, if, owing to illusion, non-Ens is taken as Ens, just as by the ophthalmic (non-existing) hair, etc. then wherefrom would even a bit of a really existing thing be apprehended ? But if through non-confusion, the real, non-imagined is perceived, as by the non-ophthalmic (real) hair, etc., then wherefrom the perception of even a bit of a non-really-existing thing, so as to infer phenomenalism (*saṁvṛttiḥ*) ?"

Our venerable Master Nāgārjuna has therefore said :

> If I did really cognize some separate things,
> I could then make an affirmation or denial,
> Upon the basis of these things perceived, or inferred.
> But these separate things do not exist for me.
> Therefore I cannot be assailed on such a basis[1].

Since it is so; since (transcendental) illusion is one thing and (transcendental) reality another; since for the transcendentalist[2], in what he considers to be absolutely real, there is no room for non-reality, what is then the meaning of Bhāvaviveka's syllogism ? He takes the phenomenal visual sensations and other mental phenomena as a minor term, (the subject of his deduction). He thus cannot escape from the criticism that his thesis is logically impossible, since it refers to a non-entity, or that this middle term is contradictory, because it appertains to an unreal substratum. The syllogism would be equivalent to the assertion that *non-existing* things do not arise out of themselves, *because they exist.*

As to the analogy with the discussions about the nature of the word, it does not exist. In those discussions there always is an agreement between every pair of contending view about what sound, in general, and what evanescence in general, are without entering into details about the nature of sound.

There is no such agreement between the radical Relativist[3] and the non-Relativist or Realist[4], in regard to what visual sensations in general are, either from the phenomenal or the transcendental point of view. For this reason the two cases are not comparable.

All that has been said about the logical impossibility of a thesis which refers to a non-entity is applicable *mutatis mutandis* as the proof of the futility of the conception of "existence" as a logical reason.

---

1 This stanza is from the Vigraha-vyāvartanī has been quoted above, text—p. 16.9.

2 *viduṣām*, they are identified with the *āryas*.

3 *śūnyatā-vādin*.

4 *aśūnyatā-vādin*.

XXII. BHĀVAVIVEKA ALSO AVAILS HIMSELF OF THE ARGUMENT THAT FOR THE MONIST ALL INDIVIDUAL EXISTENCE IS UNREAL

Such is the force of this argument[1] that even Bhāvaviveka himself, this champion of logic[2], is obliged to admit the condemnation of logic which we have exposed. He examines the following syllogism.

Thesis: The cause and conditions which produce mental phenomena[3] really exist.

Reason: Because this has been declared by Buddha.

Major premise: Whatsoever has been declared by the Buddha is true[4].

Example: As e.g., his statement that Nirvāṇa is Final Quiescence.

This syllogism has been advanced by a Hīnayānist opponent of Bhāvaviveka. He replies by the following criticism. "In what sense do you think, the word 'cause' is here used? Has Buddha spoken from the phenomenal point of view or from the transcendental one?[5]

If it is taken in the phenomenal sense, the reason has *eo ipso* no ultimate reality for Buddha himself. But supposing it is taken in the sense of something transcendentally real, then we must remember the following words of Nāgārjuna:

Neither an Ens, nor a non-Ens,
Nor any Ens-non-Ens,
No element[6] is really "turned out"[7].
How can we then assume,
The possibility of a producing cause?[8]

"Since causation[9] of things, whether real or unreal or partly real and partly unreal, is excluded, there is no such thing as a

---

1 The argument, namely that for a consistent Monist every separate thing and every separate reason is ultimately unreal.

2 *tārkika*.

3 *ādhyātmika-āyatana*.

4 Lit., "Indeed what and how is taught by the Buddha to exist, it is so.'

5 *paramārthataḥ*.

6 *dharma*.

7 *nirvartyate*.

8 *nirvartaka*.

9 *sad-asat-kārya-pratyayatva*, i.e., neither *satkārya* nor *asatkārya-vāda* is admitted.

really efficient cause." This is the meaning of the words of Nāgārjuna.

"Therefore from the transcendental point of view[1] there is altogether no efficient causality[2]. Every reason you may adduce will be either ultimately unreal or contradictory."

By adopting this line of argument against the Hīnayānist, Bhāvaviveka has himself admitted the unreality of every reason from the transcendental standpoint of the Relativist. Thus all logical demonstrations are smashed, since in all such syllogisms reasons are adduced which in the opinion of the opponent are founded on real fact, but in the opinion of the Relativist himself they are all ultimately unreal.[3]

In the following two syllogisms of Bhāvaviveka the middle term must likewise be declared faulty, on the score that it is meaningless from the Monist's transcendental point of view. E.g.

Thesis; Mental phenomena[4] do not really[5] arise from corresponding causes, separate from them.

Reason: Because these are separate entities.

Major premise; Whatsoever is a separate substance cannot really be a cause.

Example: As the causes of a jar[6] (which are not real in the absolute sense).

Or another example,

Thesis: The causes which in the opinion of our opponents[7], produce mental phenomena[8] are not understood to be causes in the absolute sense.

Reason: Because they are separate entities.

---

1 *paramārthataḥ*.

2 *nirvartya-nirvartakatva*.

3 Lit., p-31. 11-13 "Since thus he even himself by this method has admitted the unreality of the reason, therefore in all syllogisms which have middle terms suggested by attributes of real entities, since just by themselves reasons etc., are unreal, so all demonstrations are killed."

4 *ādhyātmika-āyatana*, lit. "the six subjective bases of cognition."

5 *paramārthataḥ*.

6 Read *ghaṭasya*.

7 read *paraiḥ* instead of *pare*.

8 Lit., "The six subjective bases of cognition, the faculty of vision (*cakṣuḥ*). etc.,"

Major premise: Whatsoever is a separate entity is not a cause in the absolute sense.

Example: As for example, the threads, the loom, the weaver etc. are not the causes of cloth from the transcendental point of view.

The reason "because they are separate entities" is not a valid middle term, since for the author of these syllogisms himself it has no ultimate reality.

Another example where Bhāvaviveka implicitly admits that the transcendentalist has to forego usual logical methods, is the following one. He is desirous to prove that the reason given by his opponent the Sautrāntika, is wrong, because it represents a fact whose ultimate reality he, as a Relativist, does not accept. The argument of the Sautrāntika runs thus.

Thesis: Internal facts[1] i.e., mental phenomena really arise i.e., they have a real existence.

Reason: Because they produce purposive actions directed towards the same objects as our thoughts have been directed to.

Major premise: Whatsoever is efficient is real.[2] Bhāvaviveka repudiates this conclusion by quoting the following parallel argument.

Thesis: The yogī, when merged in ecstatic meditation perceives by his supernatural faculty of vision the ultimate reality, he then apprehends causation, motion etc. as they really are[3].

The reason adduced is the same as in the foregoing syllogism, viz. "because they produce purposive actions directed to the same objects as his thoughts have been directed to." In this argument, says Bhāvaviveka, the reason does not represent a real fact from the transcendental point of view.

"It is moreover unreal," says he, "because motion does not exist[4],

---

1 *ādhyātmikā bhāvam.*

2 The definition of reality (*paramārtha-sat*) as efficiency (*arthakriyā-kāritva*) is accepted by Dignāga and Dharmakīrti, cp. Nyāya-bindu, p. 13.15. It is also shared by the Sautrāntikas, cp. N. b. Tipp. p. 19.

3 In the Santānāntara-siddhi, Art, 90 (B. B. XI), Russian trasl. p. 47. Dharmakīrti denies that the yogī perceives the ultimately real.

4 In Hīnayāna, motion is denied (*na gatir nāśāt*, Ab. Kośa. IV 1) since it represents in reality a serial of separate momentary productions (*nirantara-utpāda*), as in a cinema. In Mahāyāna, motion is denied because all the moments are relative (*svabhāva śūnya*).

Since there is no real causation, motion cannot exist.[1]"

Now this method by which Bhāvaviveka here combats the argument of his opponent can be *mutatis mutandis* applied to his own deductions which he produced bonafide, viz.,

Thesis: The future does not exist in an absolute sense[2].

Reason: Because it represents time[3].

Example: Just as the past time does not exist.

Major premise: Whatsoever is "time" does not represent an ultimate reality.

To this syllogism we may likewise apply the structure that the reason "time" represents nothing real to the author of the syllogism himself.

The student will be now able himself to extend the critique here expounded upon the unreality of the reason adduced by Bhāvaviveka in the following three syllogisms.

1. Thesis: The operating[4] sense of vision does not perceive colour.

Reason: Because it is a sense of vision in general.

Example: Just as a non-operating[5] sense of vision always is.

Major premise: Whatsoever is a sense of vision does not necessarily perceive colour[6].

---

1 Lit., p, 32. 3.7. "Just as he has said when proving the unreality (*asiddhārthatā*) of this reason given by an opponent, viz. "internal facts, *bhāvāḥ* are necessarily (*eva*) produced, since they produce actions characterised as possessing their objects;" now it is being proved that for the meditating Yogi who by his eye of wisdom sees the real path of existence (*bhāva-yāthātmya*) origination, motion etc. exist in the absolute sense (*paramārthataḥ*), then there is unreality of the reason, because they produce actions characterised as possessing their objects, and motion is denied just because origination is denied."

2 Lit., "The not-run is not at all being run in the absolute sense."

3 *adhvan*.

4 read *sabhāgam*, instead of *sāśrayam*. *Sabhāga=sva-karma-kṛt*, cp. A. Kośa, 1—39.

5 *tatsabhāga=a-sva-karma-kṛt*, cp. Ab. Kośa. 1.39.

6 For the monist, according to Candrakīrti, it would have been sufficient to deny a real perception of colour on the score that all separate facts have no ultimate reality for a consequent Monist, or only a second hand reality (*paratantra*) for a Yogācāra. But Bhāvaviveka apparently tries to corroborate this view by something like a formally correct syllogism. He seemingly has detected in the judgment "the eye is a colour-perceiving organ" the same contradiction as really appears if the copula be taken in the sense of an equation. The eye thus does not perceive colour because it does not always perceive it, perception is not its essence (*svabhāva*) as e.g. the quality of being resistant is the essence of the hard stuff.

2. Thesis: The organ of vision does not apprehend colours.
   Reason: Because it is physical[1].
   Example: Just as any physical object[2], e.g. a jar etc.
   Major premise: Whatsoever is physical does not apprehend colours[3].
3. Thesis: The solid bodies[4] do not really possess solidity.
   Reason: Because they represent Matter[5].
   Example: Just as the gaseous bodies.
   Major premise: Whatsoever is Matter is not always a solid body[6].

XXIII. ANOTHER FORMAL ERROR IN THE SYLLOGISM OF BHĀVAVIVEKA

Moreover the reason "because they (sc. mental phenomena) exist"[7] is uncertain from the standpoint of the opponent (The syllogism of Bhāvaviveka is directed against the Sāṅkhya who admits a double kind of existence, the eternal, changeless existence of the Spirit and the changing existence of Matter. It is therefore uncertain) whether the words "mental phenomena do not arise out of themselves because they already exist" means

---

1 *bhautika*.

2 *rūpa*, the first *rūpa*=the *rūpa-āyatana*, the second probably= *rūpa-skandha*.

3 Here Bhāvaviveka has recourse to an idea of the Nyāya-Vaiśeṣika school (*bhautikāni indriyāṇi*) in order to undermine the fact that colours are perceived through the eye. According to Candrakīrti this is quite superfluous for a believer in Universal Relativity (*Śūnyatā=niḥsvabhāvatā*), and moreover constitutes a fault in formal logic, since the reason, the physical character (*bhautika*) of the organ has no real force from the point of view of the author of the syllogism, it is *asiddha svataḥ*.

4 *mahī=pṛithivī*, cp. My Central Conception, p. 13.

5 *bhūta-mahā-bhūta*—*cp*. ibid. 99.

6 Solidity (*kharatva*) is the essence, *lakṣaṇa* of the solid bodies. All the work of predication being relative, it can, from this point of view, be maintained that the solid body is not solid, sc. is not solid by itself, but only in relation to others. This is a case of the *lakṣaṇa-niḥsvabhāvatā* or *śūnyatā*, cp. Triṁśikā—p. 32 For Candrakīrti, it is enough to point out this general conception in order to establish the relativity and consequent unreality of the idea of a solid stuff. But Bhāvaviveka wishes apparently to construct a formal syllogism on the same basis as the first one. i.e., he finds a contradiction in the sentence "a solid stuff is a stuff" on the score that there are stuffs that are liquid and gaseous. These three syllogisms are celebrated among the Tibetan schoolmen as baffling arguments establishing Relativity (*śūnyatā*) according to the system of the Svātantrikas founded by Bhāvaviveka.

7 Cp above, p. 26.1 *sattvāt=vidyamānatvāt*.

that they exist eternally[1] like the Spirit[2], or whether the words "because they already exist" refer to that kind of origination which is exemplified by the origination of jars and other physical existence in general, an origination which represents a change in a permanent stuff, since according to this system mental changes are in themselves physical[3].

It may be objected (that the adduced example, the identity of matter in physical objects) like jars etc., is a *petitio principii*[4] and therefore the argument is not uncertain, but wrong[5]. However this is not so, because the argument is stated not in conformity with our view, but from the standpoint of the Sāṅkhya, where mental phenomena indeed have a double nature, they are physical in themselves and at the same time, they are the reflection of the eternal changeless Spirit.

XXIV. THE MĀDHYAMIKA REPUDIATES HIS OPPONENT ON PRINCIPLES ADMITTED AS VALID BY THE SAME OPPONENT

But it may be objected that our own argument will then be liable to just the same criticism which we apply to the arguments of our opponents. All our arguments will be also wrong, because the reasons which will be adduced will either be non-entities, themselves, or they will represent something appertaining to a non-entity. When both parties are guilty of the same fault, it cannot be charged to the account of one of them alone. All this our attack on logic will thus become unfounded.

To this we reply. This objection affects only those who, being Mādhyamikas, nevertheless, like Bhāvaviveka, have recourse to *bonafide* arguments[6]. But we do not resort to direct proof by syllogism. Our arguments can have only the result of repudiating the tenets of our opponents, for us they are not valid by themselves.

1 it. "should not arise," i.e. not change. The Spirit of the Sāṅkhya is changeless.

2 *caitanya*.

3 Lit. p. 33. 4.5. "Because they exist, this reason is uncertain, what? Should the (six) internal bases (of cognition), because they exist like the Spirit, not arise out of self, or like jars etc., they should arise out of a self?"

4 *sādhya-sama*.

5 not *anaikāntika*, but *asiddha*, cp. Nyāyabindu. p. 62.

6 *svatantra-anumāna*.

Supposing some one maintains that the eye perceives external objects. He will then be repudiated on principles which he himself admits. You maintain, he will be told, that the eye lacks the capacity of introspection[1] which, in your opinion, is invariably concomitant with the capacity of apprehending external objects.

Now, we will assail it by a counter argument.

Major premise: Wheresoever introspection is absent, cognition of external objects is also absent.

Example: In physical objects like jars etc.

Minor premise: The eye lacks the capacity of introspection, it is physical.

Therefore it cannot cognise external objects.

Thus it is that the perception of an external object like a patch of blue colour is in conflict with the fact that the eye itself is deficient in self-perception. This contradiction in the argument of our opponent has been disclosed by another argument which is valid from the standpoint of the opponent himself.

This alone is elicited by our syllogism. How is then the above mentioned accusation possible? How can it be maintained that our deduction contains the same flaw which we have found in the argument of our opponent?

XXV. LOGICAL REFUTATION ON THE BASIS OF FACTS ADMITTED BY ONLY ONE PARTY

Bhāvaviveka: It is true that for us Monists all individual facts possess no reality. However a discussion is possible even then when an argument is combated on the basis of a principle admitted by one of the parties.

Answer: Yes, but it must be done on the basis of principles admitted by yourself, not on the basis of principles admitted by your opponent.

This[2] is what happens in everyday life. Indeed, sometimes in common life two contending parties appoint somebody to judge them, and according to his verdict the gain or the loss is settled. Sometimes the disputant himself declares that he has won or lost. But never is this question of gain and loss to be settled by the enemy. What is good in common life is

1 *svātma-adarśana-dharma*.
2 Read *evam* instead of *eva* p. 35.1

equally right in logic, because scientific logic is exclusively concerned with an examination of the principles which underlie purposive action in common life[1].

For this very reason some logicians have maintained that an argument cannot be exploded on the basis of the principle admitted by the opponent, because it is just these principles, by him admitted, that it is intended to reject.

Of course, Dignāga thinks that a demonstration or a refutation can be valid, if it is carried on principles admitted by both parties, not by one of them only[2]. If admitted by one of them only, it will be inconclusive. But even then he must make allowance for the just mentioned method prevailing in common life and admit the validity of arguments which start from principles admitted only by one party.

Indeed he admits that when discussions are going on about religious matters, you cannot repudiate the Scriptures adopted by your opponent on the basis of some other Scriptures which would be adopted by both parties. As to individual judgments[3] which are going on in every man's consciousness, they are guided exclusively by what people themselves think right, not by what both parties, a respondent and his possible opponent, may agree upon.

Therefore the standpoint of strict logic is to no purpose. The Buddhas have favoured their converts, who were not versed in the science of logic, with arguments which suited the occasion. Enough about this subject. Let us continue our comment.

XXVI. DENIAL OF CAUSALITY THROUGH A SEPARATE SUBSTANCE

Neither do entities arise out of something different from them just because from the monistic point of view the different does not exist[4]. This point will be elucidated later on[5], when it will be

1 Cp. text and Nyāyabindu pp. 3.5.

2 Ibid. III. 58. (p. 62).

3 *svārthānumāna* corresponds to our judgement, it includes every cognition which is not a direct passive sense perception.

4 or "just because entities do not exist in something else (=*parasmin abhāvād eva*)" as e.g., the cloth in the threads, the jar in the clay. etc.

5 cp. aphorism. 1, 3.

expressed that "what belongs to the things themselves, their own essence, does not belong to their causes and (conditions)[1]."

Therefore, just because they do not pre-exist *in* something else, they cannot be produced *out* of it. Moreover the impossibility of a substantial break[2] between cause and effect can also be established on the lines which we have laid down in our "Introduction to the Madhyamaka System" where it is said[3],

> If, to be sure, a thing were "other" in regard to causes,
> Deep darkness would then be produced from light[4]
> Then surely everything could be produced out of anything,
> Since "otherness" is just the same in causes and non-causes.[5]

The Master Buddhapālita comments, "entities cannot arise out of something essentially different from them, since it would follow that everything could arise out of anything."

The Master Bhāvaviveka assails this comment. "It is nonsense. He says, because the argument contains its own destruction[6], since (1) it is mere *deductio ad absurdum*, (2) it conflicts with the point previously established. Indeed in taking the counterpart of the reason and of the predicate we will have the following argument, "since everything must arise out of something and the origination out of non-self is rejected, entities must then arise either out of themselves or out of self and non-self combined, or without a cause, otherwise (really) everything would arise out of anything".

---

1 Lit. 36, 4 "The own existence, (*svabhāva*), of entities (*bhāvānām*) is not found in their condition, etc. "cp. infra. 1.3. This is the Vaiśeṣika view, the cloth is something different from the sum total of the threads, the jar something over and above the sum total of the atoms of clay, etc.,

2 *parata utpattiḥ*, 36. 10.

3 Madhy. av., VI 14.

4 When causality is understood as a regularity of succession, the day will be the cause of the following night and night would produce the following day, a question that has been often discussed in European philosophy.

5 Among all considerations which tend to undermine our usual conceptions of causation this one is considered by the Tibetans to be the strongest, they say it is as solid as diamond.

6 p. 37.2 read *sādhana-dūṣaṇāntaḥ*......i.e. *ity asya sādhanasya dūṣaṇam*....

It is not nonsense[1]. We have shown above that a *deductio ad absurdum* is a valid proof. As to the accusation that Buddhapālita in confuting the tenet of his opponent[2] has indirectly invalidated his own[3] previously established point, it is trivial[4]. We will not again take pains to refute this.

XXVII. COMBINED CAUSALITY DENIED

Neither do the entities arise out of both (a continuant stuff and separate factors), since all the incongruity attaching to each of these hypotheses separately will then attach to their combination.

But then both causes may perhaps work alternately, not simultaneously? No, since if they are not fit to produce something separately, (they neither will be fit to produce something separately, (they neither will be fit to produce something alternately). Indeed it will be stated later on that:—

The world[5] could be a product,
From a double set of causes,
If separately they were efficient[6].

XXVIII. NO PLURALISTIC UNIVERSE WITHOUT CAUSATION

But neither can the separate entities of this world arise without a cause. The incongruities which would follow on such an assumption will be pointed out later on, where it will be said,

If there be no causation,
All difference will vanish
Between a cause and its effect[7].

---

1 p. 37.4 read with the Tibetan *asaṁgatārthaṁ nāsti*.

2 The Vaiśeṣika who maintains *parata utpatti*.

3 sc. *paradūṣaṇena svadūṣaṇāntaḥpatitam*.

4 Lit. p. 37. 4-7 "And that he has fallen into a refutation by refuting the thesis of the opponent, this is anything but truth." i.e., by denying causation between independent substances Buddhapālita has indirectly admitted causation out of the same substance; this argument is worth nothing.

5 *duḥkha*.

6 M. s., XII 9.

7 VIII. 4.

In our Introduction to the Madhyamaka System, we have also indicated the following incongruity,

> Nothing at all could we perceive
> In a universe devoid of causes,
> It would be like the colour and the scent
> Of a lotus growing in the sky[1].

The Master Buddhapālita comments. "Entities", says he, "neither can arise without a cause, since every thing would then be possible at any time, and in any place."

This also has been assailed by Bhāvaviveka. He says, "this is again a mere *deductio ad absurdum* and it can be turned into the contrary, if the meaning of the argument be disclosed by taking the counterpart of the reason and of the predicate. You say "entities are not without a cause, since otherwise everything could appear at any time and at any place." I say, "entities must have a cause, since everything springs up at a definite time and in a definite place, and because as experience proves efficient causes produce new result." Therefore the comment of Buddhapālita on this point is wrong, because it contains the same mis-conception as his comment on the foregoing points.

As opponents[2] we will repeat that this criticism misses the mark. Its refutation has been made above.

XXIX. CAUSALITY THROUGH THE WILL OF GOD

It may be supposed that this critique of the usual notion of causality is intended in order to introduce God or similar transcendental supreme cause. But this is also impossible, because God must be included in one of the alternatives discussed, according to the idea we entertain about his essence. He is either immanent in the world, or transcends it, or he is both simultaneously immanent and transcendent.

Thus it is established that there is no causality in the ultimate sense. The dependent Origination (or Relativity) with its eight characteristics of no real origination etc., is thus established.

---

1 M. av., VI 100.

2 The same use of the term *apara* as above. text p. 9.6.

XXX MAHĀYĀNA AND HĪNAYĀNA CONTRASTED

An objection is here raised by the Hīnayānist. If it is so, he says, if your interpretation of the principle of Dependent Origination as a principle of Relativity implying that there is no real Causality is correct, how are the deliverances of Buddha to be explained which run against such a theory. Indeed it has been declared,

(1) "The forces[1] of life are influenced in this world by illusion and desire. When illusion and all desires have been suppressed in Nirvāṇa, these forces are extinct."[2] This suggests the reality of the force of illusion and Nirvāṇa.

(2) All elements[3] of life,
They all appear and disappear;
As soon as they appear they vanish.
Their final stoppage is the only bliss.

And further:—

(3) "Whether some elements of existence have appeared or whether they have not appeared, there is, according to the teaching of the Buddhas no controlling conscious Agent who makes them either appear or not appear, remains unchallenged just this eternal essence of what the elements really are, (their causal interconnection.)"[4]

---

1 saṁskāra.

2 This is the abridged formula of *pratītya-samutpāda* as applied to the development of an individual life in 12 consecutive stages, the so-called *prākarṣika or āvasthika pratītya-samutpāda*. Its first part corresponds to the direct order (*anuloma*) of the members, its second part to their reversed (*pratiloma*) order. This abridgement clearly reveals the simple meaning of the formula as it is understood in all Buddhist countries. Cp. O. Rosenberg, *Probleme*, ch. XVI and My Central Conception, p. 28n 3.

3 *saṃskāra* for *saṃskṛta-dharma*.

4 This is the celebrated formula of *pratītya-samutpāda* in its generalized sense, as given in the Śālistambha-sūtra, it is very often quoted, cp. reference in M. de la V.P.'s text edition, p. 40 n 1. The second *tathāgatānām* must be dropped and the first understood with Mādhavācārya, sarvadarś p. 41. 8. in the sense of *tathāgatānām mate*. Lit. "whether according to the Buddhas the *dharmas* originate or if they can not originate, this their essence necessarily stands". The notion of causality, as well as the idea of a gradual evolution by karma, of the world towards Nirvāṇa, the absence in this process of any controlling conscious Will, all this is included in the connotation of the term *dharma* itself. Therefore *dharma* as an element of existence and *dharma* as the doctrine about these elements are expressed by the same word. The formula is found in Hīnayānistic as well as in Mahāyānistic literature. Mādhavācārya, borrowing from some Buddhist

(4) "There is one fundamental law[1] for the subsistence of living beings, that is their fourfold nutrition."

(5) "There are two mental elements[2] which protect the world, humility and the sense of justice."

(6) "There is a descent from another world into this one, and a departure from this one into another one."[3]

Thus it is clear that Buddha has taught a principle of Dependent Origination which is not incompatible with the disappearing of some things and the appearing of others. How can you assert that it does not interfere with your principle of Relativity?[4]

It is just for this reason, because Scripture mentions a principle of Dependent Origination meaning that some elements disappear (when others appear), it is for this very reason that our Master

---

source, gives it a Hīnayānist interpretation (*dharmāṇām kārya-kāraṇa-rūpāṇām*). Candrakīrti takes it as a comprehensive formula admitting both doctrines; it very well suits his aim in this place, since he wishes to establish that the Hīnayānist view is the simpler one and the Mahāyānist the deeper one. In Aṣṭas. Prajñāp.p. 573.21. ff. and in Bodhicaryāv. t. ad IX 150 it is given a Mahāyānist interpretation as a denial of Causation and of plurality. The meaning of the formula may then be freely rendered thus; "Whether we, with the Hīnayānists, decide that according to the teaching of the Buddhas there is a causality between the separate elements of existence or whether we, with the Mahāyānists, decide that there is none, the eternal essence of elements stands as a unity". At the time when the theory of a *kāraṇa-hetu* was established in the Abhidharma, this theory which implies a universal link of a special causality between all the elements of the Universe, past, present and future, at that time the Mahāyānistic Monism was already foreshadowed.

1 Here *dharma* is not used in the Buddhist technical sense of an element. It is not one of the 75 *dharmas*. The conception of food as an abstract principle of keeping life going is inherited from the Upanishads (cp. Jacob, Concordance, s.v. anna.) The food is physical in the realms of gross bodies. It is spiritual, consisting of sensations (sparśa), volitions (cetanā), and consciousness (vijñāna) in the mystical worlds of the real bodies and pure spirits.

2 Here *dharma* is used in the technical sense, since *hrī* and *apatrapā* are included in the 75 *dharmas*. The prominence given to these moral forces (*saṃskāras*) is natural, since the reverse of them, irreverence and indifference for injustice, are supposed to be the deepest root of every immoral deed, cp. My Central Conception pp. 101, 102. Their definition is a shade different in the Triṁśikā p. 27.

3 i.e., first of all, out of this world into one of the mystic one. For the identification of all these quotations cp. the notes of M. de la V. to his edition.

4 Read *virudhyate* instead of *nirudhyate*.

Nāgārjuna has composed this Treatise on Relativity, in order to show the difference between the real and the conventional meaning of the Scripture. All the above utterances which mention a principle of Dependent Origination along with real causation do not refer to the pure essence of the objects which reveals itself when the darkness of our ignorance in philosophy is dispelled.[1] On the contrary, it refers to that condition of the world which reveals itself to the mental eyes[2] whose vision is vitiated by the darkness of illusion.

There are other utterances of Buddha which, on the contrary, refer to the absolute reality :

1. "The paramount Reality, Brethren, is Nirvāṇa, it is not a clandestine Reality.[3] All the combined forces of phenomenal life are illusions.
2. There is in this world, neither Reality, nor the absence of Illusion. It is surreptitious Reality, it is a cancelled Reality, it is a lie, childish babble, an Illusion."

Further,

All matter is a piece of foam, all feeling is a babble.
A mirage all ideas are, a (hollow) plantain trunk the forces,
The sunlike Buddha has declared
(All) consciousness is but illusion.[4]
Attentive, mindful day and night,
The recluse full of courage,
By contemplating (separate) elements,[5]
Should penetrate into Quiescence,
The bliss where all the energies repose.

5. "Because all elements that are active in the process of life contain nothing real, Plurality is an illusion."[6]

---

1 Read *āsrava* (sc. *vigata......āsrava*) instead of *anāsrava*.

2 *Mati-nayana=prajñā-cakṣuḥ*.

3 "The element having the characteristic of not being some stolen goods", i.e. the nonrelative.

4 This stanza is found in Saṁyutta N. III 142 where the illusion regarding the 5 skandhas must be understood as referring to the theory of *pudgala-nairātmya*. Here evidently Candrakīrti takes it as referring to the theory of *dharma-nairātmya*.

5 *dharma=saṃskṛta-dharma=saṃskāra*.

6 A very frequent proposition referring to the theory of *dharma-nairātmya*.

XXXI THE DIRECT AND INDIRECT MEANING OF BUDDHA'S WORDS

For the sake of those, who, having no thorough knowledge of the intention contained in the different utterances of Buddha, fall into doubt whether a particular expression refers to the absolute truth or whether it does depart from it with a special intention; and for the sake of those who, owing to their slow wits, mistake a metaphorical expression for the real intention; for the sake of both these classes of men needing instruction, is this treatise composed, in order to dispel doubt and misconception by the way of argument and references to Scripture.

The arguments have been expounded above in commenting upon the aphorism "entities do not arise out of themselves".

The Scriptural references are given by Nāgārjuna in the following chapters. e.g.

The stolen goods are of no use,
This has been said by Buddha,
And all the forces in this world
Are stolen goods, They are illusion.[1]

And further,

This world has neither beginning nor an end,
We do not see its first extremity.
The great ascetic has declared,
It has no first, it has no last.[2]

And further,

When speaking to Kātyāyana, the Buddha did elucidate,
What is existence, non-existence what?
He then denied both issues.
The possibility of affirmation and negation.[3]

In these and similar aphorisms of Nāgārjuna, Scripture is quoted.

Some supplementary scriptural evidence is here appended. In the discourse with Akṣayamati we find the following statement. "What are the scriptural texts which have a conventional meaning, and what are those which have a direct meaning? Those discourses which have been delivered in order to

1 M.s. XIII. 1.
2 M.s. XI. 1.
3 M.s. XV.7.

teach the path of salvation are metaphorically expressed. Those discourses which are delivered in order to teach the Final Result are expressed with precision. Wheresoever you find a text specifying the entrance into That kind of Final Deliverance which is Relativity, where there is no separate object, no profound meditation, no volition, no birth, no causation, no existence, no Ego, no living creatures, no individual Soul, no personality and no Lord—they are called texts having direct meaning. This, O Reverend Sāriputra, is called keeping to the precise meaning of the Scripture and not to their metaphorical expressions".

Further it is stated in the Samādhirājasūtra,

A man who knows the difference
Of the precise meaning of Scripture,
Knows in what sense the Relativity[1]
Has been conceived by Buddha.
When on the contrary, the personality,
The Being, the Spiritual Self are spoken of,
He knows that all the elements are then
Conventionally taken.

Therefore, in order to show that the doctrine which admits causality etc. is a wrong doctrine, our Master Nāgārjuna has undertaken to reconsider the doctrine of Dependent Origination.

XXXII HOW IS THE MORAL LAW TO BE VINDICATED IN AN UNREAL WORLD

Now, the following objection will eventually be made. If the Master has composed this treatise in order to prove that there is no real causation and that the plurality of the elements of life is a mere illusion, then, considering that what is an illusion does not really exist, it will follow that wicked actions do not exist, and if they do not exist, neither do miserable lives exist, nor any virtuous actions are possible, and without them no happy life. Without the happy and unhappy lives, there will be no phenomenal world[2] and thus all endeavours towards a better life will be absolutely fruitless. We answer. We teach the illusion of existence as an antidote against the obstinate

1 *śūnyatā*.
2 *saṁsāra*.

belief of common mankind in the reality of this world, we teach its relative truth. But for the Saints,[1] there is no need for that. They have reached the goal. They apprehend no plurality, nothing that could be illusion or non-illusion. And when a man has thoroughly realised the pluralistic illusion of all separate entities, there is for him no Moral Law. How can there be any virtuous actions for him, or any phenomenal life? The question whether an entity exists or does not exist will never occur to him.

Accordingly Buddha has declared in the "Ratnakūṭa Discourse", "O Kāśyapa, if we search for consciousness we do not find it. What is not to be found is not to be perceived. What is not to be perceived is neither past, nor future, nor present. What is neither past, nor future, nor present has no separate reality.[2] What has no reality has no causation. What is uncaused cannot disappear. But an ordinary man follows wrong views. He does not realize the illusive character of separate elements. He obstinately thinks that the contingent entities have a reality of their own. Swayed by this inveterate belief in the reality of separate things,[3] he takes action,[4] and as consequence of this he migrates through this phenomenal world. As long as he takes his stand on such confusion, he is not fit to attain Nirvāṇa."

But although the reality of these separate entities is an illusion, they nevertheless can produce either moral defilement or purification, just as the magical apparition of a beauty inspires passion to those who have not realized her nature, and just as a vision evoked by the Buddha is a cause of moral purification for those who have practised the roots of virtue.

This is stated in the "Discourse with the Dṛḍhāśaya". "It is similar, O noble son, to somebody watching a magical show. He contemplates the vision of a pretty woman and his heart fills with passion. Feeling shy before the audience, he gets up from his seat and disappears. After having left, he tries to persuade himself that the woman was ugly, that it is even no

1 *ārya*.

2 *svabhāvataḥ*.

3 *idaṁsatya-abhiniveśa*, i.e. regards the *dharmas* as real.

4 *karma*, technically it means that blind biotic forces (*karma*) operate, seemingly through hint.

real personality, but an assemblage of elements impermanent, disquieting and illusive etc."

The following is stated in the Vinaya. "An engineer[1] might construct a mechanical doll with the form of a beautiful young woman. It was not a real woman, but the workmanship was so perfect that it appeared as a real beauty, and an artist painter really fell in love with it. Just so it is that phenomena, although having no separate reality of their own, are nevertheless efficient producers either of moral pollution or moral purification for simple people.

We find in the Ratnakūṭasūtra[2] the following story. "At that time there were five hundred monks who did not understand the preaching of the Buddha. They did not go deep into it. They had no fervour for it. They then stood up from their seats and went away. The Buddha on this occasion produced a magical vision of two recluses on the path by which the monks were receding. The five hundred monks then reached the place where the two apparitional recluses were standing. Having met them they spoke unto them. "Where are both the Reverend Fathers going?" The magical monks answered, "We are retiring to the woods. There we will live enjoying the delightful feeling of trance. We cannot penetrate the doctrine taught by the Buddha, we cannot go deep into it. We feel no devotion, we fear it, we are trembling before it." Then the five hundred monks spoke. "Neither we can penetrate into the doctrine taught by the Buddha, nor can we go deep into it, nor are we devoted to it. We fear, we tremble, we have got quite in a tremble. Therefore we too will go to the woods and live there enjoying the delightful feeling of trance." The magical monks spoke, "Therefore, O Reverend ones, we shall be united, we shall not quarrel. Above all duties for the monk, not to quarrel is the paramount." "What do the Reverend ones think to get rid of?" They answered. "We think to get rid of covetousness, of hatred and of infatuation." The two magical monks spoke. "But are the Reverend ones really possessed of covetousness, hatred and infatuation which they want to forsake?" They answered, "They are not to be perceived, neither in us internally, nor in the things externally, nor in the

1 *yantra-kāra*.

2 Cp-Wassiliew, p. 157.

space between both. Nor can they indeed arise without having been imagined." The magical monks spoke, "Therefore, O Reverened ones, do not imagine them, do not fancy them, And if the Reverend ones will not imagine, will not fancy them, they will neither love nor hate. The man who neither loves nor hates, is called dispassionate. Merit, O Reverend ones, neither migrates, nor finally disappears. Trance, Wisdom, Deliverance, the intellectual awakening of the first glimpse of Nirvāṇa[1] they do not migrate, nor do they disappear, they are the elements, O Reverend ones, through which Nirvāṇa is suggested. But in themselves, O Reverend ones, these elements are also relative,[2] they have no essence. You must forget, O Reverend ones, even the idea of a separate Final Nirvāṇa. Do not produce conceptions about what is only an idea. For him who very much thinks about an idea as an idea, this idea becomes a prison. O Reverend ones, you must enter that mystic condition where all concepts and all feelings are extinct. We tell you that a recluse who is merged in such a trance has reached the climax after which no further progress is possible." After that these five hundred recluses got their minds delivered from all bonds, even from dispassionate bonds. Having got their minds thus enlightened, they approached the place where the Buddha was dwelling. After having approached, they saluted the feet of the Lord in touching the ground with their heads and sat aside."

"The Reverend Subhūti then spoke to the recluses thus ; "O Brethren, where did you go, wherefrom are you coming ?" They answered. "O Reverend Subhūti, the system taught by the Lord does not allow for moving to some place nor for coming from some places." Subhūti spoke. "Who is your teacher ?" They answered. "That one who never was born and never will disappear."[3] He asked. "In what spirit has philosophy been taught to you ?" They answered. "The goal was neither Bondage nor was it Deliverance." He asked. "Who has drilled you ?" They answered. "That one who neither has a body nor a mind." He asked. "What was the method of your preparation." They answered. "Neither that of foregoing ignorance nor that of acquiring knowledge." He aksed.

1 *vimukti-jñāna-darśana.*

2 *śūnya.*

3 *parinirvāsyati.* These denials evidently refer to the Hīnayānistic conceptions of Nirvāṇa.

"Whose disciples are you?" They answered. "Of that one who has not reached 'Nirvāṇa'," who has not attained the Supreme Enlightenment." He asked. "Who are your fellow disciples?" They answered. "Those who never appear in one of the three planes of existence." He asked. "O Brethren, how long will it take you to reach Supreme Nirvāṇa?" 'They answered. "We will have reached it when all the magical bodies created by The Buddhas will vanish." He asked. "How have you reached the goal?" They answered. "By analysing the idea of Self and the idea of Mine." He asked. "How have you got rid of passions?" They answered. "By the utter annihilation of all the elements of life." He asked. "How have you challenged the Tempter?" They answered. "By disregarding the tempter who is inherent in the elements of our individuality." He asked. "How have you been communicating with your Teacher?" They answered. "Neither bodily, nor vocally, nor mentally." He asked. "How have you discharged your charity obligations.?" They answered. "By taking nothing, by receiving nothing." He asked. "How have you escaped rebirth?" They answered. "By evading both annihilation and eternity." He asked. "How have you reached the goal of charity?" They answered. "By being absolutely averse to every property." He asked. "What are you going in for?" They answered. "We are going in for the same aim as all apparitional existences created by Buddha."

"During this meeting when Subhūti was starting questions and the recluses giving answers, 800 monks got rid even of their dispassionate bonds[1] and 32,000 men had their spiritual eyes cleared of all dust and filth, with regard to the reality of all elements of life."

Thus it is that the two magical apparitions which had no real existence, which were magically created by the Buddha have laid down the foundation for the purification of five hundred recluses.

It is also declared in the Vajramaṇḍadhāraṇī.[2] Thus it is, O Mañjuśrī, that and *conditioned by an effort of a man's hand by a piece of wood and by attrition*, smoke appears, and fire appears. But this conflagration is neither in the piece of wood nor in

1 i.e. they became *āryas*.

2 Cp. Burnouf, Introduction. (2) p. 484 ff.

the attrition, nor is it included in the effort of the hands. Even so it is, O Manjuśrī, that in the individuality called man one feels bewildered by an illusive unreality. The conflagration of lust, the conflagration of hatred and the conflagration of infatuation are produced. But this conflagration is not inside him, neither is it in the objects outside him, nor in the intermediate space between both. Again, O Mañjuśrī, what we call illusion, why is it so called, Illusion, O Mañjuśrī, is a condition of complete error in regard to all elements of existence. The axiom of this Dhāraṇī is that all elements are like the hells." When asked "How is it O Buddha, that this is the maxim ?" He answered. "The hells, O Mañjuśrī, are produced by imagination. Fools and simple people are cheated by error and illusion." He asks. "Wherefrom, O Blessed One, do the hells descend ?" Buddha answers. "From the Space do the hells descend." "Do you think, O Mañjuśrī, that the hells are produced by our imagination or do they exist as a separate reality ?" He answers. "The transmigration of our Soul into the hells, into animals and into ghosts is fancied by the imagination of fools and simple people. By error and imputation, they imagine that they suffer, that they live a life of misery in these three inferior planes of existence."

"These tortures of the hell exist, O Blessed One, only as far as I imagine them. Let us, e.g., suppose, O Blessed One, that somebody in a dream imagines himself gone down to the hell. He will then imagine that he is cast in an iron vessel, boiling amidst blazing fires, quite filled with many human beings.[1] There he will be tormented by a strong, acute, intense pain. This awful suffering he will imagine in his mind. He nevertheless will be frightened, will be terror-stricken. Having then awakened.[2] he will cry out, "Oh, how awful, how awful." He will be distressed and lament. His friends, acquaintances and relatives will ask, "who has made you suffer so much ?" He will reply to these friends, acquaintances and relatives. "I have suffered the tortures of the hell." He will then revile and repeat, "I am suffering the tortures of the hell, and you ask me to tell you who has made me so suffer". Then these friends, acquaintances and relatives will address the man in the

1 *eka-pauruṣa*, cp. Tib.
2 *samānaḥ*. "with self assurance". according to Tib.

following way. "Be not afraid, O man, you were asleep, you have not left this house." He will then regain memory and think, "Yes, I have been asleep, all this is wrong, it is my imagintion." And he will again recover his good spirits."

"Thus it is, O Blessed One, that this man dreaming in sleep has imagined, through a wrong imputation, that he has been in the hell. It is in the same manner, O Blessed One, that all simple and foolish people are saturated with an imagined sexual appetite. They construct for themselves the idea of a woman as the target of their desires. Having constructed it, they imagine that they enjoy themselves in her company. To such a foolish and simple man it occurs, 'I am a man, she is a woman, she is my wife.' His mind is overcome by lust and delight, he allows his mind to indulge in pleasure. Moved by such feelings he might produce a row, a dispute, an altercation. His senses become obscured, he breathes hate. With these illusions he then imagines himself passing away and suffering in the hells during many thousands of eons. The friends, acquaintances and relatives of this man, O Blessed One, will speak to him in the following way. "Don't fear, don't be frightened, O man! You were asleep, you did not leave this house".

"O Blessed One, it is just according to this relativity of the phenomenal world that the divine Buddhas have preached their doctrine to the living creatures who are imbued with the four-fold[1] illusion of the world's reality." "There is here (in this world, they teach) neither man nor woman; no living creature, no Soul, no Spirit no Personality. All this plurality of the ultimate elements[2] of existence is an illusion. They do not exist. They are misleading, they are like a trick, they are like a dream, they are like magic, they are like the reflection of the moon in water etc." Having received this instruction of the Buddha the living creatures perceive the plurality of elements without their enticement, without their illusive character, without considering them as separate existences, without this covering of plurality. They pass away with their mind merged in Space. After having passed away they will be completely

1 i.e., the illusions of a real self, its bliss, its purity, its permanence. Cp. Yoga-sū. II 5.

2 *Sarva-dharmāḥ.*

merged in the Final Reality of Nirvāṇa.[1] Thus, O Blessed One, do I regard the hells."

It is also said in the "Questions of the Venerable Upāli",[2] "I have seen the many terrors of the hell, by which thousands of creatures are tortured. But there are no creatures in this world who after death go to the tortures of the hell. There are no swords, no arrows, and no spears, by which torture is inflicted. In imagination they fancy them falling upon their bodies. There are no real weapons. And in the heavens delightful golden palaces decorated with beautiful variegated flowers appear before us, but nobody has constructed them. They are also constructed by imagination. The simple man constructs them in imagination. The fool sticks to these constructed conceptions. Whether we stick to them or do not stick to them, they are not real. These conceptions are like *fata morgana*."

Thus it is proved that these separate entities of the phenomenal world have no real independent existence of their own. To simple people who are misled by their own subjective illusions, they become a source of moral defilement in this life. In our "Introduction into the Madhyamaka System", we[3] have explained at length how it is that objects which have no reality of their own can nevertheless produce either moral defilement or moral purification. There it can be learnt.

XXXIII THE TWELVE MEMBERED CAUSAL SERIES REFERS TO THE PHENOMENAL WORLD

To this the Hīnayānist objects. If there is altogether no causation, if things arise neither out of themselves, nor out of something extraneous, nor out of both these sources, nor at random, how is the causal series preached by the Buddhas to be understood, how is it that he has declared that as long as

---

1 *Nirupādhi-śeṣa nirvāṇa-dhātu.*

2 This work is quoted in Śikṣā-samuccaya as an authority on confession, p. 164, 168, 178, 290.

3 The tenor of this work in general is probably meant.

illusion has not been extinct by knowledge and meditation, prenatal forces will always produce new lives ?[1]

We answer : This is the phenomenal point of view,[2] it is not absolute reality.[3]

The realist : Please tell, how is phenomenalism proved ?

Mādhyamika : Phenomenalism is nothing but the expression of the fact of Universal Relativity.[4] It cannot be established otherwise than by denying the four theories of causation just examined, since they necessarily imply the realistic view[5] of a plurality of substances having their own reality. But if we take our stand upon Universal Relativity, the cause and effect, being correlative, have neither of them any absolute existence, Realism[5] is thus repudiated.

Accordingly it has been said,[6]

---

1. The last but one chapter of the Madhy. śāstra is devoted to the examination of the formula of the twelve-membered Causal series. It is there given the following interpretation. There is in the world a craving for life (*punar-bhavārtham*) produced by an illusion (*avidyā*) which can be stopped by the *tattvadarśin*. In Mahāyāna, it is the Saint who intuits the world *sub specie aetertatis*. In Hīnayāna, it is the Yogin who really stops all the function of life and converts it into an eternal death. Under the influence of such illusion prenatal forces (*saṃsakāra=karma*) produce a new life (*vijñāna*), an embryo (*nāma rūpa=pañca-skandha*) is formed (*kukṣau nāma-rūpam niṣicyate*), which gradually develops the senses (*ṣaḍāyatana*), sensation (*sparśa*), feeling, (*vedanā*), sensual appetite (*tṛṣṇā*), the habits underlying (*upādāna*) life, life itself (*bhava=new karma*), and, after death, a new birth, old age and death again. The fourmula represents the rotation of the phenomenal life (*duḥkha*) in which there is no eternal principle, which is *kevala=anātma=*12 *āyatanas*, with the implication that it can be completely stopped, without any residue of life, in Nirvāṇa. If its connection with the theory of the separate elements (*dharmas*) and their total extinction in Nīrvāṇa, ultimately through yoga, is overlooked, the formula simply states that living beings come and go, are born and die. Cp. O Rosenberg, Problems, ch. XVI. The interpretation of Nāgārjuna is virtually the same as is current in all Buddhist countries, cp. Aung, Co., pendium, p. 259, ff In prof. B. Keith's interpretation op. cit. p. 99 ff. the simple formula is converted into a heap of absurdities.

2 *samvṛtiḥ*, or this is "the covering", "the face of it".

3 *tattvam.*

4 *idampratyayatā-mātram=pratītya-samutpāda-mātram, cp. text,* transl. p. 152.

5 *sa-svabhāva-vādaḥ.*

6 Lokātīta-stava, 19, Bstan-hygur, Bstod, I (M. dela V. P.)

Philosophers assume phenomenal world,[1]
Either as self-produced or as non-self produced,
Or causeless, or both self and non-self made.
But you have proved, it is contingent.[2]
And it will be stated in this treatise later on,[3]
So far as there are effects, there is a cause.
So far as there is a cause, there are effects,
We cannot realize,
For their reality another reason.

Just the same has been declared by Buddha himself in the following words;

"The theory of separate elements[4] implying the denial of personal identity[5] means that "this exists so far as that exists", "if this has appeared that will appear",[6] e.g., prenatal forces exist so far as illusion and desire have not been stopped, a new life[7] is produced so far there are prenatal forces which produce it, etc etc."

XXXIV CONTROVERSY ABOUT THE VALIDITY OF LOGIC

A vehement protest[8] is raised by some philosophers against this condemnation of logic.[9] "You maintain," they say "that separate entities are not caused (in the absolute sense). Now, is this assertion founded on argument, or is it not founded on argument? If you admit that it is founded on argument,

1 *duḥkha*.
2 *pratītya-ja*.
3 VIII. 12.
4 *dharma saṁketa=pudgala-nairātmya*=12 *āyatana s*, *Cp*. Central Conception, p., 28
5 *pudgala-nairātmya=anātma*.
6 This very ancient formulation, cp, Majjh. M., III 63, is given a realistic interpretation in Hīnayāna and a transcendental one in Mahāyāna, cp. above p. 40.
7 *vijñāna*. In the first period of the development of the embryo it is dormant (*sammūrcchita*), until sensation (*sparśa*) appears. In a bird's egg, as long as it has not lost vitality, there is *vijñāna* according to the principles of *pratītya-samutpāda*. When the term is mistranslated as "thought", "pensee" etc. confusion inevitably arises. Prof. Keith, op. cit. p. 101, has imagined that it is "visible"? Visible is termed in the Pali Canon *sanidassana*. Among the 75 ultimates there is only one, the *rūpa-āyatana*, i.e. colour, which is visible, cp. Dīgha N. III.217, Ab Kośaḥ, I, 28.
8 *pari-codanā*.
9 This and the following discussion refers to the *pramāṇaviniścayavāda* of Dignāga and others. The first step in the vindication of logic has been made by Bhāvaviveka. But he remained a Mādhyamika. The *pramāṇa-*

you are obliged to answer the following questions. How many are the sources of our knowledge? What is their essence? What is their scope? What is their origin? Have they arisen out of themselves, out of something extraneous, out of both, or out of nothing? But if your denial of causation is not founded on argument, it must be rejected, because our cognition of an object depends upon the method by which it is cognized. If something is not known, it cannot become known otherwise than by appropriate methods. If these methods do not exist, neither will cognition ever be arrived at. How is then your explicit assertion possible? You cannot assert that the separate entities are not caused. Or else just the same reason which allows you to maintain that nothing is caused will also allow me to maintain the contrary, viz. that every single thing exists. And just as you assert that all our elements of existence are uncaused,[1] I will maintain that whatsoever exists has a cause."[2]

"Or perhaps you do not really believe that nothing is being produced, you tell it just for the sake of cavilling? But then you will never persuade your opponent to believe a theory you do not yourself believe. The composition of this treatise will then serve no purpose, and the denial of Pluralism[3] will not have been really made."

Mādhyamika. We answer. If our system did allow assertive judgments implying the transcendental reality of a substratum, the question would then arise whether these judgments are founded on sound method or not. However, there is no place for them in a system of Universal Relativity. The reason for that is just the followiug one. If problematic judgements regarding reality were admitted as possible, we would then be obliged to admit the counterpart, the possibility of correspond-

---

viniścaya-vāda is expounded by Vācaspati Miśra in Tātparyaṭ. p.7.1 28 and p. 248.25 ff. cp. Garbe. Die Saṅkhya Phil. p. 203. *viniścaya* is another name for Dignāga's conception of *Kalpanā*, it represents the fundamental act of thinking appearing in such judgments as "this is Devadatta", "this is dark complexion," "this is moving" etc. where the element "this" refers to the *svalakṣaṇa*, cp. n. on. p. 137. cp. Tātparyaṭ. p. 101, 1. ff.

1 *anutpannāḥ sarva-dharmāḥ* (*dharma=bhāva*).

2 *sarva-bhāvotpattiḥ*.

3 *sarva-bhāvā apratiṣiddhāḥ*.

ing assertions. But we also absolutely deny the possibility of problematic judgments regarding the transcendental reality of a substratum, how could we then make the correlative[1] assertions, since they would not be correlative with other non-existing member of the relation. It would be like the length and the shortness of a non-existing thing, e.g., the horn of a donkey. Therefore, since we do not make any such assertion, where are the things for the sake of whose reality we should so much imagine the existence of the sources of right knowledge?[2] And how could we establish their number, their essence and their respective objects? How could we decide whether they originate out of non-self, out of both, or without a cause? It is not our business to answer all these questions.

The logician: You thus insist that you make no assertion whatsoever. But we hear from you a proposition which looks like a definite assertion,[3] viz. that entities arise neither out of

1 *Read tadviruddho.*

2 Lit., p. 56, 4. "We answer. If we would have what you call assertion, it would be produced either by right cognition or not by right cognition. But we have none. Why? Here, when non-assertion is possible, its counterpart, an assertion relative to it, might exist. But when we, first of all, don't have any non-assertion, then wherefrom the counterpart, the assertion? Since it would be disregarding the other part of the relation, just as the length and the shortness of the donkey's horn. And when there thus is no assertion, then for the sake of whose reality (*siddhi*) we would very much imagine (*parikalpa*) sources of right knowledge?" *niścaya=adhyavasāya vikalpa*, cp. Tātparyaṭ. p. 88. 22. *vikalpa* is an assertion of the form "This is that" —*evāyam*, cp. N.b.t. tipp. p. 23.4, where the element "this" refers to the "Hoc Aliquid" interpreted by Dignāga as the "thing in itself" (*svalakṣaṇa*). The judgment is regarded as synthetic (*kalpanā=nāma-jāti-yojanā*) and as dialectical (*vikalpa*); dilemma, (*aniścaya*) evidently means a problematic judgment. *iha* means either=*asmanmate*, or=*satyāṁ śūnyatāyām*. Cp. N. b. 69.22. ff. where it is stated that when something is cognized (*paricchidyate*) it means that it is contrasted (*vyavacchidyate*) with its counterpart. For both parties every assertion (*niścaya=kalpanā*) has a counterpart (*pratipakṣa*), it is a dichotomy (*dvaidhīkaraṇa*), it is relational (*apekṣā*), dialectical (*vikalpa*) If the counterpart (*sambandhyantara=pratpiakṣa*) is missing, an assertion is impossible, since it would be without a counterpart, non-relative (*nirapekṣa*). But for the Logician, every relation, as e.g. short and long has an indirect (*paratantra*) reality in the underlyng "thing in itself" (*svalakṣaṇa*). This for the Mādhyamika is like the horn of a donkey. His point seems here to be that Relativity is itself relative.

3 *niścita-rūpaṁ vākyamupapattiḥ=pramāṇam.*

themselves, nor out of something different, nor out of both, nor at random. How is that to be explained?

The Mādhyamikạ. We answer. This our statement appears decisive to simple people who try to understand it according to arguments familiar to them, but not to the Saints[1] who can intuit absolute reality.

The Logician: Do you really mean to say that these Saints believe in no argument?

The Mādhyamika. Who can say whether they have or have not any arguments? About the Absolute[2] the Saints remain silent. How is then a conversation[3] with them on this subject possible? How can we then decide whether there are arguments or not?

The Logician: If the Saints do not enlarge upon arguments, how do they manage to bring them home to simple people the idea of the Absolute?

The Mādhyamika: When the Saints are engaged in a conversation with simple folk, they do not really exhibit their own arguments. They take the arguments which are just the arguments that appeal to simple men, they provisionally admit them as a convenient method for the instruction of others, and thus give instruction to common people by just those methods which simple men can understand.

Just so it is that men influenced by sensuality invert the real condition of things. The real impurity in the body of a female they overlook. They imagine a non-existing beauty of its forms and are tormented by it. In order to liberate them from their passion, a person magically created by Buddha or a god may depict to them the impurities of the body which therefore were concealed from them under the idea of its beauty. This body, they will say, is covered with hair and contains other impurities in the intestines[4]. These men will then get rid of their conviction that it was a beauty and attain impossibility.

---

1 The Buddhist Saint (*ārya*) is here the equivalent of the Monist who by mystic intuition (*yogi-pratyakṣa*) has reached a direct vision of the world *sub specie aeternitatis*, he has entered the *dṛṣṭi-mārga*. He has absolutely no judgments (*niścaya*), strictly speaking not even the assertion of Relativity (*śūnyatā*); cp. above p. 35.

2 *paramārthaḥ*.

3 *prapañca=vāk*, M. vr. p. 373. 9i Lit. "Therefore wherefrom the possibility there of speech, so that there would be either argument or no argument".

4 The *aśubha-bhāvanā* is here alluded to, the practice of the *yogins* to concentrate upon the repulsive, loathsome particulars of every animal life.

Just the same happens here. Common mankind whose power of vision is obstructed by the darkness of ignorance imputes to separate entities a reality which they do not possess, a reality which for the Saint does not exist at all. It then happens that these ordinary men are tormented by some particular thing which they somehow imagine to exist.[1] The Saints then try to rouse their skepticism by some argument which would appeal to them. E.g., supposing the Sāṅkhya proves his tenet of identity between an effect and its material cause, the Monist then says, "If the jar did really exist in the lump of clay, it would never have needed to be produced out of it once more." This will be acquiesced in. He then concludes, "If something exists before its production, it need not be produced once more, because it exists". Thus the Sāṅkhya will be confuted in a way intelligible to everybody.

Similarly will it be said against the converse theory of the Vaiśeṣikas who admit a break between the effect and its material cause, "You agree that a sprout cannot be produced out of blazing coal because the latter *is different*, we then must conclude that it neither originates out of seeds etc., which are usually represented[2] as their cause, since they also are different.[3]

The Logician may at last maintain that causality exists because such is our direct experience.[4]

Mādhyamika: This also is wrong because of the following argument :

Thesis: This direct experience is misleading.

Reason: Because it is experience.

---

1 Lit. p. 58.1-3 "Just so here likewise, the worldlings are very much tormented (*subject to kleśas*) having imputed to something some inverted essence of entities, because their mental eyes are obstructed by the darkness or ophthalmia of ignorance, an essence whose substance is in every respect unperceived by the Saints."

2 *vivakṣita*.

3 In order to save the reality and substantiality of separate objects the Vaiśeṣikas maintain that the effect is absolutely different (*atyanta-bhinna*) from its material cause, and that the whole contains something in addition, over and above its parts. But this does not prevent them from maintaining that the parts are inherent (*samaveta*) in the whole. The Mādhyamika here resorts to his "diamond-like argument against Causality, "If the effect is different, there is no causation, if it is partly different and partly non-different the difficulty will be double." This of course should not prevent him from making use of the everyday conception of Causality when needed.

4 *anubhava*.

Example: Just as the direct experience of a double moon by a man suffering from ophthalmia.

Consequently it is wrong to oppose our argument on the basis of direct experience, since the reliability of the latter remains to be proved.[1]

We have thus established in the first chapter of our work that the separate entities of the phenomenal world have never originated and do not exist. And we have proved this by our negative method. We first assume the reality of something impossible and then condemn it.[2]

The remaining parts of the treatise are now concerned with details. They are devoted to the repudiation of all possible characteristics of reality, wheresoever they have been assumed to exist. It will be shown that in the light of Relativity, all these particular characteristics are not ultimately real, e.g., neither a moving object, nor the point to be reached,[3] nor motion[4] itself do really exist.[5]

XXXV CONTROVERSY WITH THE BUDDHIST LOGICIAN CONTINUED

However there is still a question to be considered, viz. the theory of our Buddhist epistemologists. "We are only giving, they maintain, a scientific description of what just happens in common life, in regard to the sources of knowledge and their respective objects. We do not consider their transcendental reality.[6]

---

1 *sādhya-sama*.

2 Lit., p. 58.10., "Therefore unproduced are the entities, thus, first of all, by counterargument, by imputation of a contrary essence, the first chapter is composed."

3 *gantavya*, cp. II 25.

4 C. II is devoted to the denial of motion. It is noteworthy that a splendid opportunity offered itself here to Nāgārjuna to repeat, in some form or other, some of Zeno of Elea's deductions of our usual conception of motion *ad absurdum*. The Greek philosopher was also a monist, he was anxious to prove that motion is impossible, because he followed Parmenides in denying plurality. There is no trace of Nāgārjuna having known them.

5 Lit., p. 58. 12-13, "...in order to teach that without exception every characteristic of *pratītya-samutpāda* does not exist." In this phrasing *pratītya-samutpāda* becomes a synonym of reality (*sāṁvṛtaḥ pratītya-samutpādaḥ*). Since it is synonymous with *śūnyatā*, cp. p. 431, it is quite clear that this latter term means reality, and not voidness, the voidness refers to all its determinations which have only empirical reality.

6 It seems that the first chapter originally ended with the words *pratipādanārtham*. p. 58. 12-13. The following discussion with a follower of Dignāga looks like a later addition.

The Mādhyamika asks: But what is the upshot of such a description, does it lead to the cognition of the Absolute?

The Logician: No, but bunglers in logic, the Naiyāyikas have given wrong definitions of logical processes and we have then given the right ones.

The Mādhyamika: This also is beyond the mark, we will reply, because if the realistic logicians, the Naiyāyikas, are bad logicians, and have given wrong definitions of logical processes, then there must be a gap between what humanity at large imagines about the essence of cognition and what the realists are teaching. Then alone will your emendatory work prove promising. But this is not the case. Your work, therefore, is a quite useless occupation.[1]

---

1 Lit. p. 59. 1-3 "This is wrong. If indeed bad logicians have produced inverted definitions, common mankind would have the reverse of what is being defined, for the sake of it there could be some fruitfulness of the endeavour. But it is not so. Therefore the endeavour is quite useless." The Naiyāyikas, in their conceptions about the categories of existence and the ways of cognising them, follow the every-day conceptions of common humanity. Now, if the Buddhist Logician who is here represented as likewise adhering to the every-day logic, has really no other aim than to correct the logic of the Naiyāyikas, there must be divergence between the latter and the common life views, otherwise the Buddhist would have nothing to correct in these theories of the Naiyāyikas. But "it is not so", i.e., the Naiyāyika views are much nearer to the conception of simple humanity than what the Buddhists are teaching about logical questions. Therefore, if the Buddhist really intends to remain on empirical ground, his "endeavour is quite useless"; he has nothing better to do than to accept the logic of the Realist. This the Mādhyamika has done. He accepts the categories of existence and the modes of cognising them (the 4 *pramāṇas*) of the Naiyāyikas, as well as the theory that our sense faculties (*sannikarṣa*) can apprehend the universal as well as the particular things. He accepts all this with the proviso that it is empirical cognition which has nothing to do with the cognition of the Absolute, and which, from the transcendental stand-point is an illusion (*samvṛtti*), since it is relative (*śūnya*), not absolute (*paramārthasatya*). As to Dignāga's school, it is true that it investigates that kind of cognition which is not contradicted by experience, which is *saṁvādaka*, and defines reality i.e., ultimate reality, as efficiency. They have the right to maintain that in their logic they partly remain on empirical ground. But they establish a sharp distinction between the "pure" object (*śuddha-artha*), "pure synthesis, or reason", (*śuddha-kalpanā*), pure sensation (*śuddham pratyakaṣam=nirvikalpakam*) and empirical definite cognition (*niścaya=adhyavasāya*). With regard to the latter there is no divergence, hardly any, between the logic of the Naiyāyikas and the Buddhists, *prāpya-viṣaya* (*-adhyavasite*) *nāsti vivādaḥ*. But with regard to the former, the divergence is decisive, *grāhyaviṣaye* (*=paramārthasati*), *tu mahān vivādaḥ*. In pure sensation we cognise the pure object, the "thing in itself" *svalakṣaṇa*, the *point-instant*, *kṣaṇa*, the focus of efficiency. Here we part with the empirical ground, "the thing in itself" cannot be cognised empirically (*jñānena na prāpyate*), but it is reached in pure sensation (*api tu vijñānena=pratyakṣeṇa=nirvikalpakena*). It is a kind of limit, a kind of "Grenzbegriff"

Moreover, the criticism directed against epistemology by Nāgārjuna in his "Repudiation of Contests" must not be forgotten. He there asks, "If every cognition of an object depends upon reliable sources of knowledge, these sources being in their turn objects cognised by us, on whom do they depend? If they are also cognised through other sources of knowledge, we shall be landed into a *regressus ad infinitum*". As long as this fundamental criticism has not been cleared away, all your talk about having given the right definition of logical processes is nothing.

But never mind, let us consider your views more closely. You maintain that there are two sources of knowledge, sensation and intellection, two only, and that this corresponds to the double *essentia* of every thing existing, the particular (or the unique) and the universal.[1] We will then ask, the thing possessing this double *essentia*, does it also exist or does it not?

If it does, we must then have a supplementary object of cognition, a third kind of it. What happens then to your two sources of knowledge established in exact correspondence to the double character of existence? And if the thing possessing this double essence does not exist, the double essence itself will remain in the air, unsupported by something possessing it. What will

(*loka-maryādā*), and the logicians who have established it are transcendentalists (*atipatita-loka-maryādāḥ*). It is as much the central conception in Dignāga's system as Relativity (*śūnyatā*) is the central conception of the Mādhyamikas and pluralism (*dharmāḥ*) the central conception of Hīnayāna. All these points will be put in a clearer light in the notes to my translation of the Nyāyabinduṭīkā, shortly to appear in the B.B. translation series. But it is necessary to keep them in mind in order to understand the next following discussion between Dignāga and Candrakīrti about the essence of this "thing in itself". The attitude of the Mādhyamikas towards realism corresponds to the attitude of the Roman Catholic Church towards the plain empiricism of Aristotle. Both the Mādhyamikas and the Roman Catholic Church were hostile to critical systems, they preferred realism, with the proviso that it had nothing to do with the cognition of the Absolute which is cognised by revelation or by intuition.

1 The originality of Dignāga's system of logic consists in the doctrine which admits two distinct sources of knowledge, two only. He calls them perception and inference, but they differ very widely from what is usually understood by these terms in logic and psychology. They exactly correspond to the double character of everything existing, the particular and the universal. The particular again is not the concrete object usually so designated, but the absolutely particular, the unique, the thing which neither has extension, (*deśānanugata*), nor has it duration, (*Kālānanugata*) it is the thing in itself, (*svalakṣaṇa*) apart from anything else (*sarvato vyāvṛtta*, *trailokya-vyāvṛtta*) the point-instant (*kṣaṇa*). By sense-perception (*pratyakṣa*) the knowledge corresponding to this point-instant is understood. It is a moment of pure sensation in which no synthesis, no integration at all has been

then the double knowledge mean? Nāgārjuna will state in the sequel,[1]

Without at all any characteristic
The thing itself becomes impossible
And if impossible the thing will be,
Characteristics likewise are impossible.

XXXVI CRITIQUE OF THE NOTION OF AN ABSOLUTE PARTICULAR POINT-INSTANT

But (says the logician) we should not interpret the notion of a particular essence as an essence *possessed* by something, but we should avail ourselves of the grammatical rule allowing us to interpret this term as meaning the thing itself *which possesses* that essence?[2]

The Mâdhyamika answers: Even so, even supposing that you are right, if it really means the thing possessing that essence, nevertheless a thing cannot be characterised by its own self. That by which it is characterised must be instrumentally related to it, it must be different from the thing itself which is the object of this instrumental relation. Our criticism of the notion of an absolute particular stands.[3]

The criticism is wrong, the Logician will then answer. We assume that sensation *through which* the particular essence reveals

---

produced (*kalpanāpoḍha*). Every synthetic process of thought is contrasted with the direct cognition by the senses, as an indirect cognition or inference. Dignāga's inference thus embraces, besides our inference, all that we would call judgment, intellection, ideation, thought, reason etc., every cognitive process except pure passive sensation. The point-instant corresponding to pure sensation is the central conception in Dignāga's system; it represents a differential from which, by a process of integration, all our knowledge is built up. The principle of the Differential Calculus of a planet's motion, (*tātkālikī gatiḥ*) was known to Indian astronomers. We still do not know exactly when it was first discovered. Bhāskara in the XII century knows it, but Vācaspati Miśra, in the IX centuryA.D. avers that the point-instant of the Buddhist is the mathematical point known to the astronomers (*jyotir-vidyā-siddhā*), cp. Tātparyaṭīkā, p. 386, 1. On the Differential Calculus of Hindu Astronomy cp, W. Spottiswoode, J.R.Z.S. 1869. p. 221.

1 V. 4.

2 Lit. p., 60, 1-2 "Further let it be that a characteristic or essence is not that by what it is characterised, but according to Pāṇini, III 3.13, by making the *lyuṭ* to stand for the object, a characteristic is the characterised."

3 Lt., p. 60. 2-3. "Thus also, since it is not possible that this should be characterised by that, and since by what this is characterised, its instrument is a different thing from the object, there is just the same fault."

itself is instrumentally related to it, but nevertheless it is immanent in it. We thus escape your criticism.[1]

Mādhymika: Our criticism stands, we will answer, in deed, we are here adhering to the usual conception of what a particular essence is.

The particular essence of something, in our opinion is that essence which is the exclusive characteristic of the thing, a characteristic which it does not share with anything else. Take, e.g., the following definitions.

1. Resistance is the exclusive characteristic of solid bodies.
2. Feeling is the reaction pleasant or unpleasant produced by an object,
3. Consciousness is awareness in every single case of some object present to our mind or sense.[2]

This means that by such exclusive characteristics something is characterised. But you brush aside this generally known and far-spread interpretation, and admit another one, according to which essence means not the characteristic, but the characterised.[3]

However, if you imagine that the absolutely particular, the point-instant is characterised by our awareness of it, this can only have the following meaning. The single point-instant contains a double aspect, the thing characterised and its characteristic. This, strictly speaking, will be a double particular essence, one of them will be the thing characterised, and the other will be the characteristic. If our awareness of the point-instant represents its characteristic, the thing characterised, i.e., the objective side of the relation, will nevertheless represent something different from its characteristic. Our criticism stands.[4]

---

1 Lit. p. 60. 4-5. Further it may be that this is not a fault, since cognition is instrumental, and since this instrumentality is included in the absolute particular. *Jñāna* is here used in its widest comprehension, it then includes not only pure sensation (*vijñāna*) but, according to Buddhists and Vedāntins, *vedanā*, *sukhādi* as well.

2 For these definitions of *pṛthivī*, *vedanā* and *vijñāna* cp. My Central Conception, p. 13-19.

3 Lt. p. 60.7. "Having waived off the well known and followed etymology, you assume an object-production." Before the word *prasiddha* p. 60.7, a *cheda* must be inserted.

4 Lit. p. 60.7-61.2 "By conceiving an instrumental essence in sensation, the following is expressed, just the particular essence has objectively, the character of being an instrument belongs to another particular essence, therefore if the particular essence in sensation is an instrument there should be an object different from it, thus there is the same fault."

Moreover the Logician may point to the general Buddhist denial of all substance behind the changing sense-data. The quality of existence in solid bodies etc, is but a sense datum, revealed, in our sensation, it is just the subjective part of that relation, and it does not differ from its particular essence, it is not something revealed by the sensation itself.[1]

The Mādhyamika: But then this moment of sensation[2] itself will never be objective, and then it never will be cognised, because a particular point-instant can be cognised only under the condition of its being objective in regard to our consciousness. In that case the following qualification must be added to your statement about the double essence of everything cognizable, the particular one and the universal one. "One particular essence of the point-instant will be cognizable, that one which we here have called the characterized aspect of it. Its other particular essence will not be cognizable, that one which we have called the characterizing aspect of it".

But if you go on to maintain that this second aspect is in its turn also a thing characterized, it will then likewise require some other thing as a characteristic. And if you in this case imagine a further step in awareness, an awareness of awareness as its characteristic, you will incur the danger of an infinite regress in addition to the fault of disregarding the relation of substance and quality"[3]

XXXVII INTROSPECTION

The Mādhyamika: But then you have your theory about Introspection. According to the theory, that consciousness which represents our awareness of a point-instant of reality is

1 Lit. p. 61.3-4. "Further it might be that the hardness etc. which is contained in earth etc, being apprehended by sensation, it (sc. hardness) is just the object of that (sc. sensation) and it is not different from the particular essence."

2 *vijñāna-svalakṣaṇa.*

3 Lit. p. 66.6-9 "Some particular essence which is designated 'what is characterized' is object of cognition, some is not object of cognition which is designated 'what is characterized through it.' Further it also is object-production. Then its different instrument must exist. If the instrumentality of another knowledge is with an effort (*pari-kalpanā*), the fault of an infinite regress is incurred."

apprehended by introspection. It thus contains inherent objectivity (and immanent cognizability).[1]

The Mādhyamika: We answer. In our "Introduction to the Madhyamaka System," we have already referred at length to this theory of Introspection.[2] That one particular essence (the point-instant) is characterised by another one, (i.e. by our awareness of it), and the latter by introspection—this is impossible !

Moreover, the criticism of Nāgārjuna which we have mentioned above[3] remains. That very moment of consciousness cannot be real without having an essence of its own, it cannot exist (without it). And if, on the other hand, there is nothing of which it is the essence, the latter (i.e., the essence), having no support, will have no opportunity to realize itself. What becomes then of introspection which is supposed to apprehend such consciousness which is itself impossible ?[4]

Accordingly it is said in the "Questions of Ratnacūḍa,"[5]

"Considering consciousness he the Bodhisattva investigates[6] the stream of thought,[7] and asks wherefrom does it come. The following occurs to him. Consciousness arises, if there is an immanent object. Does that mean that consciousness is one thing and the object another, or that they are identical ? In the first case we shall have a double consciousness. But if they are identical how is then consciousness to be cognized through consciousness ? Consciousness cannot apprehend its own self. The trenchancy of a sword cannot cut its own trenchancy. The tip of a finger cannot touch that very tip. Similarly this consciousness cannot be conscious of its own self."

---

1 Lt. p. 61.10-11. "Then you suppose that there is self-consciousness, therefore, objectivity existing because of apprehension through self-consciousness, there necessarily (*eva*) is inclusion in cognizability."

2 VI. 73. (p. 167: ff.)

3 Text, p. 59.10. trans. pl. 142.

4 Lit. p. 62.1-3. "Moreover this very knowledge, for sure, not being real separately from the particular essence and therefore being impossible, and in the absence of the thing characterized, not being able to operate as a characteristic without any substratum, altogether does not exist, thus wherefrom self-consciousness ?"

5 Translated partly by Burnouf, Introduction, p. 500.

6 Notwithstanding the Tibetan, we prefer here to read with Burnouf *cittaṁ samanupaśyan*, just as in the sequel, p. 62.7. 63.6. *asamanupaśyan* could only mean not having yet fully realized, what consciousness is (i.e., not having yet attained *vipaśyana*, he investigates..."

7 *citta-dhārā*, Burnouf—"le trenchant (de la pensee)."

"Thus it is that when a Saint is thoroughly attentive,[1] when he is engaged in the spiritual exercise of the Mahāyānistic application of mindfulness[2] towards his own consciousness, then it appears to him as indefinable. It neither has an end nor a beginning.[3] It is not changeless, it is not causeless, it does not conflict with the interdependence of the elements, but it is neither identical, nor non-identical, neither with itself, nor with others. He then cognizes this stream of thought, of thought as thin as a creeper, the thought-element, indefinite thought, non-manifested thought, imperceptible thought, thought as a thing in itself.[4] He intuits this (unspeakable thought) as "Thisness", the unique Reality of the Universe, he does not suppress it."[5]

"Such is the analysis of thought which he realises and intuits. This, O noble son, is the Bodhisattva's exercise of application of mindfulness consisting in the consideration of what in our consciousness represents its essence".

XXXVIII THE DISCUSSION ABOUT THE POINT-INSTANT RESUMED

We thus reject Introspection. We now return to the single moment of sensation which was supposed to be characterized by self-awareness. Since there is no such self-awareness when we say that it is a "thing in itself," a thing characterised exclusively by itself, what do we mean, who is characterized by whom?[6]

And then we ask, is there here in this thing which is its own essence any difference between the essence and the thing possessing that essence, or is there none ? In the first case, the essence will be different from the thing, and it will cease to be its essence.

---

1 *yoniśaḥ prayuktaḥ*.

2 This is the third *smṛty-upasthāna* exercise. That the Mahāyānistic exercise is meant is clear, because it results in identifying one's own consciousness with *tathatā=śūnyatā*.

3 Cp. M-vi. p. 536.15, *purānataṁ samāśritya dṛṣṭiḥ*.

4 *citta-svalakṣaṇa*, Burnouf—la pensee "contenue en elle-meme".

5 Lit. p. 63.ᶠ. "He does not produce Annihilation", sc, as the Yogin in Hīnayāna is supposed to do.

6 The Logician, i.e. Dignāga, posits as absolutely real, (*paramārtha-sat*), unimagined (*anāropita*) existence, the single moment (*kṣaṇa*) of existence which is then supposed to coalesce with the single moment of sensation characterised by self-awareness. This moment cannot be characterised by something else, since this would convert it in a relational existence. It is characterised by itself (*sva-lakṣaṇa*), it is the "thing in itself". But for the Mādhyamika, it is relational nevertheless.

It will be in same condition as any other thing which is not supposed to be its essence. Similarly the thing being different from its essence, it will not be the thing possessing that essence, just as any other thing which also does not possess it. And then, if the essence be different from the thing, the thing will be severed from its essence, and the result will be that being detached from its own essence it will be nothing, a non-entity like a flower in the sky. Now, supposing the thing and its essence are identical, in that case the thing characterized ceases to be characterized, since it has coalesced with its own characteristic, it loses its separate existence, just as the characteristic also loses its own separate existence. Neither does the essence retain its separate existence, because it has coalesced with the thing characterized. Just as the latter which has then lost its own Self it becomes also lost.

Accordingly it has been said,[1]

Characteristic from the thing is different?
The thing is then without characteristic.
And if both are identical,
'Tis clear, You have declared
That neither really does exist.

And there is no middle course to be taken between identity and otherness, if you wish to establish the reality of the thing characterized and its characteristic. The author will state this in the following verse.[2]

Supposing thus we have two things
They are not really one, nor are they two,
What are they then indeed?
How can we their reality assume?

The Logician further makes the following suggestion. Just as the Mādhyamika asserts that ultimate reality is something unspeakable, we shall also say that the relation between the thing characterized and its characteristic is something unspeakable and thus establish their reality.[3]

---

1 Lokātīta-stava, 11 (M. de la. V.P.)

2 II. 21.

3 Lit. p. 64.10-11. "Otherwise (*ucyate* to be omitted cp. Tib.) their reality (*siddhi*) could be established as unspeakable? It is not so. Indeed unspeakableness, for sure, appears when a mutual split cannot be thoroughly realized." *paraspara-vibhāga* is here the same as *dvaidhī-karaṇa* or *vikalpa*, a division of something into A and non-A involving the so called infinite judgement. Such dichotomy is then called also *vikalpa* and

Mādhyamika: This is impossible—Unspeakable reality is assumed by us when we have proved that a dichotomy does not resist scrutiny. Indeed, a dichotomy is untenable when it is proved that we cannot independently cognize "this is the characteristic, this the thing characterised". We then conclude that both are unreal.

But to establish the reality of both the members of a dichotomy, as unspeakable, is impossible.

XXXIX IS THERE A COGNISER?

Further, after having discussed the question whether our knowledge can be regarded as playing the part of an instrument through the medium of which an object becomes cognized, it is natural to ask the question whether there is something playing the part of a cognizing agent in this process of cognition, because neither an instrument, nor an action, nor its object are possible without an agent, just as the action of cutting wood is impossible without an agent.

Logician: We do not admit the reality of a cognising Soul, but the element of pure, indefinite sensation[1] may be imagined as playing the part corresponding to some sort of agent.

Mādhyamika: Even that sort of agent cannot be acquiesced in, because according to your theory, the function of pure sensation in the process of cognition is to indicate the mere presence of something. The object is, after that, qualified by other mental processes.[2] It is indeed a tenet accepted by you that "pure sensation[3] apprehends the pure object, its qualities[4] are apprehended by other mental processes".

Indeed an instrument, (an object and an agent) is assumed to be a real instrument, a real object and a real agent, when there is one single action accomplished by a variety of factors. We may then admit that every one of these factors performs some special function of its own, and thus becomes a component part of the principal action by the production of some change

identified with *kalpanā*, "arrangement", *yojanā*) it then covers, directly or indirectly, the whole range of thought, the active element of cognition. Cf. m. vr. p. 350. 12. ff.

1 *citta* 1 *citta vijñāna*. cp. Central Conception, pp. 16-18.

2 *caitaso—caitta—citta-saṃprayukta-saṃskāra*, cp. ibid. p. 18.

3 *vijñāna citta*, cp. ibid, p. 36

4 Tib. read dei khyad-par......

or of new qualities in its object.[1] But here, between definite cognition[2] and pure sensation,[3] there is no such central action. On the contrary every part has its own separate function. There is an independent action of indicating the mere presence of something, it is performed by pure sensation and there is another separate action of cognizing the qualities of the object. This is performed by constructive thought. It thus becomes impossible to impute the part of an instrument to qualifying thought,[4] and the part of an agent to pure sensation. Therefore, your theory that in the absolutely particular essence of existence, there is an immanent objectivity and an immanent instrumentality, cannot be saved. Our criticism stands.

But perhaps the Hīnayānist will, to a certain extent, concede this point about the agent, because he also maintains that there is altogether,[5] no real agent, since, according to Scripture, all elements[6] into which existence is analysed represent separate momentary flashes, there is between them no Soul[7], agent, or continuant stuff. Indeed impersonal motions and processes are clearly going on in nature without any conscious agent.

Mādhyamika: You have quite misunderstood the Scriptural teaching about the separate momentary elements of existence. Neither do these separate elements really exist. We have made this clear in our "Introduction to the Mādhyamika System".[8]

1 Lit. p. 65. 4-5." When one principal action is performed, instrument etc. possess instrumentality etc., because we admit their membership through the medium of producing qualities and actions for themselves respectively". The action of cooking rice, e.g., consists in fetching fuel, pouring water into the kettle, putting on fire, throwing the rice into the vessel, etc. All these factors (*kāraka*) concur in producing the central result, they are either instruments or object or agent. etc. But between two independent activities, as e.g., cooking rice and weaving cloth there can be no single agent in common.

2 *jñāna=savikalpaka-jñāna=artha-viśeṣa-paricchittiḥ.*

3 *vijñāna=citta=manas=artha-mātra-paricchitti=nirvikalpaka-jñāna=sattā-mātra-pradarśana.*

4 *jñānasya.*

5 *sarvathā-abhāvāt.*

6 *sarva-dharmāḥ.*

7 *anātmānaḥ*, the ātman in this context covers our notions of Soul and of substance, cp. M. vr. p. 437.4.

8 e. g. Madhy. avat, VI. 68 ff.

XL VINDICATION OF PHENOMENAL REALITY

Logician: Further, it is also possible to explain the fact that the expression *svalakṣaṇa* the thing in itself, the thing characterized only by its own self, does not involve any possessive relation by assuming that the relation is merely verbal. A relation or characterisation,[1] is possible even when there is no real characteristic beyond the characterized, e.g. when we speak about the body of a statue and the head of Rāhu, although there is nothing in the statue besides its body, and nothing in Rāhu beyond just a head. Is it not just the same as when we use the expression "solidity is the exclusive essence of solid bodies"? We use the possessive expression although there is nothing which could be called a solid body over and above this exclusive essence, (sc. the sense-datum of resistance).[2]

Mādhyamika: It is not so. Both cases are not comparable. Indeed the words, body and head are used in connection with other features usually coexisting with the, brains etc.[3] in the head, hands etc.[4] (with the body). Therefore, if a representation arises whose object is suggested by these words taken by themselves, we naturally expect to find the usually coexisting parts also. The questions "whose is that body?" "Whose is the head," naturally suggest themselves. And if some one is desirous to indicate that in the present case, the usual appurtenances are absent[5], he repudiates the expectation (of his interlocutor) by using words according to their conventional meaning in life, where they suggest such really existing appurtenances.[6]

---

1 *viśeṣaṇa-viśeṣya-bhāva.*

2 Lit. p. 66.1-3. "Further, also, it may be that in the body of a statue, the head of Rāhu, even if there is no characteristic beyond a body and a head, there is a relation of characteristic and characterised; just as in the 'proper characteristic essence of earth,' although there is no earth beyond the proper characteristic, there will be this relation."

3 *Buddhyādi.*

4 *Buddhy-upajananaḥ* for *upajāta-buddhiḥ*, or *ālambana-buddhy-upajananaḥ*, (sc. *puruṣaḥ*).

5 Read. p. 66.6—*viśeṣāntara-sambandha*, and in the Tib. khyad par-gzhan.

6 Lit. p. 66.3-7. Indeed, since the words, body and head are used in association (*sāpekṣatā-pravṛttau*) with other coexisting things, thoughts, etc. hands etc. a man who produces a thought intent upon only the words, body and head is always (*eva*) in expectation of the coexisting other things, "whose the body", "whose the head?" And another man, wishing to discard the connection with other appurtenances, cuts off the expectation of his interlocutor (*prativaktuḥ*) by availing himself of expressions suggestive

But in the other case, no relation or characterization at all is possible, because there altogether are no solid bodies[1] over and above the sense-datum of resistance.[2]

Logician: Non-Buddhists[3] assume a separate reality of substance[4] (and quality).

Are you not inclined, in order to do them pleasure,[5] to assert that the use of adjectives in speech[6] is quite all right, that it corresponds to a real relation?

Mādhyamika: No, indeed, for you it is not admissible to introduce into your system such categories as have been imagined by non-Buddhists on very poor grounds, or else you will be obliged equally to admit their number of additional sources of cognition[7] and other things also.

The Logician: But is not our example of a merely verbal relation just the same as the generally admitted among Buddhists fact of the nominal[8] personal identity[9] (in every individual's life)?

(*dhvaninā*) of the non-existing appurtenances of the statue of Rāhu, expressions which agree with their import in every day life. This is natural. But here......*Prati-kartuḥ=na vastutaḥ kartuḥ*, the "supposed agent" of the possessive relation, or the counterpart of such relation, *pratikartuḥ=pratiyoginaḥ*, (the expectation) of the counterpart."

1 *pṛthivyādi*.

2 *kāṭhinyādi*.

3 *tīrthika*.

4 *lakṣya*. C. assails the doctrine of the absolute *sva-lakṣaṇa* on the ground that there must be a *lakṣya* behind the *lakṣaṇa* and this reminds the realistic doctrine of the Vaiśeṣikas about a relation of inherence (*samavāya*) between substance and quality, a relation which no Buddhist has ever admitted to be real. The suggestion of the Logician is evidently ironical, it is a jeer at the fact that the Mādhyamika prefers the realistic logic of the *Naiyāyikas* and rejects the reforms of the Buddhist logicians.

5 *tad-anurodhena*.

6 *viśeṣaṇa-abhidhāna*.

7 C. admits the four *pramāṇas* of the Naiyāyikas, with the proviso that they will not help in the cognition of the Absolute. He here answers the gibe of the Logician with a counter gibe. He apparently wishes to say, "I can admit the realistic logic without forsaking my transcendental doctrine, but you cannot. For you the acceptance of the Naiyāyika doctrine about the sources of our knowledge (*pramāṇa*) would mean that you would be obliged to give up your doctrine of the double aspect of existence, your two sources of knowledge, your "thing in itself" "in fact all your epistemology."

8 *prajñapti*, a *cheda* is needed after *prajñapatisat*.

9 *pudgala*, the personality is different at every moment, its identity is a mental construction, it is an entity purely nominal (*prajñapti-sat=śabda-mātram*.)

Mādhyamika: No, it is not the same. Your example refers to an expression, not to a theory. The possessive relation as a mode of expressing oneself in every-day conversation, without enquiring into its reality, exists. In speaking there is a possessor of a body. The statue, we say, possesses its own body. And here is a Rāhu, the possessor of a head which is his possession, but in speech only. This your example proves nothing.[1]

Logician: However there is here nothing else than a mere body and a mere head, no possessors of them, they are the only objects apprehended. The example is quite all right.

Mādhyamika: It is not at all so. Your example is taken from common conversation; it refers only to what holds good in a conversation in which there is no philosophic investigation of reality and the usual categories are accepted as real without scrutiny.[2] Quite different is the case when the relation of substance and its appurtenances is philosophically considered. The notion of a substance[3], indeed, when critically examined, contains nothing real over and above the corresponding sense data. Nevertheless the conventional thinking of common life assumes it to exist. It imputes it to the underlying reality of the groups[4] of sense-data and mental phenomena. But your example does not mean that the same applies to the statue and to Rāhu.[5]

That there is thus no substance,[6] in solid bodies[7] over and above the quality or sense-datum of resistance[8] is proved by

1 Lit. p. 67.3-5 "Moreover like the nominal entity *prajñapti* of a person etc.? Because there exists the characteristic, being a part of usual conversation, well known without pondering, the characteristic of the statue, the possessor (*upādātṛ*) of the possession of its own body, (*sva-śarīra*) and because Rāhu, the possessor of the possession of a head, exists, this example is not suitable". Although it incidentally happens that there is no real possessive relation, nevertheless the expression is wrong, since in other cases the relation exists. The relation of substance and quality can be condemned on other philosophical grounds, not on the ground of the adequate expression.

2 Lit. p. 67.7-8. "It is not so, since in common -life-conversation there is no investigation of reality (*itthaṃvicāra*) going on and the categories of common life exist without scrutiny".

3 *ātman*, cp. *anātman*—12 *āyatana*—sense data and the mind, but no substance, *ātmaśabdo'yam svabhāva-śabda-paryāyaḥ*. M. vr. p. 437.4.

4 *skandha*.

5 Lit. p. 67.9. "There is no such establishing of the example on the score that the same applies to the *torso* and to Rāhu."

6 *lakṣya*.

7 *pṛthivyādi*.

8 *kāthinyādi*.

philosophical criticism.[1] It is true that a quality[2] cannot be imagined without the support of some substance, but this is just what we call the surface,[3] or phenomenal reality. Substance and quality are correlative terms, our Master Nāgārjuna has established their reality[4] in that sense, i.e. as a reality of mutual correlation,[5] none of them is real separately.

The Mādhyamika continues. This point is of capital importance; it must necessarily be conceded[6]. If it is not conceded, viz. if it is not admitted that phenomenal means relative, it will prove impossible to separate the phenomenal from what is logically consistent[7] and therefore real; and then every thing will be absolute reality,[8] since there will be no difference, there will be no phenomental reality at all. You must not indeed think that the body of a statue and similar relations are the only cases where a thing, upon investigation, reveals itself as merely verbal and non-existing. We will prove in our fourth chapter[9] that colour, feeling and other fundamental sense-data are likewise relational constructions and are impossible by themselves. Does it mean that we must deny their phenomenal reality, just as we deny even the phenomenal reality of e.g., a separate body in the statue?

This is impossible. Therefore your vindication of the absolute, relationless "thing in itself" and the example adduced to illustrate it is wrong.[10]

---

1 *vicāryamāṇaṁ nāsti.*

2 *lakṣaṇa.*

3 *saṁvṛtir eva iti.*

4 *siddhi.*

5 Lit. p. 67.11-12. "Nevertheless the Master has established the reality, *siddhim* (sc of the phenomenal world of the *saṁvṛti*) by the reality, (*siddhyā*) of them both inasmuch as they are mutually dependent upon one another." The idea of C. is that the "thing in itself" *svalakṣaṇa* is no exception to the law of Universal Relativity. The phenomenal here is an equivalent of the relative. In the example of the body and the statue or Rāhu and his head, there is no mutual inter-dependence of two phenomenal realities, but simply a wrong verbal expression.

6 Lit. p. 67.12 "Of all necessity, (*ca avadhāraṇāt*), this must be admitted sc. It is a point of capital importance that the world, as it is conceived phenomenally and Relatively are equivalents.

7 From these words, we must conclude that whatsoever is for C. logically consistent (*yad, yad upapannam*) represents not phenomena, but absolute reality, (*na tat saṁvṛtiḥ*). But since nothing short of the whole is logically consistent and real (the definition of reality, above p. 29) all particular objects are relative and logic dealing with them stands condemned.

8 *tattvam-eva.*

9 *skandha-parīkṣā.*

10 This is a brilliant piece of very subtle dialectics about the concep-

The Logician: Now, what is the use of such cavilling? There is a general agreement between us. Indeed I do not in the least maintain that all our familiar conceptions of cognition and cognizable represent absolute truth. I also deny the ultimate reality of the categories of substance and quality, but by

---

tion of a thing in itself. C's aim is to prove that it is also relational since it is a thing characterized by itself, and contrasted with a thing characterized not by itself, but by non-self. Dignāga, tries to prove by an example that the supposed relation is merely an inadequate expression. C. begins by criticising the example. The relation, says he (*gūḍhābhisandhiḥ*) between e.g. the elements of personality, (*pudgala*) and the personality itself is not the same as the relation between the body of a statue and its possessor. In the first case, we have a possessive relation, the identity reveals itself on philosophic examination, in the second there is no relation at all, but only a wrong expression, C. now discloses his aim (*svābhpirāyam udghāṭayati*) and vindicates the phenomenal reality of the relation of substance and quality, and at the same time he vindicates, upon Kantian lines, the necessity of assuming a transcendental reality which, however, he imagines on monistic lines. The body or bodily frame of a statue, is but an irregular and perversive manner of speaking, it means as much as "the statue of the statue" would mean. There is no real possessive relation. But in such expressions as the "resistance of solid bodies" or "the elements of a personality" there is a real possessive relation as far as phenomenal reality goes and its categories of substance and quality are regarded. It is not until philosophical analysis (*vicāra*) has condemned this relation as involved in contradictions and logically untenable (*anupapanna*) that we are obliged to reject it as ultimately unreal, whether reality be defined as efficiency (*artha-kriyā-kāra*), or as independent (*anapekṣa*) existence in itself (*sva-bhāva, svalakṣaṇa*). But empirically there is absolutely nothing cognizable which would not involve this relation. The "thing in itself" (*svalakṣaṇa*) which by Dignāga is supposed to represent the absolute reality, outside every kind of relation, C. holds equally to involve a double relation, first of all, a moment of objective reality corresponding to the moment of pure sensation, and then the relation of "the thing" to its characteristic "in itself", since this characteristic has a meaning only if contrasted with or relative to, the thing "not in itself", i.e. the general, the universal. The general and the extreme particular are thus correlative terms, the one is no more absolute than the other. This non-absolute, this being relative (*paraspara-apekṣa*), means the same as being phenomenal (*saṁvṛti*). If we do not accept that, there will be no line of demarcation between the phenomenal and the absolutely real, C. thus maintains that he has both a phenomenal reality, (*saṁvṛti*) and a transcendental one, (*sāṁvṛta*); whereas Dignāga, in admitting the absolute reality of the "thing in itself", undermines this line of demarcation and has, as a matter of fact, no phenomenal reality at all. It would be of some interest to compare this doctrine of a thing itself, (*svalakṣaṇa*), with the doctrine of Kant. The argument that if we do not admit any absolute reality, then the phenomenal will cease to be phenomenal and will itself become absolute (*tattvam eva syāt, na saṁvṛtiḥ*) is quite the same as with Kant, as well as the conception that the thing in itself is a non-representable". Kant is fully aware that his conception of a "thing in itself" is relative, it is in his words, "a correlatum to the unity of the manifold in sensuous intuition" (Critique of Pure Reason, transl. by Max Müller, p. 204). For Candrakīrti "being correlative" means "having no reality in itself (*svalakṣaṇa*), he thus charges the "thing in itself" with being also phenomenal, and he maintains that there is no other phenomenality than relativity.

this epistemology[1] I claim to have established upon a logical foundation that condition of the external world which humanity at large believes to be real.[2]

Mādhyamika: It is for me to ask you, what is the use of your sophistry? You only explain the origin of some perverse expressions current in common life. As to phenomenal reality, leave it alone, albeit its existence and shape are founded on mere confusion. It nevertheless is useful for accumulating those fundamental virtues which bring final Deliverance to those who strive after it.[3] It has some value only, as long as the philosophic comprehension of the absolute reality is not attained. But you, by your wrong logic, destroy the foundation of this phenomenal reality. The refinement of your intellect is led the wrong way, so far as the difference between what is absolutely real and what is only conventionally real is concerned. You are apparently establishing phenomenalism upon a logical basis in one point by assuming the underlying "thing in itself", but at the same time you are undermining it by your wrong logic in all other points.[4]

Now I come with a theory which really explains the importance of empirical reality.

I take my stand on our usual unsophisticated conceptions, and then I set forth a series of arguments of which every one is intended to destroy some particular usual conception of mankind. By this method, I thoroughly undermine the usual views. It is only that I, like a venerable authority, am keeping back from neglecting the rules of usual decent behaviour (i.e., of logic), but I do not undermine these rules, i.e. I do not deny their empirical reality.[5]

---

1 *amunā nyāyena.*

2 *lokaprasiddhiḥ.*

3 This is the Mādhyamika method of saving the moral law under phenomenalism. The phenomenal world is not real, but useful, since by accumulating merit and knowledge (both are inseparable) in it, we cognize its unreality. As far as I can see, this means that the phenomenal world, although unreal, is nevertheless partly real. Whether this method is a better one than the construction of a categorical imperative, in a phenomenal surrounding, must be left for the specialists to decide.

4 Perhaps to read *anyāyato' nyato nāśayati.*

5 Lit. p. 68.7-69.2. "We will also say the same ! What for is this subtlety which introduces us into an expression of common life? Let it stand, first of all, for yonder "surface", (*saṁvṛti*) which has reached an existence of its individuality, (*ātma-bhāva*) through logical inconsistency,

Therefore, if it is true that you are also taking your stand upon empirical reality in assuming your two essences, the strictly particular and the universal, you are obliged to admit the existence of a stuff which is characterized by these essences themselves. Our criticism thus stands, i.e., the criticism of the conception of an ultimate particular is not refuted. However, if we take our stand on transcendental absolute reality then indeed we will deny the separate existence of a characterised substance. But then we will also deny both these your essences, and both your sources of knowledge.

And moreover, you maintain that speech is not a source of knowledge and that the meaning of our words is purely negative,[1] you do not admit that analysis of our speech which implies the reality of actions, factors and their connection. This indeed is a very great disaster. When you speak, you make use of these very words which express actions, factors and their connection, but you yourself do not admit the reality of their meaning,

(*viparyāsa*) it is a cause of accumulating the fundamental virtues which bring salvation to those who are desirous of Deliverance, (let it stand) until the knowledge of the Absolute, (*tattva-adhigama*) is reached. But you, by your perversely sharp understanding of the division between phenomenal and absolute realities, after having introduced consistency, (*upapatti*) into some points (*kvacit*) destroy this division by wrong logic (*anyā-yataḥ*). But here I come, because I know how to establish phenomenalism (*saṃvṛtisatya*) taking my stand just on the philosophy, (*pakṣa*) of common sense, (*laukika*), I take one argument (*upapatty-antaram*) which is adduced for the critique (*nirākaraṇa*) of phenomenal reality and refute it by another (parallel) argument; like a mentor—*loka-vṛddha*. I call to order, (*nivar-tayāmi*), just yourself, whenever you set aside the rules of decency, (*ācāra*) accepted in the world, (second sense, "like an ancient authority on logic, known throughout the world, I am only refuting you whenever you depart from the ground of common sense (*lokācāra*), but I do not deny phenomenal reality)." Thus Candrakīrti maintains, (1) that the phenomenal world and the world of Relativity are equivalents and (2) since logic is in any case doomed as a means of cognizing the Absolute, he prefers simple realistic logic to a transcendental logical doctrine.

1 According to the Indian grammarians and realistic logicians, a sentence contains an expression of an action associated with an agent and factors (*kāraka*) or circumstances. This theory of speech the Mādhyamika accepted with the aforesaid proviso. But the school of Dignāga has a special theory of its own about the meaning of words according to which words express only relations, or mutual negations (*apoha=paraspara-pari-hāra=anya-vyāvṛtti=vyavaccheda=pariccheda*) between point-instants. Reality is even characterised as that which can never be expressed in speech (*paramārtha - sat-svalakṣaṇapratyakṣa - nirvikalpaka anābhilāpya*). The Mādhyamika here hints at this theory and sets forth the argument that if speech could express nothing real, nothing positive, no actions, agents etc., then it would be impossible for people to enter into conversation. This remark is of course more of a glib gibe and unfair, since the Mādhyamika's own ultimate reality is also inexpressible in speech (*niṣpra-pañca=anabhi-*

of these actions, these agents etc. Alas ! your attitude[1] is influenced by mere desires.

And if, as we have shown, the duality of every thing cognizable is a moot point, then we must agree with those who admit other sources of knowledge besides sensation and thought, as e.g. Revelation etc., since these sources of knowledge are not devised with a view strictly to agree with the duality of every thing cognizable, the particular and the universal.

XLI THE DEFINITION OF THE SENSE PERCEPTION

Mādhyamika: Further your theory of an extreme particular as the "thing in itself", is wrong, because your definition[2] of sense-perception, through which it is supported to be apprehended is deficient. It is too narrow, it does not cover such everyday expressions as the "jar is a perception", i.e. the physical object before us is perceived and these usual expressions of the ordinary man[3] should likewise be taken into account. Therefore your definition is wrong.

The Logician: It might have been wrong but for the following considerations. Perceived are directly the sense data, e.g. a patch of dark colour etc. They make up the physical object,

---

lāpya=anupākhya, prapañca=vāk). But Candrakīrti thinks that no improvement in the logic of the Realists is needed, nocritical theory of cognition, no "thing in itself" and no negative theory of speech (*apoha*). The logic of the Naiyāyikas can be accepted wholesale for the phenomenal aspect of the world, and for the Absolute, no logic at all is needed. The school of Dignāga, as well as the Hīnayānists, can maintain that they also admit a double aspect of life,-one on the surface (*saṁvṛti*) and one ultimate (*paramārtha*) or concealed (*saṁvṛta*). Cp. Ab. kośa, V 12, but C. is persuaded that his vindication of an empirical reality has a greater force. The Mādhyamikas are the inventors of the doctrine of a double truth which they probably contrasted with the "four truths" of the Hīnayāna cp. Madhyś., XXIV, 8. This is also partly the reason why the Mādhyamikas, and their followers the Vedāntins, deem it permissible freely to use the arguments of Naiyāyikas when combating Buddhist Idealism. At Śrīharṣa's time, when the enemy is no more the Buddhist, but the Naiyāyika, this attitude changes.

1 Read *pravṛttitaḥ*. C. is here playing with the double meaning of *icchā* "desire" and "tenet", "Your behaviour is bound by such theories as are merely fantastical desires". i.e. you are not acting in accordance with your tenets, if speech is only *apoha* you ought not to speak at all."

2 The definition here alluded to is Dignāga's definition: "sense perception is quite free from all synthetic operation of thought" (*kalpanāpoḍha*), cp. Nyāyabindu, p. 6.15.

3 Anārya, the non-Saint. 'The Buddhist saint, being a philosopher who has changed all usual habits of thought, directly realizes that what he perceives are only momentary sense-data, the remainder is construction. Dignāga's definition may be a right description of his perception, but will not cover the usual view.

the jar. Sense perception, as a source of knowledge, distinguishes only that. But the cognition of the physical object which is a mental construction *resulting* from sense-perception is likewise called sense-perception by a metaphor. Such metaphors we find in Scripture, e.g. when it is stated that the advent of Buddhas is a weal, instead of stating that it produces weal. We impute to the cause what really belongs to the effect. Just so, by a converse metaphor, from the cause to the effect, we say that the physical object, the jar, is perceived, while only its causes, the sense data, are really perceived.[1]

Mādhyamika: To assume a natural metaphor in such cases as the perception of a jar is impossible. Quite different is the case of the advent of a Buddha. Indeed a birth, i.e. the process of a birth, is held in ordinary life as the reverse of pleasure. (It is not the blissful Quiescence of the Forces of life). It is essentially produced through the cooperation of a plurality of biotic forces.[2] It is a cause of very much pain. By itself it is anything but a weal. Nevertheless it is here called a weal. There is a contradiction.[3] In such cases, we assume a metaphor. The advent of a Buddha, although also painful by itself, is nevertheless a weal, because it produces the weal of Quiescence in Nirvāṇa. The case is different with a perceived jar. We have no such separate thing as an invisible jar which could be called perceived metaphorically.

The Logician: On the contrary, just because there is no jar over and above the corresponding sense-data, it is convenient to maintain that its perceptibility is a metaphor.

Mādhyamika: If you take it so, the metaphor is still less possible, because the object which you metaphorically endow with perceptibility does not exist at all. You cannot speak about the sharpness of the horns on the head of the donkey even metaphorically.[4] Moreover, if you assume that the jar which

1 Lit, p. 70.1-3. "But let it be. The blue etc. the substratum of the jar, are evident, since they are being determined by perceptive cognition. Hence just as by imputing the effect to the cause, it is said that the birth of Buddha is agreeable, so the jar, although its causes are the evident blue etc., by imputing the cause to the effect, is called a perception."

2 *saṁskṛta-lakṣaṇa-svabhāva*, "it has the essence of the forces of life," about the four forms (*saṁskāra*) which are called *saṁskṛta-lakṣaṇa*, cp. my Central Conception, p. 39. There is no other weal for the Buddhist as the quiescence i.e. extinction of all life in an Absolute.

3 *asaṁbaddha eva*.

4 Lit. p. 70.9. "Because there is no substratum for what is being used as a metaphor". In the first case, the really, existing sense-data were

is a part of our every-day experience is perceived by us in a metaphorical sense, because there is no such jar over and above the sense-datum of a dark patch of colour etc. then you are bound to take the next step and condemn the patch of dark colour as well, since it also does not exist over and above the sense-datum of something resistant.[1] Then, please, assume that the patch of dark colour is also perceived in a metaphorical sense. This has been expressed in the following verse.[2]

Just as there is no jar
Beyond its colour,
Just so there is no colour
Beyond resistance.[3]

Therefore this and similar usual expressions are not covered by your definition of perception. It is quite deficient, since it does not cover the whole of its subject matter. Now, from the transcendental point of view,[4] we equally condemn the perception of the physical objects, the jar, as well as the perception of the sense-data, blue etc. On the contrary, from the empirical view of every-day life, we must admit that the jar is perceived. This has been expressed in one of the four hundred verses of Āryadeva in the following manner,

A transcendentalist[5] will never say
"We see a patch of colour, not a jar,"
Or a "jar is present before us".
In following just this line of argument
His sovereign mind will equally deny
The soft, the fragrant and the sweet.[6]

There is, however, another explanation of what perception

the substratum, and physical object jar superimposed upon them. It was answered that you cannot superimpose a thing you nowhere have perceived. In the second the relation has been reversed and it is supposed that the non-existing jar is the substratum upon which the sense-data are superimposed. This is still less possible.

1 Lit, 70.11 "There is no blue etc. beyond earth etc."

2 Catuḥśataka. XIV 14.

3 Lit, p. 71.2. "Just so there is no colour beyond wind etc. Earth, wind etc. are the four fundamental elements of Matter, (*mahābhūta*), which are cognized exclusively by touch, (*spṛṣṭavya-āyatana*), thus colour, (*rūpa-āyatana*) is here reduced to a tactile phenomenon. Cp. the contention of modern empiricism which reduces our notion of Matter to sense-data and the sense-data to the one fundamental sensation of resistance. About Matter offering resistance (*sapratighatva*) to sight, cp. Ab. Kośabh ad. 1.29.

4 *tattva-vid-apekṣayā*.

5 *tattva-vid*.

6 Catuḥśataka, XIII, 1-2.

really means. The word perception simply means a thing which is not beyond the range of our sense. (It does not mean its cognition through our senses). An object which is present and faces us is thus called a perception.[1] Jars, patches of blue colour and similar physical objects are called perceptions when they are not beyond the range of sight. A perception thus means an object which has been approached by our senses.[2] The corresponding definite cognition is also called perception by a metaphor, because it is the cause which makes the object evident, just we speak of a "straw fire" or "husk fire" metaphorically, instead of saying fire *producing* burning straw or burning husk.

There is a philosopher[3] who has given the following interpretation of the term perception. Perception is that kind of knowledge which exists in close connection with each sense faculty. (This could also mean that sense knowledge is a knowledge about the senses, a knowledge whose objects are the senses.) This interpretation is wrong, because sense perception is not a knowledge about the senses, it is a knowledge about the objects[4] of the senses. If his interpretation were correct, we should speak not of sense perception, but of "object-perception" or of "thing-perception".

Be it as the case my be, we find in the Abhidharmakośa the following explanation. Sensation[5] is produced by a double cause, the sense faculty and its object. Nevertheless it receives its name only through one of its causes, the organ in which the corresponding sense faculty is lodged, because sensation changes in degree, according to the changes by which the faculty may be affected.[6] The sharp or feeble faculties correspond to sharp or

1 The origin of this definition—*pratyakṣam aparokṣam* "perception is the object not beyond our ken," can be traced in the Bṛh. Ār. Upaniṣad, III. 4.1 and III. 5.1. It is adopted in the later scholastic Vedānta, cp. Vedānta-paribhāṣā, p. 12 (Bombay 1900 Veṅkaṭeśvar). It is also mentioned by Udayana, Pariśuddhi, p. 647 (B.I). It seems probable that the Mādhyamikas have borrowed it from the Vedāntins. To the Mādhyamikas, it suggested the omni-presence of Buddha's *dharma-kāya,* just as to the Vedāntins it suggested the omnipresence of *aparokṣam brahma* cognized by mystic intuition. Cp. above. pp. 32-33.

2. Lit, p. 70. 10-11. By meaning "in it the sense is approached, the perceptibility of jars, blue etc. not being beyond the ken, is established".

3 The definition of Praśastapāda is here alluded to, cp. Praśasta. p. 186.12. The etymological explanation of the Naiyāyikas does not differ materially, cp. Nyāyavārt. p. 30.4. Nyāyabindu, p. 6.4. makes a difference between the etymology and the real meaning.

4 *viṣaya-viṣaya.*

5 *vijñāna.*

6 Ab. Kośa. I, 45.

feeble sensations. We then have visual and other sensations. Thus, although a perception changes with every object,[1] nevertheless it receives its name according to the place where it is lodged. It exists as lodged in different sense organs, it is thus sense-perception, (not object-perception). It is customary to name a thing by its specific cause, e.g. the sound "of a drum", although it is also the sound of the sticks, the sprout "of barley" although it is also the sprout of the soil etc.

Mādhyamika: There is no analogy between the example of the sound of a drum and the above-mentioned designation of sense perception instead of object-perception. If sensation be specified according to the object, one could specify our sensations as colour-sensations etc.[2] But we could not specify in this way all the six kinds of sensations, since mental or intellectual sensation is a sixth kind of sensation, which is apprehending the same object simultaneously with the external sense. Indeed, if we include in the term sensation all its six varieties, beginning with the visual ones and including the intellectual ones, we might be quite uncertain what to think when some one would mention the term (visual) sensation. We will not know whether it means only the sensation produced by the external sense, or it is meant to include the corresponding internal sensation, the mental reaction[3] also. But if we specify sensations according to the organ in which they are lodged, although mental sensation can refer to the same object to which visual and other sensations likewise refer, nevertheless their mutual distinction will in that case, be clearly established (if they were called according to their object; since the object can be the same when different sensations are meant, confusion would arise).

However, in this case you are merely concerned with giving a definition of what the sources of knowledge are. You accordingly assume that sense-knowledge is simply that kind of knowledge where all constructive thought is brushed aside, (it is

1 Lit. p. 72.5-7. "Thus although it exists with reference to every object nevertheless, it will be sense perception, because, existing as lodged in every sense-organ, sensation is designated by its residence."

2 *nīlādi-vijñāna*.

3 *mānasa*.

pure passive sensation[1]). Just the contrast with thought is in your opinion its characteristic. No purpose is served by naming its varieties according to their specific causes.[2] Now, the number of the sources of our knowledge exactly corresponds to the number of the cognized categories of existence. You have established the character of both your sources of knowledge in strict correspondence with the double character of the cognizable. To this strict correspondence they owe their existence and their shape. You should, therefore, remain always faithful to your principle of designating cognition only according to its object. To name it according to the organ of sense would serve no purpose (from your standpoint).[3]

However the Logician may vindicate his interpretation by the following consideration. The word sense-perception is generally known to every one. The word sense-perception is not used as a designation of what we here have in our mind. For this reason, we adhere to the interpretation that the term sense-perception means perception through the sense-organs, through the place where the sensations are lodged, it does not mean the perceived object.

---

1 *kalpanāpoḍha* is the celebrated definition of Dignāga discussed almost in every Indian philosophical work. It makes a difference between the first moment in every perception, it is then pure sensation, it is passive, involving absolutely no thought-construction. But the next step, which is also perception, represents the construction of an image by synthetic thought, (*vikalpena anugamyate*). The distinction has a great importance for Dignāga, because he thinks that in this pure sensation, this so to say, "reine Sinnlichkeit", the "pure object" (*śuddha-artha*), the "thing in itself" (*svalakṣaṇa*) reveals itself to our consciousness. It is interesting to compare the controversy between Eberhard and Kant on a similar question. Eberhard assumed that he was opposing Kant when he maintained that the "thing in itself" reveals itself in our sensations (Empfindungen), but Kant conceded the point *nun ist das chen* (viz *dass die Dinge as sich der Sinnlichkeit ihren Stoff geben*) *die bestandinge Behauptungder Kritik*, *cp. Ueber, eine Entdeckung, nach der etc. p.* p. 35. (Kirchmann).

2 Lit. 73.4-6. "But here, with a view to expressing the essence of the sources of cognition (*pramāṇa*), the absence of synthesis (*kalpanā*) alone is admitted as perception, because the peculiarity of this mode of cognition is found in its difference from constructive (dichotomising, *vikalpaka*) cognition; by naming it according to its special cause, no usefulness is indicated."

3 Lit. 73. 6-8. "And since the existence of the number of the sources of cognition is dependent upon the objects of cognition and because the essence of such two sources of cognition has been established which have attained their shape (*ātmabhāva*) and existence (*sattā*) exclusively by conforming to the double form of the cognizable, the designation through the sense-organ helps nothing, thus or in every respect the designation just by the object is the right one."

The Mādhyamika answers: This is true, the word perception is very well known in common life, and we, not you, are using it just in what sense it is used in common life.[1] Your interpretation is made with utter disregard of what is established as real in common life. Generally known in your interpretation is only the utter disregard of what is really generally known, because in your interpretation, as pure sensation, it would not even mean perception.[2]

And moreover, since you give to the term a generalizing sense of what is present in all sensations, the case of single moment of visual sensation, which is produced by a single moment of the faculty of vision, will not be covered by your definition. And then, if a single moment of perception will thus (according to this definition) not be perception, neither will a number of them be perception.[3]

Now, you maintain that sense-perception is only that kind of cognition which is quite free from any participation in it of constructive thought. However with such pure sensation alone you will not be able to converse with your fellow beings. Nevertheless you pretend to analyse the course which cognition and its object take in common life. It follows that that sort of sense-knowledge which you assume, (sc. pure sensation) is quite useless.

1 *pratyakṣa* means also an object "evident", present.

2 Lit. p. 73.4. "well known could be your distortion, (*tiraskāra*) of the term "well known" and therefore it would not be thus sense-perception." The *pratyakṣa* in Dignāga's and Dharmakīrti's interpretation, meaning as it does a moment of pure, undifferentiated sensation, represents, indeed, something quite unknown in common life. The divergence between the common idea of perception and Dignāga's conception of pure sensation is much more considerable than the divergence between it and the Mādhyamika-Vedānta definition of perception as the thing perceived, since the Sanskrit term for perception (*pratyakṣa*) is a word very commonly used in the sense of a thing present, evident, perceived. Dharmottara himself calls that kind of pure perception which is imagined by Buddhist something "hardly existing" *asat-kalpa*, cp. Nyāya-bindu, p. 16. This retort of the Mādhyamika is, nevertheless, not quite fair, because the follower of Dignāga, when maintaining that perception is not the object, but its cognition, does not refer to pure sensation, but to perceptive cognition which includes a moment of sensation.

3 Lit. p. 73.3-4. "And there will be no perception-character (*pratyakṣatva*) of one visual sensation, (*cakṣur-vijñānasya*), possessing an underlying (*āśrayasya*) single moment of the sense-faculty (*indriya-kṣaṇa*), because of the absence of the meaning of generalisation. (*vīpsā*)."

Mādhyamika: You are also vindicating your theory of perception by referring to Scripture where it is stated that "a man, having a visual sensation of a patch of blue colour apprehends blue, but does not know that *it is* blue", the definite knowledge is produced by a subsequent operation of contrasting blue with not blue.[1] But in your opinion this scriptural deliverance is not meant to give any definition of sense-perception. It only is meant to notify that the sensations of the five external sense-organs alone, without the participation of a conscious element, remain unconscious. Sensation which is absolutely bare of every element of synthetic thought cannot be maintained to represent perception, even on the basis of Scripture. This would be wrong.

Therefore from the empirical,[2] (not from the transcendental), point of view, everything without exception is called present,[3] (i.e. a perception), when it is directly perceived by the senses, whether it be your strictly particular essence or the general essense of the thing[4] (possessing these both essences). A perception is thus determined as meaning the object of perception together with its cognition.[5] The double moon and similar illusions will not be sense-perceptions, if compared with the cognitions of a man with a normal capacity of vision, but for the man suffering from ophthalmia, it will be just *his* sense-perception.

As regards cognition of objects lying beyond the range of our senses, it is produced by a perceived mark which is invariably concomitant with them. It is called inference.

The words of specially qualified persons who directly perceive transcendental things[6] are called Scripture.

---

1 This very important text from an unknown *āgama* is mentioned already by Dignāga in his *pramāṇa-samuccaya-vṛtti*, I. 4, as a quotation from the abhidharma (chos-mnon-palas) in support of the theory. This could prove that Dignāga's theory of pure sensation was foreshadowed in previous Sautrāntika works. Kamalaśila examines it at length in his Nyāya-bindu-pūrva-pakṣa-saṅkṣipti (Bastan-hgyur, Mdo CXI, f. 112 fl.) Vasubandhu's definition of *pratyakṣa* is quite different, cp. Pramāṇa-samuccaya I, 15, and Nyāyavārttika, p. 42.

2 *loke.*

3 *aparokṣa.*

4 *lakṣya.*

5 *jñānena saha*, according to Dignāga *pratyakṣa*, when pure (*śuddha*) is not *jñāna*, but Dharmakīrti brings it under the head of *samyag jñāna*, cp. Tātparyaṭ, p. 102.17.

6 *atīndriyārtha.*

If something that has never been experienced is cognized through a description, so far as it has been declared to be similar to another thing which has been experienced by us—this is called analogy, e.g. when we are told that a gavaya whom we have never seen is some animal similar to a bull.

By these four methods of cognition is our knowledge of objects determined and our actions guided in common life.[1]

But if we are then asked on what transcendental basis four of these methods of usual cognition repose, we will be obliged to confess that their reality is relative.[2] The cognizable things exist so far as cognitions exist and *vice versa*, cognitions exist so far as the cognizable objects exist.

But[3] in no case is there any independent absolute reality[4] either of our cognitions, or of the objects cognised. Therefore

1 These are exactly the four sources of knowledge admitted by the Realists, the Naiyāyikas.

2 *parasparāpekṣayā siddha=śūnya.*

3 Here Candrakīrti winds up this remarkable controversy with Dignāga by admitting realistic logic in the empirical field, but not in the transcendental, and by rejecting Dignāga's reform which, although professing to be a logic of common sense (*laukika*), aimed at establishing a transcendental reality of a "thing in itself." For describing the fact that phenomenal reality is established in his system on a firm basis, he uses two words, it is *satya* "a truth," and it is *siddha*, "established as a reality". However, it is a "surface truth" (*saṁvṛti-satya*) and it is "established as a relative reality" (*parasparāpekṣayā siddha*), not absolutely (*na tu svabhāvena*). Dignāga retorts that he has also two realities, the relative reality of all our conceptions and the absolute reality of the "thing in itself." Indeed the followers of Āryasaṅga and Dignāga are frequently characterised as being also Mādhyamikas (i.e. relativists) because they adhere to the doctrine that all our conceptions have merely a relative value (*paratantra*). But Candrakīrti insists that Dignāga's "thing in itself" is also relative, that he has thus failed to grasp the real profound meaning of the doctrine of the two realities, the Relativity is the "surface" of the Absolute, it has its real stand as such a surface. Therefore in ch-XXVII and XXV 20 Nāgārjuna will emphatically assert the essential identity of the Absolute and the Phenomenal, of Nirvāṇa and Saṁsāra, cp. translation below, p. 200. The Absolute of Nāgārjuna and Candrakīrti has thus a certain similarity with the "Enzaimn of Parmenides, whereas the "thing in itself" of Dignāga has some points of similarity with the Hoc Aliquid (=kimcid idam) of Aristotle. The Mādhyamika view can be clearly realized out of the following equations. (1) *saṁvṛti* (surface),=*parasparāpekṣā* (relativity) = *loka*=*laukika-vyavastha*= *prapañca* (pluralism) =pratītya=*samutpāda*= (dependently-together-origination)=*śūnyatā*=*niḥsvabhāvatā*=*saṁsāra*=Dharma-kāya=the manifested world=onnipreaesentia Dei phaenomenon. (2) *sāṁvṛta* ('under the surface') =*anapekṣa*= (nonrelative)=*paramārtha* (absolute) = *niṣ-prapañca* (nonplural)=*anirvacanīya*=*advaita* (monistic)=*pratītyasamutpāda* (i.e., Saṁvṛtaḥ-pratīyta-samutpādaḥ)=śūnyatā i.e. Sāṁvṛtaśūnyatā=sasvabhāvatā= tathatā=dharmatā = *nirvāṇa* = *Dharma-kāya* = the world *sub specie aeternitatis.*

4. *svabhāvikī siddhiḥ.*

let us be satisfied with the usual view of the phenomenal world, just as it is cognised by us from experience.[1]

Enough of this discussion.
Let us revert to our subject matter.

The Sublime Buddhas have also preached their doctrine in adapting it just to the habits of thought of common humanity.[2]

XLII THE HĪNAYĀNA THEORY OF CAUSATION EXAMINED

From our correligionists[3] Hīnayānists, we receive regarding this our denial of causation the following reply.[4] We agree with you, they say, that entities cannot arise out of themselves, so far the production of a thing already existing out of its own self is useless. That entities cannot arise out of both sources i.e. out of a pre-existing stuff and separate agents is also true, since one half of this solution is invalidated, by our denial of a pre-existing substance.

The last eventuality, viz. that every thing exists at random without any causal link at all, is absolutely poor. It is quite right to dismiss it without much consideration. But if you also maintain that neither are existent things caused by something separate from them, this we do not admit. The Buddha has specified that existing things have causes producing them and that these causes are substantially different from the thing produced.

---

1 *yathādṛṣṭam* =*dṛṣṭam anatikramya*—

2 *laukikaṁ darśanam*, "philosophy of common sense" as opposed to *darśana*, real philosophy.

3 *svāyūthya*.

4 About the general idea of Causality, (*pratītya-samutpāda*) in Hīnayāna cp. above. p. 28. About its special application to the evolution of life in 12 consecutive stages, cp. O Resenberg, Problems, Ch-XIV, My Central Conception, p. 28 n. The schools of Hīnayāna were, moreover, engaged in classification of varieties of coordination between the separate momentary elements in which existence had been split. They thus established different *pratyayas* of the *pratītya—samutpāda*. The classification into four varieties here mentioned belongs to the school of the Sarvāstivādins. It has been supplemented by a further classification into six different *hetus*, which probably is later than Nāgārjuna, since it is not mentioned by him. The Pāli school had devised a classification into 21 *pratyayas*. The full theory of the *Sarvāsti-vādins* is given in Ab Kośa, II 50 ff. *Pratyaya* when contrasted with *hetu* means condition in general, and *hetu* cause (special). Otherwise both these terms are very often used as synonyms. All the very interesting details of their connotation can be realised only through a careful study of the *abhidharma*.

The Hīnayāna maintains

II. Four can be the conditions.
Of everything produced.
Its cause, its object, its foregoing moment,
Its most decisive factor.[1]
There is no fifth condition.

Among them, the cause is what turns out.[2] Such is the definition. Therefore, if one entity turns out the other, i.e. if their mutual position is similar to that of a seed versus a sprout,[3] it is called its cause, this is the first condition, the cause in general sense. If something when being produced, is intent upon an object, something else, as e.g. a sensation which is always intent upon an object, the latter is called its objective condition.

The foregoing condition for the production of a result is the evanescence of its material cause e.g. the foregoing destruction of the seed is a condition for the production of the sprout.

The decisive or predominant condition is that decisive fact which being efficient, the result (inevitably) appears. Such are the four kinds of possible conditions.

If there be other circumstances, previous, contemporaneous or posterior to an event, they are all to be included in one of these categories. A supreme Deity and similar transcendental conditions do not exist. Therefore the author puts limit "there is no other, fifth kind of condition". Entities arise under these conditions which are not identical with the thing produced. In such sense there is production (or coordination with) things other than the thing produced.

We answer: Neither are entities produced out of (or coordinated with) conditions which are substantially separate from them.

III. In these conditions we can find,
No self-existence of the entities,
Where self-existence is deficient,
Relational existence also lacks.

If the produced entities[4] had any pre-existence[5] at all, in their own causes and conditions which are something different from

---

1 *ādhipateya*=*adhipati-pratyaya*.
2 *nirvartaka*.
3 The seed is the *adhipati-pratyaya*=*kāraṇa-hetu*=*asādhāraṇa-kāraṇa* of the sprout, here it exemplifies a condition in general.
4 *bhāvānāṁ kāryāṇām*.
5 *utpādāt pūrvam sattvam*.

these entities themselves whether in all the combination of them or in some of them separately or both in all of them and in every one of them, or (even if they existed) somewhere outside the combination of their causes and conditions then alone could they appear out of them. But this is not so. They do not pre-exist. If they did, they would have been perceived, and their new production would have been useless. Therefore the conditions and causes of an entity do not contain any real existence of the result.[1] If they do not contain its real existence, neither do they contain its relational existence.[2] Existence, relation, production,[3] are synonyms. Production out of something extraneous means relation[4] to it, (some kind of pre-existence in it). This is impossible. Therefore it is wrong to maintain that entities can be produced out of conditions which are different from them.

But then the Hīnayānist would maintain that the produced entities, such as a sprout etc. do not really exist in their cause, such as seeds etc. as long as the latter have not undergone any change. (But when they are changed the result appears). Otherwise the latter would appear without any cause altogether. (This is what they call their relation to other entities which are their causes).

But in what sense[5] are we to understand the "otherness"[6] of causes and conditions. When both Maitra and his helpmate are present, we can assert that they are two separate entities which depend upon one another in producing a piece of work together. But this kind of co-existence is not found between a sprout and a seed. Therefore when results do not possess such separate existence of their own, their relation, the "otherness" of the sprout in regard to the seed, is absent. The designation of it as "other" becomes meaningless and this alone makes production out of something extraneous, impossible.

The Hīnayānist's appeal to Scripture betrays his utter ignorance of its real intention. Never did the Buddhas preach

1 *svabhāvaḥ*.
2 *parabhāvaḥ*.
3 *bhāvānām, bhāva, utpādaḥ*.
4 *bhāva*, cp. in *kārya-kāraṇa-bhāva*.
5 *kimapekṣam*.
6 *paratva*.

something contrary to reason.[1] What the real aim of their doctrine is we have indicated above, we have namely indicated that the doctrine of causality refers to the phenomenal world.

XLIII THE EXISTENCE OF SEPARATE ENERGIES DENIED

When the philosopher who maintains the origination of entities out of other entities which are their causes, has been thus dismissed, another one sets forth a theory of origination through special energies.[2] The organ of vision, colours and the other causes of the visual sensation are not producing it directly. They are called causes because they call forth an energy[3] capable of producing sensation. This energy[4] then actually produces visual sensation. Thus the causes, as separate entities, do not produce sensation. Its real producer[5] is a corresponding energy, an energy inherent in the causes[6] and creative[7] of sensation. Analogous is the physical energy of heat[8] which produces e.g. cooked rice.

We answer :

IV. No energies in causes,
Nor energies outside them.
No causes without energies,
Nor causes that possess them.

If an energy producing sensation does really exist, it must be associated with such causes as the organ of vision etc. But this is impossible. Why ? Because we will then be asked whether this assumed energy is supposed to appear when this sensation already exists, or before it or simultaneously with it ? The first alternative must be rejected. If the sensation is already produced, the energy is useless. The energy is supposed to produce something. But if it is already produced, what has the energy to do ? This has been expressed in our Mādhyamika Introduction thus—

1 *yukti-viruddha.*

2 Nāgārjuna avails himself of the term *kriyā* (=*jani-kriyā* in the sense of energy or function. Later, it is replaced by the term *vyāpāra* which is also used by Candrakīrti.

3 *jani-kriyā.*

4 *kriyā.*

5 *vijñāna-janika.*

6 *pratyayavatī.*

7 *vijñāna-jani-kriyā.*

8 Read *paci-kriyā.*

The second birth of something born
Should never be admitted, etc.[1]

Neither is the existence of an energy to be assumed in the causes previously to the sensation. This we have expressed in the same work thus,[2]

This energy cannot take shape,
As long as the result[3] is absent.

Neither is the existence of an energy just at the moment of production possible, because a thing is either produced or not yet produced, there is no existence between these two moments. It has been said—

What is being produced is not produced,
Because it's only half-produced.
Or else all things without exception
Would nascent always be.[4]

Since the assumed energy cannot be located in any one of the three times (past, present and future,) it does not exist altogether. Nāgārjuna, therefore, says,

No energies in causes.

We have commented upon this point in our Mādhyamika Introduction, when explaining that,

Without something characterized
There can be no characteristic feature, etc.[5]

Indeed the non-existing son of a barren woman cannot be characterized as the possessor of a cow, since he neither did nor does, nor will exist. (The non-existing energy cannot appertain to a cause.)

But then an energy might perhaps exist alone without being the possession of a cause? This is also impossible.

No energy outside the causes.

---

1. M. av. VI 8.
2. Ibid. CI. 29. cp. M.vr. p. 545.
3. *kartrā vinā*, lit. "without the maker" sc. without the result as maker or shaper of the energy. The future *vijñāna* is here envisaged as the shaper, (*karma-kāraka*) of its own producer.
4. Lit. p. 80.3-4 "Because the nascent is half-born, the nascent is not born. Otherwise the condition of being nascent would attach (*prasajyate*) to everything."
5. Ibid. VI, 57. The possessive relation is here represented in an inverted manner. Instead of speaking of causes or objects possessing energies, the author speaks of energies possessing causes (*pratyayavatī kriyā*), he means "belonging to causes."

If, therefore, there is no energy in the causes, there neither can be any energy outside them, it would then be an uncaused energy. If there is no separate cloth beside the threads composing it, this does not mean that the cloth pre-exists somewhere else, in some straw.[1] Consequently no energy producing entities do really exist.

If this is the case, if it is impossible to assume energies, then perhaps the causes alone, without possessing any energies will be sufficient for the production of entities? It is answered,

No causes without energies.

If energies do not exist, then the causes will be bereft of energy, they will not be efficient, they will not be causes. How then will they produce something?

But if causes really produce something, they must be necessarily possessors of energy.

To this it is answered,

Nor causes are there that possess them.

The[2] existence of energies is thus denied. It then becomes clear that causes cannot be possessors of non-existing energies.

What has been here said about an energy producing sensation, equally applies to the energy of heat[3] and other physical energies. Thus the word "production" is itself devoid of any meaning.

XLIV CAUSATION IS NOT CO-ORDINATION

To this the Hīnayānist replies. We are not in the least affected by your examination of the question whether the causes are possessors of energy or not. We are satisfied with establishing the fact that entities, such as sensation, arise in a certain co-ordination with other entities,[4] e.g. the organ of vision etc. (This is all what we mean, when we assert that the existence of an organ of vision etc. is the condition under which a visual sensation etc. can arise).

Nāgārjuna now states that this co-ordinational theory of causation is also wrong.

---

1 *vīraṇa*.

2 Lit. p. 81.2 "The word 'not' is the connection with the subject-matter, i.e. the negation must be taken out of the preceding sentence. The word *uta* puts emphasis."

3 Read *paci-kriyā*.

4 *pratyayān pratītya*.

V. Let those facts be causes,
With which co-ordinated other facts arise,
Non-causes will they be,
So far the other facts have not arisen.

If sensation is an entity whose origination is co-ordinated with a faculty of vision and other conditions and these co-ordinations are called causes, is it not evident that up to the moment when this so-called "result" the sensation, has really arisen, what can the organs etc. represent but non-causes? They are as good as non-causes. That is the idea of Nāgārjuna. And nothing can be produced out of its non-causes, e.g. oil cannot be pressed out of sand corns.

But the following objection is then raised. They begin by being non-causes, but they are afterwards converted into causes by combining with some other concomitant conditions. This also won't do. Because concomitant condition, concomitant with something which is not yet a condition, can be considered as a condition only if the other fact is really a condition. We are in this case faced by the same difficulty as before. Therefore this explanation cannot be accepted.

An organ of vision and an object are here assumed to represent the causes producing visual sensation. But are they the causes of an existing sensation or are they the causes of a sensation not yet existing? It is anyhow an impossibility. Nāgārjuna says,

VI. Neither non-Ens, nor Ens
Can have a cause.

Why?

If non-Ens, whose the Cause?
If Ens, what for the Cause?

Non-Ens, i.e. a non-existing thing, how could it have a cause? Its cause is perhaps so called in anticipation? It will produce the result at some future occasion. No.

Referring to a future fact
We give a name anticipating,
But never will this future come
Without a force that latently is present.[1]

The incongruities[2] (resulting from assuming latent forces) have been indicated above.

---

1 M. av. VI 58 Lit. "There is for it no futurity without a force."
2 *doṣa*.

But if a thing is really existent, if it is present, if it has taken shape, it is absolutely useless to imagine some causes producing it.

XLV THE CAUSE CONDITION

After having represented that conditions[1] in general are not really causes, since they have no capacity to produce effects, Nāgārjuna now proceeds to consider their varieties separately and to show that none of them singly is really a cause.

The following objection is raised by the Hīnayānist. If you are right, he says, there can be no conditions at all. But the notion of a condition is very well established, since we have a definition of its essence. The definition of the cause-condition[2] which is here accepted, is the following one. A cause is what "turns out." If something be altogether a non-Ens, the definition of its essence could never be given, it would be as though (some one were to teach us about the essence of a non-existing) son of a barren woman.

We answer. The producing condition (i.e., the cause), would exist if its essence were something real. (But this is not the case), since,

---

1. It would have been strictly correct to translate *pratyaya* 'condition" or "co-ordinate" and *hetu-pratyaya* cause-condition or simply cause. But *adhipati-pratyaya* is even more of a cause than *hetu-pratyaya* which, therefore, is sometimes called *sahakāri-pratyaya*. (*Sarvadarś p.*39 Poona, 1924). Only the *ālambana* and *samanantara-pratyayas* can be distinguished as "conditions." It is, therefore, impossible always to distinguish between these two terms. Yaśomitra accordingly says, ad Ab. Kośa. II. 50, *hetūnāṁ ca pratyayānāṁ ca ko viśeṣaḥ? na kaścit.*

2. *hetu-pratyaya*, the first of the four *pratyayas*. This classification of conditions into four varieties is not what to our requirements should be a strictly systematic classification, all members are not exclusive of one another. Thus the general condition is contrasted with the special one (*adhipati*), but it includes the two others which are only its varieties. It also embraces 5 causes of the *hetu*-classification, (1) *sabhāga-hetu*, relation of homogeneity between the preceding and the following moments of the same thing, producing the illusion of its duration, or moral homogeneity among the subsequent elements of a personality. This *hetu*-classification is also unsystematic, because the sixth class, the kāraṇa-hetu has two varieties, the efficient and the non-efficient one (*nus-bcas,nus-med*), the first is the same as the predominant condition *adhipati-pratyaya* or *asādhāraṇa-kāraṇa*, the second is an expression of the dependence of a given point-instant upon the condition of the whole Universe (*sarve dharmāḥ*) *sahabhū* and *saṃprayukta-hetu*, relations of co-existence according to which some elements of Matter and Mind never appear alone, but always together, (4) *vipāka-hetu* which is another name for *karma* and (5) *sarvatraga-hetu*, moral homogeneity among coexisting elements. Cp. Ab. Kośa. II 50 ff.

VII. Neither an Ens, nor a non-Ens,
Nor any Ens-non-Ens,
No element is really "turned out."
How can we then assume
The possibility of a producing cause?

Producing means creative.[1] If an element which can be produced would really be produced, then a creative cause would produce it. But it is not being (really) produced, since there is altogether no such thing that needs to be produced, whether Ens or non-Ens or (something including both) Ens and non-Ens.

Indeed Ens is not produced because it exists. Neither is non-Ens, since it does not exist. Nor Ens-non-Ens, since such mutually contradicting (characteristics) cannot exist in one thing, and because, if they did, they would be subject to both the above strictures together. So it is that, since there is no production of effects (from the Monist's point of view), neither are there any creative causes.

Consequently the argument that causes must exist because their essence (or function) has been defined does not hold good in the present case.

XLVI THE OBJECT, A CONDITION OF MENTAL PHENOMENA

The author now proceeds to deny the (second condition), the condition consisting in the fact that (every mental phenomenon) has an objective counterpart (upon which it is intent).

VIII. A mental Ens is reckoned as an element,
Separately from its objective counterpart.
Now if it begins by having no objective counterpart.,
How can it get one afterwards?

What are the elements[2] of existence which are here in the Hīnayānist's system characterised as possessors of an objective counterpart?[3] Consciousness, (i.e., pure, indefinite sensation[4] and definite mental phenomena[5] such are the words

1 Lit., what "turns out" (*nirvartaka*).
2 *dharma*.
3 *sālambana*.
4 *citta*.
5 *caitta*.

of Scripture. When consciousness is awakened, or definite mental phenomena produced, they are intent[1] upon some object (which transcends them), whether it be a patch of colour or some other object corresponding to the sensation. These are then called the objective conditions[2] of those mental elements.

It is now asked, is this objective condition imagined for sensation already existing, or for sensation not yet produced? In the first case the objective condition becomes useless. Indeed the objective condition is assumed in order to account for the production of this element,[3] (sensation). But this element then really exists before the objective cause has begun to operate.

Indeed in this case the element (consciousness) would be established as existing by itself, separately from its objective cause. Why would we then imagine it influenced by an external object?

Thus consciousness and similar elements would appear as existent and real, separately from their objective counterparts. Then it would simply be your fancy to call them possessors of an objective counterpart.[4] They would have altogether no (real) relation to objects.

Now let us examine the other alternative. We then imagine that a sensation not yet existing has already an object. This is also impossible. Because an element which has been entered into the system of elements separately from its objective counterpart is, in any case, an existing element. But (to imagine) an unexisting element combining with an object is quite impossible.[5]

The first sentence of the above verse must be supplemented thus—"you call possessor of an object" a mental Ens which in the system is reckoned as an element separately from its object.

The second sentence of the verse contains a question.

Now if it begins by having no objective counterpart, how can it get one afterwards?

---

1 *ālambanena utpadyante.*
2 *ālambana-pratyaya.*
3 *dharma.*
4 *sālambana.*
5 Lit. p. 84, 9-10. "This also is impossible, because it is stated in the aphorisms "without an object really...etc. an existing element is taught in the system." "Indeed the non-existing has no combination with the object."

This is the reason expressed in the form of a question.[1] The meaning is the following one. If an element cannot exist without being intent upon an object, if it is not real, wherefrom will then the object appear? If the object-maker[2] is absent, neither can the object exist.

But then how are we to understand the Scriptural evidence that mind and mental phenomena must have an object? The question is trivial.[3] Yes they have an object, if the rule be considered from the empirical standpoint of contingent reality, not from the transcendental standpoint of absolute reality.

XLVII THE CAUSA MATERIALIS DENIED

Nāgārjuna next proceeds to destroy the notion of an immediately preceding moment of a chain of homogeneous momentary existences which by the Hīnayānist is reckoned as a special condition.[4] He says,

IX. If separate elements do not exist,
Nor is it possible for them to disappear.
There is no moment which immediately precedes.
And if it disappears, how can it be a cause?

The[5] definition of the immediately preceding homogeneous condition is here (in the Hīnayāna) the following one. The immediately preceding destruction of the material cause is a condition of the production of the result. The following must be considered. When in a monistic system all entities,[6] all supposed results are viewed as non-produced,[7] as e.g., a sprout

1 Lit. p. 85.4 "The word *atha* for a question. Why?—for the reason."
2 *ālambanaka*.
3 *adoṣa*.
4 This condition corresponds roughly to the *samavāyi-kāraṇa* of the Nyāya-Vaiśeṣika; it represents the *upādāna*, the substratum of every appearing element. In the realistic systems, the *causa materialis* is the continuant substance in the new production. But all Buddhists deny the existence of continuant substances and reduce them to chains of discrete moments, every preceding moment representing the *upādāna* of the following one. The preceding moment is supposed to have vanished when the next one appears.

5 Precedes a grammatical explanation. Lit., p. 86. 1-3. "Here, in the last half of the verse, the quarters must be transposed. Moreover, the word "and" is at the wrong place, it should stand after the word *niruddhe*. The reading will then be, "if it has disappeared, how is it a cause?" Therefore "the foregoing", is not admissible. It has been thus expressed for the sake of versification."
6 *dharma*.
7 i.e. existing *sub specie aeternitatis*.

is not considered as a new origination,[1] then it is clear that from this standpoint, the disappearance of the cause, the seed in its last moment, is impossible. In this case, there is no disappearance of the material cause, and therefore how can there be a moment representing the immediately preceding condition for the production of the sprout?

But the Hīnayānist maintains that all existence being a chain of descrete moments, the disappearance of the seed must have happened before the result has appeared. However, if the seed is destroyed, converted into non-existence, what is then supposed to represent a cause of the sprout? Or what is the cause that has destroyed the seed? Both are without a cause. This is expressed in the words,

And if it disappears, how can it be a cause?

The word "and" refers to a non-produced sprout.[2] Indeed, since it is assumed that the sprout is not yet produced at the moment when the seed has already disappeared, both these events the disappearing of the seed and the appearing of the sprout are without a cause. For this reason, an immediately foregoing separate momentary existence as a cause is an impossibility.

Another explanation of this verse is the following one. In the first aphorism of this treatise. viz.—

There absolutely are no things,
Nowhere and none, that arise anew,
Neither out of themselves, nor out of non-self,
Nor out of both, nor at random.

The notion of origination has been cleared away altogether.

The present aphorism simply refers to that general denial and draws the consequence that—

If separate elements never appear,
Nor is it possible for them to disappear.
There is no moment which immediately precedes.[3]

As to the explanation of the last sentence of the aphorism, viz.

---

1 But as a mode of the unique substance (*tathatā*=*dharmakāya*) of the Universe.

2 It is the habit of Indian commentaries to interpret the particle 'and' as an indication of some additional circumstance.

3 i.e., there is no momentary existence which immediately disappears in order to make room for the next moment.

And if it disappears, how can it be a cause?
it remains then just the same as before.

XLVIII THE SPECIAL CAUSE ALSO DENIED

Nāgārjuna now goes on to deny the existence of a predominant condition[1] and says,

X. If entities are relative,[2]
They have no real existence.
The formula "this being, that appears."
Then loses every meaning.

The definition of the predominant condition[3] is here in Hīnayāna the following one. A predominant condition is that special fact which being present the result inevitably appears. But since all separate entities[4] from the Monist's point of view have only a relative origination[5] and no real independent existence,[6] the definition of causation expressed in the words "this being, that appears" then loses every meaning. What is indeed the meaning of the word "this" which is supposed to point to a cause, and what the meaning of the word "that" which is supposed to point to its result? It is true, a definition is given, but Causality is not thereby established.[7]

The Hīnayānist makes the following objection. After having observed that a piece of cloth is produced out of threads, we

1 This variety of causation is probably the precursor of the *nimitta-kāraṇa, asādhāraṇa kāraṇa, sādhakātma kāraṇa* or *kāraṇa* of the Nyāya-Vaiśeṣika. The eye, e.g., is the *adhipati-pratyaya* of a visual sensation. But it cannot be identified with our *causa efficiens* because such a conception has, strictly speaking, no place in the Buddhist system. Causation in the world-process is imagined as quite impersonal, the separate bits of reality are following one another automatically. *Karma* itself is a separate element, it is not personal in theory. All results are therefore automatic, the natural outflow *niṣyanda-phala* of conditions. Some results are very characteristically called anthropomorphic (*puruṣa-kāra-phala=puruṣeṇa iva kṛta*), they are also conceived as automatic, but only appearing as though they were produced by a conscious will. Cf. Ab. Kośa. II, 56 ff.

2 *niḥsvabhāva=śūnya.*

3 *adhipati-pratyaya.*

4 *bhāvānām.*

5 *pratītya-samutpannatva=śūnyatā.*

6 *svabhāva-abhāva=śūnyatā.*

7 Lit., p. 87. 1-3. "Since there is non-existence of self-existence of the entities because of their Dependently-together-origination, wherefrom that which is pointed to by "this" as a cause, wherefrom that which is pointed to by "that" as a result? Therefore, albeit from a definition, there is establishment of their conditions".

conclude that the existence of threads etc. is a necessary condition for the existence of a piece of cloth.

We answer. From the standpoint of transcendental reality, it is just the production of such separate results as cloth etc. that is ultimately[1] denied. How can we then admit that their supposed conditions are really causes? That the production of such results as cloth etc. is ultimately unreal, this Nāgārjuna makes clear in the following words,

XI. Neither singly in anyone of these conditions,
Nor together in all of them
Does the supposed result reside.
How can you out of them extract,
What in them never did exist?

The cloth, indeed, does not exist, neither in the threads, nor in the weavers brush, nor in his loom, nor in the shuttle, nor in the pins or other causes taken singly. We do not perceive in them any cloth. Moreover, from a plurality of causes a plurality of effects would be expected. And since the cloth does not exist in any one of its parts taken singly, it neither does exist in all of them, in the threads etc., taken together.

If we would admit that every single cause contributes its part to the general result, we should be obliged to admit that one result is produced piece-meal.

Therefore since there are really no results, neither can the existence of causes as separate entities[2] be admitted.

XII Supposing from these causes does appear
What never did exist in them.
This is what the Hīnayānist maintains.
Out of non-causes then
Why does it not appear?

The result does not pre-exist in these things which admittedly are not its causes. And we have seen that it neither does pre-exist in those things which admittedly are its causes. Why then is a piece of cloth never produced out of straw and other things which admittedly are not its causes? From the standpoint of ultimate reality[3] we then deny the production of results altogether.

1 *svarūpataḥ*.
2 *svabhāvataḥ*.
3 *svarūpataḥ—tattvataḥ*.

The Hīnayānist makes here the following objection. If the result were really one thing and its causes something separate, then we would understand your solicitude about the question whether the result pre-exists in the causes or not? But the result is not something outside its causes. On the contrary, it includes them in itself, the presence of the whole complex of all the causes of a given event is equivalent to the production of the latter. Nāgārjuna says,

XIII The result a cause-possessor,
But causes not even self-possessors.
How can result be cause-possessor,
If of non-self-possessors, it be a result.

You maintain that there is a possessive relation between a result and its causes, i.e., that the result is simply a modification[1] of its causes. This is wrong, because these supposed causes do not possess their own selves, i.e. they are no real causes.[2]

It is asserted that a piece of cloth consists of threads. The cloth then could be a reality if the threads themselves had ultimate reality.[3] But they consist of parts.[4] They are themselves modifications of their own parts, they are no ultimate realities.[5] Therefore, what is the use of maintaining that the result designated as a cloth consists of threads, when these threads themselves are no ultimate realities,[6] they are not "self possessors."[7] This has been expressed in the following aphorism,

Cloth is existent in its threads,
The threads again in something else.
How can these threads, unreal themselves,
Produce reality in something else?[8]

---

1 *pratyaya-vikārāḥ.*

2 *apratyaya-svabhāvāḥ.*

3 *svabhāva-siddha.*

4 *aṃśumaya,* possessing particles or filaments.

5 *asvabhāva-siddha.*

6 *asvabhāva.*

7 *asvayaṃmaya.*

8 This is against the Vaiśeṣika view that the reality of the whole is conditioned by the reality of the parts in which the whole is supposed to inhere, the atoms being the ultimate, eternal reality. For the Mādhyamikas atoms will be relative realities, constructed realities *saṃvṛti.* For the identification of this stanza cf. M. de la V.P.'s note in his ed.

XIV There is, therefore, no cause-possessor,
Nor is there a result without a cause.
Nor causes are there, nor non-causes,
If altogether no results.

Therefore there is no cause-possessing result. Then perhaps there may be a result without causes? No, there is no result outside its material cause. If the reality of a piece of cloth is not sufficiently explained by the reality of its component parts the threads, this does not mean that it will be explained any better by the reality of the straw of which mats are made.[1]

The Hīnayānist objects. Let us admit for the sake of argument that there are no results i.e., no production and no pre-existence of supposed results.[2] There is, however, a regularity[3] in the phenomenal world according to which some facts appear as coordinated and others are not so coordinated. You yourself admit it. Indeed you ask us the following question: if there are no results produced by causes and if all existence consists of discrete moments following one another why is it that certain facts appear only after those with which they are serially coordinated, why is it that they do not appear with the same evidence[4] after facts with which they are not serially coordinated? By putting this question you implicitly admit a strict regularity in the phenomenal world. If the supposed results, called a cloth or a mat, were not existent, their coordinates, the threads and the straw, would never have been called causes. In this sense we the Hīnayānists maintain the reality of results.[5]

---

1 Lit. p. 89.9 "If there is no cloth consisting of threads how can there be one consisting of *vīraṇa* straw?"

2 The theory of the non-existence or the non-pre-existence of the result in its causes, (*mā bhūt phalam=asat-phalam=asat-kāryam*) is also admitted by the Vaiśeṣikas, but they admit a new creation (*ārambha*) of the results by the causes. The Hīnayānists have substituted for a notion of efficient causality (*utpāda*) a notion of coordination, (*pratītya-samutpāda*) and converted efficient causes (*hetu, kāraṇa*) into conditions or coordinates (*pratyaya*). At the same time they have here converted every entity, every durable object, into a series of discrete momentary existences following one another with strict regularity. They have thus replaced causality by a regularity or uniformity in nature (*pratyaya-niyama*). The Mahāyānist rejects this theory from the standpoint of absolute reality, but this does not prevent him from accepting the realistic view for phenomenal reality.

3 *niyama.*

4 *abhipravartate=abhimukham pravartate.*

5 Lit. p. 89.10-12. "Here he says, let there be no result, but there is a regularity of conditions and non-conditions. Accordingly you say "if a non-existent result appears after its conditions, after its non-conditions

We answer. There would have been a real result, if conditions and non-conditions themselves really existed. We would then distinguish that, given a certain result, such and such facts are not its conditions. But if we critically examine[1] these conceptions, they reveal themselves as non-real. Therefore,

No causes are there, no non-causes,
Since altogether no result[2]

Thus we conclude that there is no coordination[3] among separate entities, when considered from the transcendental point of view.[4]

Accordingly it is stated in the Ārya-Ratnākarasūtra.[5]

Where the adept of Relativity[6] himself is lost,
What vanishes like a bird's flight in air,
What independently nowhere exists,
Will never be a cause producing something !
What independently at all does not exist,
How can it have a cause,[7] without itself existing,
Without itself existing, how can it be efficient ?[8]
Such is Causality as taught by Buddha.
All supposed forces[9] are like mountains,[10]
They are immovable and firmly seated,
Not changing, never suffering, ever quiescent
Unconscious[11] are they like aerial Space.

---

also why does it not evidently appear?" "And if the result called cloth or mat does not exist, the conditionality of the conditions, of the threads of the straw, is impossible."

1 *vicāryamāṇa*.

2 Lit. p. 90.1 "Causes and non-causes is a (dvandva) compound."

3 *samutpatti=pratītya-samutpāda*. The first chapter thus winds up with a rejection of the Hīnayānistic *pratītya-samutpāda*.

4 *svabhāvataḥ=tattvataḥ*.

5 Cp. L. Feer, Index du Kandjour, p. 248.

6 śūnya-vid. cp. Tib.

7 *para-paccayaḥ*, possibly as *bahuvrīhi*.

8 Lit. "give birth to something else."

9 *sarva-dharmāḥ=sarve saṃskārāḥ*, the totality of all the active elements of existence.

10 or "motionless", *acala*.

11 *ajānaka* Tib. *śes-pa-med-pa* does not mean that *dharma-kāya* is an unconscious materialistic principle, but that no individual things are cognized, since they are lost in the all-embracing whole.

Just as a mountain can be never shaken
So motionless are all the elements[1] of nature,
They never go and never come.
Thus should we have understood these elements
Revealed by the Victorious Buddha.
And moreover,
This one Reality Eternal,[2]
Has been revealed by the Victorious Buddha,
The lion of this mankind :
It is not born, it does not live[3]
It does not die, does not decay,
And merged[4] in it are all the beings !
If something has no essence in itself,
How can it then receive an essence from without ?[5]
There are, therefore, no things internal,
There also are no things external.
But everywhere is present our Lord.[6]
This absolute condition[7] for Quiescence
Where every individual disappears,
Has been revealed by the real Buddha.[8]
There is in it no individual life whatever.
There you will stroll[9] from birth delivered !
You will then be your Saviour,

---

1 *dharma.*

2 *dharma* evidently in the sense of *dharma-kāya*=*dharmatā*=*tathatā*. But the meaning of *dharma* "the doctrine of Buddha" is also suggested.

3 *upapadyī*, here probably in the sense of *sthita* as a member of the series *utpāda*, *sthiti*, *jarā*, *anityatā*.

4 *niveśayi*=Tib. *bkod-pa*=*saṃniveśa* "arrangement", i.e., the whole is an arrangement of parts, the parts disappear in the whole.

5 *para-bhāvatu*.

6 Lit., 91 4.5 "With whom some self-existence is not found, through something it is not reached as other-existence, it is not being reached neither from within, nor from without, in it is the Lord inherent." *nātha*= *dharma-kāya*; *niveśayi* in the same sense as in 91.2.

7 The term *gati* signifying the six kinds of worldly existence is here applied to Nirvāṇa which is not a *gati*, but the ultimate aim of all *gatis*.

8 The term *su-gata* is here evidently being interpreted as the man who has entered the "best gati", i.e., who is lost in the Absolute.

9 *voharasi* is here also used pointedly for a condition which is the negation of *vyavahāra*, but at the same time the ultimate aim of all *vyavahāra*.

And you will save the hosts of living beings !
There is no other Path discernible whatever.
There you will live, from birth delivered,
And free yourself, deliver many beings ! etc.

Finished the "Examination of Causality" the first chapter of the "Clear worded" Comment upon Relativity, the work of the venerable Master Candrakīrti.

CHAPTER XXV

EXAMINATION OF NIRVĀṆA

I. THE HĪNAYĀNISTIC NIRVĀṆA REJECTED

On this subject Nāgārjuna says,

I. If everything is relative,[1]
No real origination, no real annihilation,
How is Nirvāṇa then conceived ?
Through what deliverance,[2] through what annihilation ?[3]

With regard to this point the Buddha has taught that personalities[4] who have lived a pure life and have been initiated into Buddha's religion,[5] who have acquired a knowledge of ontology, i.e., of the elements of existence as taught in that religion,[6] can attain a double kind of Nirvāṇa, a Nirvāṇa, at lifetime, being an annihilation with some *residual substratum*, and a final Nirvāṇa, being an annihilation without any residue.

The first of them is conceived as something attainable by a complete deliverance[7] from the whole catalogue of the defiling elements,[8] e.g., the illusion of personal identity,[9] desires[10] etc., etc. A substratum is what underlies all these defiling agencies, it is the inveterate instinct of cherishing one's own life.[11] The word *residual substratum* thus refers to that foundation of our belief in personal identity[12] which is represented by the ultimate

---

1 *śūnya*.
2 *prahāṇa*.
3 *nirodha*.
4 *pudgala*.
5 *tathāgata-śāsana-pratipanna*.
6 *dharma-anu-dharma-pratipatti-yukta*; noteworthy is the use of the term *dharma* in its two chief significations side by side, the first *dharma* refers to the doctrine, or religion, the second to the 75 elements of existence, or ontology.
7 *prahāṇa*.
8 *kleśa-gaṇa*.
9 *avidyā*.
10 *rāgādi*.
11 *ātma-sneha*.
12 *ātma-prajñapti*.

elements of our mundane existence,[1] which are systematized in five different groups. A residue is what is left. A substratum is left in a partial Nirvāṇa. It exists with a *residual substratum*, hence its name.

What is the thing in which there still is a residue of personal feeling? It is Nirvāṇa. It is a residue consisting of the pure elements[2] of existence alone, delivered from the illusion of an abiding personality[3] and other stealthy defilers,[4] a state comparable to that of a town in which all criminal gangs have been executed. This is a Nirvāṇa at lifetime with some residue of personal feeling.

A Nirvāṇa in which even these purified elements themselves are absent is termed final Nirvāṇa, a Nirvāṇa without any residue of personal feeling, because of the idea that here[5] the residue of personal feeling is gone, it is impersonal. It is a state comparable to that of a town (destroyed), a town which, after all the criminal gangs have been executed, has been itself also annihilated. It has been said about this Nirvāṇa.

The body has collapsed,
Ideas[6] gone, all feelings vanished,
All energies[7] quiescent,
And consciousness[8] itself extinct.

And likewise,

With his body still at life,

---

1 *upādāna-skandhāḥ=sāsrava-dharmāḥ*, the elements of mundane existence as contrasted with the elements composing the Saint and the Buddha; *skandha* can be translated as "element" and as "group of elements" because three *skandhas* (*vedanā*, *saṃjñā*, *vijñāna*) contain one *dharma* each, *rūpa-skandha* contains 10 *dharmas*, and *saṃskāra-skandha* the remaining 59 ones, except the eternal ones *asaṃskṛta*, not included in this classification at all; *skandha* is also a group in the sense of containing past, present, future etc. *dharmas* cf. my Central Conception, p. 6.

2 *skandha-mātraka=anāsrava-dharmāḥ.*

3 *sat-kāya-dṛṣṭi.*

4 *kleśa-taskara.*

5 *nir-upadhi-śeṣa* is thus an *adhikaraṇa-sādhana madhyama-pada-lopin* composite word implying that when all the elements of life are gone, there still remains something lifeless in what there has formerly been life.

6 *ḥdu-ses=saṃjñā.*

7 ḥdu-byed=*saṃskāra.*

8 *rnam-par-ses-pa=vijñāna.*

The Saint enjoys some feeling,
But in Nirvāṇa, consciousness[1] is gone,[2]
Just as a light (when totally extinct).

This lifeless Nirvāṇa, without any residue, is attained through an extinction of all elements of life.[3]

The Mahāyānist. Now, how are we to understand the possibility of this double Nirvàṇa ?

The Hīnayānist Nirvāṇa is only possible through the annihilation of desires[4] and all active elements producing life.[5] If everything is relative,[6] if nothing really originates, nothing really disappears, where is the source of illusion and desires,[7] where all the elements[8] which must vanish, in order that Nirvāṇa should take place ? It is therefore, clear that separate entities must really exist,[9] in order that something should really vanish.

1 *cetaḥ=vijñāna-skandha.*

2 *vimokṣaḥ=nivṛttiḥ.*

3 *skandhānāṁ nirodhāt.* These two Nirvāṇas are well known in European science since the time of Childers. Of them only the second is the real and final Nirvāṇa. It is defined by Childers, according to the Pali school, as annihilation of all the *skandhas.* But the classification of existence as *skandhas* does not include *nirodha* or *asaṃskṛta-dharma. The Sarvāstivādins* and *Vaibhāṣikas*, as we have seen, assume this *nirodha* to represent a separate reality—*satya, vastu, dharma*, it is a lifeless *dharma-svabhāva* as contrasted with the living *dharma-lakṣaṇa=saṃskārāḥ.* The Mahāyānist, from his higher, monistic point of view, brushes both these Nirvāṇas aside. But there cannot be the slightest doubt that Nāgārjuna accepts their contingent reality. He thus has three Nirvāṇas. The first represents the world *sub specie aeternitatis*, it is defined below, XXV 9. The second is the condition of the Mahāyānistic Saint, the *ārya*, the *bodhisattva.* The third corresponds to his disappearance in final Nirvāṇa. The first alone is ultimately real. The two others are immanent in it; they are not separately (*svabhāvataḥ*) real. To these three Nirvāṇas, the Yogācāras have added a fourth one, called by them *apratiṣṭhita-nirvāṇa* altruistic Nirvāṇa; it represents the pure condition of their eternal Conscious Principle, that principle which they have inherited from the Sautrāntikas and the latter from earlier schools with similar theistic tendencies, the Vatsīputrīyas and the Mahāsaṅghikas, J. Masuda, Der Idealismus der Yogācāra Schule, p. 52 ff. (Heidelberg, 1926). According to consequent Mahāyānism, this fourth Nirvāṇa should be also regarded as merely an aspect of the first, but this question appears never to have been finally answered, atleast among some of the followers of that school. It is a moot point among the Tibetans, even now, whether the Absolute of an author like Dharmakīrti represents a Conscious Principle (śes-pa) or Impersonal Eternity (*rtag-pa*). According to the early Yogācāras, the *dharma-kāya* is divided into *svabhāvakāya* (no-bo-ñid-sku) and *jñāna-kāya* (je-śes-kyi-sku), the first is the motionless (*nitya*) substance of the Universe, the second is *anitya.* i.e. changing, living.

4 *kleśa.*

5 *skandha.*

6 *śūnya.*

7 *kleśāḥ=avidyā-tṛṣṇe.*

8 *skandhāḥ.*

9 *bhāvānāṃ svabhāvaḥ*, "non-relative, absolute existence."

To this the following aphorism is an answer.

II. Should everything be absolutely real,[1]
No real creation, no real destruction,
How is Nirvāṇa then conceived?
Through what deliverance, through what annihilation?

If the defiling elements[2], or all the elements in general,[3] are independent entities, existing in themselves,[4] since it is impossible for them to be deprived of their own reality, how can they be annihilated, in order that through this annihilation Nirvāṇa should be reached? Therefore Nirvāṇa is equally impossible from the standpoint of the Realists.[5] But the Relativists[6] do not admit a Nirvāṇa consisting in annihilation of all elements in general, nor do they admit a partial Nirvāṇa consisting in an annihilation of the defiling elements alone. Therefore, they are not responsible for the just mentioned incongruity.[7] The Relativists, in consequence, can never be accused of assuming a kind of Nirvāṇa which is logically impossible.

II. THE MAHĀYĀNISTIC NIRVĀṆA, WHAT?

If, to be sure, the Relativists admit neither a Nirvāṇa consisting in the extinction of illusion and desire,[8] nor a Nirvāṇa consisting in the extinction of all elements of life, what is then their idea of Nirvāṇa? The following aphorism gives the answer.

III. What neither is released, nor is it ever reached,
What neither is annihilation, nor is it eternality,
What never disappears, nor has it been created,
This is Nirvāṇa (World's Unity, the Inexpressible).

That (indefinable essence) which can neither be extinguished as, e.g., a desire, nor can be attained, as e.g., a reward for renunciation; which neither can be annihilated, as e.g., all the active elements of our life.[9] nor is everlasting,[10] as a non-

1 *aśūnya.*
2 *kleśa.*
3 *skandhānām=saṃskṛta-dharmāṇām=saṃskārāṇām.*
4 *svabhāvenavyavasthita.*
5 *svabhāva-vādin.*
6 *śūnyatā-vādin.*
7 *teṣām ayam adoṣaḥ.*
8 *kleśa=avidyā-tṛṣṇe.*
9 *skandhādivat.*
10 *śāśvata* or *nitya* "beginningless."

relative[1] absolute principle; which cannot really[2] disappear, nor can be created; that something which consists in the Quiescence[3] of all Plurality,[4] that is Nirvāṇa.

Now, if the Universe is really such a Unity, if it is no Plurality,[5] how is it then that our imagination has built up defilers[6] i.e. an illusion of personal identity and desires through a suppression of which Nirvāṇa is supposed to be attained? Or how is it that our imagination has built up separate elements through the annihilation of which Nirvāṇa reveals itself? As long as these constructions of our imagination[7] exist, Nirvāṇa cannot be reached, since it is reached just through a suppression of all Plurality.

The Hīnayānist objects. Be that as the case may be, let us admit that neither the defiling elements, nor the elements in general exist when Nirvāṇa is reached. However, they must exist on this side of Nirvāṇa, i.e., before Nirvāṇa is reached. In that case Nirvāṇa will be possible through their total annihilation.

We answer. You are haunted[8] by illusion, get rid of it!

For a real Ens which exists as an independent-entity[9] can never be converted into a non-entity. Therefore those who are really desirous to attain Nirvāṇa must first of all get rid of this imagined Plurality. Indeed Nāgārjuna himself will state that there is no line of demarcation, with the Phenomenal world on this side and the Absolute on the other.

Where is the limit of Nirvāṇa,
'T is also the limit of Saṃsāra,
There is no line of demarcation,

---

1 *aśūnyavat*, as the *svalakṣaṇa* of the Yogācāras, the Nirvāṇa of the Hīnayānists, the *pradhāna* of the Sāṅkhyas etc. etc. They are all aśūnya in that sense that their adepts suppose them to be absolute, non-relative.

2 *svabhāvataḥ*.

3 *upaśama*.

4 *sarva-prapañca*.

5 *niṣprapañca*.

6 *kleśa-kalpanā*.

7 *kalpanāḥ*.

8 *grāha*.

9 *svabhāvato vidyamāna*.

No slightest shade of difference between them.[1]

Thus it should be realized that nothing is really suppressed in Nirvāṇa, and nothing is really annihilated. Nirvāṇa consists merely in the suppression of absolutely all the false constructions of our imagination. This has been stated by the Buddha himself in the following words,

> Real ultimate elements[2] can never be annihilated,
> The things that in this world do not exist,
> They never did at all exist.
> Those who imagine existence along with non-existence
> Will never realize phenomenal[3] (Plurality's) Quiescence.

The meaning of this stanza is the following one. In the Absolute,[4] i.e., in that principle which is final Nirvāṇa[5] without any residue (of phenomenal life altogether), all elements of existence have vanished, because all of them, whether they be called defilers,[6] or the creative power of life,[7] or individual existences,[8] or groups of elements, have all totally vanished. This all systems of philosophy[9] admit, i. e., that the Absolute is a negation of the Phenomenal.

Now, these elements which do not exist there, in the Absolute, really do not exist at all; they are like that kind of terror which is experienced when , in the dark, a rope is mistaken for a snake and which dissipates as soon as a light is brought in. These elements of our life, called illusion and desire, their creative force and the consequent individual lives[10] have no real existence in the absolute sense,[11] even at any time in the phenomenal

---

1 XXV. 20.
2 *dharmāḥ*.
3 *duḥkha=saṃsāra*, cp. p. 523. 13
4 *nirvṛtti*.
5 *nirvāṇa-dhātu*.
6 *kleśa*.
7 *karma*.
8 *janma*.
9 *sarva-vādinaḥ*.
10 *kleśa-karma-janmādi*.
11 *tattvataḥ*.

condition of life.[1] Indeed, the rope which in the dark has been mistaken for the serpent, is not really in itself a serpent, since it is not apprehended by sight and touch, whether in the light or in the darkness, as a real serpent would necessarily be.

How is it then that it is called phenomenal reality ?[2]

We answer. Obsessed by the unreal devil of their "Ego" and their "Mine" the abstruse men and common worldlings imagine that they really perceive separate entities which in reality do not exist, just as the ophthalmic sees before himself hair, mosquitoes and other objects which never did exist. It has therefore been said,

Those who imagine existence along with non-existence,
Will never realize phenomenal Plurality's Quiescence.

Those who assert existence, the Realists who imagine that there is a real existence of separate entities,[3] are the followers of Jaimini, Kaṇāda, Kapila and others up to the realistic Buddhists, the Vaibhāṣikas.[4]

Those who deny future existence are the Materialists[5] who are firmly rooted in a destiny leading them to hell. The others are the Sautrāntikas who deny the existence of the past and the future,[6] deny the existence of such a separate element as the moral character of the individual, deny the existence of forces which are neither physical nor mental,[7] but admit the reality of all other separate elements. Or they are the *Yogācāras*, the Idealists who deny the existence of individual things so far as they represent logical constructions of our thought,[8] but admit 1. their contingent reality so far as they obey causal laws[9] and 2. their final reality so far they are merged into the Universal Whole.[10]

1 *saṃsāra-avasthāyām.*

2 *saṃsāra.*

3 *bhāva-sadbhāva-kalpanāvantaḥ.*

4 It is noteworthy that the Sautrāntikas are not mentioned among the Realists; it is just because they are half-realists. In addition to what has been said above, about the position of the Sautrāntikas, it must be mentioned that *Bodhidharma* and many others characterised this school as Mahāyānistic because of its moral philosophy. But their opinion was rejected, since the founders of the two main schools of the Mahāyāna, i.e., Nāgārjuna and Āryasaṅga, did not share it. (Cp. *Lanskya-hu-tuk-tu, Grub-mthah.* trans. by M. Gorsky, Ms. Mus. As. Petr.). The total silence about Vedānta is also to be noted.

5 *nāstika*, they deny retribution, moral responsibility.

6 Cp. My Central Conception p. 42.

7 *viprayukta-saṃskāra=rūpa-citta-viprayukta-saṃskāra*, cp. ibid, p. 21.

8 *pari-kalpita-svabhāva*, cp. *Triṃśikā*, p. 39

9 *paratantra*, cp. ibid.

10 *pariniṣpanna*, cp, ibid.

The phenomenal world,[1] or the phenomenal life[2] will never reach final Quiescence neither for the Realists,[3] nor for the Negativists,[4] (nor for partial Realists). Indeed,

A man, suspecting he has taken poison,
Faints even when there is no poison in his stomach.
Swayed by the care of Ego and of "Mine",
Eternally he comes and dies,
Without real knowledge[5] about his Ego[6]

Therefore it should be known that nothing is suppressed in Nirvāṇa and nothing annihilated. The essence of Nirvāṇa consists merely in the extinction of all constructions of our productive imagination.[7]

Accordingly we find it stated in the Ratnāvalī[8]

Nor is Nirvāṇa non-existence.
How can such an idea[9] come to you?
We call Nirvāṇa the cessation
Of every thought of non-existence and existence.

III NIRVĀṆA NOT AN ENS

The following aphorisms are directed against those who not being able to realize that Nirvāṇa is simply the limit of all constructions of our productive imagination continue to imagine a kind of Nirvāṇa which either represents reality or non-reality or both or neither.

IV. Nirvāṇa, first of all, is not a kind of Ens,
It would then have decay and death.
There altogether is no Ens
Which is not subject to decay and death.

There are indeed philosophers who have a preconceived idea[10] that Nirvāṇa must be something positive.[11] The following is

1 *duḥkha=pañca-upādāna-skandhāḥ*.
2 *saṃsāra*.
3 *astivādin*.
4 *nāstivādin*.
5 *bdag-der-hdu-śes-yañ dag=tad-ātma-saṃjñā*.
6 from the Tib.
7 *sarva-kalpanā-kṣaya*.
8 Ratnāvalī or Ratnamālikā, a work ascribed to Nāgārjuna.
9 *bhāvanā*.
10 *abhiniviṣṭa*.
11 *bhāva*.

their line of argument. According to our system,[1] they say, there is a positive thing which represents a barrier,[2] a definite limit[3] for the existence of a stream[4] of defiling elements, creative actions and consequent existences.[5] It is comparable to a dam checking a stream of water. This is Nirvāṇa. We know from experience[6] that a thing[7] without having a reality of its own[8] could not be efficient.[9] in that way.

The Sautrāntika objects. It has been declared that absolute indifference,[10] the extinction of desires which are associated with life,[11] of enjoyment that this kind of blank,[12] is Nirvāṇa. What in itself is a mere Extinction[13] cannot be envisaged as a kind of Ens.[14] It has been just declared,

But in Nirvāṇa consciousness itself is gone.
Just as a light when totally extinct.

To regard the extinction of the light of a lamp as a kind of Ens is logically impossible.[15]

The Vaibhāṣika answers. Your interpretation of the words "extinction of desire", as meaning "extinct desire" is wrong. The right interpretation is the following one. "That thing *in which* desire is extinct" is called extinction of desire. It can then be asserted that when that ultimate entity[16] which is called Nirvāṇa is present, every desire and consciousness are extinct. The extinction of the light of a lamp is a mere example. And even this example must be understood as an illustration of the idea that consciousness is quite extinct[17] *in something* that continues to exist.

---

1 *iha.*
2 *nirodhātmakaḥ padārthaḥ.*
3 *niyata-rodha=nirodha=nirvāṇa.*
4 *santāna.*
5 *kleśa-karma-janma.*
6 *dṛśyate.*
7 *dharma.*
8 *vidyamāna-svabhāva.*
9 *kārya-kārin.*
10 *virāga.*
11 *nandīrāga-sahagatā-tṛṣṇā.*
12 *nirodha.*
13 *kṣaya-mātram.*
14 *bhāva.*
15 *nopapadyate.*
16 *dharma.*
17 *vimokṣa.*

Our Master Nāgārjuna now examines the consequences of the theory which determines Nirvāṇa as a kind of existence. Nirvāṇa is not a positive thing he says. Why? Since it would follow that it must possess the characteristics of decay and death, because every existence is invariably connected with decay and death. He means, it would not then be Nirvāṇa, (the Absolute), since like our life[1] it would be subject to decay and death.

In order to make sure this very point, that every life is invariably connected[2] with the marks of decay and death, the Master says, there is no existence without decay and death. Indeed, that thing which is without decay and death is not at all an Ens, it is a mirage, as e.g., flowers in the sky. They never decay and never die, hence they do not exist.

Moreover,

V. If Nirvāṇa is Ens,
It is produced by causes.
Nowhere and none the entity exists
Which would not be produced by causes.

Thesis. If Nirvāṇa is a kind of Ens, it would then be produced by causes.

Reason. Because it is an Ens.

Example. Just as consciousness and the other elements of our life.

The contraposition[3] of the major premise will result in the following sentence: What is not produced by causes does not exist, like the horns on the head of a donkey. Pointing to this the author says,

Nowhere and none the entity is found
Which would not be produced by causes.

The word nowhere refers to location, the place or the time. It might be also taken as referring to a philosophic system. The word none refers to the located thing, whether it be an object of the external world or a mental phenomenon.

Moreover,

VI. If Nirvāṇa is Ens,
How can it lack substratum?

---

1 *vijñānādi=skandhāḥ.*
2 Read *avyabhicāritām.*
3 *vyatireka.*

There whatsoever is no Ens
Without any substratum.

If, in your opinion, Nirvāṇa is a positive entity, it must repose on a substratum, it must have a root in the totality of its own causes. But such a definitely located[1] Nirvāṇa is accepted by nobody. On the contrary, Nirvāṇa is the Absolute. It does not repose on any substratum. Therefore, if Nirvāṇa is an Ens, how can it be an Ens without any substratum? Indeed,

Thesis. Nirvāṇa cannot exist without substratum.

Reason. Because it is an Ens.

Example. Just as consciousness and other elements of existence. The contraposition of the major premise is further adduced as a reason.

There whatsoever is no Ens
Without any substratum.

IV NIRVĀṆA IS NOT A NON-ENS

The Sautrāntika now suggests. If Nirvāṇa is not an Ens, because of the incongruity[2] which has been pointed out, it must be a non-Ens, since it consists merely in the fact that the defiling elements and their consequence, the individual existences, are stopped. We answer. This is also impossible, because the following has been declared.

VII. If Nirvāṇa is not an Ens,
Will it then be a non-Ens?
Wherever there is absence of an Ens,
There neither is a non-Ens.

If it is not admitted that Nirvāṇa is an Ens, if the thesis "Nirvāṇa is an Ens" is rejected, then perhaps Nirvāṇa might be a non-Ens? The author's idea is that it neither can be a non-Ens.

If it be maintained that Nirvāṇa is the absence of defiling elements and individual existences produced by them,[3] then it would result that the impermanence of these defiling elements and personal existences is Nirvāṇa. Indeed, the cessation of these defiling agencies and the end of personal existences can

---

1 *upādāya.*
2 *doṣa-prasaṅga.*
3 *kleśa-janmanor abhāvaḥ.*

be envisaged as nothing but their own character of impermanence. They always have an end. Thus it will follow that impermanence is Nirvāṇa. And this cannot be admitted, since in that case Final Deliverance will be attained automatically,[1] the teaching of a Path towards Salvation would be useless. Hence this is quite inadmissible.

Moreover,

VIII. Now, if Nirvāṇa is a non-Ens,
How can it then be independent ?
For sure an independent non-Ens
Is nowhere to be found.

A non-Ens, whether it be here the impermanence or cessation of something, is constructed in our thought and expressed in speech[2] as a characteristic appertaining to some positive counterpart.[3] Absolute non-existence indeed is similar to the non-existence of horns on the head of a donkey. It is not known to be impermanent. We imagine[4] a characterised thing as relative[5] to some characteristic, and *vice versa* a characteristic as being relative to something characterized. The work of characterization[6] being thus relational,[7] what is impermanence or cessation without an entity characterised by it ? Non-existence must, therefore, be imagined along with a counterpart[8]. Therefore, if Nirvāṇa is a non-Ens, how can it be an Absolute[9] Nirvāṇa?

This argument might be formulated as follows.

Thesis. Nirvāṇa can be a non-Ens only as relative to some positive counterpart.

Reason. Because it is a non-Ens.

Example. Just as the destruction of a jar is relative to this jar.

In order to make this clear it is added,

For sure, an absolute[9] non-Ens
Is nowhere to be found.

An objection is raised. If indeed it is maintained that an absolute non-Ens is impossible, then, e.g., the negation of a son

1 *ayatnena.*
2 *prajñapyate.*
3 *bhāvam upādāya.*
4 *prajñapyate.*
5 *āśritya.*
6 *lakṣya-lakṣaṇa-pravṛtti.*
7 *paraspara-apekṣika.*
8 *upādāya.*
9 *anupādāya.*

of a barren woman must also be related[1] to a positive counterpart in the shape of the real son of a barren woman.

Answer. Who has established that the son of a barren woman etc. is a non-Ens? Just the contrary has been said above.[2]

If something is not settled as an Ens
Neither can it be settled as a non-Ens,
What people call a non-Ens
Is nothing but a change in Ens.

Thus the son of a barren woman is not really a non-Ens, a negation as something real. It has indeed been declared that,

The empty space, the horns of asses,
The sons of barren women
Are spoken of as non-Ens.
The same refers to all imagined Ens[3],

But this should be understood as a mere denial of the possibility to imagine them as real, not as conceiving them as a negation, because positive counterparts to which they could be related do not exist. The "son of a barren woman" are mere words. They do not correspond to any reality which could be cognized, which could either be an Ens or a non-Ens. How can a thing whose concrete reality has never been experienced be imagined either as existing or as not existing.[4] Therefore, it should be known that the son of a barren woman is not a real negation. Thus it is settled, there can be no non-Ens without a positive counterpart.[5]

V NIRVĀṆA IS THIS WORLD VIEWED SUB SPECIE AETERNITATIS

It is now asked, if Nirvāṇa is neither Ens nor is it non-Ens, what is it indeed? We answer. The godlike Buddhas have made about this point the following declaration.

---

1 *upādāya abhāvaḥ.*

2 XV. 5.

3 *bhāveṣu-kalpanā.*

4 Buddhist logic has established a very detailed and thorough theory of negation, where it is proved that every negative judgement is founded in a negative experience, on a possible perception which has not happened (*anupalabdhi*). It is, therefore, always related to some positive substratum, cp. Nyāyabindu II. 26 ff.

5 *anupādāya*, this kind of *upādāna* is termed in the Nyāya system a *pratiyogin*. This realistic system admits absolute non-existence (*atyanta-abhāva*) and relative non-existence (*anyonya-abhāva*).

IX. Coordinated here or caused[1] are separate things,
We call this world phenomenal.
But just the same is called Nirvāṇa,
When viewed without Causality, without Coordination.

The phenomenal world is here the run of life, hither and thither, the come and go of life, the concatenation of births and deaths. The phenomenal world is imagined as existing in the sense that its separate entities are dependent upon a complex of causes and conditions,[2] they are relatively real as, e.g., the long is real as far as there is something short with which it is contrasted. Sometimes they are imagined as produced by causes, e.g., the light is supposed to be produced by the lamp, the sprout is conceived as produced by a seed etc. But in any case, whether it be only imagined as relatively coordinated, or whether they be considered as produced by causes, when the continuity of birth and death has ceased, when there are neither relations nor causality, this same world as motionless and eternal is then called Nirvāṇa.[3] Now, the mere cessation of aspect can neither be considered as an Ens, nor as a non-Ens. Thus it is that Nirvāṇa is neither an Ens, nor a non-Ens.

---

1 From their Buddhist point of view the terms *pratītya* "relative to a cause" and *upādāya*, "relative to a substratum" are equivalents. The realistic Vaiśeṣika system imagines that the substratum (*upādāna*) is a cause (*samavāyi-kāraṇa*) really producing (*ārambhaka*) the result. In Hīnayāna the real existence of a durable substratum of a stuff or substance, is denied and the duration of the object is converted into an uninterrupted sequence of momentary flashes without any substratum, every preceding movement is the substratum (*upādāna-bhūta*) of every following one. Cause and effect are thus declared to be correlated concepts, just as the long is correlated with the short (*dīrgha-hrasva-vat,*) causation is replaced by coordination, and the causes converted into coordinates. Nāgārjuna here says that whether we, with the Vaiśeṣikas, imagine causation as a production of one thing by the other (*pratītya*), or whether we, with the Hīnayānists, imagine mere-coordination (*upādāya*) there nevertheless is a Whole in which these causes and coordinates are merged. Otherwise, *pratītya* as a part of the term *pratītya-samutpāda* refers to also causation in the sense of coordination, it then is synonymous with *upādāya*, but here both terms are contrasted from a special viewpoint.

2 *hetu-pratyaya-sāmagrī*. Since among the *hetus* we must include the *kāraṇa-hetu*; the state of the whole Universe with respect to a given point-instant is included in the totality of its causes and conditions.

3 Lit. p. 529. 5-7. "In any case whether it be established that it is imagined (*prajñapyate*) as coordinated (*upādāya*) or produced as caused (*pratītya*), in any case the non-operation (*apravṛtti*), of this duration of a lineage of births and deaths, whether as non-caused or as non-coordinated, is established as the Nirvāṇa." The non-operation or cessation of an imagined construction (*prajñapti*=*kalpanā*) is nothing but a change of aspect. Nirvāṇa is thus the Universe *sub specie aeternitatis*.

Another interpretation of this aphorism is also possible; it would then intimate that the manner of conceiving Nirvāṇa by the Hīnayānists is much the same, although they aver that their Nirvāṇa is an Ens.

They indeed maintain either, like the Sarvāstivādins, that there is in the Universe no abiding central principle[1] at all, that the world-process consists in the evolution[2] of coordinated energies.[3] They maintain that this world in which every momentary origination and every destruction obeys, in every case, causal laws,[4] when these causal laws have ceased to operate,[5] when all energies are extinct[6] is called Nirvāṇa[7].

Or they (like the *Vātsīputrīyas*) maintain that there is such a central principle, termed by them "personality"[8] which migrates out of one existence into an another. It escapes definition.[9] It neither is the eternal Soul of the Brāhmaṇa, nor is it momentary[10] like the energies of the Buddhists. Phenomenal life consists in its coming and going[11], dependent every time upon a changing substratum[12] of elements. It then evolves obeying causal laws.[13]

---

1 The anātman principle is an equivalent of *saṃskārāḥ* saṃsaranti, cp. my Central Conception, p. 25. 52 etc.

2 *saṁsaranti.*

3 *saṃ-skārāḥ=sambhūya-kāriṇaḥ.* It would be incorrect to surmise that *saṁskāraskandha* is alone meant, although the chief *saṁskāra*, *karma* or *cetanā*, the élan vital, the biotic force which arranges the coordination of all other elements, is first of all meant. But *vedanā* and *saṃjñā* are *saṁskāras*, and *vijñāna* and *rūpa* are, according to the rules of the 12 membered *pratītya-samutpāda*, always included in every life. From this whole passage, it appears clearly that the Buddhist conception of *saṃskāra* and *saṃskṛtatva* is but another name for *pratītya-samutpannatva*, cf. ibid, p. 28.

4 *pratītya pratītya ya utpādaś ca.*

5 *apratītya.*

6 *apravartamānāḥ.*

7 This absolutely lifeless something representing the picture of the Universe in which all energies are extinct reminds us, to a certain extent, of the final condition of the Universe as represented by modern science according to the Law of entropy.

8 *pudgala.*

9 *avācya.*

10 *anitya.*

11 *ājavamjavībhāva.*

12 *tad tad upādānam āśritya.*

13 *upādāya pravartate=pratītya pravartate*, so it obeys the laws of causation or coordination. The theory of the Vātsīputrīyas about an abiding personality (*pudgala*), which they nevertheless do not consider as a reality (*dharma*) or a Soul (*ātman*), is exposed with detailed argumentation by Basubandhu, ab. Kosa. XI.

This very principle which evolves on the basis of changing elements,[1] when the time comes[2] for it to assume no new substratum[3] and its evolution stops,[4] is said to have entered Nirvāṇa.[5]

Now, whether it be coordinated energies[6] alone, or some central principle like the one called "personality"[7] it is clear that the mere fact of their evolution being stopped can neither be characterised as an Ens, nor as a non-Ens.[8]

And further,

X. The Buddha has declared
That Ens and non-Ens should be both rejected.
Neither as Ens nor as a non-Ens.
Nirvāṇa therefore is conceived.

On this point, it is stated in Scripture, "O Brethren, those who seek an escape out of this phenomenal existence in a kind of new existence[9] or in annihilation[10] they have no true knowledge." Both should be rejected, the craving for eternal life and the craving for eternal death. But this Nirvāṇa is the only thing which the Buddha has characterised as the thing not to be rejected. On the contrary, he has declared it to be the only thing desirable.[11] But if Nirvāṇa had been eternal existence[12]

---

1 *upādāya pravartamānaḥ.*

2 *idānīm.*

3 *anupādāya.*

4 *apravartamānāḥ.*,

5 Lit. p. 529. 9-530.2 "Otherwise those who have the tenet that the forces (*saṃskārāḥ*) are migrating, for them it is said that in-every-case-coordinated-origination and destruction is Nirvāṇa when going on without coordination. But for those for whom the personality (*pudgala*) is migrating, for them this personality, being undefinable as to whether it is eternal or non-eternal, possesses a coming and going when reposing on different substratums, it is then going on upon a substratum; this very (personality) which is going on (*pravartamāna*) upon different substratums is now called Nirvāṇa when it no more is going on upon a substratum."

6 *saṃskārāḥ.*

7 *pudgala.*

8 This clearly is an answer to those Hīnayānists who maintain that their Nirvāṇa is an Ens. (*vastu-aharma*).

9 *bhava.*

10 *vibhava.*

11 *aprahātavya.*

12 *bhāva.*

or eternal death,[1] it also would have been rejectable. However it is not rejectable.

Neither as Ens nor as a non-Ens.
Nirvāṇa therefore is conceived.

VI. NIRVĀṆA IS NOT BOTH ENS AND NON-ENS TOGETHER

There are some Vaibhāṣikas who assume a double character in Nirvāṇa. It is a non-Ens so far it is the place in which the defiling elements and the elements of existence in general are extinct. But in itself this lifeless place is an Ens.[2] The author now proceeds to state that such double Nirvāṇa is impossible.

XI. If Nirvāṇa were both Ens and non-Ens,
Final Deliverance would be also both,
Reality and unreality together.
This never could be possible.

If Nirvāṇa had the double character of being both an Ens and a non-Ens, then Final Deliverance would be both a reality and unreality. It would then follow that the presence[3] of the energies[4] of life and their extinction, both represent Final Deliverance. However, a Final Deliverance from phenomenal life and the energies of phenomenal life cannot be the same.[5] Therefore, says the author, this is impossible.

And further,

XII. If Nirvâṇa were both Ens and a non-Ens,
Nirvāṇa could not be uncaused,
Indeed the Ens and the non-Ens
Are both dependent on causation.

If Nirvəṇa would have the double character of an Ens and a non-Ens, it would be then dependent, it would be relative to

---

1 *abhāva.*

2 This is the *Vaibhāṣika* view about the reality of Nirvāṇa with but a little change in its formulation. It is here examined once more in order to fill up the scheme of the quadrilemma.

3 *ātma-lābha.*

4 *saṃskāra.*

5 Probably the Vaibhāṣika theory about the *dharma-svabhāva* is here alluded to. According to their theory, some lifeless residue of the *saṃskāras* or dharmas remains in Nirvāṇa, but their manifestation (*dharma-lakṣaṇa*) is stopped for ever. We would then have in Nirvāṇa *saṃskāras* somehow existing and non-existing at the same time, cp. My Central Conception, p. 42-95.

the totality of its causes and conditions,[1] it would not be the Absolute.[2] Why? Because both these Ens and non-Ens are conditioned.[3] Considering that the Ens is the counterpart[4] of the non-Ens and *vice versa* the non-Ens is the counterpart of the Ens, both Ens and non-Ens[5] are necessarily dependent existences. They are not absolute.[6] If Nirvāṇa were not the absolute, it could then be partly an Ens and partly a non-Ens. But it is not so. Therefore this is impossible.

And further,

XIII. How can Nirvāṇa represent
An Ens and a non-Ens together.
Nirvāṇa is indeed uncaused,[7]
Both Ens and non-Ens are productions.[8]

An Ens is caused, since it is produced by the totality of its causes and conditions.[9] A non-Ens is likewise caused,[10] since 1. it arises as the counterpart[11] of an Ens, 2. because it has been declared in Scripture that decay and death are consequent upon a birth.[12] Thus if Nirvāṇa were essentially an Ens or a non-Ens it could not be uncaused, it would be necessarily caused. However, it is not admitted to be caused. Therefore, Nirvāṇa cannot be both Ens and non-Ens together.

Let it be so. Let Nirvāna itself not be Ens and non-Ens together. Perhaps it may be the place where Ens and non-Ens are found together. However, this is also impossible. Why? Because,

XIV. How can Nirvāṇa represent
The place of Ens and of non-Ens together?
As light and darkness in one spot
They cannot simultaneously be present.

1 *hetu-pratyaya-sāmagrīm upādāya*
2 *anupādāya-sat=paramārthasat.*
3 *upādāya=pratītya=sāpekṣika=śūnya.*
4 *upādāya=sāpekṣika=sapratiyogitāka.*
5 Read *bhāvaś cābhāvaśca.*
6 *anupādāya-sat=paramārthasat.*
7 *asaṁskṛtam=na kṛtam.*
8 *saṁskṛta=kṛtaka.*
9 *hetu-pratyaya-sāmagrī-sambhūta.*
10 *saṃskṛta.*
11 *pratītya=upādāya=pratiyogin.*
12 This simple statement that non-existence is dependent upon previous existence is here given the form of a Scriptural evidence, because it corresponds to the two last members of the 12 membered *pratītya-samutpāda*, stating that death follows upon birth.

Since Ens and non-Ens are mutually incompatible, they cannot possibly exist together in one place, in Nirvāṇa. Therefore it is said,

How can Nirvāṇa represent
The place of Ens and non-Ens together?

The interrogation means that this is absolutely impossible.

VII NOR IS NIRVĀṆA A NEGATION OF BOTH ENS AND NON-ENS TOGETHER

The author now proceeds to consider the fourth part of the quadrilemma, and indicates the incongruity of assuming that Nirvāṇa is a negation of both Ens and non-Ens. He says :

XV. If it were clear indeed
What an Ens means and what a non-Ens,
We could then understand the doctrine
About Nirvāṇa being neither Ens nor non-Ens.

The judgment[1] that Nirvāṇa is not an Ens would be possible, if we know that there is a real Ens, then by its negation Nirvāṇa would be determined. If we know that there is a real non-Ens, then by its negation we would also understand what the judgment means, that Nirvāṇa is not an Ens. But since we neither know what an Ens nor a non-Ens really is, we can neither understand their negations.[2] Therefore the result at which we have arrived, viz. that Nirvāṇa is neither an Ens nor a non-Ens, even this negative result cannot be accepted as logically consistent.[3] This also must be rejected.

---

1 *kalpanā=yojanā.*

2 From this and the following aphorisms it results that the fourth part of the quadrilemma, viz. that Nirvāṇa is neither Ens nor is it non-Ens, represents the solution favoured by the Mādhyamika. Indeed since Ens in aphorism IV and non-Ens in aphorism VIII are conceived empirically, as referring to such entities as conform to causal laws, it is evident that transcendental or absolute existence which is contrasted with both these Ens and non-Ens, can be nothing but their simultaneous negation. Since this kind of reality cannot be expressed in terms of our language, since it is *anirvācya*, the fourth part of the quadrilemma is likewise denied, but in terms which are altogether different from those used in denying the three first parts of the quadrilemma. This especially appears from the comment upon aphorism VI. It is explicitly stated above, under aphorism IX comment that both in the Hīnayānistic and in the Mahāyānistic conception, Nirvāṇa is neither an Ens nor a non-Ens, since it is transcendental and inexpressible in terms of human language.

3 *nopapadyate.*

And moreover,

XVI. If Nirvāṇa is neither Ens, nor is it non-Ens,
Who can then really understand
This doctrine which proclaims at once
Negation of them both together.

If it is imagined[1] that this Nirvāṇa neither has the essence of a non-Ens, nor has it the essence of an Ens, where is the man to understand this? Who indeed can understand, who can grasp, who can proclaim the doctrine that Nirvāṇa represents such a double negation?

But if there is nobody to understand this here, in this world, perhaps there, in Nirvāṇa, someone exists who is capable to realize[2] it? Or is this also impossible? If you admit it, you will be also obliged to admit the existence of an eternal Soul[3] in Nirvāṇa. But this you do not admit, since the existence of a Soul, or consciousness without any substratum,[4] independent of causal laws you do not admit.

But if there is nobody in the Nirvāṇa-world, if Nirvāṇa is altogether impersonal, by whom will it then be realized that there really is a Nirvāṇa of such description? If it is answered that those who remain in the phenomenal world[5] shall cognize it, we will ask, shall they cognize it empirically[6] or metaphysically[7]? If you imagine that they will cognize Nirvāṇa empirically, this is impossible. Why? Because empirical consciousness appre-

1 *kalpyate.*
2 *pratipattā.*
3 *ātman.*
4 *nirupādāna=asaṃskṛta=paramārthasat.*
5 *saṃsārāvasthitāḥ=pṛthagjanā āryāś ca.*
6 *vijñānena.*
7 *jñānena. vijñāna* as *vijñāna-skandha* is contrasted in Hīnayāna with *saṃjñā*. The first means pure sensation, and even something still more primitive, potential sensation, since sensation is *sparśa*, *Samjñā* as we have seen above, can be replaced by *jñāna*. We have then a contrast between vijñāna and jñāna, the first meaning undeveloped and the second-developed cognition. The relation between these two terms is here, to a certain extent, similar to what it is in the Bhagavadgītā, whereas the early Upanishads make no difference between them, cp Bṛh. 3.9.28, Tait. 2.5.1 3. 5. 1, Kaṭha, 3-13 Tait. 2. 1. 1. In Buddhism, however, *vijñāna* is not empirical cognition, but sensation, and *jñāna*, as is quite clear from the context, means transcendental or absolute knowledge, *sarva-pra-pañca-atīta*. The Tibetans usually translate this kind of *jñāna* not by their ordinary ses-pa, but by ye-ses, i. e. highest knowledge. *Vijñāna* again, in this context, does not mean pure sensation, but empirical knowledge, knowledge founded upon pure sensation.

hends separate objects.[1] But Nirvāṇa is the whole. There are no separate objects in Nirvāṇa. Therefore, first of all, it cannot be cognised by empirical consciousness.

But neither can it be cognized by transcendental knowledge.[2] Why? Because transcendental knowledge should be a knowledge of universal Relativity.[3] This is the absolute knowledge, which is essentially eternal, beginningless.[4] How can this knowledge which is itself undefinable[5] grasp the definite judgment "Nirvāṇa is negation of both Ens and non-Ens." Indeed, the essence[6] of absolute knowledge is such that it escapes every formulation.[7]

Therefore, the doctrine that Nirvāṇa is neither a non-Ens nor an Ens at once can be realized by no one. No one can realize it, no one can grasp it, no one can proclaim it, consequently it is logically impossible.[8]

VIII THE REAL BUDDHA, WHAT?

The author now proceeds to state that just as all the parts of the quadrilemma, are inapplicable to Nirvāṇa, just so are they inapplicable to the Buddha who enters Nirvāṇa, He says,

XVII. What is the Buddha after his Nirvāṇa?
Does he exist, or does he not exist?
Or both or neither?
We never will conceive.

---

1 'The definition *nimittālambana* or *nimittagrāhin*, or *nimitta-udgrahaṇam* is given to *saṁjñā*, and not to *vijñāna*, whose definition is *prativijñaptiḥ*, cf, My Central Conception. p. 16. But here this difference does not matter, since both *vijñāna* and *saṃjñā* are equally *nimitta-grāhin* when contrasted with the transcendental or direct knowledge of the absolute; *nimitta* has here the meaning of a mark or a particular object, *nimitta-udgrahaṇam* means abstraction or synthesis.

2 *jñānena.*

3 *śūnyatā-ālambana,*it is clear that the absolute Reality (*sāṃvṛta-śūnyatā*) is here meant which underlies the Universe of Relativity (*saṃvṛti-śūnyatā*).

4 *anutpādam eva* "quite beginningless, it is also the knowledge of the Universe in which there is no causality (anutpāda). This knowledge is also called Omniscience, *sarvajñatā=sarva-ākārajñatā=śūnyatā-jñānam=prajnā pāramitā.*

5 *avidyamāna-svarūpa*, i.e. its character, *svarūpa*, is not to be found among our human kinds of knowledge.

6 *rūpa=svārūpya.*

7 *sarva-prapañca-atīta*, (*prapañco vāk*, *cp*, M. vr. p. 373.9.)

8 *na yujyate=nopapadyate.*

Indeed it has been already stated.[1]

That one who firmly is convinced
That Buddha during lifetime did exist,
Will be convinced that after death
The Buddha cannot be existing.

Thus it is that we cannot imagine[2] what has happened after the complete extinction[3] of the Buddha, does he then exist, or does he not exist, after Nirvāṇa? Since both these solutions are unimaginable singly, they cannot be right both at once, neither is the negation of them both, therefore, imaginable.

Not alone are all these four solutions unimaginable with regard to Buddha after his demise, but his real existence before Nirvāṇa is equally unimaginable.

XVIII. What is the Buddha then at lifetime?
Does he exist or does he not exist?
Or both or neither?
We never will conceive.

This is beyond our understanding, beyond our concepts. It has been shown in the chapter devoted to the examination of Buddhahood.[4]

1. Translated according to the version in XXII 13.
2. *nohyate=na kalpyate*.
3. *nirodha*.
4. Ch. XXII. This chapter begins by stating that the Buddha is neither contained in the elements, (*skandha*) of a personality, nor is he something apart from them. (XX 1-2). It is the old formula of the Vātsīputrīyas and, probably of all the early sects who have favoured the idea of a superhuman Buddha. If the Buddha consisted of elements (*skandha*) he would be *anātmā*. (XX. 3). On this occasion, Candrakīrti remarks that the term *ātman* in this context is a synonym of substance, a real; independent or absolute substance (*ātma-śabdo'yaṁ svabhāva-śabda-paryāyaḥ*). If he were not Self-existent, he could not be the Buddha since Buddha means Self-existent, *tathāgata*—existent in reality, in absolute reality. He is then characterised as *śūnya* and *niṣ-prapañca*, the Inexpressible. Those who would attempt to give him a conceptual definition (*prapañcayanti*) are incapable of contemplating him by mystic intuition (*na paśyanti tathāgatam*) (XX. 20). The Reality, or Substantiality (*svabhāva*) of the real Buddha (*tathāgata*) is just the same as the real substance of the world (*tathāgato yatsvabhāvas tatsvabhāvam idam jagat*). And just as the phenomenal world is unreal (*niḥsvabhāva*), the personal Buddha is unreal just in the same degree (XXVII 16). Candrakīrti adds that the unreality or relativity of the phenomenal world has been established in the first chapter of this work. It is thus clear that Buddha is regarded in a pantheistic light as *deus sive substantia*. This is the strictly monistic standpoint of consequent Mahāyānism. The conception of the Buddha is here quite the same as the conception of God (īśvara) in the *advaita* system of Śaṅkara. The yogācāra school has, in this point as in others, deviated from strict Mahāyānism. Just as it had established four kinds of Nirvāṇa, instead of the former three, it has also four kinds of Buddhas or four bodies of Buddhas

IX ULTIMATE IDENTITY OF THE PHENOMENAL AND THE ABSOLUTE

Just for this reason, since both are equally inconceivable,

XIX. There is no difference at all
Between Nirvāṇa and Saṃsāra,
There is no difference at all
Between-Saṃsāra, and Nirvāṇa.

Since it is impossible to imagine a real Buddha living in this world nor to deny it, and since it is equally impossible to imagine a real Buddha after his Nirvāṇa nor to deny it, just for this reason there is no difference at all between the Phenomenal world and the Absolute. On analysis they reveal themselves as being just the same in their essence[1]. For this very reason we can now understand the words of the Buddha when he spoke, "O Brethren ! this phenomenal world[2] consisting of birth, decay and death has no under limit." This is just because there is no difference between the Phenomenal and Absolute, Indeed,

XX. What makes the limit of Nirvāṇa,
Is also then the limit of Saṃsāra.
Between the two we cannot find
The slightest shade of difference.

The phenomenal world being in its real essence nothing but the Absolute,[3] it is impossible to imagine either its beginning, or its end.

X THE ANTINOMIES

But not alone that, the antinomies established by the Buddha are insoluble for the same reason.

XXI. Insoluble are antinomic views
Regarding the existence beyond Nirvāṇa,

---

and four kinds of absolute knowledge (*bodhi*). Here Buddha abiding in "altruistic" (*apratiṣṭhita*) Nirvāṇa appears as a real God, the personified Wisdom and Love. His Spirit is not that unique substance, undifferentiated into subject and object which is the essence of *dharma-kāya* or *tathatā*, but it is a living and sympathizing Spirit which distinguishes subject, object and the other separate things of the pluriverse by *pratyavekṣaṇa-jñāna*. The constructions of the early Yogācāra school regarding Nirvāṇa, Buddha and Bodhi are extremely artificial and evidently the product of a compromise between strict Monism and the theistic tendencies of the school, cp, Vinītadeva's comment upon the closing passage of (B. B.) where he seems not to be at one with Dharma Kīrti, cp. also J. Masuda, op. cit. p. 57.

1 *rūpa=svarūpa.*

2 *saṃsāra.*

3 *nirvāṇa.*

Regarding the extinction of this world.

Regarding its beginning.[1]

All the theories about these questions are inconsistent[2] (*antinomies*). Since the phenomenal world and the Absolute, are naturally merged quiescent[3] in the Unity of the Whole.

By the indication[4] contained in the words "after Nirvāṇa", four theories are embraced, viz., 1. The Buddha exists after death; 2. after death the Buddha does not exist; 3. after death the Buddha exists and does not exist both at once; 4. after death the Buddha neither exists, nor does he not exist. These four theories are professed regarding Nirvāṇa.

The theories regarding the end of the world, are the following ones.—1. the world has limit. 2. the world has no limit; 3. the world has and has not a limit; 4. the world neither has, nor has not a limit. These four theories exist regarding the upper limit i.e., the end of the world.

Not being able to know something about our future life or about the future of the living world, we imagine that the life of the world will be stopped. This theory establishes a limit to the living world. Similarly, the theory that the living world will have no end is produced by an expectation of a future life. Those who partly expect it and partly do not expect it profess a double theory. Those who deny both profess the theory that the world-process neither has, nor has not any limit.

Regarding the beginning of the world there are likewise four theories. 1. It is eternal, i.e. it has no beginning; 2. it has a beginning; 3. it both has and has not a beginning; 4. it neither, has, nor has not beginning.

The theory that the world is beginningless[5] is based upon the view that we ourselves, or the living world, previously existed. The opposite view leads to the theory about the world having a beginning. Those who are both convinced and not convinced of it will profess the theory that the world is both eternal and

---

1 Lit. p. 536. 1-2. The theories (*dṛṣṭayaḥ*) beyond final extinction (*nirodha*) "end etc.", "eternal etc." are directed (*samāśrita*) towards Nirvāṇa, the upper limit and the under limit.

2 *nopapadyante*.

3 *prakṛti-śāntatvāt*.

4 *upalakṣaṇa*.

5 *śāśvata* means here, as appears from the context, eternal in the sense of beginningless.

non-eternal. Those who neither are convinced, nor unconvinced will profess the theory that the world is neither eternal, nor non-eternal.

How are the antinomies[1] to be solved?[2] If any one of these attributes[3] by which the world is characterised as finite, infinite etc. possessed absolute reality in itself[4] we would then understand what its affirmation or negation[5] means. But since we have established that there is no difference between the phenomenal world as constructed according to those ideas and the Absolute[6] underlying it, therefore no one of these attributes has ultimate reality, indeed—

XXII. Since everything is relative[7] we do not know
What is finite and what is infinite,
What means finite and infinite at once,
What means negation of both issues?[8]

XXIII. What is identity, and what is difference,[9]
What is eternity, what non-eternity.[10]
What means eternity and non-eternity together,
What means negation of both issues?

---

1 *dṛṣṭayaḥ=avyākṛta-vastūni.*

2 *kathaṁ yujyante.*

3 *padārtha=artha=dharma* means "any object", "everything," it contains here an allusion to the following *śūnyeṣu sarvadharmeṣu* but the predicates of finiteness, infinity, identity, otherness, etc., are more particularly aimed at, they are also *dharmas.*

4 *kaścit svabhāvaḥ.*

5 *bhāvābhāva-kalpanā=bhāvābhāva-yojanā, kalpanā* in this context means as much as our judgment.

6 Lit. p. 537. 1-2. "How are these views possible? If anything whatever possessed some self-substance, by arranging it with existence and non-existence these views would be possible."

7 This identity must evidently be understood in the sense that the Unity of the Absolute is the reality underlying the mirage of plurality.

8 *śūnya.*

9 This refers to the question of identity between the Ego and the body, it is usually formulated as a dilemma, whereas the antinomies regarding the end and the beginning of existence, as well as the question about existence after Nirvāṇa are formulated in the familiar Indian method of quadrilemma. Thus the consecrated traditional number of 14 insoluble points (*avyākṛta-vastūni*) concerning the four antonomies is arrived at. In XXVII. 4 ff. the question of personal identity between the present Ego, the past and the future one, is examined in detail with the result that there is neither identity nor otherness.

10 or "without beginning," *Śāśvata.*

These fourteen points which by the Buddha were declared insoluble, will never be solved,[1] because we do not know what reality in itself is.[2] But those who imagine some kind of absolute reality,[3] and, by either excluding or asserting[4] it, establish these dogmatical theories, are influenced by a pre-conceived bias[5]. It prevents them from entering the right Path, leading to the city of Nirvāṇa, and binds them to the turmoil of phenomenal existence. This should be noted.

XI CONCLUSION

An objection is raised. If this is so, will it not be possible to maintain that Nirvāṇa has been denied by the Buddha ? Will not his doctrine be absolutely useless, this doctrine which establishes corresponding antidotes for every kind of worldly career in order to enable mankind to reach Nirvāṇa. It has been established by the Buddha who watches the infinite hosts of living beings in their worldly career, who unmistakably knows the real intentions of all the living world, who is quite given up to his feeling of Great Commiseration, who cherishes the denizens of all the three spheres of existence as only a unique son is cherished ! We answer. This criticism would be right, if there were any absolutely real[6] doctrine, or if there were any absolutely real beings which attend to this law, or if there were any absolutely real teacher, a divine Buddha. But since in a monistic Universe that does not exist, we are not hit by your accusation.

XXIV. Our bliss consists in the cessation of all thought,
In the quiescence of Plurality.

---

1 *naiva yujyante.*

2 *asati bhāva-svarūpe*, lit. "because they are not self-subsistent things." Here again we must point out a remarkable analogy between the Indian and European philosophy with respect to the doctrine of antinomies and their solution. Kant thought that "these questions naturally suggest themselves to the human mind and he inevitably must encounter them", and the explanation he sought in the fact that the objects of the phenomenal world are not "self-subsistent things". cp. Critique of Pure Reason. (transl. by Max, Muller) p. 400.

3 *bhāva-svarūpam adhyāropya.*

4 *tad-vigama-avigamataḥ.*

5 *abhiniviśate.*

6 *svabhāva-rūpa.*

To nobody and nowhere no doctrine about separate elements[1]
By Buddha ever has been preached !

In this case how can the reproach made above affect us ! Our view[2] is that Nirvāṇa represents Quiescence, i.e. the non-applicability[3] of all the variety of names[4] and non-existence of particular objects[5]. This very Quiescence, so far as it is the natural (genuine) quiescence of the world, is called bliss. The Quiescence of Plurality is also a bliss because of the cessation of speech or because of the cessation of thought. It is also a bliss because, by putting an end to all defiling agencies, all births[6] are stopped. It is also a bliss because, by exterpating all defiling forces, all instincts (and habits of thought)[7] have been extirpated without residue. It is also a bliss because, since all the objects of knowledge have died away, knowledge itself has also died.

When the divine Buddhas have entered blissful Nirvāṇa in which all Plurality has vanished, they are like regal swans soaring in the sky without any support,[8], they are hovering in the wind produced by their two wings,[9] the wing of accumulated virtue,[10] and the wing of accumulated wisdom,[11] or they are hovering in the wind of Space, that Space which is the Void.[12]

1 *dharma* is here used in both senses, a doctrine about *dharmas*. Not a single one of the Hīnayānistic *dharmas* (elements of existence) has been taught by the real Buddha, since on p. 539. 1-2 it is stated that neither a defiling (*sāṃkleśika*) element, i.e. ignorance, and desire, nor a purifying one (*vaiyavadānika*), i.e. *prajñā* and *samādhi*, has been taught by the real Buddha, i.e. by the Buddha conceived as *Dharma-kāya*, the Cosmos. The whole catalogue of the *dharmas* is evidently meant, and their relativity and unreality from the transcendental point of view. But since Hinayāna is Pluralism, i. e. a doctrine about the elements, a *Dharma* about the *dharmas*, *dharmānudharma*, both meanings are so interwoven that in many contexts both will apply. On p. 537.13 the general meaning is evidently intended.

2 *iha*.

3 *apravṛtti*.

4 *prapañca*, *prapañco vāk*.

5 *nimitta*.

6 *janman*.

7 *vāsanā*, explained as *pūrvaṃ jñānam*, but conceived as a cosmical Force, transcendental illusion.

8 *asthāna-yogena*.

9 *pakṣa-pāta*, the meaning of bias or fervour, towards a special doctrine is equally here intended.

10 *puṇya-sambhāra*.

11 *jñāna-sambhāra*.

12 *akiṁcana*, an allusion to the doctrine of śūnyatā; the lofty Bodhisattva is hovering in the regions of Relativity, which is here poetically compared with the Void (*svabhāva-śūnyatā*.)

Then from this elevation, all separate objects having become indistinguishable[1] the Buddhas have not preached, neither about the defiling elements[2] of life, nor about its purifying elements,[3] neither in the divine worlds, nor in the human world, neither to gods, nor to men. This should be realized.

Accordingly it has been declared in the Āryatathāgataguhya—"The night, when, O Śāntamati, the Buddha has reached the highest absolute enlightenment, the night he was about to pass into Final Nirvāṇa, at that occasion the Buddha did not pronounce even one syllable, he has not spoken, nor does he speak, nor will he speak. But since all living beings, according to the intensity of their religious fervour,[4] appear as different characters[5] with different aims,[6] they imagine,[7] the Buddha proferring on different occasions a variety of discourses. On separate occasions it occurs to them "this Buddha teaches us about such a topic,"[8] "We listen to his teaching about this topic". But the real Buddha[9] is never engaged in thought-construction, in thought-division, O Śāntamati, the Buddha is averse to all plurality which is produced by our habits of thought[10] that Plurality which is the cause of an entanglement of thought constructions[11] and of the dismemberment[12] of the world's Unity.[13]

---

1 *sarva-nimitta-anupalambha.*

2 *sāṃkleśika-dharma.*

3 *vaiyavadānika-dharma.*

4 *yathādhimuktāḥ.*

5 *vividha-dhātu, dhātu* evidently in the sense of *gotra.*

6 (*vividha*)-āśaya.

7 *saṁjānanti.*

8 or element, *dharma.*

9 i.e. *dharma-kāya.*

10 *vāsanā=pūrvaṁ jñānam.*

11 *kalpanā=yojanā.*

12 *vikalpa=dvaidhīkaraṇa.*

13 This is a purely Mahāyānistic doctrine, viz. that Buddha, as soon as he became a real Buddha, did not speak, because human speech is not adapted to express, and human knowledge is incapable of realizing conceptually, that unique Substance of the Universe with which Buddha himself is identified as *dharma-kāya* and which appears directly to the intuition of the mystic. The logical value of the tenets *sarvajño na vaktā* and *asarvajño vaktā* is analysed with much subtlety by Dharmottara in the Nyāyabindu, p. 66.19 ff and by Vācaspatimiśra in the Nyāyakaṇikā, p. 110. 16 and 112. 22 ffl. M. de la V. P. /- 366. n l of his edition, thinks that this doctrine is in glaring contradiction with what is repeatedly stated in the Pali Canon. No wonder, since Mahāyāna is Monism and Hīnayāna Pluralism. Spinoza can hardly be expected to agree with Aristotle:

Indeed,

Unspeakable unpronounceable are all elements,
Relational,[1] quiescent, pure !
Those are real Buddhas and Bodhisattvas[2]
Who realize them in this their pure condition.

But if the Buddha has preached no doctrine of separate elements nowhere and to nobody, how is it then that we hear about his various discourses, constituting the Scriptures !

We answer. Mankind is plunged in the slumber of ignorance, they are as though in a dream, they have a wealth of constructive imagination.[3] It occurs to them "this Buddha, this Lord over all gods, demons and human beings in all the three worlds, teaches us about this topic."

Accordingly it has been said by Buddha,

The Buddha is but a reflexion
Of the pure passionless principle.
He is not real, he is not the Buddha.
'Tis a reflection that all creatures see.

This is likewise explained at length in the chapter about the "Secret meaning of the Buddha's words."

Since there is thus no separate teaching about separate elements[4], for the sake of reaching Nirvāṇa, how is it then possible to maintain that a kind of Nirvāṇa exists, because the discourses about the elements[5] of existence really exist. Therefore, it is established that this kind of Nirvāṇa does not really exist. Accordingly, it has been said by Buddha,

"The Ruler of the World has said
That this Nirvāṇa is not real Nirvāṇa;
A knot by empty space entwined
By empty space has been untied !"

---

1 *śūnya.*

2 *kumāra=jina-putra.*

3 *sva-vikalpa-abhyudaya.*

4 The reading of the Mss. *deśanānām* is perhaps to be retained (*abhidheya-bahutvāt*).

5 *dharma;*

Moreover, "Those who imagine that something can appear and disappear, for them O Blessed one, the real Buddha has not yet appeared ! Those, O Blessed one, who seek a realistic[1] (definite) Nirvāṇa, they never will escape out of the world migrations ! For what reason ? Because, O Blessed one, Nirvāṇa is the merger[2] of all particular signs,[3] the quiescence of every motion and commotion.[4] Ignorant indeed, O Blessed one, are all those men who having become recluses in the name of a doctrine and discipline by them imagined,[5] are seeking for a realistic Nirvāṇa and have thus fallen down into a false doctrine which is not Buddhist. They think to win Nirvāṇa is the same as to get oil out of oil-seeds or butter out of milk ! I declare, O Blessed one, that those who seek Nirvāṇa in the fact that separate elements of life will be absolutely extinct,[6] I declare, that they are not better than the most self-conceited gentiles."

"A Master of Yoga,[7] O Blessed one, the man thoroughly trained in Yoga does not really produce something new, nor does he suppress something existing,[8] nor will he admit that something, some real element,[9] can be attained, or seized by absolute knowledge.[10] etc."

Finished the Examination of Nirvāṇa, the 25th Chapter in the comment, upon Relativity by .the Venerable Master Candrakīrti.

---

1 *bhāvataḥ=sva-bhāvataḥ* i. e. not that Nirvāṇa which is immanent to the Universe.

2 *praśama.*

3 *sarva-nimittānām.*

4 *sarva-injita-saminjita.*

5 *svākhyāta.*

6 *parinirvṛta=parito niruddha.*

7 Yogācāra, here in the general sense of a Mahāyānist, not in the sense of Master of Yogācāra school.

8 as the Hīnayānist teaching about *yoga-samādhi* assumes cp. Central Conception, p. 51.

9 here *dharma* refers to the *phalas* attained by *mārga.*

10 *abhisamaya=prajñā-pāramitā.*

MADHYAMAKA ŚĀSTRA
OF
NĀGĀRJUNA
(Sanskrit TEXT)

नागार्जुनीयं

मध्यमकशास्त्रम् ।

आचार्यचन्द्रकीर्तिविरचितया प्रसन्नपदाख्यव्याख्यया संवलितम् ।

: १ :

(Containing the original of Dedication and Chapter I of the Translation.)

प्रत्ययपरीक्षा नाम प्रथमं प्रकरणम् ।

आर्यमञ्जुश्रिये कुमारभूताय नमः ।

योऽन्तद्वयावासविधूतवासः संबुद्धधीसागरलब्धजन्मा ।
सद्धर्मतोयस्य गभीरभावं यथानुबुद्धं कृपया जगाद ॥ १ ॥

यस्य दर्शनतेजांसि परवादिमतेन्धनम् ।
दहन्त्यद्यापि लोकस्य मानसानि तमांसि च ॥ २ ॥

यस्यासमज्ञानवचःशरौघा निघ्नन्ति निःशेषभवारिसेनाम् ।
त्रिधातुराज्यश्रियमादधाना विनेयलोकस्य सदेवकस्य ॥ ३ ॥

नागार्जुनाय प्रणिपत्य तस्मै तत्कारिकाणां विवृतिं करिष्ये ।
उत्तानसत्प्रक्रियवाक्यनद्धां तर्कानिलाव्याकुलितां प्रसन्नाम् ॥ ४ ॥

तत्र 'न स्वतो नापि परतो न द्वाभ्याम्' (१.३) इत्यादि वक्ष्यमाणं शास्त्रम् । तस्य कानि संबन्धाभिधानप्रयोजनानि इति प्रश्ने, मध्यमकावतारविहितविधिना अद्वयज्ञानालंकृतं महाकरुणोपायपुरःसरं प्रथमचित्तोत्पादं तथागतज्ञानोत्पत्तिहेतुमादिं कृत्वा यावदाचार्यनागार्जुनस्य विदिताविपरीतप्रज्ञापारमितानीतेः करुणया परावबोधार्थं शास्त्रप्रणयनम्, इत्येष तावच्छास्त्रस्य संबन्धः—

यच्छास्ति वः क्लेशरिपूनशेषान्संत्रायते दुर्गतितो भवाच्च।
तच्छासनात्त्राणगुणाच्च शास्त्रमेतद् द्वयं चान्यमतेषु नास्ति॥

इति। स्वयमेव चाचार्यो वक्ष्यमाणसकलशास्त्राभिधेयार्थं सप्रयोजनमुपदर्शयन्, तदविपरीतसंप्रकाशत्वेन माहात्म्यमुद्भाव्य तत्स्वभावाव्यतिरेकवर्तिने परमगुरवे तथागताय शास्त्रप्रणयननिमित्तकं प्रणामं कर्तुकाम आह—

अनिरोधमनुत्पादमनुच्छेदमशाश्वतम्।
अनेकार्थमनानार्थमनागममनिर्गमम्॥
यः प्रतीत्यसमुत्पादम्

इत्यादि। तदत्रानिरोधाद्यष्टविशेषणविशिष्टः प्रतीत्यसमुत्पादः शास्त्राभिधेयार्थः। सर्वप्रपञ्चोपशमशिवलक्षणं निर्वाणं शास्त्रस्य प्रयोजनं निर्दिष्टम्।

तं वन्दे वदतां वरम्।

इत्यनेन प्रणामः। इत्येष तावच्छ्लोकद्वयस्य समुदायार्थः॥

अवयवार्थस्तु विभज्यते। तत्र निरुद्धिर्निरोधः। क्षणभङ्गो निरोध इत्युच्यते। उत्पादनमुत्पादः। आत्मभावोन्मज्जनमित्यर्थः। उच्छित्तिरुच्छेदः। प्रबन्धविच्छित्तिरित्यर्थः। शाश्वतो नित्यः। सर्वकाले स्थाणुरित्यर्थः। एकश्चासावर्थश्चेत्येकार्थोऽभिन्नार्थः। न पृथगित्यर्थः। नानार्थो भिन्नार्थः। पृथगित्यर्थः। आगतिरागमः, विप्रकृष्टदेशावस्थितानां संनिकृष्टदेशागमनम्। निर्गतिर्निर्गमः, संनिकृष्टदेशावस्थितानां विप्रकृष्टदेशगमनम्। एतिर्गत्यर्थः, प्रतिः प्राप्त्यर्थः। उपसर्गवशेन धात्वर्थविपरिणामात्—

उपसर्गेण धात्वर्थो बलादन्यत्र नीयते।
गङ्गासलिलमाधुर्यं सागरेण यथाम्भसा॥

प्रतीत्यशब्दोऽत्र ल्यबन्तः प्राप्तावपेक्षायां वर्तते। समुत्पूर्वः पदिः प्रादुर्भावार्थ इति समुत्पादशब्दः प्रादुर्भावे वर्तते। ततश्च हेतुप्रत्ययापेक्षो भावानामुत्पादः प्रतीत्यसमुत्पादार्थः॥

अपरे तु ब्रुवते—इतिर्गमनं विनाशः। इतौ साधव इत्याः। प्रतिर्वीप्सार्थः। इत्येवं तद्धितान्तमित्यशब्दं व्युत्पाद्य प्रति प्रति इत्यानां विनाशिनां समुत्पाद इति वर्णयन्ति। तेषां "प्रतीत्यसमुत्पादं वो भिक्षवो देशयिष्यामि", "यः प्रतीत्यसमुत्पादं पश्यति स धर्मं पश्यति" इत्येवमादौ विषये वीप्सार्थस्य संभवात् समाससद्भावाच्च स्याज्ज्यायसी

व्युत्पत्तिः। इह तु "चक्षुः प्रतीत्य रूपाणि च उत्पद्यते चक्षुर्विज्ञानम्" इत्येवमादौ विषये साक्षादङ्गीकृतार्थविशेषे चक्षुः प्रतीत्येति प्रतीत्य-शब्दः एकचक्षुरिन्द्रियहेतुकायामप्येकविज्ञानोत्पत्तावभीष्टायां कुतो वीप्सार्थता? प्राप्त्यर्थस्त्वनङ्गीकृतार्थविशेषेऽपि प्रतीत्यशब्दे संभवति—प्राप्य संभवः, प्रतीत्य समुत्पाद इति। अङ्गीकृतार्थविशेषेऽपि संभवति-चक्षुः प्रतीत्य, चक्षुः प्राप्य, चक्षू रूपं चापेक्ष्येति व्याख्यानात्। तद्धितान्ते चेत्यशब्दे "चक्षुः प्रतीत्य रूपाणि च उत्पद्यते चक्षुर्विज्ञानम्" इत्यत्र प्रतीत्यशब्दस्याव्ययत्वाभावात् समासासद्भावाच्च विभक्तिश्रुतौ सत्यां चक्षुः प्रतीत्य विज्ञानं रूपाणि च इति निपातः स्यात्। न चैतदेवम्। इत्यव्ययस्यैव ल्यबन्तस्य व्युत्पत्तिरभ्युपेया॥

यस्तु—"वीप्सार्थत्वात्प्रत्युपसर्गस्य, एतेः प्राप्त्यर्थत्वात्, समुत्पादशब्दस्य च संभवार्थत्वात्, तांस्तान् प्रत्ययान् प्रतीत्य समुत्पादः प्राप्य संभव इत्येके। प्रति प्रति विनाशिनामुत्पादः प्रतीत्यसमुत्पाद इत्यन्ये"—इति परव्याख्यानमनूद्य दूषणमभिधत्ते, तस्य परपक्षानुवादाकौशलत्वमेव तावत्संभाव्यते। किं कारणम्? यो हि प्राप्त्यर्थं प्रतीत्यशब्दं व्याचष्टे, नासौ प्रतिं वीप्सार्थं व्याचष्टे, नाप्येतिं प्राप्त्यर्थम्, किं तर्हि प्रतिं प्राप्त्यर्थम्, समुदितं च प्रतीत्यशब्दं प्राप्तावेव वर्णयति।

तेन इदानीं प्राप्य संभवः प्रतीत्यसमुत्पाद इत्येवं व्युत्पादितेन प्रतीत्यसमुत्पादशब्देन यदि निरवशेषसंभविपदार्थपरामर्शो विवक्षितः, तदा तां तां हेतुप्रत्ययसामग्रीं प्राप्य संभवः प्रतीत्य समुत्पाद इति वीप्सासंबन्धः क्रियते। अथ विशेषपरामर्शः, तदा चक्षुः प्राप्य रूपाणि चेति न वीप्सायाः संबन्ध इति॥ एवं तावदनुवादाकौशलमाचार्यस्य॥

एतद्वा अयुक्तम्। किं च। अयुक्तमेतत् "चक्षुः प्रतीत्य रूपाणि च उत्पद्यते चक्षुर्विज्ञानम्" इति, अत्रार्थद्वयासंभवात् इति यदुक्तं दूषणम्, तदपि नोपपद्यते। किं कारणम्? कथमनेनैव तत्प्राप्तेः संभव इति युक्त्यनुपादानेन प्रतिज्ञामात्रत्वात्। अथायमभिप्रायः स्यात्—अरूपित्वाद्विज्ञानस्य चक्षुषा प्राप्तिर्नास्ति, रूपिणामेव तत्प्राप्तिदर्शनादिति, एतदपि न युक्तम्, 'प्राप्तफलोऽयं भिक्षुः' इत्यत्रापि प्राप्त्यभ्युपगमात्। प्राप्यशब्दस्य च अपेक्ष्यशब्दपर्यायत्वात्। प्राप्त्यर्थस्यैव आचार्यार्यनागार्जुनेन प्रतीत्यशब्दस्य

तत्तत्प्राप्य यदुत्पन्नं नोत्पन्नं तत्स्वभावतः।

इत्यभ्युपगमात्। ततो दूषणमपि नोपपद्यते इत्यपरे॥

यच्चापि स्वमतं व्यवस्थापितम्—"किं तर्हि, अस्मिन् सति इदं भवति, अस्योत्पादादिदमुत्पद्यते, इति इदंप्रत्ययतार्थः प्रतीत्यसमुत्पादार्थ इति", तदपि नोपपद्यते, प्रतीत्यसमुत्पादशब्दयोः प्रत्येकमर्थविशेषानभिधानात्, तद्व्युत्पादस्य च विवक्षिततत्वात् ॥

अथापि रूढिशब्दं प्रतीत्यसमुत्पादशब्दमभ्युपेत्य अरण्येतिलकादिवदेवमुच्यते, तदपि नोपपन्नम्, अवयवार्थानुगतस्यैव प्रतीत्यसमुत्पादस्य आचार्येण

तत्तत्प्राप्य यदुत्पन्नं नोत्पन्नं तत्स्वभावतः ।

इत्यभ्युपगमात् । अथ

अस्मिन्सतीदं भवति ह्रस्वे दीर्घं यथा सति ।

इति व्याख्यायमानेन ननु तदेवाभ्युपगतं भवति, ह्रस्वं प्रतीत्य, ह्रस्वं प्राप्यं ह्रस्वमपेक्ष्य दीर्घं भवतीति । ततश्च यदेव दूष्यते तदेवाभ्युपगम्यते इति न युज्यते । इत्यलं प्रसङ्गेन ॥

तदेवं हेतुप्रत्ययापेक्षं भावानामुत्पादं परिदीपयता भगवता अहेत्वेकहेतुविषमहेतुसंभूतत्वं स्वपरोभयकृतत्वं च भावानां निषिद्धं भवति, तन्निषेधाच्च सांवृतानां पदार्थानां यथावस्थितं सांवृतं स्वरूपमुद्भावितं भवति । स एवेदानीं सांवृतः प्रतीत्यसमुत्पादः स्वभावेनानुत्पन्नत्वाद् आर्यज्ञानापेक्षया नास्मिन्निरोधो विद्यते यावन्नास्मिन्निर्गमो विद्यते इत्यनिरोधादिभिरष्टाभिर्विशेषणैर्विशिष्यते । यथा च निरोधादयो न सन्ति प्रतीत्यसमुत्पादस्य तथा सकलशास्त्रेण प्रतिपादयिष्यति ॥

अनन्तविशेषणसंभवेऽपि प्रतीत्यसमुत्पादस्य अष्टानामेवोपादानमेषां प्राधान्येन विवादाङ्गभूतत्वात् । यथावस्थितप्रतीत्यसमुत्पाददर्शने सति आर्याणामभिधेयादिलक्षणस्य प्रपञ्चस्य सर्वथोपरमात्, प्रपञ्चानामुपशमोऽस्मिन्निति स एव प्रतीत्यसमुत्पादः प्रपञ्चोपशम इत्युच्यते । चित्तचैत्तानां च तस्मिन्नप्रवृत्तौ ज्ञानज्ञेयव्यवहारनिवृत्तौ जातिजरामरणादिनिरवशेषोपद्रवरहितत्वात् शिवः । यथाभिहितविशेषणस्य प्रतीत्यसमुत्पादस्य देशनाक्रियया ईप्सिततमत्वात् कर्मणा निर्देशः ॥

अनिरोधमनुत्पादमनुच्छेदमशाश्वतम् ।
अनेकार्थमनानार्थमनागममनिर्गमम् ॥ १ ॥

यः प्रतीत्यसमुत्पादं प्रपञ्चोपशमं शिवम्।

देशयामास संबुद्धस्तं वन्दे वदतां वरम्॥ २॥

[मङ्गलश्लोकौ]

यथोपवर्णितप्रतीत्यसमुत्पादावगमाच्च तथागतस्यैवैकस्याविपरीतार्थवादित्वं पश्यन् सर्वपरप्रवादांश्च बालप्रलापानिवावेत्य अतीव प्रसादानुगत आचार्यो भूयो भगवन्तं विशेषयति—वदतां वरमिति॥

अत्र च निरोधस्य पूर्वं प्रतिषेधः उत्पादनिरोधयोः पौर्वापर्यावस्थायाः सिद्ध्यभावं द्योतयितुम्। वक्ष्यति हि—

पूर्वं जातिर्यदि भवेज्जरामरणमुत्तरम्।
निर्जरामरणा जातिर्भवेज्जायेत चामृतः॥ [म० शा० ११.३]

इति। तस्मान्नायं नियमो यत् पूर्वमुत्पादेन भवितव्यं पश्चान्निरोधेनेति।

इदानीमनिरोधादिविशिष्टप्रतीत्यसमुत्पादप्रतिपिपादयिषया उत्पादप्रतिषेधेन निरोधादिप्रतिषेधसौकर्यं मन्यमान आचार्यः प्रथममेवोत्पादप्रतिषेधमारभते। उत्पादो हि परैः परिकल्प्यमानः स्वतो वा परिकल्प्येत, परतः, उभयतः, अहेतुतो वा परिकल्प्येत। सर्वथा च नोपपद्यत इति निश्चित्याह—

न स्वतो नापि परतो न द्वाभ्यां नाप्यहेतुतः।

उत्पन्ना जातु विद्यन्ते भावाः क्वचन केचन॥ ३॥

तत्र जात्विति कदाचिदित्यर्थः। क्वचनशब्द आधारवचनः क्वचिच्छब्दपर्यायः। केचनशब्द आधेयवचनः केचिच्छब्दपर्यायः। ततश्चैवं संबन्धः—नैव स्वत उत्पन्ना जातु विद्यन्ते भावाः, क्वचन, केचन। एवं प्रतिज्ञात्रयमपि योज्यम्॥

ननु च—नैव स्वत उत्पन्ना इत्यवधार्यमाणे परत उत्पन्ना इत्यनिष्टं प्राप्नोति। न प्राप्नोति। प्रसज्यप्रतिषेधस्य विवक्षितत्वात् परतोऽप्युत्पादस्य प्रतिषेत्स्यमानत्वात्। यया चोपपत्त्या स्वत उत्पादो न संभवति, सा—

तस्माद्धि तस्य भवने न गुणोऽस्ति कश्चि-
ज्जातस्य जन्म पुनरेव च नैव युक्तम्।

[मध्यमकावतार—६.८]

इत्यादिना मध्यमकावतारादिद्वारेणावसेया ॥

आचार्यबुद्धपालितस्त्वाह—न स्वतः उत्पद्यन्ते भावाः, तदुत्पादवैयर्थ्यात्, अतिप्रसङ्गदोषाच्च। न हि स्वात्मना विद्यमानानां पदार्थानां पुनरुत्पादे प्रयोजनमस्ति। अथ सन्नपि जायेत, न कदाचिन्न जायेत इति ॥

अत्रैके दूषणमाहुः—तदयुक्तम्, हेतुदृष्टान्तानभिधानात्परोक्तदोषापरिहाराच्च। प्रसङ्गवाक्यत्वाच्च प्रकृतार्थविपर्ययेण विपरीतार्थसाध्यतद्धर्मव्यक्तौ परस्मादुत्पन्नाभावाजन्मसाफल्यात् जन्मनिरो (धो ?) धाच्चेति कृतान्तविरोधः स्यात् ॥

सर्वमेतद्दूषणमयुज्यमानं वयं पश्यामः। कथं कृत्वा? तत्र यत्तावदुक्तं हेतुदृष्टान्तानभिधानादिति, तदयुक्तम्। किं कारणम्? यस्मात्परः स्वत उत्पत्तिमभ्युपगच्छन् पृच्छयते—स्वत इति हेतुत्वेन तदेव चोत्पद्यते इति? न च विद्यमानस्य पुनरुत्पत्तौ प्रयोजनं पश्यामः, अनवस्थां च पश्यामः। न च त्वया उत्पन्नस्य पुनरुत्पाद इष्यतेऽनवस्था चाप्यनिष्टेति। तस्मान्निरुपपत्तिक एव त्वद्वादः स्वाभ्युपगमविरोधश्चेति। किमिति चोदिते परो नाभ्युपैति यतो हेतुदृष्टान्तोपादानसाफल्यं स्यात्? अथ स्वाभ्युपगमविरोधचोदनयापि परो न निवर्तते, तदा निर्लज्जतया हेतुदृष्टान्ताभ्यामपि नैव निवर्तेत। न चोन्मत्तकेन सहास्माकं विवाद इति। तस्मात्सर्वथा प्रियानुमानतामेवात्मनः आचार्यः प्रकटयति अस्थानेऽप्यनुमानं प्रवेशयन्। न च माध्यमिकस्य सतः स्वतन्त्रमनुमानं कर्तुं युक्तं पक्षान्तराभ्युपगमाभावात्। तथोक्तमार्यदेवेन—

सदसत्सदसच्चेति यस्य पक्षो न विद्यते।
उपालम्भश्चिरेणापि तस्य वक्तुं न शक्यते ॥

(चतुःशतक—१६·२५)

विग्रहव्यावर्तन्यां चोक्तम्—

यदि काचन प्रतिज्ञा स्यान्मे तत एव मे भवेद्दोषः।
नास्ति च मम प्रतिज्ञा तस्मान्नैवास्ति मे दोषः ॥

यदि किंचिदुपलभेयं प्रवर्तयेयं निवर्तयेयं वा।
प्रत्यक्षादिभिरर्थैस्तदभावान्मेऽनुपालम्भः ॥

[विग्रहव्यावर्तनी—२९-३०]

इति। यदा चैवं स्वतन्त्रानुमानानभिधायित्वं माध्यमिकस्य, तदा कुतः "नाध्यात्मिकान्यायतनानि स्वत उत्पन्नानि" इति स्वतन्त्रा प्रतिज्ञा यस्यां सांख्याः प्रत्यवस्थाप्यन्ते। कोऽयं प्रतिज्ञार्थः किं कार्यात्मकत्वात्स्वत उत कारणात्मकत्वादिति। किं चातः ? कार्यात्मकाच्चेत् सिद्धसाधनम्, कारणात्मकाच्चेत् विरुद्धार्थता, कारणात्मना विद्यमानस्यैव सर्वस्योत्पत्तिमत उत्पादादिति। कुतोऽस्माकं विद्यमानत्वादिति हेतुर्यस्य सिद्धसाधनं विरुद्धार्थता वा स्यात्, यस्य सिद्धसाधनस्य यस्याश्च विरुद्धार्थतायाः परिहारार्थं यत्नं करिष्यामः। तस्मात्परोक्तदोषाप्रसङ्गादेव तत्परिहारः आचार्यबुद्धपालितेन न वर्णनीयः॥

अथापि स्यात्—माध्यमिकानां पक्षहेतुदृष्टान्तानामसिद्धेः स्वतन्त्रानुमानानभिधायित्वात् स्वत उत्पत्तिप्रतिषेधप्रतिज्ञातार्थसाधनं मा भूदुभयसिद्धेन वानुमानेन परप्रतिज्ञानिराकरणम्, परप्रतिज्ञायास्तु स्वत एवानुमानविरोधचोदनया स्वत एव पक्षहेतुदृष्टान्तदोषरहितैः पक्षादिभिर्भवितव्यम्। ततश्च तदनभिधानात् तद्दोषापरिहाराच्च स एव दोष इति। उच्यते। नैतदेवम्। किं कारणम्? यस्माद् यो हि यमर्थं प्रतिजानीते, तेन स्वनिश्चयवदन्येषां निश्चयोत्पादनेच्छया यया उपपत्त्या असावर्थोऽधिगतः सैवोपपत्तिः परस्मै उपदेष्टव्या। तस्मादेष तावन्न्यायः—यत्परेणैव स्वाभ्युपगतप्रतिज्ञातार्थसाधनमुपादेयम्। न चायं (चानेन ?) परं प्रति। हेतुदृष्टान्तासंभवात् प्रतिज्ञानुसारतयेव केवलं स्वप्रतिज्ञातार्थसाधनमुपादत्त इति निरुपपत्तिकपक्षाभ्युपगमात् स्वात्मानमेवायं केवलं विसंवादयन् न शक्नोति परेषां निश्चयमाधातुमिति। इदमेवास्य स्पष्टतरं दूषणं यदुत स्वप्रतिज्ञातार्थसाधनासामर्थ्यमिति किमत्रानुमानबाधोद्भावनया प्रयोजनम्? अथाप्यवश्यं स्वतोऽनुमानविरोधदोष उद्भावनीयः, सोऽप्युद्भावित एवाचार्यबुद्धपालितेन। कथमिति चेत्, न स्वत उत्पद्यन्ते भावाः, तदुत्पादवैयर्थ्यादिति वचनात्, अत्र हि तदित्यनेन स्वात्मना विद्यमानस्य परामर्शः। कस्मादिति चेत्, तथा हि तस्य संग्रहेणोक्तवाक्यस्यैतद्विवरणवाक्यम्, न हि स्वात्मना विद्यमानानां पुनरुत्पादे प्रयोजनमिति। अनेन च वाक्येन साध्यसाधनधर्मानुगतस्य परप्रसिद्धस्य साधर्म्यदृष्टान्तस्योपादानम्। तत्र स्वात्मना विद्यमानस्येत्यनेन हेतुपरामर्शः। उत्पादवैयर्थ्यादित्यनेन साध्यधर्मपरामर्शः॥ तत्र यथा–अनित्यः शब्दः। कृतकत्वात्। कृतकत्वमनित्यं दृष्टं यथा घटः। तथा च कृतकः शब्दः। तस्मात्कृतकत्वादनित्य इति कृतक-

त्वमत्र उपनयाभिव्यक्तो हेतुः। एवमिहापि—न स्वत उत्पद्यन्ते भावाः, स्वात्मना विद्यमानानां पुनरुत्पादवैयर्थ्यात्। इह हि स्वात्मना विद्यमानं पुरोऽवस्थितं घटादिकं पुनरुपादानापेक्षं दृष्टम्, तथा च मृत्पिण्डाद्यवस्थायामपि यदि स्वात्मना विद्यमानं घटादिकमिति मन्यसे, तदापि तस्य स्वात्मना विद्यमानस्य नास्त्युत्पाद इति। एवं स्वात्मना विद्यमानत्वेन उपनयाभिव्यक्तेन पुनरुत्पादप्रतिषेधाव्यभिचारिणा हेतुना स्वत एव सांख्यस्यानुमानविरोधोद्भावनमनुष्ठितमेवेति। तत्किमुच्यते तदयुक्तं हेतुदृष्टान्तानभिधानादिति ?

न च केवलं हेतुदृष्टान्तानभिधानं न संभवति, परोक्तदोषापरिहारदोषो न संभवति। कथं कृत्वा ? सांख्या हि नैव अभिव्यक्तरूपस्य पुरोऽवस्थितस्य घटस्य पुनरभिव्यक्तिमिच्छन्ति। तस्यैव च इह दृष्टान्तत्वेनोपादानम्, सिद्धरूपत्वात्। अनभिव्यक्तरूपस्य च शक्तिरूपापन्नस्य उत्पत्तिप्रतिषेधविशिष्टसाध्यत्वात् कुतः सिद्धसाधनपक्षदोषाशङ्का, कुतो वा हेतोर्विरुद्धार्थताशङ्केति। तस्मात्स्वतोऽनुमानविरोधचोदनायामपि यथोपवर्णितदोषाभावात्परोक्तदोषापरिहारासंभव एव। इत्यसंबद्धमेवैतद्दूषणमिति विज्ञेयम्॥

घटादिकमित्यादिशब्देन निरवशेषोत्पित्सुपदार्थसंग्रहस्य विवक्षितत्वादनैकान्तिकतापि पटादिभिर्नैव संभवति॥

अथवा। अयमन्यः प्रयोगमार्गः—पुरुषव्यतिरिक्ताः पदार्थाः स्वत उत्पत्तिवादिनः। तत एव न स्वत उत्पद्यन्ते। स्वात्मना विद्यमानत्वात्। पुरुषवत्। इतीदमुदाहरणमुदाहार्यम्॥

यद्यपि च अभिव्यक्तिवादिन उत्पादप्रतिषेधो न बाधकः, तथापि अभिव्यक्तावुत्पादशब्दं निपात्य पूर्वं पश्चाच्च अनुपलब्ध्युपलब्धिसाधर्म्येण उत्पादशब्देनाभिव्यक्तेरेवाभिधानादयं प्रतिषेधो न अबाधकः॥

कथं पुनरयं यथोक्तार्थाभिधानं विना व्यस्तविचारो लभ्यत इति चेत्, तदुच्यते। अथ वाक्यानि कृतानि, तानि महार्थत्वाद्यथोदितमर्थं संगृह्य प्रवृत्तानि। तानि च व्याख्यायमानानि यथोक्तमर्थात्मानं प्रसूयन्त इति नात्र किंचिदनुपात्तं संभाव्यते॥

प्रसङ्गविपरीतेन चार्थेन परस्यैव संबन्धो नास्माकम्। स्वप्रतिज्ञाया अभावात्। ततश्च सिद्धान्तविरोधासंभवः। परस्य च यावद्बहवो दोषाः प्रसङ्गविपरीतापत्त्या आपद्यन्ते, तावदस्माभिरभीष्यत एवेति। कुतो नु खलु अविपरीताचार्यनागार्जुनमतानुसारिणः आचार्यबुद्धपालितस्य

सावकाशवचनाभिधायित्वम् , यतोऽस्य परोऽवकाशं लभेत ? निःस्वभावभाववादिना सस्वभावभाववादिनः प्रसङ्गे आप (पा?) द्यमाने कुतः प्रसङ्गविपरीतार्थप्रसङ्गिता ? न हि शब्दाः दाण्डपाशिका इव वक्तारमस्वतन्त्रयन्ति, किं तर्हि सत्यां शक्तौ वक्तुर्विवक्षामनुविधीयन्ते । ततश्च परप्रतिज्ञाप्रतिषेधमात्रफलत्वात्प्रसङ्गापादनस्य नास्ति प्रसङ्गविपरीतार्थापत्तिः । तथा च आचार्यो भूयसा प्रसङ्गापत्तिमुखेनैव परपक्षं निराकरोति स्म । तद्यथा—

नाकाशं विद्यते किंचित्पूर्वमाकाशलक्षणात् ।
अलक्षणं प्रसज्येत स्यात्पूर्वं यदि लक्षणात् ॥

[म० शा०-५.१]

रूपकारणनिर्मुक्ते रूपे रूपं प्रसज्यते ।
आहेतुकं न चास्त्यर्थः कश्चिदाहेतुकः क्वचित् ॥

[म० शा०-४.२]

भावस्तावन्न निर्वाणं जरामरणलक्षणम् ।
प्रसज्येतास्ति भावो हि न जरामरणं विना ॥

[म० शा०-२४.४]

इत्यादिना । अथ अर्थवाक्यत्वादाचार्यवाक्यानां महार्थत्वे सति अनेकप्रयोगनिष्पत्तिहेतुत्वं परिकल्प्यते, आचार्यबुद्धपालितव्याख्यानान्यपि किमिति न तथैव परिकल्प्यन्ते ?

अथ स्यात्— वृत्तिकाराणामेष न्यायः, यत्प्रयोगवाक्यविस्तराभिधानं कर्तव्यमिति, एतदपि नास्ति विग्रहव्यावर्तन्या वृत्तिं कुर्वताप्याचार्येण प्रयोगवाक्यानभिधानात् ॥

अपि च । आत्मनस्तर्कशास्त्रातिकौशलमात्रमाविश्चिकीर्षया अङ्गीकृतमध्यमकदर्शनस्यापि यत्स्वतन्त्रप्रयोगवाक्याभिधानं तदतितरामनेकदोषसमुदायास्पदमस्य तार्किकस्योपलक्ष्यते । कथं कृत्वा ? तत्र यत्तावदेवमुक्तम्—अत्र प्रयोगवाक्यं भवति—न परमार्थतः आध्यात्मिकान्यायतनानि स्वत उत्पन्नानि, विद्यमानत्वात् , चैतन्यवदिति । किमर्थं पुनरत्र परमार्थत इति विशेषणमुपादीयते ? लोकसंवृत्याभ्युपगतस्य उत्पादस्य अप्रतिषिध्यमानत्वात्, प्रतिषेधे च अभ्युपेतबाधाप्रसङ्गादिति चेत्, नैतद्युक्तम् । संवृत्यापि स्वत उत्पत्त्यनभ्युपगमात् । यथोक्तं सूत्रे—

"स चायं बीजहेतुकोऽङ्कुर उत्पद्यमानो न स्वयंकृतो न परकृतो नोभयकृतो नाप्यहेतुसमुत्पन्नो नेश्वरकालाणुप्रकृतिस्वभावसंभूतः" इति।

[शालिस्तम्बसूत्रे]

तथा—

बीजस्य सतो यथाङ्कुरो न च यो बीजु स चैव अङ्कुरो।
न च अन्यु ततो न चैव तदेवमनुच्छेदअशाश्वतधर्मता॥

[ललितविस्तर–१३.१०२]

इहापि वक्ष्यति—

प्रतीत्य यद्यद्भवति न हि तावत्तदेव तत्।
न चान्यदपि तत्तस्मान्नोच्छिन्नं नापि शाश्वतम्॥

[म० शा०–१८.७]

इति॥

परमतापेक्षं विशेषणमिति चेत्, तदयुक्तम्। संवृत्यापि तदीयव्यवस्थानभ्युपगमात्। सत्यद्वयाविपरीतदर्शनपरिभ्रष्टा एव हि तीर्थिका यावदुभयथापि निषिध्यन्ते तावद् गुण एव संभाव्यत इति। एवं परमतापेक्षमपि विशेषणाभिधानं न युज्यते॥

न चापि लोकः स्वत उत्पत्तिं प्रतिपन्नः, यतस्तदपेक्षयापि विशेषणसाफल्यं स्यात्। लोको हि स्वतः परत इत्येवमादिकं विचारमनवतार्य कारणात्कार्यमुत्पद्यते इत्येतावन्मात्रं प्रतिपन्नः। एवमाचार्योऽपि व्यवस्थापयामास। इति सर्वथा विशेषणवैफल्यमेव निश्चीयते॥

अपि च। यदि संवृत्या उत्पत्तिप्रतिषेधनिराचिकीर्षुणा विशेषणमेतदुपादीयते, तदा स्वतोऽसिद्धाधारे पक्षदोषः, आश्रयासिद्धौ वा हेतुदोषः स्यात्। परमार्थतः स्वतश्चक्षुराद्यायतनानामनभ्युपगमात्। संवृत्या चक्षुरादिसद्भावाददोष इति चेत्, परमार्थत इत्येतत्तर्हि कस्य विशेषणम्? सांवृतानां चक्षुरादीनां परमार्थत उत्पत्तिप्रतिषेधाद् उत्पत्तिप्रतिषेधविशेषणे परमार्थग्रहणमिति चेत्, एवं तर्हि एवमेव वक्तव्यं स्यात्—सांवृतानां चक्षुरादीनां परमार्थतो नास्त्युत्पत्तिरिति। न चैवमुच्यते। उच्यमानेऽपि परैर्वस्तुसतामेव चक्षुरादीनामभ्युपगमात्, प्रज्ञप्तिसतामनभ्युपगमात् परतोऽसिद्धाधारः पक्षदोषः स्यादिति न युक्तमेतत्॥

अथ स्यात्—यथा अनित्यः शब्द इति धर्मधर्मिसामान्यमेव गृह्यते न विशेषः, विशेष-ग्रहणे हि सति अनुमानानुमेयव्यवहाराभावः स्यात् । तथा हि—यदि चातुर्महाभौतिकः शब्दो गृह्यते, स परस्यासिद्धः । अथाकाशगुणो गृह्यते, स बौद्धस्य स्वतोऽसिद्धः । तथा वैशेषिकस्य शब्दानित्यतां प्रतिजानानस्य यदि कार्यः शब्दो गृह्यते, स परतोऽसिद्धः । अथ व्यङ्ग्यः, स स्वतोऽसिद्धः । एवं यथासंभवं विनाशोऽपि यदि सहेतुकः, स बौद्धस्य स्वतोऽसिद्धः । अथ निर्हेतुकः, स परस्यासिद्ध इति । तस्माद् यथात्र धर्मधर्मिसामान्यमात्रमेव गृह्यते, एवमिहापि धर्मिमात्रमुत्सृष्टविशेषणं ग्रहीष्यत इति चेत्, नैतदेवम् । यस्माद् यदैवोत्पादप्रतिषेधोऽत्र साध्यधर्मोऽभिप्रेतः, तदैव धर्मिणस्तदाधारस्य विपर्यासमात्रासादितात्मभावस्य प्रच्युतिः स्वयमेवानेनाङ्गीकृता । भिन्नौ हि विपर्यासाविपर्यासौ । तद्यदा विपर्यासेन असत्सत्त्वेन गृह्यते, तैमिरिकेणेव केशादि, तदा कुतः सद्भूतपदार्थलेशस्याप्युपलब्धिः ? यदा च अविपर्यासादभूतं नाध्यारोपितं वितैमिरिकेणेव केशादि, तदा कुतोऽसद्भूतपदार्थलेशस्याप्युपलब्धिः, येन तदानीं संवृतिः स्यात् ? अत एवोक्तमाचार्यपादैः—

यदि किंचिदुपलभेयं प्रवर्तयेयं निवर्तयेयं वा ।
प्रत्यक्षादिभिरर्थैस्तदभावान्मेऽनुपालम्भः ॥ इति ॥

[वि० व्या०–३०]

यतश्चैवं भिन्नौ विपर्यासाविपर्यासौ, अतो विदुषामविपरीतावस्थायां विपरीतस्यासंभवात्कुतः सांवृतं चक्षुः यस्य धर्मित्वं स्यात् ? इति न व्यावर्ततेऽसिद्धाधारे पक्षदोषः, आश्रयासिद्धो वा हेतुदोषः । इत्यपरिहार एवायम् ॥

निदर्शनस्यापि नास्ति साम्यम् । तत्र हि शब्दसामान्यमनित्यतासामान्यं च अविवक्षितविशेषं द्वयोरपि संविद्यते । न त्वेवं चक्षुःसामान्यं शून्यताशून्यतावादिभ्यां संवृत्या अङ्गीकृतं नापि परमार्थतः । इति नास्ति निदर्शनस्य साम्यम् ॥

यश्चायमसिद्धाधारपक्षदोषोद्भावने विधिः, एष एव सत्त्वादित्यस्य हेतोरसिद्धार्थतोद्भावनेऽपि योज्यः ॥

इत्थं चैतदेवम्, यत्स्वयमप्यनेनायं यथोक्तोऽर्थोऽभ्युपगतस्तार्किकेण । सन्त्येवाध्यात्मिकायतनोत्पादका हेत्वादयः, तथा तथागतेन निर्देशात् । यद्धि यथा तथागतेनास्ति निर्दिष्टं तत्तथा, तद्यथा शान्तं निर्वाणमिति ॥

अस्य परोपक्षिप्तस्य साधनस्येदं दूषणमभिहितमनेन—को हि भवतामभिप्रेतोऽत्र हेत्वर्थः ? संवृत्या तथा तथागतेन निर्देशात्, उत परमार्थत इति ? संवृत्या चेत्, स्वतो हेतोरसिद्धार्थता। परमार्थतश्चेत्,

न सन्नासन्न सदसद्धर्मो निर्वर्तते यदा।

सदसदुभयात्मककार्यप्रत्ययत्वनिराकरणात्, तदा—

कथं निर्वर्तको हेतुरेवं सति हि युज्यते ॥

[म० शा०—१·९]

नैवासौ निर्वर्तको हेतुरिदि वाक्यार्थः। ततश्च परमार्थतो निर्वर्त्यनिर्वर्तकत्वासिद्धेः असिद्धार्थता विरुद्धार्थता वा हेतोरिति ॥

यतश्चैवं स्वयमेवामुना न्यायेन हेतोरसिद्धिरङ्गीकृतानेन, तस्मात्सर्वेष्वेवानुमानेषु वस्तुधर्मोपन्यस्तहेतुकेषु स्वत एव हेत्वादीनामसिद्धत्वात् सर्वाण्येव साधनानि व्याहन्यन्ते। तद्यथा—न परमार्थतः परेभ्यस्तत्प्रत्ययेभ्यः आध्यात्मिकायतनजन्म, परत्वात्, तद्यथा पटस्य। अथवा—न परे परमार्थेन विवक्षिताः चक्षुराद्याध्यात्मिकायतननिर्वर्तकाः प्रत्यया इति प्रतीयन्ते, परत्वात्, तद्यथा तन्त्वादय इति। परत्वादिकमत्र स्वत एवासिद्धम् ॥

यथा चानेन—उत्पन्ना एव आध्यात्मिका भावाः, तद्विषयिविशिष्टव्यवहारकरणात्—इत्यस्य पराभिहितस्य हेतोरसिद्धार्थतामुद्भावयिषुणा इदमुक्तम्, अथ समाहितस्य योगिनः प्रज्ञाचक्षुषा भावयाथात्म्यं पश्यतः उत्पादगत्यादयः सन्ति परमार्थत इति साध्यते, तदा तद्विषयिविशिष्टव्यवहारकरणादिति हेतोरसिद्धार्थता, गतेरप्युत्पादनिषेधादेव निषेधादिति। एवं स्वकृतसाधनेऽपि—परमार्थतोऽगतं नैव गम्यते, अध्वत्वात्, गताध्ववदिति अध्वत्वहेतोः स्वत एवासिद्धार्थता योज्या ॥

न परमार्थतः सभागं चक्षु रूपं पश्यति, चक्षुरिन्द्रियत्वात्, तद्यथा तत्सभागम्। तथा—न चक्षुः प्रेक्षते रूपम्, भौतिकत्वात्, रूपवत्। खरस्वभावा न मही, भूतत्वात्, तद्यथानिलः, इत्यादिषु हेत्वाद्यसिद्धिः स्वत एव योज्या ॥

सत्त्वादिति चायं हेतुः परतोऽनैकान्तिकः। किं सत्त्वात् चैतन्यवन्नाध्यात्मिकान्यायतनानि स्वत उत्पद्यन्ताम्, उताहो घटादिवत् स्वत उत्पद्यन्तामिति घटादीनां साध्यसमत्वान्नानैकान्तिकतेति चेत्, नैतदेवम्, तथानभिधानात् ॥

ननु च यथा परकीयेष्वनुमानेषु दूषणमुक्तम्, एवं स्वानुमानेष्वपि यथोक्तदूषणप्रसङ्गे सति स एव असिद्धाधारासिद्धहेत्वादिदोषः प्राप्नोति, ततश्च यः उभयोर्दोषः, न तेनैकश्चोद्यो भवतीति सर्वमेतद्दूषणमयुक्तं जायत इति। उच्यते। स्वतन्त्रमनुमानं ब्रुवतामयं दोषो जायते। न वयं स्वतन्त्रमनुमानं प्रयुञ्ज्महे परप्रतिज्ञानिषेधफलत्वादस्मदनुमानानाम्। तथा हि—परः चक्षुः पश्यतीति प्रतिपन्नः। स तत्प्रसिद्धेनैवानुमानेन निराक्रियते—चक्षुषः स्वात्मादर्शनधर्ममिच्छसि, परदर्शनधर्माविनाभावित्वं चाङ्गीकृतम्, तस्माद् यत्र यत्र स्वात्मादर्शनं तत्र तत्र परदर्शनमपि नास्ति, तद्यथा घटे, अस्ति च चक्षुषः स्वात्मादर्शनम्, तस्मात् परदर्शनमप्यस्य नैवास्ति। ततश्च स्वात्मादर्शनविरुद्धं नीलादिपरदर्शनं स्वप्रसिद्धं नैवानुमानेन विरुध्यत इति एतावन्मात्रमस्मदनुमानैरुद्भाव्यत इति कुतोऽस्मत्पक्षे यथोक्तदोषावतारः, यतः समानदोषता स्यात्?

किं पुनः—अन्यतरप्रसिद्धेनाप्यनुमानबाधा। अस्ति, सा च स्वप्रसिद्धेनैव हेतुना, न परप्रसिद्धेन, लोकत एवं दृष्टत्वात्। कदाचिद्धि लोके अर्थिप्रत्यर्थिभ्यां प्रमाणीकृतस्य साक्षिणो वचनेन जयो भवति पराजयो वा, कदाचित् स्ववचनेन। परवचनेन तु न जयो नापि पराजयः। यथा च लोके, तथा न्यायेऽपि। लौकिकस्यैव व्यवहारस्य न्यायशास्त्रे प्रस्तुतत्वात्। अत एव कैश्चिदुक्तम्—न परतः प्रसिद्धिबलादनुमानबाधा, परप्रसिद्धेरेव निराचिकीर्षितत्वादिति। यस्तु मन्यते—य एव उभयनिश्चितवादी, स प्रमाणं दूषणं वा, नान्यतरप्रसिद्धसंदिग्धवाची इति, तेनापि लौकिकीं व्यवस्थामनुरुध्यमानेन अनुमाने यथोक्त एव न्यायोऽभ्युपेयः॥

तथा हि नोभयप्रसिद्धेन वा आगमेन बाधा, किं तर्हि स्वप्रसिद्धेनापि॥

स्वार्थानुमाने तु सर्वत्र स्वप्रसिद्धिरेव गरीयसी, नोभयप्रसिद्धिः। अत एव तर्कलक्षणाभिधानं निष्प्रयोजनम्, यथास्वप्रसिद्धया उपपत्त्या बुद्धैस्तदनभिज्ञविनेयजनानुग्रहात्। इत्यलं प्रसङ्गेन। प्रकृतमेव व्याख्यास्यामः॥

परतोऽपि नोत्पद्यन्ते भावाः। पराभावादेव। एतच्च—

न हि स्वभावो भावानां प्रत्ययादिषु विद्यते।

इत्यत्र प्रतिपादयिष्यति। ततश्च पराभावादेव नापि परत उत्पद्यन्ते। अपि च—

अन्यत्प्रतीत्य यदि नाम परोऽभविष्य,
जायेत तर्हि बहुलः शिखिनोऽन्धकारः।
सर्वस्य जन्म च भवेत्खलु सर्वतश्च
तुल्यं परत्वमखिलेऽजनकेऽपि यस्मात् ॥

[मध्यमकावतार–६·१४]

इत्यादिना [मध्यमकावतारात्] परत उत्पत्तिप्रतिषेधोऽवसेयः ॥

आचार्यबुद्धपालितस्तु व्याचष्टे—न परत उत्पद्यन्ते भावाः, सर्वतः सर्वसंभवप्रसङ्गात्। आचार्यभावविवेको दूषणमाह-तदत्र प्रसङ्गवाक्यत्वात् साध्यसाधनविपर्ययं कृत्वा, स्वतः उभयतः अहेतुतो वा उत्पद्यन्ते भावाः, कुतश्चित्कस्यचिदुत्पत्तेः, इति प्राक्पक्षविरोधः। अन्यथा सर्वतः सर्वसंभवप्रसङ्गात् इत्यस्य साधनदूषणानन्तःपातित्वादसंगतार्थमेतत् [इति]। एतदप्यसंगतार्थम्। पूर्वमेव प्रतिपादितत्वाद् दूषणान्तःपातित्वाच्च परप्रतिज्ञातार्थदूषणेनेति यत्किंचिदेतदिति न पुनर्यत्न आस्थीयते ॥

द्वाभ्यामपि नोपजायन्ते भावाः, उभयपक्षाभिहितदोषप्रसङ्गात् प्रत्येकमुत्पादासामर्थ्याच्च। वक्ष्यति हि—

स्यादुभाभ्यां कृतं दुःखं स्यादेकैककृतं यदि। इति ॥

[म० शा०–१२·९]

अहेतुतोऽपि नोत्पद्यन्ते—

हेतावसति कार्यं च कारणं च न विद्यते।

[म० शा०–८·४]

इति वक्ष्यमाणदोषप्रसङ्गात्,

गृह्येत नैव च जगद्यदि हेतुशून्यं
स्याद्यद्वदेव गगनोत्पलवर्णगन्धौ ॥

[मध्यमकावतार–६·९९]

इत्यादिदोषप्रसङ्गाच्च ॥

आचार्यबुद्धपालितस्त्वाह—अहेतुतो नोत्पद्यन्ते भावाः, सदा च सर्वतश्च सर्वसंभवप्रसङ्गात्। अत्राचार्यभावविवेको दूषणमाह—अत्रापि प्रसङ्गवाक्यत्वात् यदि विपरीतसाध्यसाधनव्यक्तिवाक्यार्थ इष्यते, तदा एतदुक्तं भवति—हेतुत उत्पद्यन्ते भावाः, कदाचित्

कुतश्चित् कस्यचिदुत्पत्तेः, आरम्भसाफल्याच्च । सेयं व्याख्या न युक्ता प्रागुक्तदोषादिति । तदेतदयुक्तम्, पूर्वोदितपरिहारादित्यपरे ॥

यच्चापि ईश्वरादीनामुपसंग्रहार्थम्, तदपि न युक्तम् । ईश्वरादीनां स्वपरोभयपक्षेषु यथाभ्युपगममन्तर्भावादिति ।

तस्मात् प्रसाधितमेतन्नास्त्युत्पाद इति । उत्पादासंभवाच्च सिद्धोऽनुत्पादादिविशिष्टः प्रतीत्यसमुत्पाद इति ॥

अत्राह–यद्येवमनुत्पादादिविशिष्टः प्रतीत्यसमुत्पादो व्यवस्थितो भवद्भिः, यत्तर्हि भगवतोक्तम्–अविद्याप्रत्ययाः संस्काराः⋯अविद्यानिरोधात्संस्कारनिरोध इति, तथा–

अनित्याश्च ते (बत ?) संस्कारा उत्पादव्ययधर्मिणः ।
उत्पद्य हि निरुध्यन्ते तेषां व्युपशमः सुखः ॥

तथा–उत्पादाद्वा तथागतानामनुत्पादाद्वा तथागतानां स्थितैवैषा धर्माणां धर्मता, एको धर्मः सत्त्वस्थितये यदुत चत्वार आहाराः, द्वौ धर्मौ लोकं पालयतो ह्रीश्चापत्राप्यं चेत्यादि, तथा–परलोकादिहागमनमिहलोकाच्च परलोकगमनमिति, एवं निरोधादिविशिष्टः प्रतीत्यसमुत्पादो देशितो भगवता, स कथं न नि (वि ?) रुध्यत इति ? यत एवं निरोधादयः प्रतीत्यसमुत्पादस्योपलभ्यन्ते, अत एवेदं मध्यमकशास्त्रं प्रणीतमाचार्येण नेयनीतार्थसूत्रान्तविभागोपदर्शनार्थम् ; तत्र य एते प्रतीत्यसमुत्पादस्योत्पादादय उक्ताः, न ते विगताविद्यातिमिरानास्रवविषयस्वभावापेक्षया, किं तर्हि अविद्यातिमिरोपहतमतिनयनज्ञानविषयापेक्षया ॥

तत्त्वदर्शनापेक्षया तूक्तं भगवता–एतद्धि भिक्षवः परमं सत्यं यदुत अमोषधर्म निर्वाणम्, सर्वसंस्काराश्च मृषा मोषधर्माणः इति । तथा–नास्त्यत्र तथता वा अवितथता वा । मोषधर्मकमप्येतत्, प्रलोपधर्मकमप्येतत्, मृषाप्येतत्, मायेयं बाललापिनी इति । तथा–

फेनपिण्डोपमं रूपं वेदना बुद्बुदोपमा ।
मरीचिसदृशी संज्ञा संस्काराः कदलीनिभाः ।
मायोपमं च विज्ञानमुक्तमादित्यबन्धुना ॥ इति ॥
एवं धर्मान् वीक्षमाणो भिक्षुरारब्धवीर्यवान् ।
दिवा वा यदि वा रात्रौ संप्रजानन् प्रतिस्मृतः ।
प्रतिविध्येत्पदं शान्तं संस्कारोपशमं शिवम् ॥ इति ॥

निरात्मकत्वाच्च धर्माणामित्यादि ॥

यस्यैवं देशनाभिप्रायानभिज्ञतया संदेहः स्यात्-का ह्यत्र देशना तत्त्वार्था, का नु खलु आभिप्रायिकीति, यश्चापि मन्दबुद्धितया नेयार्थां देशनां नीतार्थामवगच्छति, तयोरुभयोरपि विनेयजनयोः आचार्यो युक्त्यागमाभ्यां संशयमिथ्याज्ञानापाकरणार्थं शास्त्रमिदमारब्धवान् ॥

तत्र 'न स्वतः' [म० शा० १·३] इत्यादिना युक्तिरुपवर्णिता ॥

तन्मृषा मोषधर्म यद्भगवानित्यभाषत ।
सर्वे च मोषधर्माणः संस्कारास्तेन ते मृषा ॥

[म० शा०–१३·१]

पूर्वा प्रज्ञायते कोटिर्नेत्युवाच महामुनिः ।
संसारोऽनवराग्रो हि नास्त्यादिर्नापि पश्चिमम् ॥

[म० शा०–११·१]

कात्यायनाववादे च अस्ति नास्तीति चोभयम् ।
प्रतिषिद्धं भगवता भावाभावविभाविना ॥

[म० शा०–१५·७]

इत्यादिना आगमो वर्णितः ॥

उक्तञ्च आर्याक्षयमतिसूत्रे–

कतमे सूत्रान्ता नेयार्थाः कतमे नीतार्थाः ? ये सूत्रान्ता मार्गावताराय निर्दिष्टाः, इम उच्यन्ते नेयार्थाः । ये सूत्रान्ताः फलावताराय निर्दिष्टाः, इम उच्यन्ते नेयार्थाः । यावद् ये सूत्रान्ताः शून्यतानिमित्ताप्रणिहितानभिसंस्काराजातानुत्पादाभावनिरात्मनिःसत्त्वनिर्जीवनिःपुद्गलास्वामिकविमोक्षमुखा निर्दिष्टाः त उच्यन्ते नीतार्थाः । इयमुच्यते भदन्त शारद्वतीपुत्र नीतार्थसूत्रान्तप्रतिशरणता, न नेयार्थसूत्रान्तप्रतिशरणता इति ॥

तथा च आर्यसमाधिराजसूत्रे–

नीतार्थसूत्रान्तविशेष जानति
यथोपदिष्टा सुगतेन शून्यता ।
यस्मिन् पुनः पुद्गलसत्त्वपूरुषा
नेयार्थतो जानति सर्वधर्मान् ॥

[समाधिराज–७·५]

तस्मादुत्पादादिदेशनां मृषार्थां प्रतिपादयितुं प्रतीत्यसमुत्पादानुदर्शनमारब्धवानाचार्यः ॥

ननु च–उत्पादादीनामभावे सति यदि सर्वधर्माणां मृषात्वप्रतिपादनार्थमिदमारब्धवानाचार्यः, नन्वेवं सति यन्मृषा न तदस्तीति न सन्त्यकुशलानि कर्माणि, तदभावान्न सन्ति दुर्गतयः, न सन्ति कुशलानि कर्माणि, तदभावान्न सन्ति सुगतयः, सुगतिदुर्गत्यसंभवाच्च नास्ति संसारः, इति सर्वारम्भवैयर्थ्यमेव स्यात् । उच्यते । संवृतिसत्यव्यपेक्षया लोकस्य इदंसत्याभिनिवेशस्य प्रतिपक्षभावेन मृषार्थता भावानां प्रतिपाद्यतेऽस्माभिः । नैव त्वार्याः कृतकार्याः किंचिदुपलभन्ते यन्मृषा अमृषा वा स्यादिति । अपि च । येन हि सर्वधर्माणां मृषात्वं परिज्ञातं किं तस्य कर्माणि सन्ति, संसारो वा अस्ति ? न चाप्यसौ कस्यचिद्धर्मस्य अस्तित्वं नास्तित्वं वोपलभते । यथोक्तं भगवता आर्यरत्नकूटसूत्रे–

चित्तं हि काश्यप परिगवेष्यमाणं न लभ्यते । यन्न लभ्यते तन्नोपलभ्यते । यन्नोपलभ्यते तन्नैव अतीतं न अनागतं न प्रत्युत्पन्नम् । यन्नैवातीतं नानागतं न प्रत्युत्पन्नम्, तस्य नास्ति स्वभावः । यस्य नास्ति स्वभावः, तस्य नास्त्युत्पादः । यस्य नास्त्युत्पादः, तस्य नास्ति निरोधः ॥ इति विस्तरः ॥

यस्तु विपर्यासानुगमान्मृषात्वं नावगच्छति, प्रतीत्य भावानां स्वभावमभिनिविशते, स धर्मेष्विदंसत्याभिनिवेशादभिनिविष्टः सन् कर्माण्यपि करोति, संसारेऽपि संसरति, विपर्यासावस्थितत्वान्न भव्यो निर्वाणमधिगन्तुम् ॥

किं पुनः—मृषास्वभावा अपि पदार्थाः संक्लेशव्यवदाननिबन्धनं भवन्ति। तद्यथा मायायुवति तत्स्वभावानभिज्ञानाम्, तथागतनिर्मितश्च उपचितकुशलमूलानाम् । उक्तं हि दृढाध्याशयपरिपृच्छासूत्रे—

तद्यथा कुलपुत्र मायाकारनाटके प्रत्युपस्थिते मायाकारनिर्मितां स्त्रियं दृष्ट्वा कश्चिद्रागपरीतचेताः पर्षच्छारद्यभयेन उत्थायासनादपक्रामेत्, सोऽपक्रम्य तामेव स्त्रियमशुभतो मनसि कुर्यात्, अनित्यतो दुःखतः शून्यतोऽनात्मतो मनसि कुर्यात् । इति विस्तरः ॥

विनये च—

यन्त्रकारकारिता यन्त्रयुवतिः सद्भूतयुवतिशून्या सद्भूतयुवतिरूपेण प्रतिभासते, तस्य च चित्रकारस्य कामरागास्पदीभूता । तथा मृषास्वभावा अपि भावा बालानां संक्लेशव्यवदाननिबन्धनं भवन्ति ॥

तथा आर्यरत्नकूटसूत्रे—

अथ खलु तानि पञ्चमात्राणि भिक्षुशतानि भगवतो धर्मदेशनामनवतरन्त्यनवगाहमानान्यनधिमुच्यमानानि उत्थायासनेभ्यः प्रक्रान्तानि। अथ भगवान् [तस्यां वेलायां] येन मार्गेणैते भिक्षवो गच्छन्ति स्म, तस्मिन् मार्गे द्वौ भिक्षू निर्मिमीतः स्म ॥

अथ तानि पञ्च भिक्षुशतानि येन [मार्गेण] तौ द्वौ भिक्षू [निर्मितकौ] तेनोपसंक्रामन्ति स्म। उपसंक्रम्य तावब्रोचन्—कुत्रायुष्मन्तौ गमिष्यथः? निर्मितकाववोचताम्—गमिष्याव आवामरण्यायतनेषु, तत्र ध्यानसुखस्पर्शविहारैर्विहरिष्यावः। यं हि भगवान् धर्मं देशयति, तमावां नावतरावो नावगाहावहे नाधिमुच्यावहे उत्त्रस्यावः संत्रासमापद्यावहे। अथ तानि पञ्च भिक्षुशतान्येतदवोचन्—वयमप्यायुष्मन्तो भगवतो धर्मदेशनां नावतरामो नावगाहामहे नाधिमुच्यामहे उत्त्रस्यामः संत्रस्यामः संत्रासमापद्यामहे। तेन वयमरण्यायतनेषु ध्यानसुखस्पर्शविहारैर्विहरिष्यामः। निर्मितकाववोचताम्—तेन हि आयुष्मन्तः संगास्यामो न विवदिष्यामः। अविवादपरमा हि श्रमणस्य धर्माः।...... कस्यायुष्मन्तः प्रहाणाय प्रतिपन्नाः? तान्यवोचन्—रागद्वेषमोहानां प्रहाणाय वयं प्रतिपन्नाः। निर्मितकाववोचताम्—किं पुनरायुष्मन्तः संविद्यन्ते रागद्वेषमोहा यान् क्षपयिष्यथ? तान्यवोचन्—न तेऽध्यात्मं न बहिर्धा नोभयमन्तरेणोपलभ्यन्ते, नापि तेऽपरिकल्पिता उत्पद्यन्ते। निर्मितकाववोचताम्—तेन हि आयुष्मन्तो मा कल्पयत, [मा विकल्पयत]। यदा चायुष्मन्तो न कल्पयिष्यथ न विकल्पयिष्यथ, तदा न रंक्ष्यथ न विरंक्ष्यथ। यश्च न रक्तो न विरक्तः, स शान्त इत्युच्यते। शीलमायुष्मन्तो न संसरति न परिनिर्वाति। समाधिः प्रज्ञा विमुक्तिर्विमुक्तिज्ञानदर्शनमायुष्मन्तो न संसरति न परिनिर्वाति। एभिश्चायुष्मन्तो धर्मैर्निर्वाणं सूच्यते। एते च धर्माः शून्याः प्रकृतिविविक्ताः। प्रजहीतैतामायुष्मन्तः संज्ञां यदुत परिनिर्वाणमिति। मा च संज्ञायां संज्ञां कार्ष्ट, मा च संज्ञायां संज्ञां परिज्ञासिष्ट। यो हि संज्ञायां संज्ञां परिजानाति, संज्ञा बन्धनमेवास्य तद्भवति। संज्ञावेदयितनिरोधसमापत्तिमायुष्मन्तः समापद्यध्वम्। संज्ञावेदयितनिरोधसमापत्तिसमापन्नस्य भिक्षोर्नास्त्युत्तरीकरणीयमिति वदावः॥

अथ तेषां पञ्चानां भिक्षुशतानामनुपादायाश्रवेभ्यश्चित्तानि विमुक्तान्यभूवन्। तानि विमुक्तचित्तानि येन भगवांस्तेनोपसंक्रान्तानि। उपसंक्रम्य भगवतः पादौ शिरसाभिवन्द्यैकान्ते न्यसीदन्॥

अथायुष्मान् सुभूतिस्तान् भिक्षूनेतदवोचत्— कुत्रायुष्मन्तो गताः कुतो वागताः? तेऽवोचन्—न क्वचिद् गमनाय न कुतश्चिदागमनाय भदन्त सुभूते भगवता धर्मो देशितः। आह—को नामायुष्मतां शास्ता? आहुः—यो नोत्पन्नो न परिनिर्वास्यति। आह—कथं युष्माभिर्धर्मः श्रुतः? आहुः न बन्धनाय न मोक्षाय। आह— केन यूयं विनीताः? आहुः—यस्य न कायो न चित्तम्। आह—कथं यूयं प्रयुक्ताः? आहुः—नाविद्याप्रहाणाय न विद्योत्पादनाय। आह—कस्य यूयं श्रावकाः? आहुः—येन न प्राप्तं नाभिसंबुद्धम्। आह—के युष्माकं सब्रह्मचारिणः? आहुः—ये त्रैधातुके नोपविचरन्ति। आह—कियच्चिरेणायुष्मन्तः परिनिर्वास्यन्ति? आहुः—यदा तथागतनिर्मिताः परिनिर्वास्यन्ति। आह—कृतं युष्माभिः करणीयम्? आहुः—अहंकारममकारपरिज्ञानतः। आह—क्षीणा युष्माकं क्लेशाः? आहुः—अत्यन्तक्षयात्सर्वधर्माणाम्। आह—धर्षितो युष्माभिर्मारः? आहुः—स्कन्धमारानुपलम्भात्। आह—परिचरितो युष्माभिः शास्ता? आहुः—न कायेन न वाचा न मनसा। आह—विशोधिता युष्माभिर्दक्षिणीयभूमिः? आहुः—अग्राहतोऽप्रतिग्राहतः। आह—उत्तीर्णो युष्माभिः संसारः? आहुः—अनुच्छेदतोऽशाश्वततः। आह—प्रतिपन्ना युष्माभिर्दक्षिणीयभूमिः? आहुः—सर्वग्राहविनिर्मुक्तितः। आह—किंगामिन आयुष्मन्तः? आहुः—यंगामिनस्तथागतनिर्मिताः। इति ह्यायुष्मतः सुभूतेः परिपृच्छतस्तेषां भिक्षूणां प्रतिविसर्जयतां तस्यां पर्षदि अष्टानां भिक्षुशतानामनुपादायाश्रवेभ्यश्चित्तानि विमुक्तानि, द्वात्रिंशतश्च प्राणिसहस्राणां विरजो विगतमलं धर्मचक्षुर्विशुद्धम्। इति ॥

इत्येवं मृषास्वभावाभ्यां तथागतनिर्मिताभ्यां भिक्षुभ्यां पञ्चानां भिक्षुशतानां व्यवदाननिबन्धनं कृतमिति ॥

उक्तं च आर्यवज्रमण्डायां धारण्याम्—

तद्यथा मञ्जुश्रीः काण्डं च प्रतीत्य मथनीं च प्रतीत्य पुरुषस्य हस्तव्यायामं च प्रतीत्य धूमः प्रादुर्भवतीति अग्निरभिनिर्वर्तते। स चाग्निसंतापो न काण्डसंमिश्रितो न मथनीसंमिश्रितो न पुरुषहस्तव्यायामसंमिश्रितः। एवमेव मञ्जुश्रीः असद्विपर्यासमोहितस्य पुरुषपुद्गलस्य उत्पद्यते रागपरिदाहो द्वेषपरिदाहो मोहपरिदाहः। स च परिदाहो नाध्यात्मं न बहिर्धा नोभयमन्तरेण स्थितः ॥

अपि तु मञ्जुश्रीः यदुच्यते मोह इति, तत्केन कारणेनोच्यते मोह इति ? अत्यन्तमुक्तो हि मञ्जुश्रीः सर्वधर्मैर्मोहस्तेनोच्यते मोह इति। तथा नरकमुखा मञ्जुश्रीः सर्वधर्मा इदं धारणीपदम्। आह—कथं भगवन्निदं धारणीपदम् ? आह—नरका मञ्जुश्रीः बालपृथग्जनैरसद्विपर्यासविठपिताः स्वविकल्पसंभूताः। आह—कुत्र भगवन्नरकाः समवसरन्ति ? भगवानाह—आकाशसमवसरणा मञ्जुश्रीः नरकाः। तत्किं मन्यसे मञ्जुश्रीः स्वविकल्पसंभूता नरका उत स्वभावसंभूताः ? आह— स्वविकल्पेनैव भगवन् सर्वबालपृथग्जना नरकतिर्यग्योनियमलोकं संजानन्ति। ते च असत्समारोपेण दुःखां वेदनां वेदयन्ति दुःखमनुभवन्ति त्रिष्वप्यपायेषु ॥

यथा चाहं भगवन् नरकान् पश्यामि तथा नारकं दुःखम्। तद्यथा भगवन कश्चिदेव पुरुषः सुप्तः स्वप्नान्तरगतो नरकगतमात्मानं संजानीते। स तत्र क्वथितायां संप्रज्वलितायामनेकपौरुषायां लोहकुम्भ्यां प्रक्षिप्तमात्मानं संजानीयात्। स तत्र खरां कटुकां तीव्रां दुःखां वेदनां वेदयेत्। स तत्र मानसं परिदाहं संजानीयात् उत्त्रसेत् संत्रासमापद्येत। स तत्र प्रतिबुद्धः समानः-अहो दुःखम्, अहो दुःखम्, इति क्रन्देत् शोचेत् परिदेवेत्। अथ तस्य मित्रज्ञातिसालोहिताः परिपृच्छेयुः-केन तत्ते दुःखमिति। स तान् मित्रज्ञातिसालोहितानेवं वदेत्-नैरयिकं दुःखमनुभूतम्। स तानाक्रोशेत् परिभाषेत्—अहं च नाम नैरयिकं दुःखमनुभवामि। यूयं च मे उत्तरि परिपृच्छथ केनैतत्तव दुःखमिति। अथ ते मित्रज्ञातिसालोहितास्तं पुरुषमेवं वदेयुः—मा भैर्भोः पुरुष। सुप्तो हि त्वम्। न त्वमितो गृहात् कचिन्निर्गतः। तस्य पुनरपि स्मृतिरुत्पद्यते—सुप्तोऽहमभूवम्। वितथमेतन्मया परिकाल्पतमिति। स पुनरपि सौमनस्यं प्रतिलभते ॥

तद्यथा भगवन् स पुरुषोऽसत्समारोपेण सुप्तः स्वप्नान्तरगतो नरकगतमात्मानं संजानीयात्, एवमेव भगवन् सर्वबालपृथग्जना असद्रागपर्यवनद्धाः स्त्रीनिमित्तं कल्पयन्ति। ते स्त्रीनिमित्तं कल्पयित्वा ताभिः सार्धं रममाणमात्मानं संजानन्ति। तस्य बालपृथग्जनस्यैवं भवति—अहं पुरुषः, इय स्त्री, ममैषा स्त्री। तस्य तेन च्छन्दरागपर्यवस्थितेन चित्तेन भोगपर्येष्टिं चित्तं क्रामयति ? स ततो निदानं कलहविग्रहविवादं संजनयति। तस्य प्रदुष्टेन्द्रियस्य वैरं संजायते। स तेन संज्ञाविपर्यासेन कालगतः समानो बहूनि कल्पसहस्राणि नरकेषु दुःखां वेदनां वेदयमानमात्मानं संजानाति ॥

तद्यथा भगवन् तस्य पुरुषस्य मित्रज्ञातिसालोहिता एवं वदन्ति—मा भैः, मा भैः, भो पुरुष। सुप्तो हि त्वम्। न त्वमितो गृहात् कुतश्चिन्निर्गतः इति। एवमेव बुद्धा भगवन्तश्चतुर्विपर्यासविपर्यस्तानां सत्त्वानामेवं धर्मं देशयन्ति—नात्र स्त्री न पुरुषो न सत्त्वो न जीवो न पुरुषो न पुद्गलः। वितथा इमे सर्वधर्माः। असन्त इमे सर्वधर्माः। विठपिता इमे सर्वधर्माः। मायोपमा इमे सर्वधर्माः। स्वप्नोपमा इमे सर्वधर्माः। निर्मितोपमा इमे सर्वधर्मा। उदकचन्द्रोपमा इमे सर्वधर्माः। इति विस्तरः। ते इमां तथागतस्य धर्मदेशनां श्रुत्वा विगतरागान् सर्वधर्मान् पश्यन्ति। विगतमोहान् सर्वधर्मान् पश्यन्ति अस्वभावाननावरणान्। ते आकाशस्थितेन चेतसा कालं कुर्वन्ति। ते कालगताः समाना निरुपधिशेषे निर्वाणधातौ परिनिर्वान्ति। एवमहं भगवन् नरकान् पश्यामि। इति॥

उक्तं च आर्योपालिपरिपृच्छायाम्—

भय दर्शित नैरयिकं मे
सत्त्वसहस्र सवेजित नैके।
न च विद्यति कश्चिह सत्त्व
यो च्युतु गच्छति घोरमपायम्॥

न च कारकु कारण सन्ति
येहि कृता असितोमरशस्त्राः।
कल्पवशेन तु पश्यति तत्र
कायि पतन्ति अपायित शस्त्राः॥

चित्रमनोरम सज्जितपुष्पाः
स्वर्णविमान जलन्ति मनोज्ञाः।
तेष्वपि कारकु नास्तिह कश्चि
तेऽपि च स्थापित कल्पवशेन॥

कल्पवशेन विकल्पितु लोकः
संज्ञगहेण विकल्पितु बालः।
सो च गहो अगहो असभूतो
मायमरीचिसमा हि विकल्पाः॥

तदेवमेतेऽस्वभावा भावाः स्वविपर्यासविठपिता बालानां संक्लेशहेतवो भवन्ति संसारे इति स्थितम्॥

यथा च मृषास्वभावानां पदार्थानां संक्लेशव्यवदानहेतुत्वं तथा मध्यमकावताराद्विस्तरेणावसेयम् ॥

अत्राह—यदि स्वतः परतः उभयतोऽहेतुतश्च नास्ति भावानामुत्पादः, तत्र कथमविद्याप्रत्ययाः संस्कारा इत्युक्तं भगवता ? उच्यते । संवृतिरेव न तत्त्वम् ॥

किं संवृतेर्व्यवस्थानं वक्तव्यम् ? इदंप्रत्ययतामात्रेण संवृतेः सिद्धिरभ्युपगम्यते । न तु पक्षचतुष्टयाभ्युपगमेन सस्वभाववादप्रसङ्गात्, तस्य चायुक्तत्वात् । इदंप्रत्ययतामात्राभ्युपगमे हि सति हेतुफलयोरन्योन्यापेक्षत्वान्नास्ति स्वाभाविकी सिद्धिरिति नास्ति सस्वभाववादः । अत एवोक्तम्—

स्वयं कृतं परकृतं द्वाभ्यां कृतमहेतुकम् ।
तार्किकैरिष्यते दुःखं त्वया तूक्तं प्रतीत्यजम् ॥
[लोकातीतस्तव-९]

इहापि वक्ष्यति—

प्रतीत्य कारकः कर्म तं प्रतीत्य च कारकम् ।
कर्म प्रवर्तते नान्यत्पश्यामः सिद्धिकारणम् ॥ इति ॥
[म० शा०-८. १२]

भगवताप्येतावन्मात्रमेवोक्तम्—

तत्रायं धर्मसंकेतो यदुतास्मिन् सतीदं भवति, अस्योत्पादादिदमुत्पद्यते, यदुत अविद्याप्रत्ययाः संस्काराः, संस्कारप्रत्ययं विज्ञानमित्यादि ॥

अत्र केचित्परिचोदयन्ति—अनुत्पन्ना भावा इति किमयं प्रमाणजो निश्चय उताप्रमाणजः ? तत्र यदि प्रमाणज इष्यते, तदेदं वक्तव्यम्—कति प्रमाणानि किंलक्षणानि किंविषयाणि, किं स्वत उत्पन्नानि किं परत उभयतोऽहेतुतो वेति । अथाप्रमाणजः, स न युक्तः, प्रमाणाधीनत्वात्प्रमेयाधिगमस्य । अनधिगतो ह्यर्थो न विना प्रमाणैरधिगन्तुं शक्यत इति प्रमाणाभावादर्थाधिगमाभावे सति कुतोऽयं सम्यङ्निश्चय इति न युक्तमेतदनिष्पन्ना भावा इति । यतो वायं निश्चयो भवतोऽनुत्पन्ना भावा इति भविष्यति, तत एव ममापि सर्वभावाः सन्तीति । यथा चायं ते निश्चयः— अनुत्पन्नाः सर्वधर्मा इति, तथैव ममापि सर्वभावोत्पत्तिर्भविष्यति । अथ ते नास्ति निश्चयोऽनुत्पन्नाः सर्वभावा इति, तदा स्वयमनिश्चितस्य परप्रत्यायनासंभवाच्छास्त्रारम्भवैयर्थ्यमेवेति सन्त्यप्रतिषिद्धाः सर्वभावा इति ॥

उच्यते। यदि कश्चिन्निश्चयो नामास्माकं स्यात्, स प्रमाणजो वा स्यादप्रमाणजो वा। न त्वस्ति। किं कारणम्? इहानिश्चयसंभवे सति स्यात्तत्प्रतिपक्षस्तदपेक्षो निश्चयः। यदा त्वनिश्चय एव तावदस्माकं नास्ति, तदा कुतस्तद्विरुद्धाविरुद्धो निश्चयः स्यात् संबन्ध्यन्तरनिरपेक्षत्वात्, खरविषाणस्य ह्रस्वदीर्घतावत्। यदा चैवं निश्चयस्याभावः, तदा कस्य प्रसिद्ध्यर्थं प्रमाणानि परिकल्पयिष्यामः? कुतो वैषां संख्या लक्षणं विषयो वा भविष्यति—स्वतः परत उभयतोऽहेतुतो वा समुत्पत्तिरिति सर्वमेतन्न वक्तव्यमस्माभिः॥

यद्येवं निश्चयो नास्ति सर्वतः, कथं पुनरिदं निश्चितरूपं वाक्यमुपलभ्यते भवताम्—न स्वतो नापि परतो न द्वाभ्यां नाप्यहेतुतो भावा भवन्तीति? उच्यते। निश्चितमिदं वाक्यं लोकस्य स्वप्रसिद्धयैवोपपत्त्या, नार्याणाम्। किं खलु आर्याणामुपपत्तिर्नास्ति? केनैतदुक्तमस्ति वा नास्ति वेति। परमार्थो ह्यार्याणां तूष्णींभावः। ततः कुतस्तत्र प्रपञ्चसंभवो यदुपपत्तिरनुपपत्तिर्वा स्यात्?

यदि ह्यार्या उपपत्तिं न वर्णयन्ति, केन खल्विदानीं परमार्थं लोकं बोधयिष्यन्ति? न खल्वार्या लोकसंव्यवहारेणोपपत्तिं वर्णयन्ति, किं तु लोकत एव या प्रसिद्धोपपत्तिः, तां परावबोधार्थमभ्युपेत्य तयैव लोकं बोधयन्ति। यथैव हि विद्यमानामपि शरीराशुचितां विपर्यासानुगता रागिणो नोपलभन्ते, शुभाकारं चाभूतमध्यारोप्य परिक्लिश्यन्ते, तेषां वैराग्यार्थं तथागतनिर्मितो देवो वा शुभसंज्ञया प्राक् प्रच्छादितान् कायदोषानुपवर्णयेत्—सन्त्यस्मिन् काये केशा इत्यादिना। ते च तस्याः शुभसंज्ञाया विमुक्ता वैराग्यमासादयेयुः। एवमिहाप्यार्यैः सर्वथाप्यनुपलभ्यमानात्मकं भावानामविद्यातिमिरोपहतमतिनयनतया विपरीतं स्वभावमध्यारोप्य कचिच्च कंचिद्विशेषमतितरां परिक्लिश्यन्ति पृथग्जनाः। तानिदानीमार्याः तत्प्रसिद्धयैवोपपत्त्या परिबोधयन्ति। यथा विद्यमानस्य घटस्य न मृदादिभ्य उत्पाद इत्यभ्युपेतम्, एवमुत्पादात्पूर्वं विद्यमानस्य विद्यमानत्वान्नास्त्युत्पाद इत्यवसीयताम्। यथा च परभूतेभ्यो ज्वालाङ्गारादिभ्योऽङ्कुरस्योत्पत्तिर्नास्ति इति अभ्युपेतम्, एवं विवक्षितेभ्योऽपि बीजादिभ्यो नास्तीत्यवसीयताम्॥

अथापि स्यात्—अनुभव एषोऽस्माकमिति, एतदप्ययुक्तम्। यस्मादनुभव एष मृषा, अनुभवत्वात्, तैमिरिकद्विचन्द्राद्यनुभववदिति। ततश्चानुभवस्यापि साध्यसमत्वात्तेन प्रत्यवस्थानं न युक्तमिति। तस्माद-

नुत्पन्ना भावा इत्येवं तावद्विपरीतस्वरूपाध्यारोपप्रतिपक्षेण प्रथमप्रकरणारम्भः। इदानीं क्वचिद्यः कश्चिद्विशेषोऽध्यारोपितः, तद्विशेषापाकरणार्थं शेषप्रकरणारम्भः, गन्तृगन्तव्यगमनादिकोऽपि निरवशेषो विशेषो नास्ति प्रतीत्यसमुत्पादस्येति प्रतिपादनार्थम् ॥

अथ स्यात्—एष एव प्रमाणप्रमेयव्यवहारो लौकिकोऽस्माभिः शास्त्रेणानुवर्णित इति, तदनुवर्णनस्य तर्हि फलं वाच्यम्। कुतार्किकैः स नाशितो विपरीतलक्षणाभिधानेन, तस्यास्माभिः सम्यग्लक्षणमुक्तमिति चेत्, एतदप्ययुक्तम्। यदि हि कुतार्किकैर्विपरीतलक्षणप्रणयनात्कृतं लक्ष्यवैपरीत्यं लोकस्य स्यात्, तदर्थं प्रयत्नसाफल्यं स्यात्। न चैतदेवम्। इति व्यर्थ एवायं प्रयत्न इति ॥

अपि च। यदि प्रमाणाधीनः प्रमेयाधिगमः, तानि प्रमाणानि केन परिच्छिद्यन्त इत्यादिना विग्रहव्यावर्तन्यां विहितो दोषः। तदपरिहारात् सम्यग्लक्षणद्योतकत्वमपि नास्ति ॥

किं च। यदि स्वसामान्यलक्षणद्वयानुरोधेन प्रमाणद्वयमुक्तं यस्य तल्लक्षणद्वयम्, तल्लक्ष्यमस्ति अथ नास्ति? यद्यस्ति, तदा तदपरं प्रमेयमस्तीति कथं प्रमाणद्वयम्? अथ नास्ति लक्ष्यम्, तदा लक्षणमपि निराश्रयं नास्तीति कथं प्रमाणद्वयम्? वक्ष्यति हि—

लक्षणासंप्रवृत्तौ च न लक्ष्यमुपपद्यते।
लक्ष्यस्यानुपपत्तौ च लक्षणस्याप्यसंभवः॥ इति ॥

[म० शा०–५.४]

अथ स्यात्—न लक्ष्यतेऽनेनेति लक्षणम्, किं तर्हि 'कृत्यल्युटो बहुलम्' [पा०-३.३ ११३] इति कर्मणि ल्युटं कृत्वा लक्ष्यते तदिति लक्षणम्। एवमपि तेनैतस्य लक्ष्यमाणत्वासंभवाद्येनैतल्लक्ष्यते, तस्य करणस्य कर्मणोऽर्थान्तरत्वात् स एव दोषः ॥

अथ स्यात्—ज्ञानस्य करणत्वात्तस्य च स्वलक्षणान्तर्भावादयमदोष इति, उच्यते। इह भावानामन्यासाधारणमात्मीयं यत्स्वरूपं तत्स्वलक्षणम्, तद्यथा पृथिव्याः काठिन्यं वेदनाया विषयानुभवो विज्ञानस्य विषयप्रतिविज्ञप्तिः। तेन हि तल्लक्ष्यत इति कृत्वा प्रसिद्धानुगतां च व्युत्पत्तिमवधूय कर्मसाधनमभ्युपगच्छति। विज्ञानस्य च करणभावं प्रतिपद्यमानेनेत्युक्तं भवति स्वलक्षणस्यैव कर्मता स्वलक्षणान्तरस्य करणभावश्चेति। तत्र यदि विज्ञानस्वलक्षणं करणम्, तस्य व्यतिरिक्तेन कर्मणा भवितव्यमिति स एव दोषः ॥

अथ स्यात्-यत्पृथिव्यादिगतं काठिन्यादिकं विज्ञानगम्यं तत्तस्य कर्मास्त्येव, तच्च स्वलक्षणाव्यतिरिक्तमिति। एवं तर्हि विज्ञानस्वलक्षणस्य कर्मत्वाभावात्प्रमेयत्वं न स्यात्, कर्मरूपस्यैव स्वलक्षणस्य प्रमेयत्वात्। ततश्च द्विविधं प्रमेयं स्वलक्षणं सामान्यलक्षणं च इत्येतद्विशेष्य वक्तव्यम्—किंचित्स्वलक्षणं प्रमेयं यल्लक्ष्यत इत्येवं व्यपदिश्यते, किंचिदप्रमेयं यल्लक्ष्यतेऽनेनेति व्यपदिश्यत इति। अथ तदपि कर्मसाधनं तदा तस्यान्येन करणेन भवितव्यम्। ज्ञानान्तरस्य करणभावपरिकल्पनायामनवस्थादोषश्चापद्यते॥

अथ मन्यसे—स्वसंवित्तिरस्ति, ततस्तया स्वसंवित्त्या ग्रहणात्कर्मतायां सत्यामस्त्येव प्रमेयान्तर्भाव इति, उच्यते। विस्तरेण मध्यमकावतारे स्वसंवित्तिनिषेधात् स्वलक्षणं स्वलक्षणान्तरेण लक्ष्यते, तदपि स्वसंवित्त्या इति न युज्यते। अपि च। तदपि नाम ज्ञानं स्वलक्षणव्यतिरेकेणासिद्धेरसंभवाल्लक्ष्याभावे निराश्रयलक्षणप्रवृत्त्यसंभवात् सर्वथा नास्तीति कुतः स्वसंवित्तिः? तथा चोक्तमार्यरत्नचूडपरिपृच्छायाम्—

स चित्तमसमनुपश्यन् चित्तधारां पर्येषते कुतश्चित्तस्योत्पत्तिरिति। तस्यैवं भवति-आलम्बने सति चित्तमुत्पद्यते। तत्किमन्यदालम्बनमन्यच्चित्तम्, अथ यदेवालम्बनं तदेव चित्तम्? यदि तावदन्यदालम्बनमन्यच्चित्तम्, तदा द्विचित्तता भविष्यति। अथ यदेवालम्बनं तदेव चित्तम्, तत्कथं चित्तेन चित्तं समनुपश्यति? न च चित्तं चित्तं समनुपश्यति। तद्यथापि नाम तयैवासिधारया सैवासिधारा न शक्यते छेत्तुम्, न तेनैवाङ्गुल्यग्रेण तदेवाङ्गुल्यग्रं शक्यते स्प्रष्टुम्, एवमेव न तेनैव चित्तेन तदेव चित्तं शक्यं द्रष्टुम्। तस्यैवं योनिशः प्रयुक्तस्य या चित्तस्यानवस्थानता अनुच्छेदादशाश्वतता न कूटस्थतानाहैतुकी न प्रत्ययविरुद्धा न ततो नान्यतो न सैव नान्या। तां चित्तधारां चित्तलतां चित्तधर्मतां चित्तानवस्थिततां चित्ताप्रचारतां चित्तादृश्यतां चित्तस्वलक्षणतां तथा जानाति तथा पश्यति यथातथतां न च निरोधयति। तां च चित्तविवेकतां तथा प्रजानाति तथा पश्यति। इयं कुलपुत्र [बोधिसत्त्वस्य] चित्ते चित्तानुपश्यना स्मृत्युपस्थानमिति॥

तदेवं नास्ति स्वसंवित्तिः। तदभावात् किं केन लक्ष्यते?

किं च। भेदेन वा तल्लक्षणं लक्ष्यात्स्यादभेदेन वा? तत्र यदि तावद् भेदेन, तदा लक्ष्याद् भिन्नत्वादलक्षणवल्लक्षणमपि न लक्षणम्।

लक्षणाच्च भिन्नत्वादलक्ष्यवल्लक्ष्यमपि न लक्ष्यम्। तथा लक्ष्याद्भिन्नत्वाल्लक्षणस्य लक्षणनिरपेक्षं लक्ष्यं स्यात्। ततश्च न तल्लक्ष्यं लक्षणनिरपेक्षत्वात् खपुष्पवत्। अथाभिन्ने लक्ष्यलक्षणे, तदा लक्षणादव्यतिरिक्तत्वाल्लक्षणस्वात्मवद्विहीयते लक्ष्यस्य लक्ष्यता। लक्ष्याच्चाव्यतिरिक्तत्वाल्लक्ष्यस्वात्मवल्लक्षणमपि न लक्षणस्वभावम्। यथा चोक्तम्—

लक्ष्याल्लक्षणमन्यच्चेत्स्यात्तल्लक्ष्यमलक्षणम।
तयोरभावोऽनन्यत्वे विस्पष्टं कथितं त्वया॥ इति॥

[लोकातीतस्तव-११]

न च विना तत्त्वान्यत्वेन लक्ष्यलक्षणसिद्धौ अन्या गतिरस्ति। तथा च वक्ष्यति—

एकीभावेन वा सिद्धिर्नानाभावेन वा ययोः।
न विद्यते, तयोः सिद्धिः कथं नु खलु विद्यते॥ इति॥

[म० शा०-२.२१]

अथवोच्यते-अवाच्यतया सिद्धिर्भविष्यतीति चेत्, नैतदेवम्। अवाच्यता हि नाम परस्परविभागपरिज्ञानाभावे सति भवति। यत्र च विभागपरिज्ञानं नास्ति, तत्र इदं लक्षणम्, इदं लक्ष्यम्, इति विशेषतः परिच्छेदासंभवे सति द्वयोरप्यभाव एवेति। तस्मादवाच्यतयापि नास्ति सिद्धिः॥

अपि च। यदि ज्ञानं करणं विषयस्य परिच्छेदे, कः कर्ता? न च कर्तारमन्तरेणास्तिकरणादीनां संभवः छिदिक्रियायामिव। अथ चित्तस्य तत्र कर्तृत्वं परिकल्प्यते, तदपि न युक्तम्, यस्मादर्थमात्रदर्शनं चित्तस्य व्यापारः, अर्थविशेषदर्शनं चैतसानाम्,

तत्रार्थदृष्टिर्विज्ञानं तद्विशेषे तु चैतसाः।

इत्यभ्युपगमात्। एकस्यां हि प्रधानक्रियायां साध्यायां यथास्वं गुणक्रियानिर्वृत्तिद्वारेणाङ्गीभावोपगमात् करणादीनां करणादित्वम्। न चेह ज्ञानविज्ञानयोरेका प्रधानक्रिया, किं तर्हि, अर्थमात्रपरिच्छित्तिर्विज्ञानस्य प्रधानक्रिया, ज्ञानस्य तु अर्थविशेषपरिच्छेद इति नास्ति ज्ञानस्य करणत्वं नापि चित्तस्य कर्तृत्वम्। ततश्च स एव दोषः॥

अथ स्यात्-अनात्मानः सर्वधर्मा इत्यागमात् कर्तुः सर्वथाभावात् कर्तारमन्तरेणापि विद्यत एव क्रियादिव्यवहार इति, एतदपि नास्ति। आगमस्य सम्यगर्थानवधारणात्। एतदेवोक्तं मध्यमकावतारे॥

अथापि स्यात्-यथा शिलापुत्रकस्य शरीरम्, राहोः शिरः, इति शरीरशिरोव्यतिरिक्तविशेषणासंभवेऽपि विशेषणविशेष्यभावोऽस्ति,

एवं पृथिव्याः स्वलक्षणमिति स्वलक्षणव्यतिरिक्तपृथिव्यसंभवेऽपि भविष्यतीति, नैतदेवम्। अतुल्यत्वात्। शरीरशिरःशब्दयोर्हि बुद्ध्यादिपाण्यादिवत्सहभाविपदार्थान्तरसापेक्षताप्रवृत्तौ शरीरशिरःशब्दमात्रालम्बनो बुद्ध्युपजननः सहचारिपदार्थान्तरसाकाङ्क्ष एव वर्तते, कस्य शरीरम्, कस्य शिर इति। इतरोऽपि विशेषणान्तरसंबन्धनिराचिकीर्षया शिलापुत्रकराहुविशेषणध्वनिना लौकिकसंकेतानुविधायिना प्रतिकर्तुः काङ्क्षामपहन्तीति युक्तम्। इह तु काठिन्यादिव्यतिरिक्तपृथिव्याद्यसंभवे सति न युक्तो विशेषणविशेष्यभावः। तीर्थिकैर्व्यतिरिक्तलक्ष्याभ्युपगमात्तदनुरोधेन विशेषणाभिधानमदुष्टमिति चेत्, नैतदेवम्। न हि तीर्थिकपरिकल्पिता युक्तिविधुराः पदार्थाः स्वसमयेऽभ्युपगन्तुं न्याय्याः, प्रमाणान्तरादेरप्यभ्युगमप्रसङ्गात्। अपि च। पुद्गलादिप्रज्ञप्तिवत् सशरीरोपादानस्य शिलापुत्रकस्योपादातुर्लौकिकव्यवहाराङ्गभूतस्य विशेषणस्याविचारप्रसिद्धस्य सद्भावात्, शिरउपादानस्य च राहोरुपादातुः सद्भावादयुक्तमेतन्निदर्शनम्। शरीरशिरोव्यतिरिक्तस्यार्थान्तरस्यासिद्धेस्तन्मात्रस्योपलम्भात् सिद्धमेव निदर्शनमिति चेत्, नैतदेवम्। लौकिके व्यवहारे इत्थं विचाराप्रवृत्तेरविचारतश्च लौकिकपदार्थानामस्तित्वात्। यथैव हि रूपादिव्यतिरेकेण विचार्यमाण आत्मा न संभवति, अपि च लोकसंवृत्या स्कन्धानुपादाय अस्यास्तित्वम्, एवं राहुशिलापुत्रकयोरपीति नास्ति निदर्शनसिद्धिः॥

एवं पृथिव्यादीनां यद्यपि काठिन्यादिव्यतिरिक्तं विचार्यमाणं लक्ष्यं नास्ति, लक्ष्यव्यतिरेकेण च लक्षणं निराश्रयम्, तथापि संवृतिरेवेति परस्परापेक्षया तयोः सिद्ध्या सिद्धिं व्यवस्थापयांबभूवुराचार्याः। अवश्यं चैतदेवमभ्युपेयम्। अन्यथा हि संवृतिरुपपत्त्या न वियुज्येत, तदेव तत्त्वमेव स्यान्न संवृतिः। न च उपपत्त्या विचार्यमाणानां शिलापुत्रकादीनामेवासंभवः, किं तर्हि वक्ष्यमाणया युक्त्या रूपवेदनादीनामपि नास्ति संभव इति तेषामपि संवृत्या शिलापुत्रकादिवन्नास्तित्वमास्थेयं स्यात्। न चैतदेवमित्यसदेतत्॥

अथ स्यात्—किमनया सूक्ष्मेक्षिकिया? नैव हि वयं सर्वप्रमाणप्रमेयव्यवहारं सत्यमित्याचक्ष्महे, किं तु लोकप्रसिद्धिरेषा अमुना न्यायेन व्यवस्थाप्यत इति। उच्यते। वयमप्येवं ब्रूमः—किमनया सूक्ष्मेक्षिकया लौकिकव्यवहारेऽवतारिक (त?) या? तिष्ठतु तावदेषा विपर्यासमात्रासादितात्मभावसत्ताका संवृतिः मुमुक्षूणां मोक्षावाहककुशलमूलोपचयहेतुः, यावन्न तत्त्वाधिगम इति। भवांस्तु एतां संवृति-

परमार्थसत्यविभागदुर्विदग्धबुद्धितया क्वचिदुपपत्तिमवतार्य अन्यायतो नाशयति। सोऽहं संवृतिसत्यव्यवस्थावैलक्षण्याल्लौकिक एव पक्षे स्थित्वा संवृत्येकदेशनिराकरणोपक्षिप्तोपपत्त्यन्तरमुपपत्त्यन्तरेण विनिवर्तयन् लोकवृद्ध इव लोकचारात्परिभ्रश्यमानं भवन्तमेव निवर्तयामि न तु संवृतिम्। तस्माद् यदि लौकिको व्यवहारः, तदा अवश्यं लक्षणवल्लक्ष्येणापि भवितव्यम्। ततश्च स एव दोषः। अथ परमार्थः, तदा लक्ष्याभावाल्लक्षणद्वयमपि नास्तीति कुतः प्रमाणद्वयम्?

अथ शब्दानामेवं क्रियाकारकसंबन्धपूर्विका व्युत्पत्तिर्नाङ्गीक्रियते, तदिदमतिकष्टम्। तैरेव क्रियाकारकसंबन्धप्रवृत्तैः शब्दैर्भवान् व्यवहरति, शब्दार्थं क्रियाकरणादिकं च नेच्छतीति अहो बत इच्छामात्रप्रतिबद्धप्रवृत्तितो (वृत्तिः?) भवतः।

यदा चैवं प्रमेयद्वयमव्यवस्थितं तदा स्वसामान्यलक्षणाविषयत्वेन आगमादीनां प्रमाणान्तरत्वम्। किं च घटः प्रत्यक्ष इत्येवमादिकस्य लौकिकव्यवहारस्यासंग्रहादनार्यव्यवहाराभ्युपगमाच्च अव्यापिता लक्षणस्येति न युक्तमेतत्॥

अथ स्यात्—घटोपादाननीलादयः प्रत्यक्षाः प्रत्यक्षप्रमाणपरिच्छेद्यत्वात्। ततश्च यथैव कारणे कार्योपचारं कृत्वा बुद्धानां सुख उत्पाद इति व्यपदिश्यते, एवं प्रत्यक्षनीलादिनिमित्तकोऽपि घटः कार्ये कारणोपचारं कृत्वा प्रत्यक्ष इति व्यपदिश्यते। नैवंविषये उपचारो युक्तः। उत्पादो हि लोके सुखव्यतिरेकेणोपलब्धः, स च संस्कृतलक्षणस्वभावत्वादनेकदुष्करशतहेतुत्वादसुख एव, स सुख इति व्यपदिश्यमानः असंबद्ध एवेत्येवंविषये युक्त उपचारः। घटः प्रत्यक्ष इत्यत्र तु—न हि घटो नाम कश्चिद्योऽप्रत्यक्षः पृथगुपलब्धो यस्योपचारात्प्रत्यक्षत्वं स्यात्। नीलादिव्यतिरिक्तस्य घटस्याभावादौपचारिकं प्रत्यक्षत्वमिति चेत्, एवमपि सुतरामुपचारो न युक्तः उपचर्यमाणस्याश्रयस्याभावात्। न हि खरविषाणे तैक्ष्ण्यमुपचर्यते। अपि च। लोकव्यवहाराङ्गभूतो घटो यदि नीलादिव्यतिरिक्तो नास्तीति कृत्वा तस्यौपचारिकं प्रत्यक्षत्वं परिकल्प्यते, नन्वेवं सति पृथिव्यादिव्यतिरेकेण नीलादिकमपि नास्तीति नीलादेरस्यौपचारिकं प्रत्यक्षत्वं कल्प्यताम्। यथोक्तम्—

रूपादिव्यतिरेकेण यथा कुम्भो न विद्यते।
वाय्वादिव्यतिरेकेण तथा रूपं न विद्यते॥ इति॥

[चतुःशतक–१४·१४]

तस्मादेवमादिकस्य लोकव्यवहारस्य लक्षणेनासंग्रहादव्यापितैव लक्षणस्येति। तत्त्वविदपेक्षया हि—

प्रत्यक्षत्वं घटादीनां नीलादीनां च नेष्यते।

लोकसंवृत्या त्वभ्युपगन्तव्यमेव प्रत्यक्षत्वं घटादीनाम्। यथोक्तं शतके—

सर्व एव घटोऽदृष्टो रूपे दृष्टे हि जायते।
ब्रूयात्कस्तत्त्वविन्नाम घटः प्रत्यक्ष इत्यपि॥
एतेनैव विचारेण सुगन्धि मधुरं मृदु।
प्रतिषेधयितव्यानि सर्वाण्युत्तमबुद्धिना॥ इति।

[चतुःशतक—१३·१–२]

अपि च। अपरोक्षार्थवाचित्वात्प्रत्यक्षशब्दस्य साक्षादभिमुखोऽर्थः प्रत्यक्षः, प्रतिगतमक्षमस्मिन्निति कृत्वा घटनीलादीनामपरोक्षाणां प्रत्यक्षत्वं सिद्धं भवति। तत्परिच्छेदकस्य ज्ञानस्य तृणतुषाग्निवत् प्रत्यक्षकारणत्वात् प्रत्यक्षत्वं व्यपदिश्यते। यस्तु अक्षमक्षं प्रति वर्तत इति प्रत्यक्षशब्दं व्युत्पादयति, तस्य ज्ञानस्येन्द्रियाविषयत्वाद् विषयविषयत्वाच्च न युक्ता व्युत्पत्तिः। प्रतिविषयं तु स्यात् प्रत्यर्थमिति वा॥

अथ स्यात्—यथा उभयाधीनायामपि विज्ञानप्रवृत्तौ आश्रयस्य पटुमन्दतानुविधानाद् विज्ञानानां तद्विकारविकारित्वादाश्रयेणैव व्यपदेशो भवति चक्षुर्विज्ञानमिति, एवं यद्यपि अर्थमर्थं प्रति वर्तते, तथापि अक्षमक्षमाश्रित्य वर्तमानं विज्ञानमाश्रयेण व्यपदेशात् प्रत्यक्षमिति भविष्यति। दृष्टो हि असाधारणेन व्यपदेशो भेरीशब्दो यवाङ्कुर इति। नैतत्पूर्वेण तुल्यम्। तत्र हि विषयेण विज्ञाने व्यपदिश्यमाने रूपविज्ञानमित्येवमादिना विज्ञानषट्कस्य भेदो नोपदर्शितः स्यात्, मनोविज्ञानस्य चक्षुरादिविज्ञानैः सहैकविषयप्रवृत्तत्वात्। तथा हि नीलादिविज्ञानषट्के विज्ञानमित्युक्ते साकाङ्क्ष एव प्रत्ययाज्जायते किमेतद्रूपीन्द्रियजं विज्ञानमाहोस्विन्मानसमिति। आश्रयेण तु व्यपदेशे मनोविज्ञानस्य चक्षुरादिविज्ञानविषये प्रवृत्तिसंभवेऽपि परस्परभेदः सिद्धो भवति। इह तु प्रमाणलक्षणविवक्षया कल्पनापोढस्य प्रत्यक्षत्वाभ्युपगमे सति विकल्पादेव तद्विशेषत्वाभिमतत्वादसाधारणकारणेन व्यपदेशे सति न किंचित् प्रयोजनमुपलक्ष्यते। प्रमेयपरतन्त्रायां च प्रमाणसंख्याप्रवृत्तौ प्रमेयाकारानुकारि-

तामात्रतया च समासादितात्मभावसत्ताकयोः प्रमाणयोः स्वरूपस्य व्यवस्थापनान्नेन्द्रियेण व्यपदेशः किंचिदुपकरोतीति सर्वथा विषयेणैव व्यपदेशो न्याय्यः ॥

लोके प्रत्यक्षशब्दस्य प्रसिद्धत्वाद्विवक्षितेऽर्थे प्रत्यक्षशब्दस्याप्रसिद्धत्वादाश्रयेणैव व्युत्पत्तिराश्रीयत इति चेत्, उच्यते। अस्त्ययं प्रत्यक्षशब्दो लोके प्रसिद्धः। स तु यथा लोके, तथा अस्माभिरुच्यत एव। यथास्थितलौकिकपदार्थतिरस्कारेण तु तद्व्युत्पादे क्रियमाणे प्रसिद्धशब्दतिरस्काः प्रसिद्धः स्यात्, ततश्च प्रत्यक्षमित्येवं न स्यात्। एकस्य च चक्षुर्विज्ञानस्य एकेन्द्रियक्षणाश्रयस्य प्रत्यक्षत्वं न स्याद् वीप्सार्थाभावात्, एकैकस्य च प्रत्यक्षत्वाभावे बहूनामपि न स्यात् ॥

कल्पनापोढस्यैव च ज्ञानस्य प्रत्यक्षत्वाभ्युपगमात्, तेन च लोकस्य संव्यवहाराभावात्, लौकिकस्य च प्रमाणप्रमेयव्यवहारस्य व्याख्यातुमिष्टत्वाद् व्यर्थैव प्रत्यक्षप्रमाणकल्पना संजायते। चक्षुर्विज्ञानसामग्री नीलं जानाति नो तु नीलमिति चागमस्य प्रत्यक्षलक्षणाभिधानार्थस्याप्रस्तुतत्वात, पञ्चानामिन्द्रियविज्ञानानां जडत्वप्रतिपादकत्वाच्च नागमादपि कल्पनापोढस्येव विज्ञानस्य प्रत्यक्षत्वमिति न युक्तमेतत्। तस्माल्लोके यदि लक्ष्यं यदि वा स्वलक्षणं सामान्यलक्षणं वा, सर्वमेव साक्षादुपलभ्यमानत्वादपरोक्षम्, अतः प्रत्यक्षं व्यवस्थाप्यते तद्विषयेण ज्ञानेन सह। द्विचन्द्रादीनां तु अतैमिरिकज्ञानापेक्षया अप्रत्यक्षत्वम्, तैमिरिकाद्यपेक्षया तु प्रत्यक्षत्वमेव ॥

परोक्षविषयं तु ज्ञानं साध्याव्यभिचारिलिङ्गोत्पन्नमनुमानम् ॥
साक्षादतीन्द्रियार्थविदामाप्तानां यद्वचनं स आगमः ॥
सादृश्यादननुभूतार्थाधिगम उपमानं गौरिव गवय इति यथा ॥
तदेवं प्रमाणचतुष्टयाल्लोकस्यार्थाधिगमो व्यवस्थाप्यते ॥

तानि च परस्परापेक्षया सिध्यन्ति—सत्सु प्रमाणेषु प्रमेयार्थाः, सत्सु प्रमेयेष्वर्थेषु प्रमाणानि। नो तु खलु स्वाभाविकी प्रमाणप्रमेययोः सिद्धिरिति। तस्माल्लौकिकमेवास्तु यथादृष्टमित्यलं प्रसङ्गेन। प्रस्तुतमेव व्याख्यास्यामः। लौकिक एव दर्शने स्थित्वा बुद्धानां भगवतां धर्मदेशना ॥ ३ ॥

आत्राहुः स्वयूथ्याः—यदिदमुक्तं न स्वत उत्पद्यन्ते भावा इति, तद्युक्तम्, स्वत उत्पत्तिवैयर्थ्यात्। यच्चोक्तं न द्वाभ्यामिति, तदपि युक्तम्, एकांशवैकल्यात्। अहेतुपक्षस्तु एकान्तनिकृष्ट इति तत्प्रतिषेधोऽपि

युक्तः। यत्तु खल्विदमुच्यते नापि परत इति, तदयुक्तम्, यस्मात्परभूता एव भगवता भावानामुत्पादका निर्दिष्टाः।

चत्वारः प्रत्यया हेतुश्चालम्बनमनन्तरम्।
तथैवाधिपतेयं च प्रत्ययो नास्ति पञ्चमः॥ ४॥

तत्र निर्वर्तको हेतुरिति लक्षणात्, यो हि यस्य निर्वर्तको बीजभावेनावस्थितः, स तस्य हेतुप्रत्ययः। उत्पद्यमानो धर्मो येनालम्बनेनोत्पद्यते, स तस्यालम्बनप्रत्ययः। कारणस्यानन्तरो निरोधः कार्यस्योत्पत्तिप्रत्ययः, तद्यथा बीजस्यानन्तरो निरोधोऽङ्कुरस्योत्पादप्रत्ययः। यस्मिन् सति यद्भवति तत्तस्याधिपतेयमिति। त एते चत्वारः प्रत्ययाः। ये चान्ये पुरोजातसहजातपश्चाज्जातादयः, ते एतेष्वेव अन्तर्भूताः। ईश्वरादयस्तु प्रत्यया एव न संभवन्तीति, अत एवावधारयति–प्रत्ययो नास्ति पञ्चम इति। तस्मादेभ्यः परभूतेभ्यो भावानामुत्पत्तिरस्ति परत उत्पत्तिरिति॥ ४॥

अत्रोच्यते– नैव हि भावानां परभूतेभ्यः प्रत्ययेभ्य उत्पत्तिरिति। यस्मात्—

न हि स्वभावो भावानां प्रत्ययादिषु विद्यते।
अविद्यमाने स्वभावे परभावो न विद्यते॥ ५॥

इति। यदि हि हेत्वादिषु परभूतेषु प्रत्ययेषु समस्तेषु व्यस्तेषु व्यस्तसमस्तेषु हेतुप्रत्ययसामग्र्या अन्यत्र वा कचिद् भावानां कार्याणामुत्पादात्पूर्वं सत्त्वं स्यात्, स्यात्तेभ्य उत्पादः। न चैवं यदुत्पादात्पूर्वं संभवः स्यात्। यदि स्यात्, गृह्येत च, उत्पादवैयर्थ्यं च स्यात्। तस्मान्न चास्ति भावानां प्रत्ययादिषु स्वभावः। अविद्यमाने च स्वभावे नास्ति परभावः। भवनं भाव उत्पादः, परेभ्य उत्पादः, परभावः, स न विद्यते। तस्मादयुक्तमेतत् परभूतेभ्यो भावानामुत्पत्तिरिति॥

अथवा भावानां कार्याणामंकुरादीनां बीजादिषु प्रत्ययेषु सत्स्वविकृतरूपेषु नास्ति स्वभावो निर्हेतुकत्वप्रसङ्गात्॥

तत्किमपेक्षं परत्वं प्रत्ययादीनाम्? विद्यमानयोरेव हि मैत्रोपग्राहकयोः परस्परापेक्षं परत्वम्? न चैवं बीजाङ्कुरयोर्यौगपद्यम्। तस्मादविद्यमाने स्वभावे कार्याणां परभावः परत्वं बीजादीनां नास्तीति परव्यपदेशाभावादेव न परत उत्पाद इति। तस्मादागमाभिप्रायान-

भिज्ञतैव परस्य। न हि तथागता युक्तिविरुद्धं वाक्यमुदाहरन्ति। आगमस्य चाभिप्रायः प्रागेवोपवर्णितः ॥ ५ ॥

तदेवं प्रत्ययेभ्य उत्पादवादिनि प्रतिषिद्धे क्रियात उत्पादवादी मन्यते-न चक्षूरूपादयः प्रत्ययाः साक्षाद्विज्ञानं जनयन्ति। विज्ञान-जनिक्रियानिष्पादकत्वात्तु प्रत्यया उच्यन्ते। सा च क्रिया विज्ञानं जनयति। तस्मात्प्रत्ययवती विज्ञानजनिक्रिया विज्ञानजनिका, न प्रत्ययाः यथा पचिक्रिया ओदनस्येति। उच्यते-

क्रिया न प्रत्ययवती

यदि क्रिया काचित् स्यात्, सा चक्षुरादिभिः प्रत्ययैः प्रत्ययवती विज्ञानं जनयेत्। न त्वस्ति। कथं कृत्वा ? इह क्रियेयमिष्यमाणा जाते वा विज्ञाने इष्यते, अजाते वा जायमाने वा ? तत्र जाते न युक्ता। क्रिया हि भावनिष्पादिका। भावश्चेन्निष्पन्नः, किमस्य क्रियया ?

जातस्य जन्म पुनरेव च नैव युक्तम्।

[मध्यमकावतार–६·८]

इत्यादिना च मध्यमकावतारे प्रतिपादितमेतत्। अजातेऽपि न युक्ता,

कर्त्रा विना जनिरियं न च युक्तरूपा।

[मध्यमकावतार–६·१९]

इत्यादिवचनात्। जायमानेऽपि भावे क्रिया न संभवति, जाताजात-व्यतिरेकेण जायमानाभावात्। यथोक्तम्—

जायमानार्धजातत्वाज्जायमानो न जायते।
अथ वा जायमानत्वं सर्वस्यैव प्रसज्यते॥ इति ॥

[चतुःशतक–१५·१६]

यतश्चैवं त्रिषु कालेषु जनिक्रियाया असंभवः, तस्मान्नास्ति सा। अत एवाह—क्रिया न प्रत्ययवती इति।

विशेषणं नास्ति विना विशेष्यम्।

[मध्यमकावतार–६·५७]

इत्यादिना प्रतिपादितमेतन्मध्यमकावतारे। न हि वन्ध्यापुत्रो गोमानित्युच्यते ॥

यद्येवम्, अप्रत्ययवती तर्हि भविष्यतीति, एतदप्ययुक्तमित्याह—

नाप्रत्ययवती क्रिया।

यदा प्रत्ययवती नास्ति, तदा कथमप्रत्ययवती निर्हेतुका स्यात् ? न हि तन्तुमयः पटो न युक्त इति वीरणमयोऽभ्युपगम्यते। तस्मात्क्रिया न भावजनिका ॥

अत्राह—यद्येवं क्रियाया असंभवः, प्रत्ययास्तर्हि जनका भविष्यन्ति भावानामिति। उच्यते—

प्रत्यया नाक्रियावन्तः

यदा क्रिया नास्ति, तदा क्रियारहिता अक्रियावन्तो निर्हेतुकाः प्रत्ययाः कथं जनकाः? अथ क्रियावन्त एव जनका इति, उच्यते—

क्रियावन्तश्च सन्त्युत ॥ ६ ॥

नेति प्रकृतेनाभिसंबन्धः। उतशब्दोऽवधारणे। तत्र क्रियाया अभाव उक्तः, कथं क्रियावत्त्वं प्रत्ययानामिति? यथा च विज्ञानजनिक्रियोक्ता, एवं परिक्रियादयोऽपि भावा उक्ता वेदितव्या इति नास्ति क्रियातोऽपि समुत्पत्तिर्भावानामिति भवत्युत्पादाभिधानमर्थशून्यम् ॥ ६ ॥

अत्राह—किं न एतेन क्रियावन्तः प्रत्यया इत्यादिविचारेण? यस्माच्चक्षुरादीन् प्रतीत्य प्रत्ययान् विज्ञानादयो भावा जायन्ते, तस्माच्चक्षुरादीनां प्रत्ययत्वं तेभ्यश्चोत्पादो विज्ञानादीनामिति। एतदप्ययुक्तमित्याह—

उत्पद्यते प्रतीत्येमानितीमे प्रत्ययाः किल।
यावन्नोत्पद्यत इमे तावन्नाप्रत्ययाः कथम् ॥ ७ ॥

यदि चक्षुरादीन् प्रत्ययान् प्रतीत्य विज्ञानमुत्पद्यते इति अस्य इमे प्रत्यया उच्यन्ते, ननु यावत्तद्विज्ञानाख्यं कार्यं नोत्पद्यते तावदिमे चक्षुरादयः कथं नाप्रत्ययाः? अप्रत्यया एवेत्यभिप्रायः। न चाप्रत्ययेभ्य उत्पत्तिः सिकताभ्य इव तैलस्य।

अथ मतम्—पूर्वमप्रत्ययाः सन्तः किंचिदन्यं प्रत्ययमपेक्ष्य प्रत्ययत्वं प्रतिपद्यन्त इति, एतदप्ययुक्तम्। यत् तत् प्रत्ययान्तरमप्रत्ययस्य तस्य प्रत्ययत्वेन कल्प्यते, तदपि प्रत्ययत्वे सति अस्य प्रत्ययो भवति। तत्राप्येषैव चिन्तनेति न युक्तमेतत् ॥ ७ ॥

किं च। इह इमे चक्षुरादयो विज्ञानस्य प्रत्ययाः कल्प्यमानाः सतो वा अस्य कल्प्येरन्, असतो वा? सर्वथा च न युज्यते इत्याह—

नैवासतो नैव सतः प्रत्ययोऽर्थस्य युज्यते।

कस्मादित्याह—

असतः प्रत्ययः कस्य सतश्च प्रत्ययेन किम् ॥ ८ ॥

असतो ह्यर्थस्य अविद्यमानस्य कथं प्रत्ययः स्यात्? भविष्यता व्यपदेशो भविष्यतीति चेत्, नैवम्—

भविष्यता चेद्व्यपदेश इष्टः
शक्तिं विना नास्ति हि भावितास्य।
[मध्यमकावतार–६.५८]

इत्यादिनोक्तदोषत्वात्। सतोऽपि विद्यमानस्य लब्धजन्मनो निष्फलैव प्रत्ययकल्पना॥

एवं समस्तानां प्रत्ययानां कार्योत्पादनासामर्थ्येन अप्रत्ययत्वमुद्भाव्य अतः परं व्यस्तानामप्रत्ययत्वं प्रतिपाद्यते॥

अत्राह—यद्यप्येवं प्रत्ययानामसंभवः, तथापि अस्त्येव लक्षणोपदेशात्प्रत्ययप्रसिद्धिः। तत्र निर्वर्तको हेतुरिति लक्षणमुच्यते हेतुप्रत्ययस्य। न चाविद्यमानस्य लक्षणोपदेशो युक्तो वन्ध्यासुतस्येवेति। उच्यते। स्याद्धेतुप्रत्ययो यदि तस्य लक्षणं स्यात्। यस्मात्—

न सन्नासन्न सदसन् धर्मो निर्वर्तते यदा।
कथं निर्वर्तको हेतुरेवं सति हि युज्यते॥ ९॥

तत्र निर्वर्तक उत्पादकः। यदि निर्वर्त्यो धर्मो निर्वर्तेत, तमुत्पादको हेतुरुत्पादयेत्। न तु निर्वर्तते, सदसदुभयरूपस्य निर्वर्त्यस्याभावात्। तत्र सन्न निर्वर्तते विद्यमानत्वात्। असन्नपि, अविद्यमानत्वात्। सदसन्नपि, परस्परविरुद्धस्यैकार्थस्याभावात्, उभयपक्षाभिहितदोषत्वाच्च। यत एवं कार्यस्योत्पत्तिर्नास्ति, हेतुप्रत्ययोऽप्यतो नास्ति। ततश्च यदुक्तं लक्षणसंभवाद्विद्यते हेतुप्रत्यय इति, तदेवं सति न युज्यते॥९॥

इदानीमालम्बनप्रत्ययनिषेधार्थमाह—

अनालम्बन एवायं सन् धर्म उपदिश्यते।
अथानालम्बने धर्मे कुत आलम्बनं पुनः॥ १०॥

इह सालम्बनधर्माः कतमे? सर्वचित्तचैत्ता इत्यागमात्। चित्तचैत्ता येनालम्बनेनोत्पद्यन्ते यथायोगं रूपादिना, स तेषामालम्बनप्रत्ययः। अयं च विद्यमानानां वा परिकल्प्येत अविद्यमानानां वा। तत्र विद्यमानानां नार्थस्तदालम्बनप्रत्ययेन। धर्मस्य हि उत्पत्त्यर्थमालम्बनं परिकल्प्यते, स चालम्बनात्पूर्वं विद्यमान एवेति। अथैवमनालम्बने धर्मे स्वात्मना प्रसिद्धे किमस्य आलम्बनयोगेन परिकल्पि-

तेन, इत्यनालम्बन एवायं सन् विद्यमानो धर्मः चित्तादिकः केवलं सालम्बन इत्युच्यते भवद्भिः स्वमनीषिकया, न त्वस्य आलम्बनेन कश्चित्संबन्धोऽस्ति। अथाविद्यमानस्यालम्बनं परिकल्प्यते, तदपि न युक्तम्, अनालम्बन एवायमित्यादि। अविद्यमानस्य हि नास्ति आलम्बनेन योगः॥

अनालम्बन एवायं सन् धर्म उपदिश्यते।

भवद्भिः सालम्बन इति वाक्यशेषः।

अथानालम्बने धर्मे कुत आलम्बनं पुनः॥

अथशब्दः प्रश्ने। कुत इति हेतौ। तेनायमर्थः—अथैवमनालम्बने धर्मेऽसति अविद्यमाने भूयः कुत आलम्बनम्? आलम्बनकाभावादालम्बनस्याप्यभाव इत्यभिप्रायः। कथं तर्हि सालम्बनाश्चित्तचैत्ताः? सांवृतमेतल्लक्षणं न पारमार्थिकमित्यदोषः॥ १०॥

इदानीं समनन्तरप्रत्ययनिषेधार्थमाह—

अनुत्पन्नेषु धर्मेषु निरोधो नोपपद्यते।

नानन्तरमतो युक्तं निरुद्धे प्रत्ययश्च कः॥ ११॥

तत्र पश्चिमे श्लोकस्यार्धे पादव्यत्ययो द्रष्टव्यः, चशब्दश्च भिन्नक्रमो निरुद्धे चेति। तेनैवं पाठः—निरुद्धे च प्रत्ययः कः? नानन्तरमतो युक्तम् इति। श्लोकबन्धार्थं त्वेवमुक्तम्॥

तत्र कारणस्यानन्तरो निरोधः कार्यस्योत्पादप्रत्ययः समनन्तरप्रत्ययलक्षणम्। अत्र विचार्यते—अनुत्पन्नेषु धर्मेषु कार्यभूतेष्वङ्कुरादिषु निरोधो नोपपद्यते कारणस्य बीजादेः। यदैतदेवम्, तदा कारणस्य निरोधाभावादङ्कुरस्य कः समनन्तरप्रत्ययः? अथानुत्पन्नेऽपि कार्ये बीजनिरोध इष्यते, एवं सति निरुद्धबीजे अभावीभूते अङ्कुरस्य कः प्रत्ययः? को वा बीजनिरोधस्य प्रत्यय इति। उभयमेतदहेतुकमित्याह—निरुद्धे च कः प्रत्यय इति। चशब्दोऽनुत्पन्नशब्दापेक्षः। तेन अनुत्पन्ने चाङ्कुरे बीजादीनां निरोधे इष्यमाणेऽप्युभयमेतदहेतुकमापद्यत इति नानन्तरमतो युक्तम्। अथ वा। न स्वतो नापि परत इत्यादिना उत्पादो निषिद्धः, तमभिसंधायाह—

अनुत्पन्नेषु धर्मेषु निरोधो नोपपद्यते।

नानन्तरमतो युक्तम् इति।

अपि च।

निरुद्धे प्रत्ययश्च कः॥

इत्यत्र पूर्वकमेव व्याख्यानम् ॥ ११ ॥

इदानीमधिपतिप्रत्ययस्वरूपनिषेधार्थमाह—बीजादीनां

भावाना निःस्वभावानां न सत्ता विद्यते यतः ।

सतीदमस्मिन् भवतीत्येतन्नैवोपपद्यते ॥ १२ ॥

इह यस्मिन् सति यद्भवति, तत्तस्य आधिपतेयमित्यधिपतिप्रत्ययलक्षणम् । भावानां च प्रतीत्यसमुत्पन्नत्वात् स्वभावाभावे कुतस्तद् यदस्मिन्निति कारणत्वेन व्यपदिश्यते, कुतस्तद् यदिदमिति कार्यत्वेन ? तस्मान्नास्ति लक्षणतोऽपि प्रत्ययसिद्धिः ॥ १२ ॥

अत्राह—तन्त्वादिभ्यः पटादिकमुपलभ्य पटादेस्तन्त्वादयः प्रत्यया इति । उच्यते । पटादिफलप्रवृत्तिरेव स्वरूपतो नास्ति, कुतः प्रत्ययानां प्रत्ययत्वं सेत्स्यति ? यथा च पटादिफलप्रवृत्तिरसती, तथा प्रतिपादयन्नाह—

न च व्यस्तसमस्तेषु प्रत्ययेष्वस्ति तत्फलम् ।

प्रत्ययेभ्यः कथं तच्च भवेन्न प्रत्ययेषु यत् ॥ १३ ॥

तत्र व्यस्तेषु तन्तुतुरीवेमतसरशलाकादिषु प्रत्ययेषु पटो नास्ति, तत्रानुपलभ्यमानत्वात्, कारणबहुत्वाच्च कार्यबहुत्वप्रसङ्गात् । समुदितेष्वपि तन्त्वादिषु नास्ति पटः, प्रत्येकमवयवेष्वविद्यमानत्वात्, एकस्य कार्यस्य खण्डश उत्पत्तिप्रसङ्गात् । तस्मात्फलाभावान्न सन्ति प्रत्ययाः स्वभावत इति ॥ १३ ॥

अथासदपि तत्तेभ्यः प्रत्ययेभ्यः प्रवर्तते ।

इत्यभिप्रायः स्यात्—

अप्रत्ययेभ्योऽपि कस्मात्फलं नाभिप्रवर्तते ॥ १४ ॥

अप्रत्ययेष्वपि नास्ति फलमिति । अप्रत्ययेभ्योऽपि वीरणादिभ्यः कस्मान्नाभिप्रवर्तते पट इति नास्ति फलप्रवृत्तिः स्वरूपतः ॥ १४ ॥

अत्राह—यदि अन्यत् फलं स्यादन्ये च प्रत्ययाः, तदा किं प्रत्ययेषु फलमस्ति नास्तीति चिन्ता स्यात् । नास्ति तु व्यतिरिक्तं फलम्, किं तर्हि प्रत्ययमयमेवेति ? उच्यते—

फलं च प्रत्ययमयं प्रत्ययाश्चास्वयंमयाः ।

फलमस्वमयेभ्यो यत्तत्प्रत्ययमयं कथम् ॥ १५ ॥

यदि प्रत्ययमयं प्रत्ययविकारः फलमिति व्यवस्थाप्यते, तदयुक्तम् । यस्मात्तेऽपि प्रत्यया अस्वयंमया अप्रत्ययस्वभावा इत्यर्थः । तन्तुमयो हि पट इत्युच्यते । स्यात् पटो यदि तन्तव एव स्वभावसिद्धाः स्युः । ते हि अंशुमया अंशुविकारा न स्वभावसिद्धाः । ततश्च तेभ्योऽस्वयंमयेभ्योऽस्वभावेभ्यो यत्फलं पटाख्यम्, तत्कथं तन्तुमयं भविष्यति ? यथोक्तम्—

पटः कारणतः सिद्धः सिद्धं कारणमन्यतः ।
सिद्धिर्यस्य स्वतो नास्ति तदन्यज्जनयेत्कथम् ॥ इति ॥ १५ ॥

[शून्यतासप्तति]

तस्मान्न प्रत्ययमयं

फलं संविद्यते । अप्रत्ययमयं तर्हि अस्तु—

नाप्रत्ययमयं फलम् ।

संविद्यते

इति तन्तुमयो यदा पटो नास्ति, तदा कथं वीरणमयः स्यात् ?

अत्राह—मा भूत्फलम्, प्रत्ययाप्रत्ययनियमस्तु विद्यते । तथा च भवान् ब्रवीति—यदि असत् फलं प्रत्ययेभ्यः प्रवर्तते, अप्रत्ययेभ्योऽपि कस्मान्नाभिप्रवर्तते इति । न चासति फले पटकटाख्ये तन्तुवीरणानां प्रत्ययानां प्रत्ययत्वं युक्तम्, अतः फलमप्यस्तीति । उच्यते । स्यात्फलं यदि प्रत्ययाप्रत्यया एव स्युः । सति हि फले इमेऽस्य प्रत्यया इमेऽप्रत्यया इति स्यात् । तच्च विचार्यमाणं नास्तीति—

फलाभावात्प्रत्ययाप्रत्ययाः कुतः ॥ १६ ॥

प्रत्ययाश्च अप्रत्ययाश्चेति समासः ॥ तस्मान्नास्ति भावानां स्वभावतः समुत्पत्तिरिति । यथोक्तमार्यरत्नाकरसूत्रे—

शून्यविद्य न हि विद्यते कचि
अन्तरीक्षि शकुनस्य वा पदम् ।
यो न विद्यति सभावतः कचि
सो न जातु परहेतु भेष्यति ॥
यस्य नैव हि सभावु लभ्यति
सोऽस्वभावु परपच्चयः कथम् ।
अस्वभावु परु किं जनीष्यति
एष हेतु सुगतेन देशितः ॥

सर्वं धर्म अचला दृढं स्थिता
निर्विकार निरुपद्रवाः शिवाः ।
अन्तरीक्षपथतुल्यऽजानका
तत्र मुह्यति जर्ग अजानकम् ॥
शैलपर्वत यथा अकम्पिया
एवं धर्म अविकम्पियाः सदा ।
नो च्यवति न पि चोपपद्ययु
एवं धर्मत जिनेन देशिता ॥ इत्यादि ।

तथा—

यो न पि जायति ना चुपपद्यी
नो च्यवते न पि जीर्यति धर्मः ,
तं जिनु देशयती नरसिंहः
तत्र निवेशयि सत्त्वशतानि ॥
यस्य सभावु न विद्यति कश्चि
नो परभावतु केनचि लब्धः ।
नान्तरतो न पि बाहिरतो वा
लभ्यति तत्र निवेशयि नाथः ॥
शान्त गती कथिता सुगतेन
नो च गति उपलभ्यति काचि ।
तत्र च बोहरसी गतिमुक्तो
मुक्तकु मोचयमी बहुसत्त्वान् ॥ इति विस्तरः ॥ १६ ॥

इत्याचार्यचन्द्रकीर्तिपादोपरचितायां प्रसन्नपदायां मध्यमकवृत्तौ
प्रत्ययपरीक्षा नाम प्रथमं प्रकरणम् ॥

निर्वाणपरीक्षा पञ्चविंशतितमं प्रकरणम् ।

(Containing the original of ch. XXV of the translation)

अत्राह—

> यदि शून्यमिदं सर्वमुदयो नास्ति न व्ययः ।
> प्रहाणाद्वा निरोधाद्वा कस्य निर्वाणमिष्यते ॥ १ ॥

इह हि भगवता उषितब्रह्मचर्याणां तथागतशासनप्रतिपन्नानां धर्मानुधर्मप्रतिपत्तियुक्तानां पुद्गलानां द्विविधं निर्वाणमुपवर्णितं सोपधिशेषं निरुपधिशेषं च। तत्र निरवशेषस्य अविद्यारागादिकस्य क्लेशगणस्य प्रहाणात् सोपधिशेषं निर्वाणमिष्यते। तत्र उपधीयतेऽस्मिन्नात्मस्नेहः इति उपधिः। उपधिशब्देन आत्मप्रज्ञप्तिनिमित्ताः पञ्चोपादानस्कन्धा उच्यन्ते। शिष्यत इति शेषः, उपधिरेव शेषः उपधिशेषः, सह उपधिशेषेण वर्तते इति सोपधिशेषम्। किं तत्? निर्वाणम्। तच्च स्कन्धमात्रकमेव केवलं सत्कायदृष्ट्यादिक्लेशतस्कररहितमवशिष्यते निहताशेषचौरगणग्राममात्रावस्थानसाधर्म्येण। तत् सोपधिशेषं निर्वाणम्। यत्र तु निर्वाणे स्कन्धपञ्चकमपि नास्ति, तन्निरुपधिशेषं निर्वाणम्। निर्गतः उपधिशेषोऽस्मिन्निति कृत्वा। निहताशेषचौरगणस्य ग्राममात्रस्यापि विनाशसाधर्म्येण। तदेव च अधिकृत्य उच्यते—

> अभेदि कायो निरोधि सञ्ञा
> वेदना पि ति तहंसु सब्बा।
> वूपसमिंसु संखारा
> विञ्ञाणमत्थमगमा ति ॥

[उदान-८.९]

तथा—

> असंलीनेन कायेन वेदनामध्यवासयत्।
> प्रद्योतस्येव निर्वाणं विमोक्षस्तस्य चेतसः ॥ इति ॥

[थेरगाथा-९०६]

तदेवं निरुपधिशेषं निर्वाणं स्कन्धानां निरोधाल्लभ्यते। एतच्च द्विविधं निर्वाणं कथं युज्यते यदि क्लेशानां स्कन्धानां च निरोधो

भवति ? यदा तु सर्वमिदं शून्यम्, नैव किंचिदुत्पद्यते नापि किंचिन्निरुध्यते, तदा कुतः क्लेशाः, कुतो वा स्कन्धाः, येषां निरोधे निर्वाणं स्यादिति ? तस्माद्विद्यत एव भावानां स्वभाव इति ॥ १ ॥

अत्रोच्यते ननु एवमपि सस्वभावाभ्युपगमे—

यद्यशून्यमिदं सर्वमुदयो नास्ति न व्ययः ।
प्रहाणाद्वा निरोधाद्वा कस्य निर्वाणमिष्यते ॥ २ ॥

स्वभावेन हि व्यवस्थितानां क्लेशानां स्कन्धानां च स्वभावस्यानपायित्वात् कुतो निवृत्तिः, यतस्तन्निवृत्त्या निर्वाणं स्यादिति ? तस्मात् स्वभाववादिनां नैव निर्वाणमुपपद्यते । न च शून्यतावादिनः स्कन्धनिवृत्तिलक्षणं क्लेशनिवृत्तिलक्षणं वा निर्वाणमिच्छन्ति यतस्तेषामयं दोषः स्यादिति । अतः अनुपालम्भ एवायं शून्यवादिनाम् ॥ २॥

यदि खलु शून्यतावादिनः क्लेशानां स्कन्धानां वा निवृत्तिलक्षणं निर्वाणं नेच्छन्ति, किंलक्षणं तर्हि इच्छन्ति ? उच्यते--

अप्रहीणमसंप्राप्तमनुच्छिन्नमशाश्वतम् ।
अनिरुद्धमनुत्पन्नमेतन्निर्वाणमुच्यते ॥ ३ ॥

यद्धि नैव प्रहीयते रागादिवत्, नापि प्राप्यते श्रामण्यफलवत्, नाप्युच्छिद्यते स्कन्धादिवत्, यच्चापि न नित्यमशून्यवत्, तत् स्वभावतोऽनिरुद्धमनुत्पन्नं च सर्वप्रपञ्चोपशमलक्षणं निर्वाणमुक्तम् । तत् कुतस्तस्मिन्नित्थंविधे निष्प्रपञ्चे क्लेशकल्पना येषां क्लेशानां प्रहाणान्निर्वाणं भवेत् ? कुतो वा स्कन्धकल्पना तत्र, येषां स्कन्धानां निरोधात् तद्भवेत् ? यावद्धि एताः कल्पनाः प्रवर्तन्ते, तावन्नास्ति निर्वाणाधिगमः, सर्वप्रपञ्चपरिक्षयादेव तदधिगमात् ॥

अथ स्यात्—यद्यपि निर्वाणे न सन्ति क्लेशाः, न चापि स्कन्धाः, तथापि निर्वाणादर्वाग् विद्यन्ते । ततस्तेषां परिक्षयान्निर्वाणं भविष्यतीति । उच्यते । त्यज्यतामयं ग्राहः, यस्मान्निर्वाणादर्वाक् स्वभावतो विद्यमानानां न पुनरभावः शक्यते कर्तुम् । तस्मान्निर्वाणाभिलाषिणा त्याज्यैषा कल्पना । वक्ष्यति हि—

निर्वाणस्य च या कोटिः कोटिः संसरणस्य च ।
न तयोरन्तरं किंचित्सुसूक्ष्ममपि विद्यते ॥ इति ।

[म० शा०—२५.२०]

तदेवं निर्वाणे न कस्यचित् प्रहाणं नापि कस्यचिन्निरोध इति विज्ञेयम्। ततश्च निरवशेषकल्पनाक्षयरूपमेव निर्वाणम्। उक्तं च भगवता--

निर्वृति धर्माण न अस्ति धर्मा
ये नेह अस्ती न ते जातु अस्ति।
अस्तीति नास्तीति च कल्पनावता-
मेवं चरन्तान न दुःख शाम्यति॥ इति।

[समाधिराजसूत्र-९.२६]

अस्या गाथाया अयमर्थः-निर्वृतौ निरुपधिशेषे निर्वाणधातौ धर्माणां क्लेशकर्मजन्मलक्षणानां स्कन्धानां वा सर्वथा अस्तंगमादस्तित्वं नास्ति, एवं च सर्ववादिनामभिमतम्। ये तर्हि धर्मा इह निर्वृतौ न सन्ति, प्रदीपोदयादन्धकारोपलब्धरज्जुसर्पभयादिवत्, न ते जातु अस्ति, न ते धर्माः क्लेशकर्मजन्मादिलक्षणाः कस्मिंश्चित् काले संसारावस्थायामपि तत्त्वतो विद्यन्ते। न हि रज्जुः अन्धकारावस्थायां स्वरूपतः सर्पोऽस्ति, सद्भूतसर्पवत् अन्धकारेऽपि आलोकेऽपि कायचक्षुर्भ्यामग्रहणात्। कथं तर्हि संसारः इति चेत्, उच्यते। आत्मात्मीयासद्ग्रहग्रस्तानां बालपृथग्जनानामसत्स्वरूपा अपि भावाः सत्यतः प्रतिभासन्ते तैमिरिकाणामिव असत्केशमशकादय इवेति। आह—

अस्तीति नास्तीति च कल्पनावता-
मेवं चरन्तान न दुःख शाम्यति। इति।

अस्तीति भावसद्भावकल्पनावतां जैमिनीयकाणादकापिलादीनां वैभाषिकपर्यन्तानाम्। नास्तीति च कल्पनावतां नास्तिकानामपायगतिनिष्ठानाम्। तदन्येषां च अतीतानागतसंस्थानां विज्ञप्तिविप्रयुक्तसंस्काराणां नास्तिवादिनां तदन्यदस्तिवादिनाम्, परिकल्पितस्वभावस्य नास्तिवादिनाम्, परतन्त्रपरिनिष्पन्नस्वभावयोरस्तिवादिनाम्, एवमस्तिनास्तिवादिनामेवं चरतां न दुःखं संसारः शाम्यतीति। तथा-

यथ शङ्कितेन विषसंज्ञ अभ्युपेति
नो चापि कोष्ठ गन्तु आविष्ट पपद्यते।
एवमेव बालुऽपगतो.......
.......जायि म्रियते सदा अभूतो॥ इति।

तदेवं न कस्यचिन्निर्वाणे प्रहाणं नापि कस्यचिन्निरोध इति विज्ञेयम्। ततश्च सर्वकल्पनाक्षयरूपमेव निर्वाणम्। यथोक्तमार्यरत्नावल्याम्-

न चाभावोऽपि निर्वाणं कुत एवास्य भावना।
भावाभावपरामर्शक्षयो निर्वाणमुच्यते॥

इति॥ ३॥

ये तु सर्वकल्पनोपशमरूपं निर्वाणमप्रतिपद्यमानाः भावाभावतदुभयानुभयरूपं निर्वाणं परिकल्पयन्ति, तान् प्रति उच्यते-

भावस्तावन्न निर्वाणं जरामरणलक्षणम्।
प्रसज्येतास्ति भावो हि न जरामरणं विना॥ ४॥

तत्रैके भावतो निर्वाणमभिनिविष्टा एवमाचक्षते-इह क्लेशकर्मजन्मसंतानप्रवृत्तिनियतरोधभूतो जलप्रवाहरोधभूतसेतुस्थानीयो निरोधात्मकः पदार्थः, तन्निर्वाणम्। न च अविद्यमानस्वभावो धर्मः एवं कार्यकारी दृश्यते। ननु च योऽस्या नन्दीरागसहगतायास्तृष्णायाः क्षयो विरागो निरोधो निर्वाणमित्युक्तम्, न च क्षयमात्रं भावो भवितुमर्हति। तथा-

प्रद्योतस्येव निर्वाणं विमोक्षस्तस्य चेतसः।

इत्युक्तम्। न च प्रद्योतस्य निवृत्तिर्भाव इत्युपपद्यते। उच्यते। नैतदेवं विज्ञेयं तृष्णायाः क्षयः तृष्णाक्षयः इति। किं तर्हि तृष्णायाः क्षयोऽस्मिन्निति निर्वाणाख्ये धर्मे सति भवति, स तृष्णाक्षय इति वक्तव्यम्। प्रदीपश्च दृष्टान्तमात्रम्। तत्रापि यस्मिन् सति चेतसो विमोक्षो भवतीति वेदितव्यमिति॥

एवं भावे निर्वाणव्यवस्थापिते आचार्यो निरूपयति-भावस्तावन्न निर्वाणम्। किं कारणम्? यस्माज्जरामरणलक्षणं प्रसज्येत, भावस्य जरामरणलक्षणाव्यभिचारित्वात्। ततश्च निर्वाणमेव तन्न स्यात्, जरामरणलक्षणत्वाद्विज्ञानवत्, इत्यभिप्रायः॥

तामेव च जरामरणलक्षणाव्यभिचारितां स्पष्टयन्नाह- अस्ति भावो हि न जरामरणं विनेति। यो हि जरामरणरहितः, स भाव एव न संभवति, खपुष्पवत्, जरामरणरहितत्वात्॥ ४॥

किं चान्यत्-

भावश्च यदि निर्वाणं निर्वाणं संस्कृतं भवेत्।
नासंस्कृतो हि विद्यते भावः क्वचन कश्चन॥५॥

यदि निर्वाणं भावः स्यात्, तदा तन्निर्वाणं संस्कृतं भवेत्, विज्ञानादिवत् भावत्वात् । यस्तु असंस्कृतः, नासौ भावः, तद्यथा खरविषाणवदिति व्यतिरेकमुपदर्शयन्नाह–

नासंस्कृतो हि विद्यते भावः क्वचन कश्चन ।

क्वचनेत्यधिकरणे देशे काले सिद्धान्ते वा । कश्चनेत्याधेये । आध्यात्मिको बाह्यात्मिको वेत्यर्थः ॥ ५ ॥

किं चान्यत्—

भावश्च यदि निर्वाणमनुपादाय तत्कथम् ।

निर्वाणं नानुपादाय कश्चिद् भावो हि विद्यते ॥ ६ ॥

यदि भवन्मतेन निर्वाणं भावः स्यात्, तदुपादाय भवेत्, स्वकारणसामग्रीमाश्रित्य भवेदित्यर्थः । न चैवमुपादाय निर्वाणमिष्यते, किं तर्हि अनुपादाय । तद्यदि भावो निर्वाणमनुपादाय, तत् कथं निर्वाणं स्यात् ? नैव अनुपादाय स्यात्, भावत्वात् विज्ञानादिवत् । व्यतिरेककारणमाह–नानुपादाय कश्चिद्भावो हि विद्यते इति ॥ ६ ॥

अत्राह–यदि भावो हि न निर्वाणम्, यथोदितदोषप्रसङ्गात्, किं तर्हि अभाव एव निर्वाणम्, क्लेशजन्मनिवृत्तिमात्रत्वादिति ? उच्यते । एतदप्ययुक्तम्, यस्मात्–

यदि भावो न निर्वाणमभावः किं भविष्यति ।

निर्वाणं यत्र भावो न नाभावस्तत्र विद्यते ॥ ७ ॥

यदि भावो निर्वाणं नेष्यते, यदि निर्वाणं भाव इति नेष्यते, तदा किमभावो भविष्यति निर्वाणम् ? अभावोऽपि न भविष्यतीत्यर्थः । क्लेशजन्मनोरभावो निर्वाणमिति चेत्, एवं तर्हि क्लेशजन्मनोरनित्यता निर्वाणमिति स्यात् । अनित्यतैव हि क्लेशजन्मनोरभावो नान्यत्, इत्यतः अनित्यतैव निर्वाणं स्यात् । न चैतदिष्टम्, अयत्नेनैव मोक्षप्रसङ्गादित्युक्तमेवैतत् ॥ ७ ॥

किं चान्यत्–

यद्यभावश्च निर्वाणमनुपादाय तत्कथम् ।

निर्वाणं न ह्यभावोऽस्ति योऽनुपादाय विद्यते ॥ ८ ॥

तत्र अभावः अनित्यता वा भावमुपादाय प्रज्ञप्यते, खरविषाणादीनामनित्यतानुपलम्भात्। लक्षणमाश्रित्य लक्ष्यं प्रज्ञप्यते, लक्ष्यमाश्रित्य च लक्षणम्। अतः परस्परापेक्षिक्यां लक्ष्यलक्षणप्रवृत्तौ कुतो लक्ष्यं भावमपेक्ष्य अनित्यता भविष्यति? तस्मादभावोऽप्युपादाय प्रज्ञप्यते। ततो यदि अभावश्च निर्वाणम्, तत् कथमनुपादाय निर्वाणं भवेत्? उपादायैव तद्भवेत्, अभावत्वाद्विनाशवत्। एतदेव स्पष्टयन्नाह– न ह्यभावोऽस्ति योऽनुपादाय विद्यते इति॥

यदि तर्हि अभावः अनुपादाय नास्ति, किमिदानीमुपादाय वन्ध्यापुत्रादयोऽभावा भविष्यन्ति? केनैतदुक्तं वन्ध्यापुत्रादयोऽभावा इति? उक्तं हि पूर्वम्–

भावस्य चेदप्रसिद्धिरभावो नैव सिध्यति।
भावस्य ह्यन्यथाभावमभावं ब्रुवते जनाः॥ इति।

[म० शा०–१५.५]

तस्मान्न वन्ध्यापुत्रादीनामभावत्वम्। यच्चाप्युच्यते–

आकाशं शशशृङ्गं च वन्ध्यायाः पुत्र एव च।
असन्तश्चाभिलप्यन्ते तथा भावेषु कल्पना॥ इति,

[लङ्कावतारसूत्र–२.१६६, १०.४५३]

तत्रापि भावकल्पनाप्रतिषेधमात्रम्, न अभावकल्पना, भावत्वासिद्धेरेवेति विज्ञेयम्। वन्ध्यापुत्र इति शब्दमात्रमेवैतत्, न अस्य अर्थः उपलभ्यते, यस्यार्थस्य भावत्वमभावत्वं वा स्यादिति। कुतः अनुपलभ्यमानस्वभावस्य भावाभावकल्पना योक्ष्यते? तस्मात् न वन्ध्यापुत्रोऽभाव इति विज्ञेयम्। ततश्च स्थितमेव न ह्यभावोऽस्ति योऽनुपादाय विद्यते इति॥ ८॥

अत्राह–यदि भावो निर्वाणं न भवति, अभावोऽपि, किं तर्हि निर्वाणमिति? उच्यते। इह हि भगवद्भिस्तथागतैः–

य आजवंजवीभाव उपादाय प्रतीत्य वा।
सोऽप्रतीत्यानुपादाय निर्वाणमुपदिश्यते॥ ९॥

तत्र आजवंजवीभावः आगमनगमनभावजन्ममरणपरंपरेत्यर्थः। स चायमाजवंजवीभावः कदाचिद्धेतुप्रत्ययसामग्रीमाश्रित्य अस्तीति प्रज्ञप्यते दीर्घह्रस्ववत्। कदाचिदुत्पद्यत इति प्रज्ञप्यते प्रदीपप्रभावद्

बीजाङ्कुरवत् । सर्वथा यद्ययमुपादाय प्रज्ञप्यते, यदि वा प्रतीत्य जायत इति व्यवस्थाप्यते, सर्वथास्य जन्ममरणपरंपराप्रबन्धस्य अप्रतीत्य वा अनुपादाय वा अप्रवृत्तिस्तन्निर्वाणमिति व्यवस्थाप्यते । न च अप्रवृत्तिमात्रं भावोऽभावो वेति परिकल्पितुं पार्यत इति । एवं न भावो नाभावो निर्वाणम् ॥

अथवा । येषां संस्काराः संसरन्तीति पक्षः, तेषां प्रतीत्य प्रतीत्य य उत्पादश्च विनाशश्च, सोऽप्रतीत्या प्रवर्तमानो निर्वाणमिति कथ्यते । येषां तु पुद्गलः संसरति, तेषां तस्य नित्यानित्यत्वेनावाच्यस्य तत्तदुपादानमाश्रित्य य आजवंजवीभावः स उपादाय प्रवर्तते, स एवोपादायोपादाय प्रवर्तयमानः सन्निदानीमनुपादायाप्रवर्तयमानो निर्वाणमिति व्यपदिश्यते । न च संस्काराणां पुद्गलस्य वा अप्रवृत्तिमात्रकं भावोऽभावो वेति शक्यं परिकल्पयितुम् । इत्यतोऽपि न भावो नाभावो निर्वाणमिति युज्यते ॥ ९ ॥

किं चान्यत्–

प्रहाणं चाब्रवीच्छास्ता भवस्य विभवस्य च ।
तस्मान्न भावो नाभावो निर्वाणमिति युज्यते ॥ १० ॥

तत्र सूत्र उक्तम्–ये केचिद्भिक्षवो भवेन भवस्य निःसरणं पर्येषन्ते विभवेन वा, अपरिज्ञानं [तं ?] तत्तेषामिति । उभयं ह्येतत् परित्याज्यं भवे तृष्णा विभवे तृष्णा च । न चैतन्निर्वाणं प्रहातव्यमुक्तं भगवता, किं तर्हि अप्रहातव्यम् । तद्यदि निर्वाणं भावरूपं स्यादभावरूपं वा, तदपि प्रहातव्यं भवेत् । न च प्रहातव्यम् ।

तस्मान्न भावो नाभावो निर्वाणमिति युज्यते ।

येषामपि क्लेशजन्मनोस्तत्राभावादभावरूपं निर्वाणं स्वयं च भावरूपत्वाद्भावरूपमित्युभयरूपम्, तेषामुभयरूपमिति निर्वाणं नोपपद्यते, इति प्रतिपादयन्नाह–

भवेदभावो भावश्च निर्वाणमुभयं यदि ।
भवेदभावो भावश्च मोक्षस्तच्च न युज्यते ॥ ११ ॥

यदि भावाभावोभयरूपं निर्वाणं स्यात्, तदा भावश्च अभावश्च मोक्ष इति स्यात् । ततश्च यः संस्काराणामात्मलाभः तस्य च विगमः, स एव मोक्षः स्यात् । न च संस्कारा एव मोक्ष इति युज्यते । अत एवाह–तच्च न युज्यते इति ॥ ११ ॥

किं चान्यत्–

भवेदभावो भावश्च निर्वाणमुभयं यदि ।
नानुपादाय निर्वाणमुपादायोभयं हि तत् ॥ १२ ॥

यदि भावाभावरूपं निर्वाणं स्यात्, तदा हेतुप्रत्ययसामग्रीमुपादाय आश्रित्य भवेत्, न अनुपादाय। किं कारणम्? यस्मादुपादायोभयं हि तत्। भावमुपादाय अभावः, अभावं चोपादाय भावः, इति कृत्वा उभयमेतद् भावं च अभावं च उपादायैव भवति, न अनुपादाय। एवं निर्वाणं भवेद् भावाभावरूपम्। न चैतदेवम्, इति न युक्तमेतत् ॥ १२ ॥

किं चान्यत्–

भवेदभावो भावश्च निर्वाणमुभयं कथम् ।
असंस्कृत च निर्वाणं भावाभावौ च संस्कृतौ ॥ १३ ॥

भावो हि स्वहेतुप्रत्ययसामग्रीसंभूतत्वात् संस्कृतः। अभावोऽपि [भावं] प्रतीत्य संभूतत्वात्, जातिप्रत्ययजरामरणवचनाच्च संस्कृतः। तद्यदि भावाभावस्वभावं निर्वाणं स्यात्, तदा न असंस्कृतम् [किं तु] संस्कृतमेव। यस्मान्न च संस्कृतमिष्यते, तस्मान्न भावाभावस्वरूपं निर्वाणं युज्यते ॥ १३ ॥

अथापि स्यात्–नैव हि निर्वाणं भावाभावस्वरूपम्, किं तर्हि निर्वाणे भावाभावाविति। एवमपि न युक्तम्। कुतः? यस्मात्–

भवेदभावो भावश्च निर्वाणे उभयं कथम् ।
[तयोरेकत्र नास्तित्वमालोकतमसोर्यथा] ॥ १४ ॥

भावाभावयोरपि परस्परविरुद्धयोरेकत्र निर्वाणे नास्ति संभव इति, अतः,

भवेदभावो भावश्च निर्वाणे उभयं कथम् ।

नैव भवेदित्यभिप्रायः ॥ १४ ॥

इदानीं यथा नैव भावो नैवाभावो निर्वाणं युज्यते, तथा प्रतिपादयन्नाह–

नैवाभावो नैव भावो निर्वाणमिति याञ्जना ।
अभावे चैव भावे च सा सिद्धे सति सिध्यति ॥ १५ ॥

यदि हि भावो नाम कश्चित् स्यात्, तदा तत्प्रतिषेधेन नैव भावो निर्वाणमित्येषा कल्पना, यदि कश्चिदभावः स्यात्, तदा तत्प्रतिषेधेन नैवाभावो निर्वाणं स्यात्। यदा च भावाभावावेव न स्तः, तदा तत्प्रतिषेधोऽपि नास्तीति। तस्मान्नैव भावो नैवाभावो निर्वाणमिति या कल्पना, सापि नोपपद्यत एव। इति न युक्तमेतत्॥ १५॥

किं चान्यत्—

नैवाभावो नैव भावो निर्वाणं यदि विद्यते।
नैवाभावो नैव भाव इति केन तदज्यते॥ १६॥

यदि एतन्निर्वाणं नैवाभावरूपं नैव भावरूपमस्तीति कल्प्यते, केन तदानीं तदित्थंविधं नोभयरूपं निर्वाणमस्तीति अज्यते गृह्यते प्रकाशते वा ? किं तत्र निर्वाणे कश्चिदेवंविधः प्रतिपत्तास्ति, अथ नास्ति ? यदि अस्ति, एवं सति निर्वाणेऽपि तवात्मा स्यात्। न चेष्टम्, निरुपादानस्यात्मनोऽस्तित्वाभावात्। अथ नास्ति, केनैतदित्थंविधं निर्वाणमस्तीति परिच्छिद्यते ? संसारावस्थितः परिच्छिनत्तीति चेत्, यदि संसारावस्थितः परिच्छिनत्ति, स किं विज्ञानेन परिच्छिनत्ति, उत ज्ञानेन ? यदि विज्ञानेनेति परिकल्प्यते, तन्न युज्यते। किं कारणम् ? यस्मान्निमित्तालम्बनं विज्ञानम्, न च निर्वाणे किंचिन्निमित्तमस्ति, तस्मान्न तत्तावद्विज्ञानेनालम्ब्यते। ज्ञानेनापि न ज्ञायते। किं कारणम् ? यस्माद् ज्ञानेन हि शून्यतालम्बनेन भवितव्यम्, तच्च अनुत्पादरूपमेवेति, कथं तेनाविद्यमानस्वरूपेण नैवाभावो नैव भावो निर्वाणमिति गृह्यते, सर्वप्रपञ्चातीतरूपत्वाद् ज्ञानस्येति। तस्मान्न केनचिन्निर्वाणं नैवाभावो नैव भाव इत्यज्यते। अनज्यमानमप्रकाश्यमानमगृह्यमाणं तदेवमस्तीति न युज्यते॥ १६॥

सर्वथा यथा च निर्वाणे एताश्चतस्रः कल्पना न संभवन्ति, एवं निर्वाणाधिगन्तर्यपि तथागते एताः कल्पना नैव संभवन्तीति प्रतिपादयन्नाह—

परं निरोधाद्भगवान् भवतीत्येव नोह्यते।
न भवत्युभयं चेति नोभयं चेति नोह्यते॥ १७॥

उक्तं हि पूर्वम्—

घनग्राहगृहीतस्तु येनास्तीति तथागतः।
नास्तीति वा कल्पयन् स निर्वृतस्य विकल्पयेत्॥

[म० शा०—२२.१३]

एवं तावत् परं निरोधाद्भवति तथागतो न भवति चेति नोह्यते। एतद्द्वयस्याभावादुभयमित्यपि नोह्यते। उभयस्याभावादेव नोभयमिति नोह्यते न गृह्यते ॥ १७ ॥

न च केवलं परं निरोधाच्चतुर्भिः प्रकारैर्भगवान्नोह्यते, अपि च-

तिष्ठमानोऽपि भगवान् भवतीत्येव नोह्यते।
न भवत्युभयं चेति नोभयं चेति नोह्यते ॥ १८ ॥

यथा नाह्यं न चोह्यं तथा तथागतपरीक्षायां प्रतिपादितम् ॥१८॥
अत एव—

न संसारस्य निर्वाणात्किंचिदस्ति विशेषणम्।
न निर्वाणस्य संसारात्किंचिदस्ति विशेषणम् ॥ १९ ॥

यस्मात्तिष्ठन्नपि भगवान् भवतीत्येवमादिना नोह्यते, परिनिर्वृतोऽपि नोह्यते भवतीत्येवमादिना, अत एव संसारनिर्वाणयोः परस्परतो नास्ति कश्चिद्विशेषः, विचार्यमाणयोस्तुल्यरूपत्वात्। यच्चापीदमुक्तं भगवता- अनवराग्रो हि भिक्षवो जातिजरामरणसंसार इति, तदपि अत एवोपपन्नम्, संसारनिर्वाणयोर्विशेषस्याभावात् ॥ १९ ॥

तथाहि—

निर्वाणस्य च या कोटिः कोटिः संसरणस्य च।
न तयोरन्तरं किंचित्सुसूक्ष्ममपि विद्यते ॥ २० ॥

न च केवलं संसारस्य निर्वाणेनाविशिष्टत्वात् पूर्वापरकोटिकल्पना न संभवति, या अप्येताः—

परं निरोधादन्ताद्याः शाश्वताद्याश्च दृष्टयः।
निर्वाणमपरान्तं च पूर्वान्तं च समाश्रिताः ॥ २१ ॥

ता अपि अत एव नोपपद्यन्ते, संसारनिर्वाणयोरुभयोरपि प्रकृतिशान्तत्वेनैकरसत्वात् ॥

तत्र परं निरोधादित्यनेनोपलक्षणेन चतस्रो दृष्टयः परिगृह्यन्ते। तद्यथा-भवति तथागतः परं मरणात्, न भवति तथागतः परं मरणात्, भवति च न भवति च तथागतः परं मरणात्, नैव भवति न न भवति तथागतः परं मरणादिति। एताश्चतस्रो दृष्टयो निर्वाणपरामर्शेन प्रवृत्ताः ॥

अन्ताद्या अपि दृष्टयः । तद्यथा—अन्तवान् लोकः, अनन्तवांश्च, अन्तवांश्चानन्तवांश्च, नैवान्तवान नानन्तवान् लोकः इति । एताश्चतस्रो दृष्टयोऽपरान्तं समाश्रित्य प्रवृत्ताः । तत्र आत्मनो लोकस्य वा अनागतमुत्पादमपश्यन् अन्तवान् लोक इत्येवं कल्पयन् अपरान्तमालम्ब्य प्रवर्तते । एवमनागतमुत्पादं पश्यन् अनन्तवान् लोक इति प्रवर्तते । पश्यंश्च अपश्यंश्च उभयथा प्रतिपद्यते । द्वयप्रतिषेधेन नैवान्तवान् नानन्तवानिति प्रतिपद्यते । शाश्वतो लोकः, अशाश्वतो लोकः, शाश्वतश्चाशाश्वतश्च, नैव शाश्वतो नैवाशाश्वतो लोकः, इत्येताश्चतस्रो दृष्टयः पूर्वान्तं समाश्रित्य प्रवर्तन्ते । तत्र आत्मनो लोकस्य वा अतीतमुत्पादं पश्यन् शाश्वतो लोक इति प्रतिपद्यते, अपश्यन्नशाश्वत इति प्रतिपद्यते, पश्यंश्च अपश्यंश्च शाश्वतश्चाशाश्वतश्चेति प्रतिपद्यते, नैव पश्यन्नैवापश्यन् नैव शाश्वतो नाशाश्वतश्चेति प्रतिपद्यते पूर्वान्तमाश्रित्य । ताश्चैता दृष्टयः कथं युज्यन्ते ? यदि कस्यचित्पदार्थस्य कश्चित् स्वभावो भवेत्, तस्य भावाभावकल्पनात् स्युरेता दृष्टयः । यदा तु संसारनिर्वाणयोरविशेषः प्रतिपादितः, तदा—

> शून्येषु सर्वधर्मेषु किमनन्तं किमन्तवत् ।
> किमन्तमन्तवच्च नानन्तं नान्तवच्च किम् ।। २२ ।।
> किं तदेव किमन्यत्किं शाश्वतं किमशाश्वतम् ।
> अशाश्वतं शाश्वतं च किं वा नोभयमप्यतः ।। २३ ।।

चतुर्दशाप्येतानि अव्याकृतवस्तूनि असति भावस्वरूपे नैव युज्यन्ते । यस्तु भावस्वरूपमध्यारोप्य तद्विगमाविगमतः एता दृष्टीरुत्पाद्य अभिनिविशते, तस्यायमभिनिवेशो निर्वाणपुरगामिनं पन्थानं निरुणद्धि, सांसारिकेषु च दुःखेषु नियोजयतीति विज्ञेयम् ।। २३ ।।

अत्राह—यदि एवं भवता निर्वाणमपि प्रतिषिद्धम्, ननु च य एष भगवता अनन्त-चरितसत्त्वराश्यनुवर्तकेन विदिताविपरीतसकलजगदाशयस्वभावेन महाकरुणापरतन्त्रेण प्रियैकपुत्रकप्रेमानुगताशेषत्रिभुवनजनेन चरित-प्रतिपक्षानुरूपो धर्मो देशितो लोकस्य निर्वाणाधिगमार्थम्, स एवं सति व्यर्थ एव जायते । उच्यते—यदि कश्चिद्धर्मो नाम स्वभावरूपतः स्यात्, केचिच्च सत्त्वास्तस्य धर्मस्य श्रोतारः स्युः, कश्चिद्वा देशिता बुद्धो भगवान्नाम भावस्वभावः स्यात्, स्यादेतदेवम् । यदा तु—

सर्वोपलम्भोपशमः प्रपञ्चोपशमः शिवः ।

न क्वचित्कस्यचित्कश्चिद्धर्मो बुद्धेन देशितः ॥ २४ ॥

तदा कुतोऽस्माकं यथोक्तदोषप्रसङ्गः? इह हि सर्वेषां प्रपञ्चानां निमित्तानां य उपशमोऽप्रवृत्तिस्तन्निर्वाणम् । स एव चोपशमः प्रकृत्यैवोपशान्तत्वाच्छिवः । वाचामप्रवृत्तेर्वा प्रपञ्चोपशमश्चित्तस्याप्रवृत्तेः शिवः । क्लेशानामप्रवृत्त्या वा जन्मनोऽप्रवृत्त्या शिवः शिवः । क्लेशप्रहाणेन वा प्रपञ्चोपशमो निरवशेषवासनाप्रहाणे शिवः । ज्ञेयानुपलब्ध्या वा प्रपञ्चोपशमो ज्ञानानुपलब्ध्या शिवः । यदा चैवं बुद्धा भगवन्तः सर्वप्रपञ्चोपशान्तरूपे निर्वाणे शिवेऽस्थानयोगेन नभसीव हंसराजाः स्थिताः स्वपुण्यज्ञानसंभारपक्षपातवाते वातगगने वा गगनस्याकिंचनत्वात्, तदा सर्वनिमित्तानुपलम्भान्न क्वचिद्देवेषु वा मनुष्येषु वा न कस्यचिद्देवस्य वा मनुष्यस्य वा न कश्चिद्धर्मः सांक्लेशिको वा वैयवदानिको वा देशित इति विज्ञेयम् । यथोक्तमार्यतथागतगुह्यसूत्रे—"यां च रात्रिं शान्तमते तथागतोऽनुत्तरां सम्यक्संबोधिमभिसंबुद्धः, यां च रात्रिमनुपादाय परिनिर्वास्यति, अत्रान्तरे तथागतेनैकमप्यक्षरं नोदाहृतं न व्याहृतं नापि प्रव्याहरति नापि प्रव्याहरिष्यति । अथ च यथाधिमुक्ताः सर्वसत्त्वा नानाधात्वाशयास्तां तां विविधां तथागतवाचं निश्चरन्तीं संजानन्ति । तेषामेवं पृथक् पृथग्भवति—अयं भगवानस्मभ्यमिमं धर्मं देशयति, वयं च तथागतस्य धर्मदेशनां शृणुमः । तत्र तथागतो न कल्पयति न विकल्पयति । सर्वकल्पविकल्पजालवासनाप्रपञ्चविगतो हि शान्तमते तथागतः" । इति विस्तरः ॥

तथा—

अवाचऽनक्षराः सर्वशून्याः शान्तादिनिर्मलाः ।

य एवं जानति धर्मान् कुमारो बुद्ध सोच्यते ॥

यदि तर्ह्येवं न क्वचित्कस्यचित्कश्चिद्धर्मो बुद्धेन देशितः, तत्कथमिमे एते विचित्राः प्रवचनव्यवहाराः प्रज्ञायन्ते? उच्यते । अविद्यानिद्रानुगतानां देहिनां स्वप्नायमानानामिव स्वविकल्पाभ्युदय एषः—अयं भगवान् सकलत्रिभुवनसुरासुरनरनाथः इमं धर्ममस्मभ्यं देशयतीति । यथोक्तं भगवता—

तथागतो हि प्रतिबिम्बभूतः

कुशलस्य धर्मस्य अनास्रवस्य ।

नैवात्र तथता न तथागतोऽस्ति
बिम्बं च संदृश्यति सर्वलोके ॥ इति ।

एतच्च तथागतवाग्गुह्यपरिवर्ते विस्तरेण व्याख्यातम् । ततश्च निर्वाणार्थं धर्मदेशनाया अभावात् कुतो धर्मदेशनायाः सद्भावेन निर्वाणस्यास्तित्वं भविष्यति ? तस्मान्निर्वाणमपि नास्तीति सिद्धम् । उक्तं च भगवता—

अनिर्वाणं हि निर्वाणं लोकनाथेन देशितम् ।
आकाशेन कृतो ग्रन्थिराकाशेनैव मोचितः ॥ इति ।

तथा—न तेषां भगवन् संसारसमतिक्रमो ये निर्वाणं भावतः पर्येषन्ते । तत्कस्य हेतोः ? निर्वाणमिति भगवन् यः प्रशमः सर्वनिमित्तानामुपरतिः सर्वेञ्जितसमिञ्जितानाम् । तदिमे भगवन् मोहपुरुषा ये स्वाख्याते धर्मविनये प्रव्रज्य तीर्थिकदृष्टौ निपतिता निर्वाणं भावतः पर्येषन्ते तद्यथा तिलेभ्यस्तैलं क्षीरात्सर्पिः । अत्यन्तपरिनिर्वृतेषु भगवन् सर्वधर्मेषु ये निर्वाणं मार्गन्ति तानहमाभिमानिकान् तीर्थिकानिति वदामि । न भगवन् योगाचारः सम्यक् प्रतिपन्नः कस्यचिद्धर्मस्योत्पादं वा निरोधं वा करोति, नापि कस्यचिद्धर्मस्य प्राप्तिमिच्छति नाभिसमयमिति विस्तरः ॥

इत्याचार्यचन्द्रकीर्तिपादोपरचितायां प्रसन्नपदायां मध्यमकवृत्तौ
निर्वाणपरीक्षा नाम पञ्चविंशतितमं प्रकरणम् ॥

INDEX TO THE INTRODUCTION

INDEX TO STCHERBATSKY'S TEXT

INDEX OF SAṀSKRIT & PĀLĪ WORDS

INDEX OF TIBETAN WORDS

INDEX OF MONGOLIAN WORDS

INDEX OF SANSKRIT AND PĀLĪ WORKS

INDEX OF PROPER NAMES

SUBJECTS

in nature. The mystic worlds also imagined as obeying special causal laws 13. Similarity of this Buddhist conception of causality with the modern conception of causation as meaning of the formula of *pratītya-samutpāda*, to be distinguished from the 12 membered special formula (c. c.). A general causal interdependence (*kāraṇahetu*) between all elements, past, present and future of the whole universe. This conception the forerunner (or corollary) of Monism, causes and conditions (*hetu-pratyaya*), the difference how far observed, both terms used as synonyms. Classification of condition, not always required to be strictly systematical. The classification of conditions in the school of the Sarvāstivādins. The preceding condition of *causa materialis* (samanantara-pratyaya). The special condition or *causa effeciens* (*Adhipati-pratyaya*). The objective condition (*ālambana-pratyaya*). The general or cooperating condition (*hetupratyaya or sahakāripratyaya*). The homogeneous (*sabhāga*) the simultaneous (*sahabhū-samprayukta*) and the moral (*vipākahetukarma*) causations. Anthropomorphic (*puruṣa-karmaphala*) conception of causation rejected.

Causality II. In Mahāyāna. The conception of interdependent momentary elements replaced by the idea of their Relativity (q. c.) 94 ff. Origination, existence, relation conceived as synonyms. The relativity of separate elements conceived as their ultimate unreality, therefore causality denied altogether 97. The adamantine argument against causation; the effect can be neither identical with the cause nor can it be different. The current views of causality involved in contradiction. A new manifestation not to be distinguished from a new production. A new production of an existing thing useless. Meaning of such arguments. Critique of the converse (*Vaiśeṣika*) view of a break between the effect and its material cause, impossibility of efficient causes. Causation not to be established on the basis of direct experience. Causality as coordination denied. The denial of identity between cause and effect does not entail the acceptance of a difference between them. Impossibility of a double causation, when the effect is supposed to be partly identical and partly different from its cause 127. Impossibility of a (pluralistic) Universe without causation

Saint (*ārya=yogin*) ibid. Attained suddenly in the 24 consecutive moments, 21.

Mystic world, higher planes of existence corresponding to degrees of absorption in trance, where the faculty of concentration and the special powers which it confers are predominant and control the character of life and the number of elements entering the composition for shaping individual existences, 16. These worlds projected by imagination on the basis of observation of the states of ecstatic meditation, by transferring actual experiences into separate higher planes of existence, Opinion of Śrīlābha, ibid. Whereas in the worlds of gross bodies the formula of an individual being contains elements of 27 different kinds (5 sense faculties, 5 corresponding sense data, 5 corresponding sensations, the mind, ideas and mental sensations,) in the worlds of trance (the four *dhyānas*) the olfactory and gustatory faculties and the corresponding sensations being in abeyance, the formula is reduced to elements of 14 kinds, 16. The experimental foundation of this feature. Life shapes under the changed condition that neither food, nor clothes, nor houses, are needed. The consequent moral perfection of those beings, ibid; their transparent bodies ibid. The condition of their life described, ibid. In the highest planes of trance the appearance of all physical elements being suppressed by Yoga, the formula of a personal existence comprised only mental elements (3 kinds of them). The denizens are pure spirits, merged in almost eternal catalepsy.

Nirvāṇa, I, Hīnayānistic, a designation of the Absolute as an absolute end of all phenomenal existence 4 possibly pre-Buddhistic, unlike a survival in heaven, extinction of all active elements (*saṃskāras*) of life, even the thinnest vestige of life, still existing in cateleptic states, extinct in N. Yoga as the expedient through which a gradual extinction of all elements, is attained. Protest against annihilation of life as the ultimate goal of life, meaning of N. as immortality, it is a place where there is neither life, nor (repeated) death, a place of eternal death, how far similar to the materialistic conception, similar to the Nyāya Vaiśeṣika conception of a "stone-like" condition of the Soul as the absolute end, how far comparable to the conception of modern science about the absolute end (Entropy), the 'difficulties of giving a clear definition of the Absolute realized in Hīnayāna, the antinomies, their solution similar to the answer given by Kant, the reluctance of the Buddha to go into details when pressed by inquisitive questioners. N. final and non-final their definitions in the Hīnayāna, ibid.! The Vaibhāṣikas, the only school of later Buddhism which kept faithful to the idea of a lifeless N. their idea of this N, as being a reality (vastu), in the sense of materialistic, lifeless reality, their line of argument, the denial of such a N. by the Sautrāntikas definition of the latter presupposes the acceptance of the Mahāyānistic idea of *dharma-kāya*, The moral side of the problem of N., Buddha's emphatic protest against Materialism in the Indian conception of the term as connoting a denial of moral obligations and of retribution, such materialism is a direct way not to Nirvāṇa; but to hell, N., although extinction of life, nevertheless a "desirable" aim, contrasted with phenomenal life as the aim to be shunned. The world-process as a process of gradual moral purification and spiritualization of life, which nevertheless leads towards Annihilation of all life. The strangeness, for our habits of thought, of the "desirability" of such a solution, 4, but Buddha finds the conception of an eternal Soul equally strange. The grip of the idea of Quiescence upon the Indian mind. The protest of several early schools against a lifeless N. The idea of a surviving consciousness in the Vātsīputrīya, Mahāsaṅghika and other schools, 46, their line of argument. The Sautrāntika-school a continuator of this tendency leading to Mahāyānism 35. Nirvāṇa II Mahāyānistic, a designation of the Absolute harmonizing with a system of Philosophical Monism, 41ff. its identity with the Vedānta conception n. influence of the Upaniṣads probable, its contrast with the Pluralism of Hīnayāna, it is neither an Ens, nor a non-Ens, 203 nor both, nor neither 209. The last solution (neither Ens nor non-Ens) how far favoured in Mahāyāna, N. means non-plurality, non-duality (*advaita*), extinction of Plurality, no Origination, no motion, no real extinction but it is the extinction of all constructions of human (pluralistic) thought N. inexpressible, N. is this world viewed *sub specie aeternitatis* 205; thus there is a substantial identity between

Saint, 10 (cp. the similar change that Buddha wished to inculcate in the meaning of the term Brāhmin (Rhys Davids, Dialogues), *ārya-pudgala* represents an assemblage of morally pure elements, 95; he is the man who has through accumulated virtue (*puṇya-sambhāra*) and accumulated knowledge (*jñāna-sambhāra*) entered the Path of Illumination, (*dṛṣṭi-mārga*) consisting in a direct intuition of the real condition of the Universe, as Pluralism in Hīnayāna, as Monism in Mahāyāna, 10; is called the Yogin 24, the Yogācāra. His intuition called mystic intuition (*yogi-pratyakṣa*) 18 ff. All habits of thought changed, ibid. This intuition only felt internally (*pratyātma-vedya*) cannot be expressed in words. The real attitude of the Saint in the discussion about the Absolute should be silence. He nevertheless can adapt himself to the habitual ways of thinking and instruct mankind by arguments intelligible to them. All arguments will be negative and point out the hopeless contradictions in the usual ways of thinking, ibid.

Sāṅkhya views 3.

Sarvāstivādins, their idea of the world as an assembly of cooperating elements, 207

Sautrāntika, as intermediate school between Hīnayāna and Mahāyāna, 34 their role comparable to Occam's Razor, their conception of reality, regarded as Mahāyānist.

Scholasticism in Early Buddhism 26

Scriptures, their conventional and real meaning 89, 132

Sense-data, the only reality in Matter according to Hīnayāna,

Sense-perception, its definition as pure sensation, the Mādhyamika definition n.

Sophisms of Bhāvaviveka, 61 cf. Zeno of Elea.

Soul, eternal, individual 2, denial of its existence as a separate substance in Early Buddhism, 6 as inanimate ubiquitous "stonelike" substance in Nyāya-Vaiśeṣika, 64

Sound, theories about its essence, 156

Sources of Knowledge only two, (intellect and senses) the four sources of realistic logic accepted by the Mādhyamika.

Space, a reality in Hīnayāna,

Speech, the Buddhist theory of speech (*apoha*) 144

Sphere of purified matter of ethereal bodies, 8 of pure spirits, 8 cp. s-v-Mystic worlds.

of producing a radical change in the composition of individual existences by suppressing the operation of elements composing a normal existence Individuals with a highly developed faculty of concentration and having much practised it considered to be purified. This power capable of transferring human beings out of this world of gross bodies into higher mystic worlds (q.c.) where it becomes the predominant faculty controlling the character of life and the composition of individual existences (the gradually reduced number of elements entering into cooperation for producing an individual personal life) 18. The ultimate end of this process of suppression in Nirvāṇa. Buddhist yoga has nothing to do with magic and sorcery, Yoga exercises in Zen monasteries in Japan, Origin and history of the Buddhist doctrine of meditation, its denial as a mystic power by the Mīmāṁsakas, its importance in the Nyāya Vaiśeṣika system.

Yogācāras, the school of 36 ff. their idea that all elements of life are eternally quiescent, their conception of reality, the synonym of a Mahāyānist.

TECHNICAL TERMS

Ati-prasaṅga, a generalized *reductio ad absurdum.* e.g. "if cause and effect are identical, everything will be eternally nascent, if they really are different, all things being different from one another, everything will be produced out of anything", 98

Adhikaraṇa-sādhana, a noun denoting the place where an action is going on, e.g. *dhyāna* from the root *dhyai* (to meditate) in the sense of a world of which the denizens possess thought-concentration as their normal condition, 7.

Adhipati-pratyaya, a ruling or determining cause, e.g., the organ of vision in regard to visual sensation, 175 c.p. *samanantara-ālambana.*—and *hetu-pratyaya.*

Adhyavasita-viṣaya , see prāpya-viṣaya,

Adhvan, transition, time; past, present and future, 48. 121

Anapekṣaḥ, sva-bhāvaḥ "one's own" independent existence non-relative, absolute Ens. a conception corresponding to a certain extent, to Spinoza's 'Substance', 53

Anāsrava, "uninfluenced" by kleśas q.c. cp. āsrava.

Anātma-(*vāda*) the theory maintaining that the Whole whether a Soul, a Psyche or a Substance, does not exist separately, over and above its separate elements (dharma) linked together by causal laws. This is the principal tenet of Hīnayāna. Buddhism, synon. *pudgala nairātmya, pratītya-samutpāda* (Hīnayānistic) *dharmatā* (Hīnayānistic) *dharma-saṅketa, skandha-āyatana-dhātavaḥ* etc. q.c. The converse theory, viz. the Whole really exists, but not the parts, is the central conception in Mahāyāna, 55

Anupākhya, inexpressible in speech, beyond words, and discursive concepts-*anirvacanīya niṣprapañca.*

Anupalabdhi , negation of the hypothetically-assumed presence of something, e.g. there is on this place no jar, because if it were present it would be perceived, 205 A theory of negative judgments very similar to that introduced into European Logic by Sigwart, cp. Logic, 3 p. 155. "die Verneinung setzt eine zumuthung (āropa) voraus", cp. Nyāya-bindu, II 26 ff.

Anupādāya-sat, existence independent of any substratum

uncaused, non-relative, absolute existence, 210

Anubhava, immediate experience, as contrasted with philosophic interpretation 146

Anaikāntika (*-hetu*) inconclusive, indefinite argument, synon. savyabhicāra

Anya-vyāvṛtti (existence of an object established by) contrast with its negations, e.g. "blue colour is established and exists only insofar as there are non-blue colours", synon. *apoha*, *paraspara-apekṣa*, *svabhāva-śūnya*, etc.

Anvaya jñāna, a momentary mystic intuition of the "Four Truths" in the mystic worlds, i.e. of the elements out of which these worlds are constructed in accordance with special causal laws, 20.

Aparokṣa (=artha) the presence of an object in one's own ken, the essence of sense-perception according to Vedānta and Mādhyamika.

Apratiṣṭhita (*nirvāṇa*) "altruistic" Nirvāṇa, cp. in the preceding Index s.v. Nirvāṇa, M. de la V.P. explains it (Museon, 1914, p. 34) as a Nirvāṇa into which a Buddha could have entered, if he did not prefer to remain in Saṁsāra, and to work for the Salvation of all living beings. A similar explanation is also current in Japan. O. Rosenberg, Die Welt anschaung des moderenen Buddhismus p. 30 J. Rahder, Daśabhūmikasūtra, p. XXIV, thinks that the Mahāyānistic Buddha does not reside in 'aprat'. n., "il niest pas separe du samsara, ni ne se rejouit du nirvana." But a Buddha who does not reside in Nirvāṇa is not a complete Buddha in his Dharmakāya. However aprat n. is always represented as the highest form of Dharmakāya, the most perfect Mahāyānistic Nirvāṇa. It is contrasted with the Hīnayānistic Nirvāṇa.

The latter is attained by the Saint for his own, personal salvation. It is "egoistic", The Mahāyānistic Buddha does not reside in that kind of Hīnayānistic Nirvāṇa, his Nirvāṇa is altruistic and represents all-embracing Love and Wisdom as the highest manifestation of Dharma-kāya, just as every creature and every object is also but a manifestation of it. The Tibetan Grubmthah is perfectly aware that the Mahāyānistic Buddha represents the motionless Cosmos and cannot be an active principle, but the empirically existing virtues are conceived as a special manifestation of the eternal principle; *apratiṣṭhitanirvāṇa* is thus defined negatively, it is not a Nirvāṇa which is reached exclusively for one's own Salvation, it is altruistic (ran kho-nai don-du-zh-ba-la mi-gnas = svārthamātreṇa upaśame na pratiṣṭhitaḥ). The manifestations of Love and Wisdom in the Universe are viewed as a special manifestation of the eternal Buddha and this is called the altruistic aspect of Nirvāṇa. The Hīnayānist, i.e. the Śrāvaka and the Pratyeka, are characterized as persons degraded by their bias for personal egoistic quietisms (zhi-mthar-lhun-bai gan-zag = apasamante patitau pudgalau). Suzuki's words (Mahāyāna p. 345.) that the Buddha does not cling to Nirvāṇa etc. are apparently intended to suggest the same explanation as the one here given.

Abhisamaya, (1) In Hīnayāna-*prajñā-amalā*, direct intuition of a monistic Universe (=*prajñā-pāramitā*). Nāgārjuna in his Prajñā-mūla has taught Monism directly and the Mahāyānistic mārga indirectly. Maitreya-Asaṅga in his Abhisamaya-alamkāra, has taught this *mārga* directly; it is thus, a synonym of *prajñā-pāramitopadeśa* or *mārga*, 55, 95, 222.

Arūpadhātu, immaterial plane of existence, the mystic worlds, of pure spirits, 8, 9, 10. The formula of individual existence in these worlds, includes three kinds (*dhātu*) of elements (*dharmāḥ*) and (*mano-vijñāna*), cp. Central Conception, 10, 17, 120.

Arūpiṇo dharmāḥ, non-material mental elements, 9

Artha-kriyā-kāritva, efficiency of an Ens. existence characterized as efficiency in the schools of Sautrāntikas and Yogācāras, 120.

Artha-vākya, an aphorism implying a wide connotation, 110

Avidyā, naive realism, as contrasted with prajñā-amalā "philosophic insight", 10, 193.

Avyākṛta-vastūni, the four insoluble antinomies established by Buddha, (they are 14, according to the Indian mode of reckoning), 217

Asaṁskṛta, not being produced by co-operating causes, eternal absolute, (three such elements in the Sarvāstivādin system), 18, 40, 49, 194.

Ātman, (1) Soul, personality, 8, 36, etc.; the equivalent of *pudgala* according to most schools; different from it according to the Vātsīputrīyas; (2) Substance = (*sva-bhāva*), 160, 212.

Ātma-bhāva, Individual existence; ātman means here body, and is usually in this context translated into. Tib as lus, Cf. Buddhaghoṣa Asl 240, 287.

Ātma-lābha, taking shape, actual existence, = *ātma-bhāva-pratilābha*, having a body in one of the three spheres of existence either as a gross or an ethereal or immaterial (*mano-maya*) body, cp. Rhys Davids, Dialogues I, 259.

Ādi-śānta-dharma eternally quiescent existence. 40, a theory denying a real transition from the phenomenal into absolute existence and maintaining that the phenomenal world itself is the Absolute; if viewed *sub specie eternitatis*.

Ādhyātmika-āyatana, the 6 internal bases of cognition, viz. consciousness (pure) and the 5 sense-faculties; the translation "mental phenomena" will be found applicable in many cases, although it is not quite correct, since *sañjñā*, *vedanā*, *saṁskāra* are classified as *bāhya-āyatana* with regard to pure consciousness (*manas*),

Ārambha-vāda, the "creative" theory of causality, advocated in the Nyāya Vaiśeṣika schools, the reverse of the Sāṅkhya theory of an identity (*tādātmya*) between the cause and effect and of a mere change of manifestation (*pariṇāma-vāda*).

Ārya, a Buddhist Saint, cp. prec. Index. s.v. Saint, ārya-satya (—āryasya catvāri satyāni) the four aspects of the Universe (of its elements) as it appears to the Saint in mystic intuitions 18-23; replaced in Mahāyāna by two aspects (the phenomenal and the absolute).

Ālambana-pratyaya, the object of a cognition, viewed as a cause or a condition of every knowledge, 183

Ālambanaka, the agency producing the intentness of cognition upon an object, 181, 183.

Ālaya-vijñāna, the granary of consciousness, containing the "seeds" of all future ideas and the residue of all past thoughts and deeds, 35, 37, 75

Āvasthika (or prakarṣika), *pratītya-samutpāda*.

Āśraya-asiddha, devoid of a real substratum, e.g. the quality length of the (non-existing) horns of a donkey, 113

Āsrava, originally a physical "influx" of the subtle defiling matter through the pores of the skin to fill up the Soul; in Buddhism, spiritual "influence" by kleśa q.c. from (root) √sru. Buddhaghoṣa derives Pāli āsava from (root) √su, and interprets it etymologically as an "intoxicant", 66, 131.

Idaṁtā,—tathatā, 55

Idampratyayatā, causation in its Buddhist interpretation 55 Causality.

Indriya 1 the six, 5 sense faculties and *manas* (pure sensation) the 22 agencies determining the shape or formulas of life in the different planes of ordinary or mystic existence.

Indriya-kṣaṇa, a moment of the operating sense-faculty, which together with a moment of the object and a moment of consciousness (*vijñāna*) produces actual sensation (the *sparśa*); before such actual sensation, consciousness in an embryo is latent *sammūrchita,* 171.

Uccheda-vāda, the theory denying future life, Materialism in the sense of a denial of retribution and of a moral law; according to this theory every death is Nirvāṇa; Buddhism maintains that this theory does not lead to Nirvāṇa, but to hell, 38, 58.

Utkarṣa, either growth (avayava-upacaya), or increased intensity, 9

Utpāda, production or causation, Mahāyāna a synon. of existence (bhava), of becoming (bhavana), and relation (bhāva), 102, 189.

Upapatti, 1) being logically admissible, 113; 2) being reborn in one of the worlds, 9

Upapatti-dhyāna, being born in the lower 4 mystic worlds whose denizens possess ethereal bodies, 9 cp. samāpatti-*dhyāna.*

Upapāduka, apparitional, born miraculously or according to special laws, 13.

Upādāna, substratum, 141, 206

Upādāna-skandha, sc. *kleśa upādāna-skandha,* the elements of a personality as influenced by *avidyā* and *tṛṣṇā-sāsrava dharmāḥ-duḥkha-satya-duḥkha,* 194

Upādāya, having a substratum, co-ordinated, caused, relative, 203, 204, 206.

Upādāya-prajñapti, a synonym of the Mahāyānistic *madhyamā pratipad* q.c. 85

Ekāgratā, the concentration of thought upon one point (samâdhi), 7

Karaṇa-sādhana, noun meaning the instrument of an action, 7

Karman, (1) Volition and purposive action—following the volition (*—cetanaṁ cetayitvaṁ ca karaṇam,* Ab; K. IV), (2) the will of the Universe, the general force which keeps life going and models its forms in the different worlds, the elan vital, Every system of philosophy in India has its own construction regarding the origin, the essence, the operation, the immediate and the remote result of *karman.* It has accordingly a place assigned to it in the ontology of each system. The materialists deny its existence altogether, i.e. they deny the reality of an influence of past deeds, whether good or bad, upon man's destiny. The Jainas classify *karman,* among their elements of Matter. Gosāla admitted that volition is only half-karman since the real *karman* is physical, cp. D.N. I. 454. The Mīmāṁsakas analyse it into their conceptions of *vidhi, bhāvanā, apūrva, niyoga* etc. The Nyāya Vaiśeṣika system finds a place for it among the *guṇas* where its different aspects can be recognized under the mental qualities of *dharma, adharma, adṛṣṭa* and *saṁskāra.* The Buddhists place it into their *saṁskāra-skandha* where it originally held the place of a predominant ruling force of life (cp. my Central Conception) p. 20. In the Sarvāstivādin list of ultimate realities it is classified as the *citta:mahā-bhūmika-samprayukta-saṁskāra,* under the name of *cetanā* (will) cp. my Central Conception p. 19, 100

Karma-sādhana, a noun meaning the object of an action, 7

Kalpanā, a mental act of linking together an indefinite something (Hoc Aliquid) either with a name or a universal or a quality or an action (*=nāma-jāti-ādi-yojanā*); a judgment of the form "this is that" (sa evāyam). According to Sigwart, cp Logic, (3) I, p. 67 the judgments of the Form this is Socrates' ile, (sa evāyam) are also the fundamental form of all judgment. Hence it is identified with *Vikalpa* q.c., 50, 144, 155.

Kalpanāpoḍha a pure sensation without any participation of synthetic thought, 21, 149, 165, 170

Kleśa, morally impure elements (mental in Buddhism) physical in Jainism; illusion and desire (*avidyā-tṛṣṇe*) are the principal ones; when residues (*saṁskāra*) of former deeds (karman) are moistened (*abhisyandita*) by them, they like "seeds" produce new existences (*janma*), 10 146, 195, 198

Kāraṇa-hetu, notion of a universal link between all elements of existence, past, present and future, also called *sahakārihetu* as contrasted with the *adhipati-hetu* q.c. this notion is a forerunner of Monism, 48, 130, 187, 206

Kālānanugata, having no duration in time, point-instant, cp. deśanānugata, 149

Kriyā, (=vyāpāra), energy supplying a link between the cause and the effect, such as the energy, heat (pacikriyā), 177

Kṣaṇa, a moment, point-instant, identified with the "thing-in-itself", the differential of motion; its principle known to Indian astronomers and philosophers, 41, 149, 54

Kṣānti, satisfaction (=ruci) 20

Kharatva, resistance, 122

Khyāti=Jñāna=upalabdhi,

Gati, (1) motion (2) individual existence in one of the six kinds of bodies, 191, 192.

Grahaṇaka-vākya, a short statement to be developed (*vivaraṇa*) in the sequel, 104

Grāhyaviṣaya, the prima facie object, the first moment in the cognition of an object, cp. prāpyaviṣaya, 149

Citta, pure consciousness or pure sensation, manas and vijñāna (sa-vijñāna-skandha), its synonyms in Hīnayāna cp. Vijñāna 157.

Citta-mahā-bhūmika, (dharma) the mental elements always represented in every conscious moment cp. Central Conceptions, p. 100

Cetanā, will, conscious volition, a purposive action (karman) q.c. 130.

Caitta, mental phenomena 182 (citta-samprayukta saṁskāra). cp—C. C.

Jani-kriyā, energy, function 127 (vyāpāra)

Jñāna, (1) knowledge in general in the sense of mental phenomena, (2) definite cognition as contrasted with pure indefinite sensation (vijñāna q.c.) (3) transcendental metaphysical knowledge. (B) omniscience (Tib-yeśes) 151

Tat-sabhāga, non-active non-operating sense faculty (a-sva-*karma-kṛta*) cp.Sabhāga. 121

Tattva, absolute reality, (=*tattvam eva*) 154

Tathatā, "thisness" absolute reality, (many, synonyms) 48, 141.

Tātkālikī-gatiḥ, the differential of a planet's motion, 150

Duḥkha, (1) *vedanā duḥkha*, suffering (2) *pariṇāma-duḥkha*, phenomenal existence (=*upādāna-skandha*)

Dṛṣṭi, (1) intuition, 19; (2) wrong view, (=mithyā dṛṣṭi), (3) antinomy.

Dṛṣṭi-mārga, the path of illumination, momentary mystic intuition of the real condition of the universe, (yogi-pratykṣa) 19, 21, 145.

Deśanānugata, having no existence, a point-instant.

Dvaidhi-karaṇa, dichotomizing (thought), thought operating, by contrast of A with non=A 144.

Dharma, doctrine (2) quality, (3) element of existence, 191 194.

Dharma-anu-dharma, a doctrine about elements or an element according to that doctrine its connotation (*dharma-saṅketa*) includes strict Uniformity of Nature (asmin-sati idambhavati); hence the translation 2 "norm" "normalism"which is not quite correct since norm is *niyama*, *dharmāṇāṁ niyama-pratyaya-niyama-pratītya-samutpāda*, q.c. 4 a synonym of *saṁskṛta-dharma* and *saṁskāra*. q.c- 5) Nyāya-Vaiśeṣika. a meritorious action (=karman) 6) In Jainism, a special ubiquitous substance, the medium of motion.

Dharma-kāya, The Cosmical Body of Buddha, i.e. the Cosmos regarded as the personification of the eternal Buddha, divided into *svabhāva-kāya*, which is *nitya* and *Jñāna-kāya* which is *anitya* 98; identified with Buddha's final Nirvāṇa, when mentioned in Hīnayānistic lore (e.g. D.N., III. 84, with the synonyms *brahma-kāya* and *dharma-bhūta*) it probably has no clearly Mahāyānistic sc. monistic, connotation. Synon. *tathatā*.

Dhātu, has many different meanings which are summarized in the Bahu-dhātuka-sūtra, the principal are 1) when three are reckoned, the 3 spheres or planes of existence of gross bodies (*kāma*=) of ethereal bodies, passim) when six are reckoned, the component principles of an existence in the material worlds, sc. the four general elements of Matter, (*mahā-bhūta*), *ākāśa* and *vijñāna*, this *ākāśa* is not the *asaṁ-*

skṛta ākāśa in the next classification and *vijñāna* here comprises all mental elements, it is also quite different from the *vijñāna-dhātu* of the next classification, cp. Ab. Kośa, I 283) when eighteen are reckoned, a special division of all elements of existence into ten material and eight spiritual ones, (cp. Central Conception p. 9), 4) *dhātu-gotra*.

Dhyāna — 1) concentrated contemplation (—*samādhi-yoga*); 2) a mystic world where the denizens normally possess thought-concentration.

Nāstika, when used by Buddhists as an invective means Materialism as a denial of *Karman*, i.e. of the moral law and of every survival after death.

Niḥ-svabhāva, having no independent existence of its own, relative, ultimately unreal—*śūnya* 173.

Niyama, strict uniformity in nature, norm, causality between elements of existence, cp. dharma.

Nirodhasatya, 1) in Hīnayāna, the reality of the Annihilation of all energies (*saṁskāra*), comparable with the idea of Entropy in modern science 30; 2) in Mahāyāna, the cessation of all differentiation in a monistic Universe, (sarva-kalpanā-kṣaya).

Nirmāṇa-kāya, the apparitional body of Buddha, Buddha in the docetic sense, 66

Nirvāṇa. cp. prec. Index.

Nirvāṇa-dhātu, ditto

Nir-vikalpaka, pure sensation, devoid of any synthesis or thought-construction.

Niṣprapañca, inexpressible in speech and irrealizable in concepts,—the Absolute, 50, 52, 96, 164, 197, 214.

Niṣyanda-phala, natural result, automatic out-flow out of preceding homogeneous conditions (sabhāga-hetu), 186

Pakṣa, tenet, theists, minor term in a Syllogism.

Pakṣa-doṣa, impossible thesis (=bādhita viṣaya) 113

Pakṣa-dharma, minor premise (=upanaya).

Padārtha, a thing, an entity, 217

Parata-utpatti, a break between cause and effect, production out of something different, the Nyāya-Vaiśeṣika view of causality, extreme realism, involving *ārambhavāda* q.c. and the doctrine of *samavāya* as a semi-substantial universal substratum, a ubiquitous thing invented in order to bridge over the gap between a result and its material cause, 126, 127

Paratantra, relative with the connotation attached to it in the Yogācāra school which admits the reality of relative things obeying causal laws, 38, 144, 173, 199

Paramārtha-sat, existing in an absolute, non-relative, sense, 120, 149, 164

Paramārtha-satya, absolute reality as contrasted with *saṁvṛti-satya*.

Paraspara-apekṣa, mutually relative, relative, synon. *śūnya*, *pratītya-samutpanna*, 162, 173, 204.

Parikalpita-lakṣaṇa, see *lakṣaṇa niḥsvabhāvatā*

Pariṇāma-duḥkhatā, the changing, impermanent or phenomenal world, synon. duḥkha-satya, or duḥkha, cp. duḥkha-vedanā—suffering 20

Pariniṣpanna, absolute reality in a monistic sense with the connotation attached to it in the Yogācāra school, 38, 39, 199.

Pudgala-nairātmya—anātman, q.c. 48, 131.

Pudgala, "the fleeting union of elements that make up, for a time only, an unstable individuality (Rhys Davids, Dialogues, 1 260), synon. *ātma-bhāva*, *santāna*. Vātsīputrīya and others assume a kind of surviving *pudgala*; this tendency, the forerunner of Mahāyāna, 8, 48, 58, 162, 193, 207, 208.

Puruṣa-kāra-phala, = (*puruṣeṇa iva kṛta*); anthropomorphic result, anthropomorphic conception of causation 186

Pṛthivi, the resistant hard stuff in Matter, imagined as an atomic force of resistance, 151

Prati-vijñapti, the momentary awareness of the presence of an object in one's ken.

Prati-saṅkhyā-nirodha, the blank created by the extinction of element (*dharma*) through *yoga* 66

Pratītya, different interpretations of the term, 90, 92, 206

Pratītya-samutpāda, 1) Hīnayāna, inter-connection according to causal laws of all the elements co-operating in the formulation of life, contrasted with *adhītya-samutpāda* (production at random) synon. *Pratyaya-niyama-saṁskṛtatva-dharma-saṅketa*, 2) in Mahāyāna, Relativity synon. *paraspara-apekṣatā* = *svabhāva-śūnyatā-saṁvṛti*; 3) its general formula in Śālistamba-sūtra, in Hīnayānistic and Mahāyānistic interpretation, 4) *āvasthika* or *prākarṣika* pr. s. utp.-12 *nidānas* a special case of the general law, its application to the evolution of an individual life under the influence of illusion (*avidyā*) and passion as long as they are not extinct by philosophic insight (*prajñā*) and ecstatic meditation and the mystic power (Yoga), derived from it. Prenatal forces, (*saṁskāras*) then produce a new life (*vijñāna*), 4-7, develops into full life (n 8-10) decay and death and is continued in a new life (n-11-12) in a new individual and so on without an end, until Nirvāṇa is attained, which according to strict Hīnayāna represents a complete Annihilation of every life (Entropy). This twelve-membered formula refers to the phenomenal world.

Pratyakṣa, sense-perception of object perceived, 50, 144, 171.

Pratyaya-niyama, see niyama, 189

Pratyavekṣaṇa-jñāna, a special kind of Omniscience with which the Buddha, according to Yogācāras, is endowed when representing *apratiṣṭhita-nirvāṇa* q.c. 215

Prapañca, speech, (-vāk) the expression of conceptually differentiated reality in words, 123, 219

Pramāṇa-viniścaya-vāda, vindication of logic, anti-scepticism the standpoint of Diṅnāga and Dharmakīrti as opposed to the Mādhyamika school 142.

Prayoga (-vākya), formulation, syllogism, (-prayogānta), 110

Prayoga-mārga, path of practice, the second division of the Path of Salvation 19, 21.

Prasaṅga-vākya. deductio ad absurdum, 99

Prasajya-pratiṣedha, a simple negation, not necessitating any affirmation of the opposite 98.

Prākarṣika, cp. *āvasthika* sc, *pratītya-samutpāda*, 129.

Prāpya-viṣaya, the object as cognized in a definite representation the final object, synon. *adhyavaseya*—cf. *grāhya-viṣaya*,

Bhāva, existence, "becoming (=*bhavana*) relation, production, 176

Bhāvanā, (1) profound meditation, (samādhi), 200—vāsanā, karman.

Bhāvanā-heya, an element of existence to be neutralized or extirpated by profound Meditation, cp. 10 *dṛṣṭi-heya*.

*Bhāva-sadbhā*va-kalpanā, Realism, 199

Bhāvābhāva, affirmation and negation, 217

Bhūta-mahābhūta, Matter, 122.

Madhyamā-pratipad, the Middle Path, (1) in Hīnayāna, a middle course between materialism (*uccheda-vāda*) and the doctrine of an Eternal Soul, (*ātma-vāda, śāśvatavāda*), (2) in Mahāyāna, Relativity, *śūnyatā*, the theory which maintains that the Relativity of all the objects of the empirical world is the surface, (*saṁvṛti*), of its monistic Essence, 85

Mahā-karuṇā, Great Commiseration (Hīnayānistic, different from Mahāyānistic) 87

Mahā-bhūta, the four fundamental elements or atomic forces of Matter; repulsion, cohesion, heat and lightness (or motion) 167

Yathādhimukta, being in accordance with one's religious fervour (either Hīnayāna or Mahāyāna) 220.

Yoga, v. 2, 5, 6, 7, 8, 10, 11, 12, 17, etc.

Rūpa, (1) *svarūpa*, essence, real essence, (2) *rūpāyatana*, colour and shape, the external basis (*bāhya āyatana*) of visual cognition, (3) *rūpa-skandha*, the assemblage of all physical elements involved in the constitution of an individual life, the elements of its body and of its external world, 122 (4) *rūpa-dhātu*, the mystic worlds of ethereal (accha) bodies, 11.

Lakṣaṇa-niḥ-svabhāvatā, the unreality of logical construction (*prakalpita*), according to the Yogācāras, 38, 122

Lakṣya-lakṣaṇa-pravṛtti, imagined entities as something continuant characterized by changing characteristics 204

Vāsanā, the Yogācāra idea of karman, q.c. explained as *pūrvaṁ jñānam* and derived either from root *vās* to perfume or from the causal form of root *vas* 'to live'

Vāsanā = bhāvanā to make live, to produce empirical existence, 219, 220.

Vikalpa, dilemma, dichotomizing thought, the differentiation of the object into A and non-A, hence productive imagination, thought in general and a synonym of kalpanā q.c. 50, 144, 155.

Vijñāna, (1) in Hīnayāna synon. of *citta* and *manas*, *vijñāna-skandha* = *mana-āyatana* = *mano-dhātu*, pure indefinite sensation, pure consciousness, the principle of every conscious life, the third member of the 12 membered formula of *pratītya-samutpāda*, it is latently (sammūrcchita) present even in an egg as long as it has not lost its vitality; this *vijñāna* is regarded by the Yogâcāras as an *ālaya-vijñāna*, by the Hīnayānists and Mādhyamikas as a *mano-vijñāna-dhātu*; in the moment of conception the masculine and feminine sperma unite with Vijñāna under the influence of *saṁskāras* (=karman) the physical part of the new being comes from the parents, but the *vijñāna* element as causally connected with some previous existence, not necessarily that of the parents; this theory, possibly founded upon some observation, has led to the doctrine of reincarnation; *vijñāna* is here to be translated as "life", "the vital principle" and must be distinguished from sensation, sparśa, which is a further step of the formula empirical knowledge, when contrasted with absolute knowledge (*Jñāna*=*sarvajñatā*=tib ye-śes, 149, 202, 4) in the idealist Yogâcāra system (*vijñāna-vāda*) everything becomes *vijñāna*, it then means idea in general, *vijñāna-skandha*, 202, 212,

Vipāka-hetu, moral causation, =*karman*, 181.

Viprayukta-saṁskāra, forces which cannot be classified either as Matter or as Mind (=*rūpa-citta-viprayukta-saṁskāra*), cp. Central Conception 1, 199.

Vaiyavadānika-dharma, those elements of an individual life (santāna, pudgala) which have a purifying, soothing force, conducing to Nirvāṇa, e.g. *prajñā and samādhi.*

Śāśvata, eternal, beginningless (cp. *pūrvantaṁ samāśritya-dṛṣṭi*), 196, 216, 217

Śūnya, devoid of independent reality (=*svabhāva-śūnya*), dependent, relative, unreal; in Mahāyāna, a synonym of *Pratītya samutpanna*, q.c. 217, 221.

Śūnyatā, Relativity, the theory that nothing short of the whole is real, the parts being always dependent are ultimately unreal; its synonym is *pratitya-samutpāda, madhyamā pratipad*, etc. as saṁvṛta-śūnyatā q. c. represents the absolute, 213

Saṁvādaka, agreeing with experience, supported by successful purposive action=*avisaṁvādaka* not contradicted by experience.

Saṁvṛti-satya, the surface reality, empirical reality, identified with Relativity, with the Dialectic of Being, 164, 173.

Saṁskāra, (1) the forces, the four forces, (*saṁskṛta-lakṣaṇa*) accompanying the appearance of every momentary existence (*jāti-sthiti-jarā-anityatā*), (2)—*viprayukta saṁskāra* q.c

(3) *citta-saṁprayukta-saṁskāra* = all mental phenomena, (4) a synonym of *saṁskṛta-dharma* in general (5) = *karman* cp. Central Conception, p. 207

Samjñā, idea, conception produced by abstraction (*nimitta-udgrahaṇa*).

Satya, truth, reality, four stages of reality in Hīnayāna and in all realistic systems, replaced by two stages in Mahāyāna,

Sanidassana the visible = rūpāyatana.

Santāna, continuity or synthesis of moments of existence of either an element or an assemblage of elements, a personality (*pudgala* = *ātman*), 10

Sabhāga, 1) hetu, homogeneity between cause and effect, 2) indriya, active operating efficient, = *sva-karma-kṛt*, cp. *tat-sabhāga*, 121

Samanantara-pratyaya, the immediately preceding moment of every effect, its substratum (*upādāna-kṣaṇa*), 38, 181

Samāpatti-dhyāna, being transferred in ecstatic meditation to one of the mystic worlds, 7

Sambhāra-mārga the accumulation of virṭue and knowledge, the preparatory path to Salvation, 19

Sarva, a techn. term, denoting the totality of all elements of the Universe including the Absolute, 63

Sarvajñatā, Omniscience in the sense of an intuition of the Absolute, 95

Sa-svabhāva-vāda, Realism, 109

Saṁvṛta, "under the surface,"; Relativity (*pratītya-samut*-pāda-śūnyatā) is the "surface" (*saṁvṛti*) of the absolute reality, this same absolute reality viewed as the thing lying "under the surface" is metaphorically also called *pratītya-samutpāda* or *śūnyatā* which, in this sense, becomes designation of the absolute, and it is in this sense that Nirvāṇa the Absolute is declared to be the equivalent of Saṁsāra, the Phenomenal.

Sādhya-sama, petitio principii, 147

Sāṅkleśika, associated with kleśa q.c. defiling, disquieting, relegating Nirvāṇa, 220.

Sāmagrī = *heṭu-kāraṇa-sāmagrī*), the sum total of causes and conditions relative to a given entity, the entire setting in which the thing exists, (J.S. Mill), 73

Sālambana, intentness upon an object as a characteristic of mind and mental phenomena, 183

Sāsrava, see āsrava 10

Skandha-āyatana-dhātavaḥ, classification of the elements (*dharma*) of existence from different points of view,—*anātman* q.c. cp. Central Conception, p. 48, 49.

Sparśa, sensation as a mental element (*citta-samprayukta-saṁskāra*), the sixth member of the twelve member formula of life's development, it is sensation in which a sense faculty and its object partake, it must be distinguished from *vijñāna*, the third member, which then represents the quite indefinite and even latent principle of life.

Svabhāva-abhāva—niḥsvabhāvatā, śūnyatā, 186

Svalakṣaṇa, the "thing in itself", 143, 149.

Hīnādhimukta—a Hīnayānist.

Hetu-pratyaya, causes and conditions, terms also used as synonyms, 206, 210

Heya-dharma, elements of phenomenal existence to be extinguished by the Saint.